Android™ Wireless Application Development

Volume II: Advanced Topics

Third Edition

Barnes & Noble Special Edition

Android™ Wireless Application Development

Volume II: Advanced Topics

Third Edition

Barnes & Noble Special Edition

Lauren Darcey
Shane Conder

✦✦Addison-Wesley

Upper Saddle River, NJ · Boston · Indianapolis · San Francisco
New York · Toronto · Montreal · London · Munich · Paris · Madrid
Cape Town · Sydney · Tokyo · Singapore · Mexico City

The publisher offers excellent discounts on this book when ordered in quantity for bulk purchases or special sales, which may include electronic versions and/or custom covers and content particular to your business, training goals, marketing focus, and branding interests. For more information, please contact:

U.S. Corporate and Government Sales
(800) 382-3419
corpsales@pearsontechgroup.com

For sales outside the United States, please contact:

International Sales
international@pearsoned.com

Visit us on the Web: informit.com/aw

Library of Congress Cataloging-in-Publication Data

Darcey, Lauren, 1977-

  Android wireless application development : Android essentials / Lauren Darcey and Shane Conder. — 3rd ed., Barnes & Noble Special ed.

     p. cm.

  Includes bibliographical references and index.

  ISBN 978-0-321-81496-8 (v. 1 : pbk. : alk. paper) — ISBN 978-0-321-81497-5 (v. 2 : pbk. : alk. paper) 1. Application software—Development. 2. Android (Electronic resource) 3. Mobile computing. I. Conder, Shane, 1975- II. Title.

  QA76.76.A65D258 2012b

  005.1—dc23

                2011049389

Copyright © 2012 Lauren Darcey and Shane Conder

ISBN-13: 978-0-321-81497-5
ISBN-10: 0-321-81497-5

Text printed in the United States on recycled paper at R.R. Donnelley in Crawfordsville, Indiana.
First printing, July 2012

Editor-in-Chief
Mark Taub

Acquisitions Editor
Laura Lewin

Development Editor
Songlin Qiu

Managing Editor
Kristy Hart

Project Editor
Betsy Harris

Copy Editor
Deadline-Driven Publishing

Indexer
Lisa Stumpf

Proofreader
Paula Lowell

Technical Reviewers
Tony Hillerson
Douglas Jones
Ray Rischpater

Publishing Coordinator
Olivia Basegio

Multimedia Developer
Dan Scherf

Book Designer
Gary Adair

Senior Compositor
Gloria Schurick

❖

This book is dedicated to ESC.

❖

Contents

III: Leveraging Common Android APIs

11 Using Android Networking APIs   169

12 Using Android Web APIs   183

VI: Advanced Topics in Application Publication and Distribution

26 Internationalizing Your Applications 415

27 An Overview of Third-Party In-App Billing APIs for Android   423

28 Enabling Application Statistics with Google Analytics 429

Acknowledgments

This book would never have been written without the guidance and encouragement we received from a number of supportive individuals, including our editorial team, coworkers, friends, and family. We'd like to thank the Android developer community, Google, and the Open Handset Alliance for their vision and expertise. Throughout this project, our editorial team at Pearson Education (Addison-Wesley) always had the right mix of professionalism and encouragement. Thanks especially to Trina MacDonald and Laura Lewin, Olivia Basegio, Songlin Qiu, and our crack team of technical reviewers: Doug Jones, Ray Rischpater, and Tony Hillerson, (as well as Dan Galpin, Tony Hillerson, Ronan Schwarz, Charles Stearns, Mike Wallace, and Mark Gjoel, who reviewed previous editions and incarnations of this book). Dan Galpin also graciously provided the clever Android graphics used for tips, notes, and warnings. Amy Badger must be commended for her wonderful waterfall illustration, and we also thank Hans Bodlaender for letting us use the nifty chess font he developed as a hobby project.

About the Authors

Lauren Darcey is responsible for the technical leadership and direction of a small software company specializing in mobile technologies, including Android, Apple iOS, Blackberry, Palm Pre, BREW, J2ME, and consulting services. With more than two decades of experience in professional software production, Lauren is a recognized authority in application architecture and the development of commercial-grade mobile applications. Lauren received a B.S. in computer science from the University of California, Santa Cruz.

She spends her free time traveling the world with her geeky mobile-minded husband and daughter. She is an avid nature photographer. Her work has been published in books and newspapers around the world. In South Africa, she dove with 4-meter-long great white sharks and got stuck between a herd of rampaging hippopotami and an irritated bull elephant. She's been attacked by monkeys in Japan, gotten stuck in a ravine with two hungry lions in Kenya, gotten thirsty in Egypt, narrowly avoided a coup d'état in Thailand, geocached her way through the Swiss Alps, drank her way through the beer halls of Germany, slept in the crumbling castles of Europe, and had her tongue stuck to an iceberg in Iceland (while being watched by a herd of suspicious wild reindeer).

Shane Conder has extensive development experience and has focused his attention on mobile and embedded development for the past decade. He has designed and developed many commercial applications for Android, iOS, BREW, Blackberry, J2ME, Palm, and Windows Mobile—some of which have been installed on millions of phones worldwide. Shane has written extensively about the mobile industry and evaluated mobile development platforms on his tech blogs. He is well-known within the blogosphere. Shane received a B.S. in computer science from the University of California.

A self-admitted gadget freak, Shane always has the latest smartphone, tablet, or other mobile device. He can often be found fiddling with the latest technologies, such as cloud services and mobile platforms, and other exciting, state-of-the-art technologies that activate the creative part of his brain. He is a very hands-on geek dad. He also enjoys traveling the world with his geeky wife, even if she did make him dive with 4-meter-long great white sharks and almost got him eaten by a lion in Kenya. He admits that he has to take at least two phones with him when backpacking—even though there is no coverage—and that he snickered and whipped out his Android phone to take a picture when Laurie got her tongue stuck to that iceberg in Iceland, and that he is catching on that he should be writing his own bio.

The authors have also published several other Android books, including *Android Wireless Application Development, Android Wireless Application Development Volume I: Android Essentials, Sams Teach Yourself Android Application Development, Learning Android™ Application Programming for the Kindle Fire™*, and the mini-book *Introducing Android Development with Ice Cream Sandwich*. Lauren and Shane have also published numerous articles on mobile software development for magazines, technical journals, and online publishers of educational content. You can find dozens of samples of their work in *Linux User and Developer*, *Smart Developer* magazine (Linux New Media), developer.com, Network World, Envato (MobileTuts+ and CodeCanyon), and InformIT, among others. They also publish articles of interest to their readers at their own Android website, http://androidbook.blogspot.com. You can find a full list of the authors' publications at http://goo.gl/f0Vlj.

Preface

Thank you for picking up this special edition of *Android Wireless Application Development, Third Edition, Volume II: Advanced Topics.* We hope the special features in this version of the book help you master Android quickly and thoroughly with a minimum of fuss and frustration. Hopefully, you've picked up this book after reading *Android Wireless Application Development, Third Edition, Volume I: Android Essentials* and you're now ready to dive deeper into the Android platform.

Features of the Special Edition

The features of this special edition include the following:

- **A companion CD with all the source code:** This book comes with dozens of completely functional code examples, packaged in Android project files ready for importing into Eclipse. These projects are organized by chapter. Simply load them up in Eclipse and run them to illustrate concepts discussed in each chapter. Note that you can also download the latest version of the source code from the book's website: http://www.informit.com/BNandroidVol2 (Register your book to download a zip file of the code. If you are unable to access the files after registering, visit www.informit.com/about/contact_us and select Site Problems/Comments.) All standard-edition code is also available on the authors' book website: http://androidbook.blogspot.com/p/book-code-downloads.html

- **Appendix C, "Java for Android Developers":** Android applications are written in Java, it's true, but often the sample applications—whether they come from our books or the Android development team—contain some Java syntax that those not familiar with the programming language might find unusual. This appendix covers a brief rundown of some of the Java syntax commonly used in Android that you won't necessarily find in your average beginner's Java reference.

- **Appendix D, "Architecting Android Apps: An Example":** Learn by example with this walkthrough of a completely functional Android application. Whereas most of the code provided in this book is "cookbook" style—short and "to the point"—this appendix and its accompanying source code provide a "fully baked" sample application that combines many Android concepts discussed in this book into a single cohesive example. There's a little of everything in this app: databases, content providers, loaders, voice recognition, device storage usage, and more. If you're just getting started, this appendix might be a bit overwhelming, so you may want to simply skim it at first and return to it after you have mastered some of the skills covered in this book.

Introduction

Pioneered by the Open Handset Alliance and Google, Android is a popular, free, open-source mobile platform that has taken the wireless world by storm. This book and *Android Wireless Application Development Volume I: Android Essentials* provide comprehensive guidance for software development teams on designing, developing, testing, debugging, and distributing professional Android applications. If you're a veteran mobile developer, you can find tips and tricks to streamline the development process and take advantage of Android's unique features. If you're new to mobile development, these books provide everything you need to make a smooth transition from traditional software development to mobile development—specifically, its most promising platform: Android.

Who Should Read This Book?

This book includes tips for successful mobile development based upon our years in the mobile industry and it covers everything you need to know to run a successful Android project from concept to completion. We cover how the mobile software process differs from traditional software development, including tricks to save valuable time and pitfalls to avoid. Regardless of the size of your project, this book is for you.

This book was written for several audiences:

- **Software developers who want to learn to develop professional Android applications.** The bulk of this book is targeted at software developers with Java experience who do not necessarily have mobile development experience. More seasoned developers of mobile applications can learn how to take advantage of Android and how it differs from the other technologies of the mobile development market today.

- **Quality assurance personnel tasked with testing Android applications.** Whether they are black box or white box testing, quality assurance engineers can find this book invaluable. We devote several chapters to mobile QA concerns, including topics such as developing solid test plans and defect tracking systems for mobile applications, how to manage handsets, and how to test applications thoroughly using all the Android tools available.

- **Project managers planning and managing Android development teams.** Managers can use this book to help plan, hire, and execute Android projects from start to finish. We cover project risk management and how to keep Android projects running smoothly.

- **Other audiences.** This book is useful not only to a software developer, but also for the corporation looking at potential vertical market applications, the entrepreneur thinking about a cool phone application, and the hobbyists looking for some fun with their new phones. Businesses seeking to evaluate Android for their specific needs (including feasibility analysis) can also find the information provided valuable. Anyone with an Android handset and a good idea for a mobile application can put the information provided in this book to use for fun and profit.

Why Two Volumes in the Third Edition?

We wrote the first edition of this book before the Android SDK was released. Now, three years and 14 Android SDK releases later, there is so much to talk about that we've had to divide the content of the Android wireless application development process into two separate volumes for this, the third edition.

Android Wireless Application Development Volume I: Android Essentials focuses on Android essentials, including setting up your development environment, understanding the application lifecycle and the user interface design, developing for different types of devices, and understanding the mobile software process from design and development to testing and publication of commercial-grade applications.

Android Wireless Application Development Volume II: Advanced Topics focuses on advanced Android topics, including leveraging various Android APIs for threading, networking, location-based services, hardware sensors, animation, graphics, and more. Coverage of advanced Android application components, such as services, application databases, content providers, and intents, is also included. Developers learn to design advanced user interface components and integrate their applications deeply into the platform. Finally, developers learn how to extend their applications beyond traditional boundaries using optional features of the Android platform, including the Android Native Development Kit (NDK), Cloud-To-Device Messaging service (C2DM), Android Market In-Application Billing APIs, Google Analytics APIs, and more.

Android Wireless Application Development Volume II: Advanced Topics is divided into seven parts. Here is an overview of the various parts in this book:

- **Part I: Advanced Android Application Design Principles**

  Part I picks up where *Android Wireless Application Development Volume I: Android Essentials* leaves off in terms of application design techniques. We begin by talking about asynchronous processing. We then move on to some of the more complex Android application components, such as services, application databases (SQLite), content providers, and intents and notifications.

- **Part II: Advanced Android User Interface Design Principles**

  Part II dives deeper into some of the more advanced user interface tools and techniques available as part of the Android SDK, including working with action bars and menus, gathering input through nonstandard methods such as gestures and voice recognition, and much more. You also learn more about how to develop applications that are accessible to different types of users with impairments.

- **Part III: Leveraging Common Android APIs**

    Part III dives deeper into some of the more advanced and specialty APIs available as part of the Android SDK, including networking, location-based services, multimedia (including the camera), telephony, and hardware sensors.

- **Part IV: Drawing, Animations, and Graphics Programming with Android**

    Part IV is for those developers incorporating graphics of any kind into their applications. We cover both 2D and 3D graphics (OpenGL ES and RenderScript), animation, and the Android NDK.

- **Part V: Maximizing Android's Unique Features**

    Part V discusses some of the many ways the Android platform is different from other mobile platforms and how your applications can leverage its unique features. Here you learn how to extend your application features beyond the traditional borders of mobile applications, integrating them with the Android operating system. App Widgets, enabling searches, leveraging cloud-based services, and backups are just some of the topics discussed.

- **Part VI: Advanced Topics in Application Publication and Distribution**

    Part VI covers some more specialized topics in the realm of application publication and distribution, including how to internationalize your applications, enable In-App billing with the Android Market, track application usage patterns with Google Analytics, and take measures to protect your intellectual property from software pirates.

- **Part VII: Appendixes**

    Part VII includes a helpful quick start guide for the Android Debug Bridge tool and a refresher course on using SQLite.

Key Questions Answered in Volume II

This volume of the book answers the following questions:

1. How can developers write responsive applications?
2. How are Android applications structured? How are background operations handled with services? What are broadcast intents and how can applications use them effectively?
3. How do applications store data persistently using SQLite? How can applications act as content providers and why would they want to do so?
4. How do applications interact with the Android operating system? How do applications trigger system notifications, access underlying device hardware, and monitor device sensors?

5. How can developers design the best user interfaces for the devices of today and tomorrow? How can developers work with 2D and 3D graphics and leverage animation opportunities on Android?

6. How can developers write high-performance, computationally intensive applications using native code or RenderScript?

7. What are some of the most commonly used APIs for networking, location-based services, multimedia, telephony, and Internet access?

8. What do managers, developers, and testers need to look for when planning, developing, and testing a mobile development application?

9. How do mobile teams design bulletproof Android applications for publication?

10. How can developers make their applications leverage everything Android has to offer in the form of App Widgets, live wallpapers, and other system perks?

11. How can applications take advantage of some of the optional third-party APIs available for use, such as the Android Market's In-App billing and license verification libraries, Google's Analytics, and Cloud-to-Device Messaging (C2DM) services?

An Overview of Changes in This Edition

When we began writing the first edition of this book, there were no Android devices on the market. One Android device became available shortly after we started writing, and it was available only in the United States. Today there are hundreds of devices shipping all over the world—smartphones, tablets, e-book readers, wrist watches, and specialty devices such as the Google TV. The Android platform has gone through extensive changes since the first edition of this book was published. The Android SDK has many new features and the development tools have received much-needed upgrades. Android, as a technology, is now on solid footing in the mobile marketplace.

In this new edition, we took the opportunity to do a serious overhaul on book content—but don't worry, it's still the book readers loved the first (and second!) time, just bigger, better, and more comprehensive. To cover more of the exciting topics available to Android developers, we had to divide the book into two volumes. In addition to adding tons of new content, we've retested and upgraded all existing content (text and sample code) for use with the latest Android SDKs available while still remaining backwards compatible. The Android development community is diverse, and we aim to support all developers, regardless of which devices they are developing for. This includes developers who need to target nearly all platforms, so coverage in some key areas of older SDKs continues to be included as it's often the most reasonable option for compatibility.

Here are some of the highlights of the additions and enhancements we've made to this edition:

- Coverage of the latest and greatest Android tools and utilities.
- Updates to all existing chapters, often with entirely new sections.
- New chapters, which cover new SDK features or expand upon those covered in previous editions.
- Updated sample code and applications, conveniently organized by chapter.
- Topics such as threading and asynchronous processing, creating content providers, broadcast intents, and animation frameworks now have their own chapters.
- Coverage of hot topics such as tablet and TV design, best practices, Renderscript, in-app billing, and Google Analytics.
- Even more tips and tricks from the trenches to help you design, develop, and test applications for different device targets, including an all-new chapter on tackling compatibility issues.

As you can see, we cover many of the hottest and most exciting features that Android has to offer. We didn't take this review lightly; we touched every existing chapter, updated content, and added many new chapters. Finally, we included many additions, clarifications, and, yes, even a few fixes based upon the feedback from our fantastic (and meticulous) readers. Thank you!

The Development Environment Used in This Book

The Android code in this book was written using the following development environments:

Windows 7 and Mac OS X 10.7.x

- Eclipse Java IDE Version 3.7 (Indigo)
- Eclipse JDT plug-in and Web Tools Platform (WTP)
- Java SE Development Kit (JDK) 6 Update 26
- Android SDK Version 2.3.4, API Level 10 (Gingerbread MR1), Android SDK Version 3.2, API Level 13 (Honeycomb MR2), Android SDK Version 4.0.3, API Level 15 (Ice Cream Sandwich MR1)

  1. ADT plug-in for Eclipse 16.0.1
  2. SDK Tools Revision 16
  3. Android Support Package r4
  4. Android NDK r7

- Android devices: Samsung Galaxy Nexus, Motorola Droid 3, Samsung Galaxy tab 10.1, Asus Transformer Prime, Motorola Atrix 4G, and Logitech Revue

The Android platform continues to aggressively grow in market share against competing mobile platforms, such as Apple iOS and BlackBerry. New and exciting types of devices reach consumers' hands at a furious pace, with new editions of the Android platform appearing all the time. Developers can no longer ignore Android as a target platform if they want to reach the smartphone (or smart-device) users of today and tomorrow.

Android's latest major platform update, Android 4.0, frequently called by its code-name, Ice Cream Sandwich or just ICS, merges the smartphone-centric Android 2.3.x (Gingerbread) and the tablet-centric Android 3.x (Honeycomb) platform editions into a single SDK for all smart-devices, be they phones, tablets, televisions, or toasters. This book features the latest SDK and tools available, but it does not focus on them to the detriment of popular legacy versions of the platform. This book is meant to be an overall reference to help developers support all popular devices on the market today. As of the writing of this book, only a small percentage (less than 5 percent) of users' devices run Android 3.0 or 4.0. Of course, some devices receive upgrades, and users purchase new devices as they become available, but for now, developers need to straddle this gap and support numerous versions of Android to reach the majority of users in the field.

So what does this mean for this book? It means we provide both legacy API support and discuss some of the newer APIs available only in later versions of the Android SDK. We discuss strategies for supporting all (or at least most) users in terms of compatibility. And we provide screenshots that highlight different versions of the Android SDK, because each major revision has brought with it a change in the look and feel of the overall platform. That said, we are assuming that you are downloading the latest Android tools, so we provide screenshots and steps that support the latest tools available at the time of writing, not legacy tools. Those are the boundaries we set when trying to determine what to include or leave out of this book.

Supplementary Materials Available

The source code that accompanies this book is available for download on the publisher website: http://www.informit.com/title/9780321813848. The source code is also available for download from our book website: http://androidbook.blogspot.com/p/book-code-downloads.html (http://goo.gl/kyAsN). You can also find a variety of Android topics discussed at our book website (http://androidbook.blogspot.com). For example, we present reader feedback, questions, and additional information. You can also find links to our various technical articles on our book website.

Where to Find More Information

There is a vibrant, helpful Android developer community on the Web. Here are a number of useful websites for Android developers and followers of the wireless industry:

- **Android Developer Website:** The Android SDK and developer reference site: http://developer.android.com/

- **Stack Overflow:** The Android website with great technical information (complete with tags) and an official support forum for developers:

  http://stackoverflow.com/questions/tagged/android

- **Open Handset Alliance:** Android manufacturers, operators, and developers:

  http://www.openhandsetalliance.com/

- **Android Market:** Buy and sell Android applications:

  http://www.android.com/market/

- **Mobiletuts+:** Mobile development tutorials, including Android:

  http://mobile.tutsplus.com/category/tutorials/android/

- **anddev.org:** An Android developer forum:

  http://www.anddev.org

- **Google Team Android Apps:** Open source Android applications:

  http://apps-for-android.googlecode.com/

- **Android Tools Project Site:** The tools team discusses updates and changes:

  https://sites.google.com/a/android.com/tools/recent

- **FierceDeveloper:** A weekly newsletter for wireless developers:

  http://www.fiercedeveloper.com/

- **Wireless Developer Network:** Daily news on the wireless industry:

  http://www.wirelessdevnet.com/

- **XDA-Developers Android Forum**: From general development to ROMs:

  http://forum.xda-developers.com/forumdisplay.php?f=564

- **Developer.com:** A developer-oriented site with mobile articles:

  http://www.developer.com/

Conventions Used in This Book

This book uses the following conventions:

- ➥ is used to signify to readers that the authors meant for the continued code to appear on the same line. No indenting should be done on the continued line.

- Code or programming terms are set in `monospace` text.

- Java import statements, exception handling, and error checking are often removed from printed code samples for clarity and to keep the book a reasonable length.

This book also presents information in the following sidebars:

Tip

Tips provide useful information or hints related to the current text.

Note

Notes provide additional information that might be interesting or relevant.

Warning

Warnings provide hints or tips about pitfalls that may be encountered and how to avoid them.

Contacting the Authors

We welcome your comments, questions, and feedback. We invite you to visit our blog at:

http://androidbook.blogspot.com
Or, email us at:

androidwirelessdev+awad3ev2@gmail.com
Circle us on Google+:

- Lauren Darcey: http://goo.gl/P3RGo
- Shane Conder: http://goo.gl/BpVJh

## 1

Threading and Asynchronous Processing

Offloading intensive operations provides a smoother, more stable experience to the user. The Android SDK provides two easy ways to manage offload processing from the main UI thread: the `AsyncTask` class and the standard Java `Thread` class. An `Activity` or `Fragment` often needs to load data upon launch, which can be done asynchronously using a `Loader` class. In this chapter, you learn how to make your applications more responsive by knowing when and how to move intensive operations off the main UI thread to be handled asynchronously.

The Importance of Processing Asynchronously

Users demand responsive applications, time-intensive operations such as networking should not block the main UI thread. Some common blocking operations include:

- Any lengthy or complex calculation or operation
- Querying a data set of indeterminate size
- Parsing a data set
- Processing multimedia files, such as images, video, or audio
- Iterating over a data structure of indeterminate size
- Accessing network resources
- Accessing location-based services
- Accessing a content provider interface
- Accessing a local database
- Accessing a local file
- Accessing any service that uses any of the previous services

If your application is not responsive enough, it might be plagued with Application Not Responding (ANR) events. ANR events occur when the Android operating system decides that your application is not responding in a reasonable time and shuts that application down. Typically, these events happen when your application takes longer than 5 seconds to respond or complete a task.

On API Level 11 and later, moving certain operations off the main UI thread is mandatory. For example, networking code must be completed asynchronously. Your code violates system-wide `StrictMode` policies otherwise. Make sure to test on devices.

Offloading intensive operations from the main UI thread helps avoid the dreaded ANR event and provides a smoother, more stable experience to the user. However, you must still perform all UI operations on the main thread so some communication between these tasks may be desired. Even certain nonintensive operations are important to offload, such as reading or writing to the file system. While these are normally fast, occasionally a read or write might block for various reasons, including contention on the file or the file system itself. Mobile devices often use flash-based storage that uses wear-reduction algorithms that can significantly delay disk writes on occasion.

The Android SDK provides several ways to manage offload processing from the main UI thread:

- Use the `AsyncTask` helper class to easily complete tasks asynchronously and communicate back to the main UI thread.

- Use the standard `Thread` class to complete your processing, as you would in any Java application.

- Use the `Loader` class to facilitate the loading of data for use in an `Activity` or `Fragment` while still starting up quickly.

We discuss all three of these in this chapter.

Tip

Many of the code examples provided in this chapter are taken from the SimpleAsync application. The source code for the SimpleAsync application is provided for download on the book's websites.

Working with the `AsyncTask` Class

The `AsyncTask` class (`android.os.AsyncTask`) is a special class for Android development that encapsulates background processing and helps facilitate communication to the UI thread while managing the lifecycle of the background task within the context of the `Activity` lifecycle.

The `AsyncTask` class is an abstract helper class for managing background operations that eventually are posted back to the UI thread. It creates a simpler interface for asynchronous operations than manually creating a `Thread` class. Internally, `AsyncTask` improves with the Android SDK, and in later versions, it can manage multiple tasks simultaneously using multiple physical cores and an internal thread pool.

Instead of creating threads for background processing and using messages and message handlers for updating the UI, you can create a subclass of `AsyncTask` and implement the appropriate callback methods. The important callbacks are:

- The `onPreExecute()` method runs on the UI thread before background processing begins.
- The `doInBackground()` method runs in the background and is where all the real work is done.
- The `publishProgress()` method, called from the `doInBackground()` method, periodically informs the UI thread about the background process progress. This method sends information to the UI process. Use this opportunity to send updated progress for a progress bar that the user can see.
- The `onProgressUpdate()` method runs on the UI thread whenever the `doInBackground()` method calls `publishProgress()`. This method receives information from the background process. Use this opportunity to update a `ProgressBar` control that the user can see.
- The `onPostExecute()` method runs on the UI thread once the background processing is completed.

When launched with the `execute()` method, the `AsyncTask` class handles processing in a background thread without blocking the UI thread.

Let's look at a simple example. Here we have an `Activity` class that simply displays a `TextView` control on the screen. In its `onCreate()` method, it launches an asynchronous task called `CounterTask`, which slowly counts to 100. Every time it makes some progress (defined here as 5 percent), it updates the `TextView` control in the UI. Here is the complete implementation:

```java
public class SimpleAsyncActivity extends Activity {

    @Override
    public void onCreate(Bundle savedInstanceState) {
        super.onCreate(savedInstanceState);
        setContentView(R.layout.main);

        CountingTask tsk = new CountingTask();
        tsk.execute();
    }

    private class CountingTask extends AsyncTask<Void, Integer, Integer> {

        CountingTask() {}

        @Override
        protected Integer doInBackground(Void... unused) {
```

```
            int i = 0;
            while (i < 100) {
                SystemClock.sleep(250);
                i++;

                if (i % 5 == 0) {
                    // update UI with progress every 5%
                    publishProgress(i);
                }
            }
            return i;
        }

        protected void onProgressUpdate(Integer... progress) {
            TextView tv = (TextView) findViewById(R.id.counter);
            tv.setText(progress[0] + "% Complete!");
        }

        protected void onPostExecute(Integer result) {
            TextView tv = (TextView) findViewById(R.id.counter);
            tv.setText("Count Complete! Counted to " + result.toString());
        }
    }
}
```

There are two ways to start the task. The first, and default, is to simply instantiate the task and call the execute() method. Each task instantiation can be executed only once.

```
CountingTask tsk = new CountingTask();
tsk.execute();
```

On devices running at least API Level 11, tasks can be executed in parallel. On devices with multiple cores, this can allow execution to complete faster and, in the process, potentially increase your application performance and smoothness. If you modify the previous code to take an identifier for what TextView to update with the counter, you can execute several in parallel. Each task still has to be instantiated separately.

```
CountingTask tsk = new CountingTask();
tsk.executeOnExecutor(AsyncTask.THREAD_POOL_EXECUTOR, id1);
CountingTask tsk2 = new CountingTask();
tsk2.executeOnExecutor(AsyncTask.THREAD_POOL_EXECUTOR, id2);
```

Warning

On API Level 11, the execute() method behaves as if it were using a thread pool. If you do not want parallel execute, call executeOnExecute(AsyncTask.SERIAL_ EXECUTOR). Although the documentation lists the plan to return execute to serial behavior after API Level 11, you can only confirm that the behavior is serial on API Level 14.

Working with the `Thread` Class

If you need to control a thread yourself, use the `Thread` class (`java.lang.Thread`).
Porting existing code might be simpler using the `Thread` class directly, instead of
`AsyncTask`. The `Activity` class that owns the thread is responsible for managing the
lifecycle of the thread. Generally speaking, the `Activity` includes a member variable of
type `Handler`. Then, when the `Thread` is instantiated and started, the `post()` method of
the `Handler` is used to communicate with the main UI thread. You can also communicate to the main UI thread using the `runOnUiThread()` method of the `Activity` class
and the `post()` and `postDelayed()` methods of the `View` class. For example, here is a
simple `Activity` class that performs a similar operation to the `AsyncTask` example
shown earlier in this chapter.

```
public class SimpleThreadActivity extends Activity {
    @Override
    public void onCreate(Bundle savedInstanceState) {
        super.onCreate(savedInstanceState);
        setContentView(R.layout.main);

        final TextView tv = (TextView) findViewById(R.id.counter);
        new Thread(new Runnable() {
            public void run() {

                int i = 0;

                while (i < 100) {
                    SystemClock.sleep(250);
                    i++;

                    final int curCount = i;
                    if (curCount % 5 == 0) {
                        // update UI with progress every 5%
                        tv.post(new Runnable() {
                            public void run() {
                                tv.setText(curCount + "% Complete!");
                            }
                        });
                    }
                }

                tv.post(new Runnable() {
                    public void run() {
                        tv.setText("Count Complete!");
                    }
                });
            }
```

```
        }).start();
    }
}
```

Here we create a new `Thread` object on the fly in the `onCreate()` method of the `Activity` class. Again, we count to 100 using the `post()` method to update the `TextView` with our progress in a thread-safe manner.

Working with `Loaders`

Android 3.0 (API Level 11) introduced the concept of a `Loader` class, which helps asynchronously load data for an `Activity` or `Fragment` from a data source such as a content provider or the network. When configured properly, a `Loader` also monitors the data source for changes, updating the `Activity` or `Fragment` as necessary, which helps avoid unnecessary queries. The most common reason to use a `Loader` involves pulling data from a content provider. To use a `Loader`, take the following steps:

1. Use your `Activity` or `Fragment` class's `LoaderManager` to initialize a `Loader`.

2. Provide an implementation of the `LoaderManager.LoaderCallbacks`.

3. The `onCreateLoader()` method is used to return a new `Loader` instance, typically a `CursorLoader` that queries a content provider that the `Activity` or `Fragment` wants to display data from.

4. The `onLoadFinished()` method signals that all data has been loaded and is ready for use. Typically, your screen contains some sort of control, such as a `ListView`, that leverages the `CursorAdapter` associated with the `CursorLoader`, so you want to swap the old and new `Cursor` objects in the adapter at this time.

5. The `onLoaderReset()` method is used to signify that that the data is unavailable, and thus, the `Cursor` used by the adapter is no longer valid. Typically, you need to swap out the `Cursor` again at this time, because it is no longer valid.

Although the `Loader` class was added in API Level 11, it is part of the Android Support Package, so it can be used as far back as Android 1.6.

Tip

You can find an example of a `CursorLoader` in Chapter 4, "Building Android Content Providers." There are also numerous examples in the Android SDK samples.

Understanding StrictMode

Strict mode is a method developers can use to detect operations that should not be performed on the main thread. Beginning in API Level 9, developers can enable strict mode in their own applications to detect when they were, for instance, performing network or disk operations on the main thread. In API Level 11, strict mode was expanded with system-wide settings. These settings disallow some operations on the main thread and instead throw exceptions. To enable strict mode in your own applications to behave like API Level 11 or later, use the following code:

```
StrictMode.ThreadPolicy policy = new StrictMode.ThreadPolicy.Builder()
        .detectAll().penaltyDeath().build();

StrictMode.setThreadPolicy(policy);
```

If you're not writing a production application and want to run some quick code without wiring up a full thread, you can disable the crashing and simply flash the screen instead (on API Level 11) or log the mistakes. You can also call `permitAll()` to skip strict mode entirely. This is not recommended for production applications.

On Android 4.0 and later devices, a Developer options setting screen is available to turn on and off the screen flashing with strict mode; however, it doesn't detect quite as many mistakes. It can be enlightening to turn it on, though.

Summary

Android applications perform many intensive operations on a regular basis, such as accessing resources on disk, services, content providers, databases, and the network. Other operations that can block the main thread include long processing and calculations, and even simple tasks that are performed on a large set of data. All of these tasks should be moved from the main UI thread of the application using some sort of asynchronous method, whether it uses the `Thread` class, an `AsyncTask` implementation, a `Loader`, or a background service, which we talk about in the next chapter. Developers can use `StrictMode` to help identify areas of their applications that could be more responsive.

References and More Information

Android Dev Guide: "Designing for Responsiveness":
   http://d.android.com/guide/practices/design/responsiveness.html
Android Dev Guide: "Processes and Threads":
   http://d.android.com/guide/topics/fundamentals/processes-and-threads.html
Android SDK documentation on the `Thread` class:
   http://d.android.com/reference/java/lang/Thread.html
Android SDK documentation on the `AsyncTask` class:
   http://d.android.com/reference/android/os/AsyncTask.html
Android Dev Guide: "Loaders":
   http://d.android.com/guide/topics/fundamentals/loaders.html
Android SDK documentation on the `StrictMode` class:
   http://d.android.com/reference/android/os/StrictMode.html

2

Working with Services

One important Android application component that can greatly enhance an application is a service. An Android service might be used to perform functions in the background that do not require user input or to supply information to other applications. In this chapter, learn how to create and interact with an Android service. Then learn how to define a remote interface using the Android Interface Definition Language (AIDL). Finally, learn how to pass objects through this interface by creating a class that implements a `Parcelable` object.

Determining When to Use Services

A service in the Android Software Development Kit (SDK) can mean one of two things. First, a service can mean a background process, performing some useful operation at regular intervals. Second, a service can be an interface for a remote object, called from within your application. In both cases, the service object extends the `Service` class from the Android SDK, and it can be a standalone component or part of an application with a complete user interface.

Certainly, not all applications require or use services. However, you might want to consider a service if your application meets certain criteria, such as the following:

- The application performs lengthy or resource-intensive processing that does not require input from the user.
- The application must perform certain functions routinely, or at regular intervals, such as uploading or downloading fresh content or logging the current location.
- The application performs a lengthy operation that, if cancelled because the application exits, would be wasteful to restart. An example of this is downloading large files.
- The application performs a lengthy operation while the user might be using multiple activities. A service can be used to span processing across the bounds of activity lifecycles.
- The application needs to expose and provide data or information services (think web services) to other Android applications without the need of a user interface.

Understanding the Service Lifecycle

Before we get into the details of how to create a service, let's look at how services interact with the Android operating system. First, it should be noted that a service implementation must be registered in that application's manifest file using the `<service>` tag. The service implementation might also define and enforce any permissions needed for starting, stopping, and binding to the service, as well as make specific service calls.

After it's been implemented, an Android service can be started using the `Context.startService()` method. If the service was already running when the `startService()` method was called, these subsequent calls don't start further instances of the service. The service continues to run until either the `Context.stopService()` method is called or the service completes its tasks and stops itself using the `stopSelf()` method.

To connect to a service, interested applications use the `Context.bindService()` method to obtain a connection. If that service is not running, it is created at that time. After the connection is established, the interested applications can begin making requests of that service, if the applications have the appropriate permissions. For example, a Magic Eight Ball application might have an underlying service that can receive yes-or-no questions and provide Yoda-style answers. Any interested application can connect to the Magic Eight Ball service, ask a question ("Will my app flourish on the Android Market?"), and receive the result ("Signs point to Yes."). The application can then disconnect from the service when finished using the `Context.unbindService()` method.

Warning

Like applications, services can be killed by the Android operating system under low-memory conditions. Also like applications, services have a main thread that can be blocked, causing the system to become unresponsive. Always offload intensive processing to worker threads using whatever methodology you like, even when implementing a service.

Creating a Service

Creating an Android service involves extending the `Service` class and adding a service block to the `AndroidManifest.xml` permissions file. The `GPXService` class, discussed later in this section, overrides the `onCreate()`, `onStart()`, `onStartCommand()`, and `onDestroy()` methods to begin with. Defining the service name enables other applications to start the service that runs in the background and stop it. Both the `onStart()` and `onStartCommand()` methods are essentially the same, with the exception that `onStart()` is deprecated in API Levels 5 and above. (The default implementation of the `onStartCommand()` on API Level 5 or greater is to call `onStart()`, which returns an appropriate value so that behavior is compatible to previous versions.) In the following example, both methods are implemented.

Tip

Many of the code examples provided in this chapter are taken from the SimpleService and UseService applications. The source code for these applications is provided for download on the book's websites.

For this example, we implement a simple service that listens for GPS changes, displays notifications at regular intervals, and then provides access to the most recent location data via a remote interface. The following code gives a simple definition to the `Service` class called `GPXService`:

```
public class GPXService extends Service {
    public static final String GPX_SERVICE =
        "com.androidbook.GPXService.SERVICE";

    private LocationManager location = null;
    private NotificationManager notifier = null;

    @Override
    public void onCreate() {
        super.onCreate();
    }
    @Override
    public void onStart(Intent intent, int startId) {
        super.onStart(intent, startId);
    }

    @Override
    public void onStartCommand(Intent intent, int flags, int startId) {
        super.onStart(intent, startId);
    }

    @Override
    public void onDestroy() {
        super.onDestroy();
    }
}
```

You need to understand the lifecycle of a service because it's different from that of an activity. If a service is started by the system with a call to the `Context.startService()` method, the `onCreate()` method is called just before the `onStart()` or `onStartCommand()` methods. However, if the service is bound to with a call to the `Context.bindService()` method, the `onCreate()` method is called just before the `onBind()` method. The `onStart()` and `onStartCommand()` methods are not called in this case. We talk more about binding to a service later in this chapter. Finally, when the service is finished—that is, it is stopped and no other process is bound to it—the `onDestroy()` method is called. Everything for the service must be cleaned up in this method.

With this in mind, here is the full implementation of the `onCreate()` method for the GPXService class previously introduced:

```
public void onCreate() {
    super.onCreate();

    location = (LocationManager)
        getSystemService(Context.LOCATION_SERVICE);
    notifier = (NotificationManager)
        getSystemService(Context.NOTIFICATION_SERVICE);
}
```

Because the object doesn't yet know if the next call is to either of the start methods or the `onBind()` method, we make a couple of quick initialization calls, but no background processing is started. Even this might be too much if neither of these objects is used by the interface provided by the binder.

Because we can't always predict what version of Android our code runs on, we can simply implement both the `onStart()` and `onStartCommand()` methods and have them call a third method that provides a common implementation. This enables us to customize behaviors on later Android versions while being compatible with earlier versions. To do this, the project needs to be built for an SDK of Level 5 or higher while having a `minSdkValue` of whatever earlier versions are supported. Of course, we highly recommend testing on multiple platform versions to verify that the behavior is as you expect. Here are sample implementations of the `onStartCommand()` and `onStart()` methods:

```
@Override
public int onStartCommand(Intent intent, int flags, int startId ) {
    Log.v(DEBUG_TAG, "onStartCommand() called, must be on L5 or later");

    if (flags != 0) {
        Log.w(DEBUG_TAG, "Redelivered or retrying service start: "+flags);
    }

    doServiceStart(intent, startId);
    return Service.START_REDELIVER_INTENT;
}

@Override
public void onStart(Intent intent, int startId) {
    super.onStart(intent, startId);
    Log.v(DEBUG_TAG, "onStart() called, must be on L3 or L4");
    doServiceStart(intent,startId);
}
```

Next, let's look at the implementation of the doServiceStart() method in greater detail:

```
@Override
public void doServiceStart(Intent intent, int startId) {
    updateRate = intent.getIntExtra(EXTRA_UPDATE_RATE, -1);
    if (updateRate == -1) {
        updateRate = 60000;
    }

    Criteria criteria = new Criteria();
    criteria.setAccuracy(Criteria.NO_REQUIREMENT);
    criteria.setPowerRequirement(Criteria.POWER_LOW);

    location = (LocationManager)
        getSystemService(Context.LOCATION_SERVICE);

    String best = location.getBestProvider(criteria, true);

    location.requestLocationUpdates(best,
        updateRate, 0, trackListener);

    Notification notify = new
        Notification(android.R.drawable.stat_notify_more,
        "GPS Tracking", System.currentTimeMillis());
    notify.flags |= Notification.FLAG_AUTO_CANCEL;

    Intent toLaunch = new Intent(getApplicationContext(),
        ServiceControl.class);
    PendingIntent intentBack =
        PendingIntent.getActivity(getApplicationContext(),
        0, toLaunch, 0);

    notify.setLatestEventInfo(getApplicationContext(),
        "GPS Tracking", "Tracking start at " +
        updateRate+"ms intervals with [" + best +
        "] as the provider.", intentBack);
    notifier.notify(GPS_NOTIFY, notify);
    }
```

The background processing starts in the two start methods. In this example, though, the background processing is actually just registering for an update from another service. For more information about using location-based services and the LocationManager, see Chapter 13, "Using Location-Based Services APIs," and for more information on Notification calls, see Chapter 6, "Working with Notifications."

> **Tip**
>
> The use of a callback to receive updates is recommended over doing background process-
> ing to poll for updates. Most mobile devices have limited battery life. Continual running in
> the background, or even just polling, can use a substantial amount of battery power. In
> addition, implementing callbacks for the users of your service is also more efficient for the
> same reasons.

In this case, we turn on the GPS for the duration of the process, which might affect battery life even though we request a lower power method of location determination. Keep this in mind when developing services.

The `Intent` extras object retrieves data passed in by the process requesting the service. Here, we retrieve one value, `EXTRA_UPDATE_RATE`, for determining the length of time between updates. The string for this, `update-rate`, must be published externally, either in developer documentation or in a publicly available class file so that users of this service know about it.

The implementation details of the `LocationListener` object, `trackListener`, are not interesting to the discussion on services. However, processing should be kept to a minimum to avoid interrupting what the user is doing in the foreground. Some testing might be required to determine how much processing a particular phone can handle before the user notices performance issues.

There are two common methods to communicate data to the user. The first is to use notifications. This is the least-intrusive method and can be used to drive users to the application for more information. It also means the users don't need to be actively using their phone at the time of the notification because it is queued. For instance, a weather application might use notifications to provide weather updates every hour.

The other method is to use `Toast` messages. From some services, this might work well, especially if the user expects frequent updates and those updates work well overlaid briefly on the screen, regardless of what the user is currently doing. For instance, a background music player could briefly overlay the current song title when the song changes.

The `onDestroy()` method is called when no clients are bound to the service and a request for the service to be stopped has been made via a call to the `Context.stopService()` method, or a call has been made to the `stopSelf()` method from within the service. At this point, everything should be gracefully cleaned up because the service ceases to exist.

Here is an example of the `onDestroy()` method:

```
@Override
public void onDestroy() {
    if (location != null) {
        location.removeUpdates(trackListener);
        location = null;
    }

    Notification notify = new
```

```
        Notification(android.R.drawable.stat_notify_more,
            "GPS Tracking", System.currentTimeMillis());
    notify.flags |= Notification.FLAG_AUTO_CANCEL;

    Intent toLaunch = new Intent(getApplicationContext(),
        ServiceControl.class);
    PendingIntent intentBack =
        PendingIntent.getActivity(getApplicationContext(),
        0, toLaunch, 0);
    notify.setLatestEventInfo(getApplicationContext(),
        "GPS Tracking", "Tracking stopped", intentBack);

    notifier.notify(GPS_NOTIFY, notify);
    super.onDestroy();
}
```

Here, we stop updates to the `LocationListener` object. This stops all our background processing. Then, we notify the user that the service is terminating. Only a single call to the `onDestroy()` method happens, regardless of how many times the start methods are called.

The system does not know about a service unless it is defined within the `AndroidManifest.xml` permissions file using the `<service>` tag. Here is the `<service>` tag we must add to the Android Manifest file:

```
<service
    android:enabled="true"
    android:name="GPXService">
    <intent-filter>
        <action android:name=
            "com.androidbook.GPXService.SERVICE" />
    </intent-filter>
</service>
```

This block of XML defines the service name, `GPXService`, and that the service is enabled. Then, using an intent filter, we use the same string that we defined within the class. This is the string that is used later on when controlling the service. With this block of XML inside the application section of the manifest, the system now knows that the service exists and it can be used by other applications.

Controlling a Service

At this point, the example code has a complete implementation of a `Service`. Now we write code to control the service we previously defined.

```
Intent service = new Intent("com.androidbook.GPXService.SERVICE");
service.putExtra("update-rate", 5000);
startService(service);
```

Starting a service is as straightforward as creating an `Intent` with the service name and calling the `startService()` method. In this example, we also set the `Intent` extra parameter called `update-rate` to 5 seconds. That rate is quite frequent but works well for testing. For practical use, we probably want this set to 60 seconds or more. This code triggers a call to the `onCreate()` method, if the Service isn't bound to or running already. It also triggers a call to the `onStart()` or `onStartCommand()` methods, even if the service is already running.

Later, when we finish with the service, it needs to be stopped using the following code:

```
Intent service = new Intent("com.androidbook.GPXService.SERVICE");
stopService(service);
```

This code is essentially the same as starting the service but with a call to the `stopService()` method. This calls the `onDestroy()` method if there are no bindings to it. However, if there are bindings, `onDestroy()` is not called until those are also terminated. This means background processing might continue despite a call to the `stopService()` method. If there is a need to control the background processing separate from these system calls, a remote interface is required.

Implementing a Remote Interface

Sometimes it is useful to have more control over a service than just system calls to start and stop its activities. However, before a client application can bind to a service for making other method calls, you need to define the interface. The Android SDK includes a useful tool and file format for remote interfaces for this purpose.

To define a remote interface, you must declare the interface in an AIDL file, implement the interface, and then return an instance of the interface when the `onBind()` method is called.

Using the example `GPXService` service we already built in this chapter, we now create a remote interface for it. This remote interface has a method, which can be called especially for returning the last location logged. You can use only primitive types and objects that implement the `Parcelable` (`android.os.Parcelable`) protocol with remote service calls. This is because these calls cross process boundaries where memory can't be shared. The AIDL compiler handles the details of crossing these boundaries when the rules are followed. The `Location` object implements the `Parcelable` interface so it can be used.

Here is the AIDL file for this interface, `IRemoteInterface`:

```
package com.androidbook.services;


interface IRemoteInterface {
    Location getLastLocation();
}
```

When using Eclipse, you can add this AIDL file, IRemoteInterface.aidl, to the project under the appropriate package and the Android SDK plug-in does the rest. Now we must implement the code for the interface. Here is an example implementation of this interface:

```
private final IRemoteInterface.Stub
    mRemoteInterfaceBinder = new IRemoteInterface.Stub() {
        public Location getLastLocation() {
            Log.v("interface", "getLastLocation() called");
            return lastLocation;
        }
    };
```

The service code already stored off the last location received as a member variable, so we can simply return that value. With the interface implemented, it needs to be returned from the onBind() method of the service:

```
@Override
public IBinder onBind(Intent intent) {
    // we only have one, so no need to check the intent
    return mRemoteInterfaceBinder;
}
```

If multiple interfaces are implemented, the Intent passed in can be checked within the onBind() method to determine what action is to be taken and which interface should be returned. In this example, though, we have only one interface and don't expect any other information within the Intent, so we simply return the interface.

We also add the class name of the binder interface to the list of actions supported by the intent filter for the service within the AndroidManifest.xml file. Doing this isn't required but is a useful convention to follow and allows the class name to be used. The following block is added to the service tag definition:

```
<action android:name =
    "com.androidbook.services.IRemoteInterface" />
```

The service can now be used through this interface. This is done by implementing a ServiceConnection object and calling the bindService() method. When finished, the unbindService() method must be called so the system knows that the application is done using the service. The connection remains even if the reference to the interface is gone.

Here is an implementation of a ServiceConnection object's two main methods, onServiceConnected() and onServiceDisconnected():

```
public void onServiceConnected(ComponentName name,
    IBinder service) {

    mRemoteInterface =
```

```
        IRemoteInterface.Stub.asInterface(service);
    Log.v("ServiceControl", "Interface bound.");
}

public void onServiceDisconnected(ComponentName name) {
    mRemoteInterface = null;
    Log.v("ServiceControl",
        "Remote interface no longer bound");
}
```

When the `onServiceConnected()` method is called, an `IRemoteInterface` instance that can be used to make calls to the interface we previously defined is retrieved. A call to the remote interface looks like any call to an interface now:

```
Location loc = mRemoteInterface.getLastLocation();
```

Tip

Remember that remote interface calls operate across process boundaries and are completed synchronously. As such, you should place it within a separate thread, as any lengthy call would be.

To use this interface from another application, you should place the AIDL file in the project and appropriate package. The call to `onBind()` triggers a call to the `onServiceConnected()` after the call to the service's `onCreate()` method. Remember, the `onStart()` and `onStartCommand()` methods are not called in this case.

```
bindService(new Intent(IRemoteInterface.class.getName()),
    this, Context.BIND_AUTO_CREATE);
```

In this case, the `Activity` we call from also implements the `ServiceConnection` interface. This code also demonstrates why it is a useful convention to use the class name as an intent filter. Because we have both intent filters and we don't check the action on the call to the `onBind()` method, we can also use the other intent filter, but the code here is clearer.

When done with the interface, a call to `unbindService()` disconnects the interface. However, a callback to the `onServiceDisconnected()` method does not mean that the service is no longer bound; the binding is still active at that point, just not the connection.

Implementing a `Parcelable` Class

In the example so far, we have been lucky in that the `Location` class implements the `Parcelable` interface. What if a new object needs to be passed through a remote interface?

Let's take the following class, `GPXPoint`, as an example:

```
public final class GPXPoint {

    public int latitude;
    public int longitude;
    public Date timestamp;
    public double elevation;

    public GPXPoint() {
    }
}
```

The GPXPoint class defines a location point that is similar to a GeoPoint but also includes the time the location was recorded and the elevation. This data is commonly found in the popular GPX file format. On its own, this is not a basic format that the system recognizes to pass through a remote interface. However, if the class implements the Parcelable interface and we then create an AIDL file from it, the object can be used in a remote interface.

To fully support the Parcelable type, we need to implement a few methods and a Parcelable.Creator<GPXPoint>. The following is the same class now modified to be a Parcelable class:

```
public final class GPXPoint implements Parcelable {

    public int latitude;
    public int longitude;
    public Date timestamp;
    public double elevation;

    public static final Parcelable.Creator<GPXPoint>
        CREATOR = new Parcelable.Creator<GPXPoint>() {

        public GPXPoint createFromParcel(Parcel src) {
            return new GPXPoint(src);
        }

        public GPXPoint[] newArray(int size) {
            return new GPXPoint[size];
        }

    };

    public GPXPoint() {
    }

    private GPXPoint(Parcel src) {
        readFromParcel(src);
```

```
    }

    public void writeToParcel(Parcel dest, int flags) {
        dest.writeInt(latitude);
        dest.writeInt(longitude);
        dest.writeDouble(elevation);
        dest.writeLong(timestamp.getTime());
    }

    public void readFromParcel(Parcel src) {
        latitude = src.readInt();
        longitude = src.readInt();
        elevation = src.readDouble();
        timestamp = new Date(src.readLong());
    }

    public int describeContents() {
        return 0;
    }
}
```

The writeToParcel() method is required and flattens the object in a particular order using supported primitive types within a Parcel. When the class is created from a Parcel, the Creator is called, which, in turn, calls the private constructor. For readability, we also created a readFromParcel() method that reverses the flattening, reading the primitives in the same order that they were written and creating a new Date object.

Now you must create the AIDL file for this class. You should place it in the same directory as the Java file and name it GPXPoint.aidl to match. You should make the contents look like the following:

```
package com.androidbook.services;


parcelable GPXPoint;
```

Now the GPXPoint class can be used in remote interfaces. This is done in the same way as any other native type or Parcelable object. You can modify the IRemoteInterface.aidl file to look like the following:

```
package com.androidbook.services;


import com.androidbook.services.GPXPoint;

interface IRemoteInterface {
    Location getLastLocation();
    GPXPoint getGPXPoint();
}
```

Additionally, we can provide an implementation for this method within the interface, as follows:

```
public GPXPoint getGPXPoint() {
    if (lastLocation == null) {
        return null;
    } else {
        Log.v("interface", "getGPXPoint() called");
        GPXPoint point = new GPXPoint();

        point.elevation = lastLocation.getAltitude();
        point.latitude =
            (int) (lastLocation.getLatitude() * 1E6);
        point.longitude =
            (int) (lastLocation.getLongitude() * 1E6);
        point.timestamp =
            new Date(lastLocation.getTime());

        return point;
    }
}
```

As can be seen, nothing particularly special needs to happen. Just by making the object `Parcelable`, it can now be used for this purpose.

Using the `IntentService` Class

Offloading regularly performed tasks to a work queue is an easy and efficient way to process multiple requests without the cumbersome overhead of creating a full `Service`. The `IntentService` class (`android.app.IntentService`) is a simple type of service that can be used to handle such tasks asynchronously by way of `Intent` requests. Each `Intent` is added to the work queue associated with that `IntentService` and handled sequentially. You can send data back to the application by simply broadcasting the result as an `Intent` object and using a broadcast receiver to catch the result and use it within the application.

Certainly, not all applications require or use a `Service`, or more specifically an `IntentService`. However, you may want to consider one if your application meets certain criteria, such as:

- The application routinely performs the same or similar blocking or resource-intensive processing operations that do not require input from the user in which requests for such operations can "pile up," requiring a queue to handle the requests in an organized fashion. Image processing or data downloading are examples of such processing.

- The application performs certain blocking operations at regular intervals but does not need to perform these routine tasks so frequently as to require a permanent, "always on" `Service`. Examples of such operations are accessing local storage content providers, application database, network, as well as heavy image processing, or math to chug through.

- The application routinely dispatches "work" but doesn't need an immediate response. For example, an email application might use an `IntentService` work queue to queue up each message to be packaged up and sent out to a mail server. All networking code would then be separated from the main user interface of the application.

Now let's look at an example of how you might use `IntentService`.

Tip

The code examples in this section are taken from the SimpleIntentService sample application. The source code for this application is provided for download on the book's websites.

Let's assume you have an application with a screen that performs some processing each time the user provides some input, and then displays the result. For example, you might have an `EditText` control for taking some textual input, a `Button` control to commit the text and start the processing, and a `TextView` control for displaying the result. The code in the `Button` click handler within the `Activity` class would look something like this:

```
EditText input = (EditText) findViewById(R.id.txt_input);
String strInputMsg = input.getText().toString();
SystemClock.sleep(5000);
TextView result = (TextView) findViewById(R.id.txt_result);
result.setText(strInputMsg + " "
  + DateFormat.format("MM/dd/yy h:mmaa", System.currentTimeMillis()));
```

All this click handler does is retrieve some text from an `EditText` control on the screen, hang around doing nothing for 5 seconds, and then generate some information to display in the `TextView` control as a result. In reality, your application would probably not just sit around sleeping, but do some real work. As written, the click processing runs on the main UI thread. This means that every time the user clicks on the `Button` control, the entire application becomes unresponsive for at least 5 seconds. The user must wait for the task to finish before he can continue using the application because the task is being completed on the main thread.

Wouldn't it be great if we could dispatch the processing request each time the user clicked the `Button`, but let the user interface remain responsive so the user can go about his business? Let's implement a simple `IntentService` that does just that. Here's our simple `IntentService` implementation:

```
public class SimpleIntentService extends IntentService {
    public static final String PARAM_IN_MSG = "imsg";
    public static final String PARAM_OUT_MSG = "omsg";

    public SimpleIntentService() {
        super("SimpleIntentService");
    }

    @Override
    protected void onHandleIntent(Intent intent) {
        String msg = intent.getStringExtra(PARAM_IN_MSG);
        SystemClock.sleep(5000);
        String resultTxt = msg + " "
            + DateFormat.format("MM/dd/yy h:mmaa",
              System.currentTimeMillis());
    Intent broadcastIntent = new Intent();
    broadcastIntent.setAction(ResponseReceiver.ACTION_RESP);
    broadcastIntent.addCategory(Intent.CATEGORY_DEFAULT);
    broadcastIntent.putExtra(PARAM_OUT_MSG, resultTxt);
    sendBroadcast(broadcastIntent);
    }
}
```

We use `Intent` extras to send some data associated with the specific task request, in a manner similar to passing data between `Activity` classes. In this case, we take the incoming `EditText` text value and package it into the `PARAM_IN_MSG` extra. Once the processing is complete, we use a broadcast intent to tell anyone interested that the service has finished the task. Your `IntentService` needs to do this only if the user interface needs to be updated. If the task simply updated the underlying application database or the shared preferences or what have you, then your application would not need to be informed directly, as `Cursor` objects and such would be updated automatically when some underlying data changed.

Now, turn your attention back to the `Activity` class that hosts your application user interface with the `Button` control. Update the `Button` click handler to send a new task request to the `SimpleIntentService`. The request is packaged as an `Intent`, the incoming parameter is set (the data associated with the task), and the request is fired off using the `startService()` method.

```
EditText input = (EditText) findViewById(R.id.txt_input);
String strInputMsg = input.getText().toString();
Intent msgIntent = new Intent(this, SimpleIntentService.class);
msgIntent.putExtra(SimpleIntentService.PARAM_IN_MSG, strInputMsg);
startService(msgIntent);
```

Finally, define a `BroadcastReceiver` object for use by the application `Activity`, to listen for the results of each task completing and update the user interface accordingly:

```
public class ResponseReceiver extends BroadcastReceiver {
   public static final String ACTION_RESP =
      "com.mamlambo.intent.action.MESSAGE_PROCESSED";

  @Override
   public void onReceive(Context context, Intent intent) {
      TextView result = (TextView) findViewById(R.id.txt_result);
      String text = intent.getStringExtra(SimpleIntentService.PARAM_OUT_MSG);
      result.setText(text);
   }
}
```

The `BroadcastReceiver` class's `onReceive()` callback method does the work of reacting to a new broadcast from your `SimpleIntentService`. It updates the `TextView` control based upon the `Intent` extra data, which is the "result" from the task processing. Your application should register the broadcast receiver only when it needs to listen for results, and then unregister it when it's no longer needed. To manage this, first add a private member variable to your `Activity`, like this:

```
private ResponseReceiver receiver;
```

Activities typically register for broadcasts in their `onCreate()` or `onResume()` methods by creating an `IntentFilter`, like this:

```
IntentFilter filter = new IntentFilter(ResponseReceiver.ACTION_RESP);
filter.addCategory(Intent.CATEGORY_DEFAULT);
receiver = new ResponseReceiver();
registerReceiver(receiver, filter);
```

Similarly, it is typical to unregister the receiver when the `Activity` class no longer needs to react to results. For example, in the `onPause()` or `onDestroy()` methods.

```
unregisterReceiver(receiver);
```

Finally, don't forget to register your `SimpleIntentService` in your Android Manifest file, like this:

```
<service android:name="SimpleIntentService"/>
```

That's the complete implementation of our example `IntentService`. The `Activity` shoots off requests to the `SimpleIntentService` each time the `Button` control is clicked. The service handles the queuing, processing, and broadcasting of the result of each task asynchronously. The service shuts itself down when there's nothing left to do and starts back up if a new request comes in. Meanwhile, the application `Activity` remains responsive because it is no longer processing each request on the same thread that handles the UI. The user interface is responsive throughout all processing, allowing the user to continue to use the application. The user can press the `Button` control five times in succession and trigger five tasks to be sent to the `IntentService` without having to wait 5 seconds between each click.

Summary

The Android SDK provides the `Service` mechanism that can be used to implement background tasks and to share functionality across multiple applications. By creating an interface through the use of AIDL, a `Service` can expose functionality to other applications without having to distribute libraries or packages. Creating objects with the `Parcelable` interface enables developers to extend the data that can also be passed across process boundaries.

Care should be taken when creating a background service. Poorly designed background services might have substantial negative impact on handset performance and battery life. In addition to standard testing, you should test a `Service` implementation with respect to these issues.

Prudent creation of a `Service`, though, can dramatically enhance the appeal of an application or service you might provide. `Service` creation is a powerful tool provided by the Android SDK for designing applications simply not possible on other mobile platforms. The `IntentService` class can be used to create a simple service that acts as a work queue.

References and More Information

Android Reference: The `Service` class:
   http://d.android.com/reference/android/app/Service.html
Android Dev Guide: "Service Lifecycle":
   http://d.android.com/guide/topics/fundamentals/services.html#Lifecycle
Android Dev Guide: "Processes and Threads":
   http://d.android.com/guide/topics/fundamentals/processes-and-threads.html
Android Application Framework FAQ:
   http://d.android.com/guide/appendix/faq/framework.html

## 3

Leveraging SQLite Application Databases

Applications use a combination of application preferences, the file system, and database support to store information. In this chapter, we explore one of the most powerful ways you can store, manage, and share application data with Android: an application database powered by SQLite. Application databases provide structured data storage that is quick to access, search, and manipulate.

Note

For more information about designing SQLite databases and interacting with them via the `sqlite3` command-line tool, please see Appendix B, "The SQLite Quick-Start Guide." This appendix is divided into two parts. The first half is an overview of the most commonly used features of the `sqlite3` command-line interface and the limitations of SQLite compared to other flavors of SQL; the second half of the appendix includes a fully functional tutorial in which you build a SQLite database from the ground up and then use it. If you are new to SQLite or a bit rusty on your syntax, this appendix is for you.

Storing Structured Data Using SQLite Databases

When your application requires a more robust data storage mechanism, you'll be happy to hear that the Android file system includes support for application-specific relational databases using SQLite. SQLite databases are lightweight and file-based, making them ideally suited for embedded devices.

Tip

Many of the code examples provided in this section are taken from the SimpleDatabase application. This source code for the SimpleDatabase application is provided for download on the book's websites.

These databases and the data in them are private to the application. To share application data with other applications, you must expose the data you want to share by making your application a content provider.

The Android SDK includes a number of useful SQLite database management classes. Many of these classes are found in the `android.database.sqlite` package. Here you can find utility classes for managing database creation and versioning, database management, and query builder helper classes to help you format proper SQL statements and queries. The package also includes specialized `Cursor` objects for iterating query results. You can also find all the specialized exceptions associated with SQLite.

In this chapter, we focus on creating databases in our Android applications. For that, we use the built-in SQLite support to programmatically create and use a SQLite database to store application information. However, if your application works with a different sort of database, you can also find more generic database classes (in the `android.database` package) to help you work with data from other providers.

In addition to programmatically creating and using SQLite databases, developers can also interact directly with their application's database using the `sqlite3` command-line tool that's accessible through the ADB shell interface. This can be a helpful debugging tool for developers and quality assurance personnel who might want to manage the database state (and content) for testing purposes.

Creating a SQLite Database

You can create a SQLite database for your Android application in several ways. To illustrate how to create and use a simple SQLite database, let's create an Android project called SimpleDatabase.

Creating a SQLite Database Instance Using the Application Context

The simplest way to create a new `SQLiteDatabase` instance for your application is to use the `openOrCreateDatabase()` method of your application `Context`, like this:

```
import android.database.sqlite.SQLiteDatabase;
...
SQLiteDatabase mDatabase;
mDatabase = openOrCreateDatabase(
    "my_sqlite_database.db",
    SQLiteDatabase.CREATE_IF_NECESSARY,
    null);
```

Finding the Application Database File on the Device File System

Android applications store their databases (SQLite or otherwise) in a special application directory:

```
/data/data/<application package name>/databases/<databasename>
```

So, in this case, the path to the database would be

`/data/data/com.androidbook.SimpleDatabase/databases/my_sqlite_database.db`

You can access your database using the `sqlite3` command-line interface using this path.

Configuring the SQLite Database Properties

Now that you have a valid `SQLiteDatabase` instance, it's time to configure it. Some important database configuration options include version, locale, and the thread-safe locking feature:

```
import java.util.Locale;
...
mDatabase.setLocale(Locale.getDefault());
mDatabase.setLockingEnabled(true);
mDatabase.setVersion(1);
```

Creating Tables and Other SQLite Schema Objects

Creating tables and other SQLite schema objects is as simple as forming proper SQLite statements and executing them. The following is a valid CREATE TABLE SQL statement. This statement creates a table called `tbl_authors`. The table has three fields: a unique `id` number, which auto-increments with each record and acts as our primary key, and `firstname` and `lastname` text fields:

```
CREATE TABLE tbl_authors (
id INTEGER PRIMARY KEY AUTOINCREMENT,
firstname TEXT,
lastname TEXT);
```

You can encapsulate this CREATE TABLE SQL statement in a `static final String` variable (called `CREATE_AUTHOR_TABLE`) and then execute it on your database using the `execSQL()` method:

```
mDatabase.execSQL(CREATE_AUTHOR_TABLE);
```

The `execSQL()` method works for nonqueries. You can use it to execute any valid SQLite SQL statement. For example, you can use it to create, update, and delete tables, views, triggers, and other common SQL objects. In our application, we add another table called `tbl_books`. The schema for `tbl_books` looks like this:

```
CREATE TABLE tbl_books (
id INTEGER PRIMARY KEY AUTOINCREMENT,
title TEXT,
dateadded DATE,
authorid INTEGER NOT NULL CONSTRAINT authorid REFERENCES tbl_authors(id) ON DELETE
CASCADE);
```

Unfortunately, SQLite does not enforce foreign key constraints. Instead, we must enforce them ourselves using custom SQL triggers. So we create triggers, such as this one that enforces that books have valid authors:

```
private static final String CREATE_TRIGGER_ADD =
"CREATE TRIGGER fk_insert_book BEFORE INSERT ON tbl_books
FOR EACH ROW
BEGIN
SELECT RAISE(ROLLBACK, 'insert on table \"tbl_books\" violates foreign key
constraint \"fk_authorid\"') WHERE  (SELECT id FROM tbl_authors WHERE id =
NEW.authorid) IS NULL;
END;";
```

We can then create the trigger simply by executing the CREATE TRIGGER SQL statement:

```
mDatabase.execSQL(CREATE_TRIGGER_ADD);
```

We need to add several more triggers to help enforce our link between the author and book tables, one for updating tbl_books and one for deleting records from tbl_authors.

Creating, Updating, and Deleting Database Records

Now that we have a database set up, we need to create some data. The SQLiteDatabase class includes three convenience methods to do that. They are, as you might expect, insert(), update(), and delete().

Inserting Records

We use the insert() method to add new data to our tables. We use the ContentValues object to pair the column names to the column values for the record we want to insert. For example, here we insert a record into tbl_authors for J.K. Rowling:

```
import android.content.ContentValues;
...
ContentValues values = new ContentValues();
values.put("firstname", "J.K.");
values.put("lastname", "Rowling");
long newAuthorID = mDatabase.insert("tbl_authors", null, values);
```

The insert() method returns the identifier of the newly created record. We use this author identifier to create book records for this author.

Tip

There is also another helpful method called `insertOrThrow()`, which does the same thing as the `insert()` method but throws a `SQLException` on failure, which can be helpful, especially if your inserts do not seem to be working and you'd like to know why. Generally, you'll want to check values before inserting and not rely on exceptions for common constraints.

You might want to create simple classes (that is, class `Author` and class `Book`) to encapsulate your application record data when it is used programmatically.

Updating Records

You can modify records in the database using the `update()` method. The `update()` method takes four arguments:

- The table to update records
- A `ContentValues` object with the modified fields to update
- An optional `WHERE` clause, in which `?` identifies a `WHERE` clause argument
- An array of `WHERE` clause arguments, each of which is substituted in place of the `?`s from the second parameter

Passing `null` to the `WHERE` clause modifies all records within the table, which can be useful for making sweeping changes to your database.

Most of the time, we want to modify individual records by their unique identifier. The following function takes two parameters: an updated book title and a `bookId`. We find the record in the table called `tbl_books` that corresponds with the `id` and update that book's title. Again, we use the `ContentValues` object to bind our column names to our data values:

```
public void updateBookTitle(Integer bookId, String newtitle) {
    ContentValues values = new ContentValues();
    values.put("title", newtitle);
    mDatabase.update("tbl_books",
        values, "id=?", new String[] { bookId.toString() });
}
```

Because we are not updating the other fields, we do not need to include them in the `ContentValues` object. We include only the `title` field because it is the only field we change.

Deleting Records

You can remove records from the database using the `remove()` method. The `remove()` method takes three arguments:

- The table to delete the record from
- An optional `WHERE` clause, in which `?` identifies a `WHERE` clause argument

- An array of WHERE clause arguments, each of which is substituted in place of the ?s from the second parameter

Passing null to the WHERE clause deletes all records in the table. For example, this function call deletes all records in the table called tbl_authors:

```
mDatabase.delete("tbl_authors", null, null);
```

Most of the time, though, we want to delete individual records by their unique identifiers. The following function takes a parameter bookId and deletes the record corresponding to that unique id (primary key) in the table called tbl_books:

```
public void deleteBook(Integer bookId) {
    mDatabase.delete("tbl_books", "id=?",
        new String[] { bookId.toString() });
}
```

You need not use the primary key (id) to delete records; the WHERE clause is entirely up to you. For instance, the following function deletes all book records in the table tbl_books for a given author by the author's unique identifier:

```
public void deleteBooksByAuthor(Integer authorID) {
    int numBooksDeleted = mDatabase.delete("tbl_books", "authorid=?",
        new String[] { authorID.toString() });
}
```

Working with Transactions

Often you have multiple database operations you want to happen all together or not at all. You can use SQL transactions to group operations together; if any of the operations fails, you can handle the error and either recover or roll back all operations. If the operations all succeed, you can then commit them. Here we have the basic structure for a transaction:

```
mDatabase.beginTransaction();
try {
    // Insert some records, update others, delete a few.
    // Do whatever you need to do as a unit, then commit it.

    mDatabase.setTransactionSuccessful();
} catch (Exception e) {
    // Transaction failed. Failed! Do something here.
    // It's up to you.
} finally {
    mDatabase.endTransaction();
}
```

Now let's look at the transaction in a bit more detail. A transaction always begins with a call to `beginTransaction()` method and a `try/catch` block. If your operations are successful, you can commit your changes with a call to the `setTransactionSuccessful()` method. If you do not call this method, all your operations are rolled back and not committed. Finally, you end your transaction by calling `endTransaction()` in the finally clause, guaranteeing that it'll be called. It's as simple as that.

In some cases, you might recover from an exception and continue with the transaction. For example, if you have an exception for a read-only database, you can open the database and retry your operations.

Finally, note that transactions can be nested, with the outer transaction either committing or rolling back all inner transactions.

Querying SQLite Databases

Databases are great for storing data in any number of ways, but retrieving the data you want is what makes databases powerful. This is partly a matter of designing an appropriate database schema and partly achieved by crafting SQL queries, most of which are SELECT statements.

Android provides many ways in which you can query your application database. You can run raw SQL query statements (strings), use a number of different SQL statement builder utility classes to generate proper query statements from the ground up, and bind specific user interface controls such as container views to your backend database directly.

Working with Cursors

When results are returned from a SQL query, you often access them using a `Cursor` found in the `android.database.Cursor` class. `Cursor` objects are like file pointers; they allow random access to query results.

You can think of query results as a table, in which each row corresponds to a returned record. The `Cursor` object includes helpful methods for determining how many results were returned by the query the `Cursor` represents and methods for determining the column names (fields) for each returned record. The columns in the query results are defined by the query, not necessarily by the database columns. These might include calculated columns, column aliases, and composite columns.

`Cursor` objects are generally kept around for a time. If you do something simple (such as get a count of records or in cases when you know you retrieved only a single simple record), you can execute your query and quickly extract what you need; don't forget to close the `Cursor` when you're done, as shown here:

```
// SIMPLE QUERY: select * from tbl_books
Cursor c = mDatabase.query("tbl_books",null,null,null,null,null,null);
// Do something quick with the Cursor here...
c.close();
```

Managing Cursors as Part of the Application Lifecycle

When a `Cursor` returns multiple records, or you do something more intensive, you need to consider running this operation on a thread separate from the UI thread. You also need to manage your `Cursor`.

`Cursor` objects must be managed as part of the application lifecycle. When the application pauses or shuts down, the `Cursor` must be deactivated with a call to the `deactivate()` method, and when the application restarts, the `Cursor` should refresh its data using the `requery()` method. When the `Cursor` is no longer needed, a call to `close()` must be made to release its resources.

As the developer, you can handle this by implementing `Cursor` management calls within the various lifecycle callbacks, such as `onPause()`, `onResume()`, and `onDestroy()`.

If you're lazy, like us, and you don't want to bother handling these lifecycle events, you can hand off the responsibility of managing `Cursor` objects to the parent `Activity` by using the `Activity` method called `startManagingCursor()`. The `Activity` handles the rest, deactivating and reactivating the `Cursor` as necessary and destroying the `Cursor` when the `Activity` is destroyed. You can always begin manually managing the `Cursor` object again later by simply calling `stopManagingCursor()`.

Here we perform the same simple query and then hand over `Cursor` management to the parent `Activity`:

```
// SIMPLE QUERY: select * from tbl_books
Cursor c = mDatabase.query("tbl_books",null,null,null,null,null,null);
startManagingCursor(c);
```

Note that, generally, the managed `Cursor` object is a member variable of the class, in terms of scope. You may notice that the `startManagingCursor()` and `stopManagingCursor()` calls are deprecated. In the context of using data on Android, most databases are exposed as content providers. Using a content provider, one can perform queries similar to these, but on more abstract URIs rather than directly on a database using table names. In doing this, you use the higher-level `query()` method of the `ContentResolver` class rather than directly on the database. The proper current method of doing this in a managed way is through the use of the `CursorLoader` class (`android.content.CursorLoader` for API Level 11 and higher, and in the support package for API Level 4 and higher).

Iterating Rows of Query Results and Extracting Specific Data

You can use the `Cursor` to iterate those results, one row at a time using various navigation methods such as `moveToFirst()`, `moveToNext()`, and `isAfterLast()`.

On a specific row, you can use the `Cursor` to extract the data for a given column in the query results. Because SQLite is not strongly typed, you can always pull fields out as Strings using the `getString()` method, but you can also use the type-appropriate extraction utility function to enforce type safety in your application.

For example, the following method takes a valid `Cursor` object, prints the number of returned results, and then prints some column information (name and number of columns). Next, it iterates through the query results, printing each record.

```java
public void logCursorInfo(Cursor c) {
    Log.i(DEBUG_TAG, "*** Cursor Begin *** " + " Results:" +
        c.getCount() + " Columns: " + c.getColumnCount());

    // Print column names
    String rowHeaders = "|| ";
    for (int i = 0; i < c.getColumnCount(); i++) {
        rowHeaders = rowHeaders.concat(c.getColumnName(i) + " || ");
    }

    Log.i(DEBUG_TAG, "COLUMNS " + rowHeaders);

    // Print records
    c.moveToFirst();
    while (c.isAfterLast() == false) {

        String rowResults = "|| ";
        for (int i = 0; i < c.getColumnCount(); i++) {
            rowResults = rowResults.concat(c.getString(i) + " || ");
        }

        Log.i(DEBUG_TAG,
            "Row " + c.getPosition() + ": " + rowResults);

        c.moveToNext();
    }
    Log.i(DEBUG_TAG, "*** Cursor End ***");
}
```

The output to the LogCat for this function might look something like Figure 3.1.

Figure 3.1   Sample log output for the `logCursorInfo()` method.

Executing Simple Queries

Your first stop for database queries should be the `query()` methods available in the `SQLiteDatabase` class. This method queries the database and returns any results as in a `Cursor` object. The `query()` method we mainly use takes the following parameters:

- [`String`]: The name of the table to compile the query against
- [`String Array`]: List of specific column names to return (use `null` for all)
- [`String`] The `WHERE` clause: Use `null` for all; might include selection args as `?`s
- [`String Array`]: Any selection argument values to substitute in for the `?`s in the earlier parameter
- [`String`] `GROUP BY` clause: `null` for no grouping
- [`String`] `HAVING` clause: `null` unless `GROUP BY` clause requires one
- [`String`] `ORDER BY` clause: If `null`, default ordering used
- [`String`] `LIMIT` clause: If `null`, no limit

Previously, we called the `query()` method with only one parameter set to the table name, as shown in the following code:

```
Cursor c = mDatabase.query("tbl_books",null,null,null,null,null,null);
```

This is equivalent to the SQL query

```
SELECT * FROM tbl_books;
```

Tip

The individual parameters for the clauses (`WHERE`, `GROUP BY`, `HAVING`, `ORDER BY`, `LIMIT`) are all `String`s, but you do not need to include the keyword, such as `WHERE`. Instead, you include the part of the clause after the keyword.

Add a `WHERE` clause to your query, so you can retrieve one record at a time:

```
Cursor c = mDatabase.query("tbl_books", null,
    "id=?", new String[]{"9"}, null, null, null);
```

This is equivalent to the SQL query

```
SELECT * tbl_books WHERE id=9;
```

Selecting all results might be fine for tiny databases, but it is not terribly efficient. You should always tailor your SQL queries to return only the results you require with no extraneous information included. Use the powerful language of SQL to do the heavy lifting for you whenever possible, instead of programmatically processing results yourself. For example, if you need only the titles of each book in the book table, you might use the following call to the `query()` method:

```
String asColumnsToReturn[] = { "title", "id" };
String strSortOrder = "title ASC";
```

```
Cursor c = mDatabase.query("tbl_books", asColumnsToReturn,
    null, null, null, null, strSortOrder);
```

This is equivalent to the SQL query

```
SELECT title, id FROM tbl_books ORDER BY title ASC;
```

Executing More Complex Queries Using SQLiteQueryBuilder

As your queries get more complex and involve multiple tables, you should leverage the SQLiteQueryBuilder convenience class, which can build complex queries (such as joins) programmatically.

When more than one table is involved, you need to make sure you refer to columns in a table by their fully qualified names. For example, the title column in the tbl_books table is tbl_books.title. Here we use a SQLiteQueryBuilder to build and execute a simple INNER JOIN between two tables to get a list of books with their authors:

```
import android.database.sqlite.SQLiteQueryBuilder;
...
SQLiteQueryBuilder queryBuilder = new SQLiteQueryBuilder();

queryBuilder.setTables("tbl_books, tbl_authors");
queryBuilder.appendWhere("tbl_books.authorid=tbl_authors.id");

String asColumnsToReturn[] = {
    "tbl_books.title",
    "tbl_books.id",
    "tbl_authors.firstname",
    "tbl_authors.lastname",
    "tbl_books.authorid" };
String strSortOrder = "title ASC";

Cursor c = queryBuilder.query(mDatabase, asColumnsToReturn,
    null, null, null, null,strSortOrder);
```

First, we instantiate a new SQLiteQueryBuilder object. Then we can set the tables involved as part of our JOIN and the WHERE clause that determines how the JOIN occurs. Then, we call the query() method of the SQLiteQueryBuilder that is similar to the query() method we have been using, except we supply the SQLiteDatabase instance instead of the table name. The earlier query built by the SQLiteQueryBuilder is equivalent to the SQL query:

```
SELECT tbl_books.title,
tbl_books.id,
tbl_authors.firstname,
tbl_authors.lastname,
tbl_books.authorid
FROM tbl_books
INNER JOIN tbl_authors on tbl_books.authorid=tbl_authors.id
ORDER BY title ASC;
```

Executing Raw Queries Without Builders and Column-Mapping

All these helpful Android query utilities can sometimes make building and performing a nonstandard or complex query too verbose. In this case, you might want to consider the rawQuery() method. The rawQuery() method simply takes a SQL statement String (with optional selection arguments if you include ?s) and returns a Cursor of results. If you know your SQL and you don't want to bother learning the ins and outs of all the different SQL query building utilities, this is the method for you.

For example, let's say we have a UNION query. These types of queries are feasible with the QueryBuilder, but their implementation is cumbersome when you start using column aliases and the like.

Let's say we want to execute the following SQL UNION query, which returns a list of all book titles and authors whose names contain the substring ow (that is Hallows, Rowling), as in the following:

```
SELECT title AS Name,
'tbl_books' AS OriginalTable
FROM tbl_books
WHERE Name LIKE '%ow%'
UNION
SELECT (firstname||' '|| lastname) AS Name,
'tbl_authors' AS OriginalTable
FROM tbl_authors
WHERE Name LIKE '%ow%'
ORDER BY Name ASC;
```

We can easily execute this by making a string that looks much like the original query and executing the rawQuery() method, as shown in the following code:

```
String sqlUnionExample = "SELECT title AS Name, 'tbl_books' AS
    OriginalTable from tbl_books WHERE Name LIKE ? UNION SELECT
    (firstname||' '|| lastname) AS Name, 'tbl_authors' AS OriginalTable
    from tbl_authors WHERE Name LIKE ? ORDER BY Name ASC;";

Cursor c = mDatabase.rawQuery(sqlUnionExample,
    new String[]{ "%ow%", "%ow%"});
```

We make the substrings (ow) into selection arguments, so we can use this same code to look for other substrings' searches.

Closing and Deleting a SQLite Database

Although you should always close a database when you are not using it, you might on occasion also want to modify and delete tables and delete your database.

Deleting Tables and Other SQLite Objects

You delete tables and other SQLite objects in exactly the same way you create them. Format the appropriate SQLite statements and execute them. For example, to drop our tables and triggers, we can execute three SQL statements:

```
mDatabase.execSQL("DROP TABLE tbl_books;");
mDatabase.execSQL("DROP TABLE tbl_authors;");
mDatabase.execSQL("DROP TRIGGER IF EXISTS fk_insert_book;");
```

Closing a SQLite Database

You should close your database when you are not using it. You can close the database using the close() method of your SQLiteDatabase instance, like this:

```
mDatabase.close();
```

Deleting a SQLite Database Instance Using the Application Context

The simplest way to delete a SQLiteDatabase is to use the deleteDatabase() method of your application Context. You delete databases by name and the deletion is permanent. You lose all data and schema information.

```
deleteDatabase("my_sqlite_database.db");
```

Designing Persistent Databases

Generally speaking, an application creates a database and uses it for the rest of the application's lifetime—by which we mean until the application is uninstalled from the device. So far, we've talked about the basics of creating a database, using it, and then deleting it.

In reality, most mobile applications do not create a database on-the-fly, use them, and then delete them. Instead, they create a database the first time they need it and then use it. The Android SDK provides a helper class called SQLiteOpenHelper to help you manage your application's database.

To create a SQLite database for your Android application using the SQLiteOpenHelper, you need to extend that class and then instantiate an instance of it as a member variable for use in your application. To illustrate how to do this, let's create a new Android project called PetTracker.

> **Tip**
>
> Many of the code examples provided in this section are taken from the PetTracker application. The source code for the PetTracker application is provided for download on the book's websites.

Keeping Track of Database Field Names

You've probably realized by now that it is time to start organizing your database fields programmatically to avoid typos and such in your SQL queries. One easy way you do this is to make a class to encapsulate your database schema in a class, such as PetDatabase, shown here:

```
import android.provider.BaseColumns;


public final class PetDatabase {

    private PetDatabase() {}

    public static final class Pets implements BaseColumns {
        private Pets() {}
        public static final String PETS_TABLE_NAME="table_pets";
        public static final String PET_NAME="pet_name";
        public static final String PET_TYPE_ID="pet_type_id";
        public static final String DEFAULT_SORT_ORDER="pet_name ASC";
    }

    public static final class PetType implements BaseColumns {
        private PetType() {}
        public static final String PETTYPE_TABLE_NAME="table_pettypes";
        public static final String PET_TYPE_NAME="pet_type";
        public static final String DEFAULT_SORT_ORDER="pet_type ASC";
    }
}
```

By implementing the BaseColumns interface, we begin to set up the underpinnings for using database-friendly user interface controls in the future, which often require a specially named column called _id to function properly. We rely on this column as our primary key.

Extending the SQLiteOpenHelper Class

To extend the SQLiteOpenHelper class, we must implement several important methods, which help manage the database versioning. The methods to override are onCreate() and onUpgrade() and optionally onDowngrade() and onOpen(). We use our newly defined PetDatabase class to generate appropriate SQL statements, as shown here:

```
import android.content.Context;
import android.database.sqlite.SQLiteDatabase;
import android.database.sqlite.SQLiteOpenHelper;

import com.androidbook.PetTracker.PetDatabase.PetType;
import com.androidbook.PetTracker.PetDatabase.Pets;
```

```
class PetTrackerDatabaseHelper extends SQLiteOpenHelper {

    private static final String DATABASE_NAME = "pet_tracker.db";
    private static final int DATABASE_VERSION = 1;

    PetTrackerDatabaseHelper(Context context) {
        super(context, DATABASE_NAME, null, DATABASE_VERSION);
    }

    @Override
    public void onCreate(SQLiteDatabase db) {
        db.execSQL("CREATE TABLE " +PetType.PETTYPE_TABLE_NAME+" ("
            + PetType._ID + " INTEGER PRIMARY KEY AUTOINCREMENT ,"
            + PetType.PET_TYPE_NAME + " TEXT"
            + ");");
        db.execSQL("CREATE TABLE " + Pets.PETS_TABLE_NAME + " ("
            + Pets._ID + " INTEGER PRIMARY KEY AUTOINCREMENT ,"
            + Pets.PET_NAME + " TEXT,"
            + Pets.PET_TYPE_ID + " INTEGER" // FK to pet type table
            + ");");
    }

    @Override
    public void onUpgrade(SQLiteDatabase db, int oldVersion,
        int newVersion){
        // Housekeeping here.
        // Implement how to "move" your application data
        // during an upgrade of schema versions.
        // Move or delete data as required. Your call.
    }

    @Override
    public void onOpen(SQLiteDatabase db) {
        super.onOpen(db);
    }
}
```

Now we can create a member variable for our database like this:

```
PetTrackerDatabaseHelper mDatabase = new
    PetTrackerDatabaseHelper(this.getApplicationContext());
```

Now, whenever our application needs to interact with its database, we request a valid database object. We can request a read-only database or a database that we can also write to. We can also close the database. For example, here we get a database we can write data to:

```
SQLiteDatabase db = mDatabase.getWritableDatabase();
```

Binding Data to the Application User Interface

In many cases with application databases, you want to couple your user interface with the data in your database. You might want to fill drop-down lists with values from a database table, or fill out form values, or display only certain results. There are various ways to bind database data to your user interface. You, as the developer, can decide whether to use built-in data-binding functionality provided with certain user interface controls, or build your own user interfaces from the ground up.

Working with Database Data Like Any Other Data

If you peruse the PetTracker application provided on the book's websites, you notice that its functionality includes no magical data-binding features, yet the application clearly uses the database as part of the user interface.

Specifically, the database is leveraged:

- When you fill out the Pet Type field, the `AutoComplete` feature is seeded with pet types already in listed in the `table_pettypes` table (Figure 3.2, left).
- When you save new records using the Pet Entry Form (Figure 3.2, middle).
- When you display the Pet List screen, you query for all pets and use a `Cursor` to programmatically build a `TableLayout` on-the-fly (Figure 3.2, right).

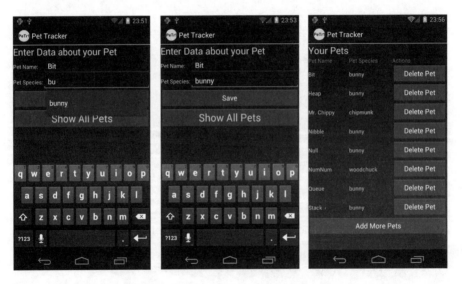

Figure 3.2   The PetTracker application: Entry Screen (left, middle) and Pet Listing Screen (right).

This might work for small amounts of data; however, there are various drawbacks to this method. For example, all the work is done on the main thread, so the more records you add, the slower your application response time becomes. Second, there's quite a bit of custom code involved to map the database results to the individual user interface components. If you decide you want to use a different control to display your data, you have quite a lot of rework to do. Third, we constantly requery the database for fresh results, and we might be requerying far more than necessary.

> **Note**
>
> Yes, we really named our pet bunnies after data structures and computer terminology. We are that geeky. Null, for example, is a rambunctious little black bunny. Shane enjoys pointing at him and calling himself a Null pointer.

Binding Data to Controls Using Data Adapters

Ideally, you'd like to bind your data to user interface controls and let them take care of the data display. For example, we can use a fancy `ListView` to display the pets instead of building a `TableLayout` from scratch. We can spin through our `Cursor` and generate `ListView` child items manually, or even better, we can simply create a data adapter to map the `Cursor` results to each `TextView` child within the `ListView`.

The PetTracker2 application behaves much like the PetTracker sample application, except that it uses the `SimpleCursorAdapter` with `ListView` and an `ArrayAdapter` to handle `AutoCompleteTextView` features.

> **Tip**
>
> The source code for subsequent upgrades to the series of PetTracker applications is provided for download on the book's websites.

Binding Data Using `SimpleCursorAdapter`

Let's now look at how we can create a data adapter to mimic our Pet Listing screen, with each pet's name and species listed. We also want to continue to have the ability to delete records from the list.

A `ListView` container can contain children such as `TextView` objects. In this case, we want to display each Pet's name and type. We therefore create a layout file called `pet_item.xml` that becomes our `ListView` item template:

```xml
<?xml version="1.0" encoding="utf-8"?>
<RelativeLayout
    xmlns:android="http://schemas.android.com/apk/res/android"
    android:id="@+id/RelativeLayoutHeader"
    android:layout_height="wrap_content"
    android:layout_width="fill_parent">
    <TextView
        android:id="@+id/TextView_PetName"
        android:layout_width="wrap_content"
```

```
        android:layout_height="?android:attr/listPreferredItemHeight"
        android:layout_alignParentLeft="true" />
    <TextView
        android:id="@+id/TextView_PetType"
        android:layout_width="wrap_content"
        android:layout_height="?android:attr/listPreferredItemHeight"
        android:layout_alignParentRight="true" />
</RelativeLayout>
```

Next, in our main layout file for the Pet List, we place our `ListView` in the appropriate place on the overall screen. The `ListView` portion of the layout file might look something like this:

```
<ListView
    android:layout_width="wrap_content"
    android:layout_height="wrap_content"
    android:id="@+id/petList" android:divider="#000" />
```

Now to programmatically fill our `ListView`, we must take the following steps:

1. Perform our query and return a valid `Cursor` (a member variable).
2. Create a data adapter that maps the `Cursor` columns to the appropriate `TextView` controls within our `pet_item.xml` layout template.
3. Attach the adapter to the `ListView`.

In the following code, we perform these steps:

```
SQLiteQueryBuilder queryBuilder = new SQLiteQueryBuilder();
queryBuilder.setTables(Pets.PETS_TABLE_NAME +", " +
    PetType.PETTYPE_TABLE_NAME);

queryBuilder.appendWhere(Pets.PETS_TABLE_NAME + "." +
    Pets.PET_TYPE_ID + "=" + PetType.PETTYPE_TABLE_NAME + "." +
    PetType._ID);

String asColumnsToReturn[] = { Pets.PETS_TABLE_NAME + "." +
    Pets.PET_NAME, Pets.PETS_TABLE_NAME +
    "." + Pets._ID, PetType.PETTYPE_TABLE_NAME + "." +
    PetType.PET_TYPE_NAME };

mCursor = queryBuilder.query(mDB, asColumnsToReturn, null, null,
    null, null, Pets.DEFAULT_SORT_ORDER);

startManagingCursor(mCursor);

ListAdapter adapter = new SimpleCursorAdapter(this,
    R.layout.pet_item, mCursor,
```

```
new String[]{Pets.PET_NAME, PetType.PET_TYPE_NAME},
new int[]{R.id.TextView_PetName, R.id.TextView_PetType });
```

```
ListView av = (ListView)findViewById(R.id.petList);
av.setAdapter(adapter);
```

Notice that the _id column and the expected name and type columns appear in the query. This is required for the adapter and ListView to work properly.

Using a ListView (Figure 3.3, left) instead of a custom user interface enables us to take advantage of the ListView control's built-in features, such as scrolling when the list becomes longer, and the ability to provide context menus as needed. The _id column is used as the unique identifier for each ListView child node. If we choose a specific item on the list, we can act on it using this identifier, for example, to delete the item.

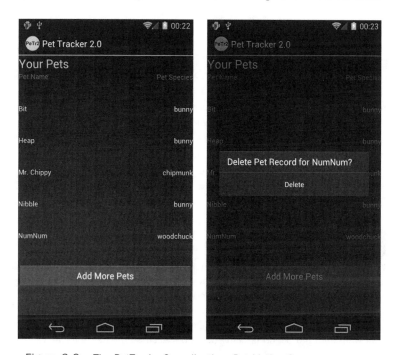

Figure 3.3   The PetTracker2 application: Pet Listing Screen ListView
(left) with Delete feature (right).

Now we reimplement the Delete functionality by listening for onItemClick() events and providing a Delete Confirmation dialog (Figure 3.3, right):

```
av.setOnItemClickListener(new AdapterView.OnItemClickListener() {
    public void onItemClick(AdapterView<?> parent, View view,
            int position, long id) {
        final long deletePetId = id;
```

```
            RelativeLayout item = (RelativeLayout) view;
            TextView nameView = (TextView) item
                    .findViewById(R.id.TextView_PetName);
            String name = nameView.getText().toString();
            new AlertDialog.Builder(PetTrackerListActivity.this)
                    .setMessage("Delete Pet Record for " + name + "?")
                    .setPositiveButton("Delete",
                            new DialogInterface.OnClickListener() {
                                public void onClick(DialogInterface dialog,
                                        int which) {

                                    deletePet(deletePetId);
                                    mCursor.requery();
                                }
                    }).show();
    }
});
```

Note that within the PetTracker2 sample application, we also use an `ArrayAdapter` to bind the data in the pet_types table to the `AutoCompleteTextView` on the Pet Entry screen. Although our next example shows you how to do this in a preferred manner, we left this code in the PetTracker sample to show you that you can always intercept the data your `Cursor` provides and do what you want with it. In this case, we create a `String` array for the AutoText options by hand. We use a built-in Android layout resource called `android.R.layout.simple_dropdown_item_1line` to specify what each individual item within the AutoText listing looks like. You can find the built-in layout resources provided within your appropriate Android SDK version's resource subdirectory.

A Note on Design

In this example, we've followed the traditional Android use of context menus with the press-and-hold, as the SDK provides for. However, in Android 4.0, the design guidelines have changed to recommend using press-and-hold for selection. See http://developer.android.com/design/patterns/new-4-0.html (http://goo.gl/aBH6n) for more information. When you are using contextual menus, be sure the dialog contains the context of what item the action is being taken on, such as the name as we've shown here.

Storing Nonprimitive Types (Such as Images) in the Database

Because SQLite is a single file, it makes little sense to try to store binary data in the database. Instead store the *location* of data, as a file path or a URI in the database, and access it appropriately.

Summary

There are a variety of different ways to store and manage application data on the Android platform. The method you use depends on what kind of data you need to store. Application-specific SQLite databases are secure and efficient mechanisms for structured data storage. You now know how to design persistent data-access mechanisms in your Android application, and you also learned how to bind data from various sources to user interface controls, such as `ListView` objects.

References and More Information

Android Dev Guide: "Data Storage":
   http://d.android.com/guide/topics/data/data-storage.html
Android SDK Documentation for the `android.database.sqlite` package:
   http://d.android.com/reference/android/database/sqlite/package-summary.html
SQLite website:
   http://www.sqlite.org/index.html
SQLzoo.net:
   http://sqlzoo.net/

## 4

Building Android Content Providers

Applications can access data in other applications on the Android system through content provider interfaces and they can expose internal application data to other applications by becoming a content provider. Typically, a content provider is backed by a SQLite database where the underlying data is stored. In this chapter, you build upon the knowledge of SQLite application databases from Chapter 3, "Leveraging SQLite Application Databases," by working through two content provider examples.

Acting as a Content Provider

Do you have data in your application? Can another application do something interesting with that data? To share the information in your application with other applications, you need to make the application a content provider by providing the standardized content provider interface for other applications; then you must register your application as a content provider in the Android manifest file. The most straightforward way to make an application a content provider is to store the information you want to share in a SQLite database.

We work through two content provider exercises in this chapter. The first is a content provider for GPS track points. This content provider enables users of it to query for points and store points. The data for each point contains a time stamp, the latitude and longitude, and the elevation.

Tip

The code examples provided in this section are taken from the Tracks application. This source code for the Tracks application is provided for download on the book's websites.

Implementing a Content Provider Interface

Implementing a content provider interface is relatively straightforward. The following code shows the basic interface that an application needs to implement to become a content provider, requiring implementations of five important methods:

```java
public class TrackPointProvider extends ContentProvider {

    public int delete(Uri uri,
        String selection, String[] selectionArgs) {
        return 0;
    }

    public String getType(Uri uri) {
        return null;
    }

    public Uri insert(Uri uri, ContentValues values) {
        return null;
    }

    public boolean onCreate() {
        return false;
    }

    public Cursor query(Uri uri, String[] projection,
        String selection, String[] selectionArgs, String sortOrder) {
        return null;
    }

    public int update(Uri uri, ContentValues values,
        String selection, String[] selectionArgs) {
        return 0;
    }
}
```

Tip

You can use Eclipse to easily create a new class and include the basic overrides that you need. To do this, right-click on the package you want to add the new class to, choose New, and then choose Class. Type the name of your content provider in the Name field, choose `android.content.ContentProvider` as your superclass, and check the box next to Inherited abstract methods.

Defining the Data URI

The provider application needs to define a base URI that other applications will use to access this content provider. This must be in the form of a `public static final Uri` named `CONTENT_URI`, and it must start with `content://`. The URI must be unique. The best practice for this naming is to use the fully qualified class name of the content provider. Here, we have created a URI name for our GPS track point provider book example:

```
public static final Uri CONTENT_URI =
    Uri.parse("content://com.androidbook.TrackPointProvider");
```

Defining Data Columns

The user of the content provider needs to know what columns the content provider has available to it. In this case, the columns used are timestamp, latitude and longitude, and the elevation. We also include a column for the record number, which is called _id.

```
public final static String _ID = "_id";
public final static String TIMESTAMP = "timestamp";
public final static String LATITUDE = "latitude";
public final static String LONGITUDE = "longitude";
public final static String ELEVATION = "elevation";
```

Users of the content provider use these same strings. A content provider for data such as this often stores the data in a SQLite database. If this is the case, matching these columns' names to the database column names simplifies the code.

Implementing Important Content Provider Methods

This section shows example implementations of each of the methods that are used by the system to call this content provider when another application wants to use it. The system, in this case, is the `ContentResolver` interface that was used indirectly in the previous section when built-in content providers were used.

Some of these methods can make use of a helper class provided by the Android SDK, `UriMatcher`, which is used to match incoming `Uri` values to patterns that help speed up development. The use of `UriMatcher` is described and then used in the implementation of these methods.

Implementing the `query()` Method

Let's start with a sample query implementation. Any query implementation needs to return a `Cursor` object. One convenient way to get a `Cursor` object is to return the `Cursor` from the underlying SQLite database that many content providers use. In fact, the interface to `ContentProvider.query()` is compatible with the `SQLiteQueryBuilder.query()` call. This example uses it to quickly build the query and return a `Cursor` object.

```
public Cursor query(Uri uri, String[] projection,
    String selection, String[] selectionArgs,
    String sortOrder) {

    SQLiteQueryBuilder qBuilder = new SQLiteQueryBuilder();

    qBuilder.setTables(TrackPointDatabase.TRACKPOINTS_TABLE);

    if ((sURIMatcher.match(uri)) == TRACKPOINT_ID) {
        qBuilder.appendWhere("_id=" + uri.getLastPathSegment());
    }

    Cursor resultCursor = qBuilder.query(mDB
        .getReadableDatabase(), projection,
        selection, selectionArgs, null, null,
        sortOrder, null);

    resultCursor.setNotificationUri(getContext()
        .getContentResolver(), uri);
    return resultCursor;
}
```

First, the code gets an instance of a SQLiteQueryBuilder object, which builds up a query with some method calls. Then, the setTables() method configures which table in the database is used. The UriMatcher class checks to see which specific rows are requested. UriMatcher is discussed in greater detail later.

Next, the actual query is called. The content provider query has fewer specifications than the SQLite query, so the parameters are passed through and the rest is ignored. The instance of the SQLite database is read-only. Because this is only a query for data, it's acceptable.

Finally, the Cursor needs to know if the source data has changed. This is done by a call to the setNotificationUri() method telling it which URI to watch for data changes. The call to the application's query() method might be called from multiple threads, as it calls to update(), so it's possible the data can change after the Cursor is returned. Doing this keeps the data synchronized.

Exploring the UriMatcher Class

The UriMatcher class is a helper class for pattern matching on the URIs that are passed to this content provider. It is used frequently in the implementations of the content provider functions that must be implemented. Here is the UriMatcher used in these sample implementations:

```
public static final String AUTHORITY =
    "com.androidbook.TrackPointProvider"

private static final int TRACKPOINTS = 1;
```

```
private static final int TRACKPOINT_ID = 10;

private static final UriMatcher sURIMatcher =
    new UriMatcher(UriMatcher.NO_MATCH);
static {
    sURIMatcher.addURI(AUTHORITY, "points", TRACKPOINTS);
    sURIMatcher.addURI(AUTHORITY, "points/#", TRACKPOINT_ID);
}
```

First, arbitrary numeric values are defined to identify each different pattern. Next, a static UriMatcher instance is created for use. The code parameter that the constructor wants is merely the value to return when there is no match. A value for this is provided for use within the UriMatcher class itself.

Next, the URI values are added to the matcher with their corresponding identifiers. The URIs are broken up in to the authority portion, defined in AUTHORITY, and the path portion, which is passed in as a literal string. The path can contain patterns, such as the "#" symbol to indicate a number. The "*" symbol is used as a wildcard to match anything.

Implementing the `insert()` Method

The insert() method is used for adding data to the content provider. Here is a sample implementation of the insert() method:

```
public Uri insert(Uri uri, ContentValues values) {

    int match = sURIMatcher.match(uri);
    if (match != TRACKPOINTS) {
        throw new IllegalArgumentException(
            "Unknown or Invalid URI " + uri);
    }

    SQLiteDatabase sqlDB = mDB.getWritableDatabase();

    long newID = sqlDB.
        insert(TrackPointDatabase.TRACKPOINTS_TABLE, null, values);

    if (newID > 0) {
        Uri newUri = ContentUris.withAppendedId(uri, newID);
        getContext()
            .getContentResolver().notifyChange(newUri, null);
        return newUri;
    }

    throw new SQLException("Failed to insert row into " + uri);
}
```

The Uri is first validated to make sure it's one where inserting makes sense. A Uri targeting a particular row would not, for instance. Next, a writeable database object instance is retrieved. Using this, the database insert() method is called on the table defined by the incoming Uri and with the values passed in. At this point, no error checking is performed on the values. Instead, the underlying database implementation throws exceptions that can be handled by the user of the content provider.

If the insert was successful, a Uri is created for notifying the system of a change to the underlying data via a call to the notifyChange() method of the ContentResolver. Otherwise, an exception is thrown.

Implementing the update() Method

The update() method is used to modify an existing row of data. It has elements similar to the insert() and query() methods. The update is applied to a particular selection defined by the incoming Uri.

```
public int update(Uri uri, ContentValues values,
    String selection, String[] selectionArgs) {

    SQLiteDatabase sqlDB = mDB.getWritableDatabase();
    int match = sURIMatcher.match(uri);
    int rowsAffected;

    switch (match) {
        case TRACKPOINTS:
            rowsAffected = sqlDB.update(
                TrackPointDatabase.TRACKPOINTS_TABLE,
                values, selection, selectionArgs);
            break;

        case TRACKPOINT_ID:
            String id = uri.getLastPathSegment();
            if (TextUtils.isEmpty(selection)) {
                rowsAffected = sqlDB.update(
                    TrackPointDatabase.TRACKPOINTS_TABLE,
                    values, _ID + "=" + id, null);
            } else {
                rowsAffected = sqlDB.update(
                    TrackPointDatabase.TRACKPOINTS_TABLE,
                    values, selection + " and " + _ID + "="
                    + id, selectionArgs);
            }
            break;
        default:
            throw new IllegalArgumentException(
                "Unknown or Invalid URI " + uri);
```

```
    }

    getContext().getContentResolver().notifyChange(uri, null);
    return rowsAffected;
}
```

In this block of code, a writable SQLiteDatabase instance is retrieved and the Uri type the user passed in is determined with a call to the match() method of the UriMatcher. No checking of values or parameters is performed here. However, to block updates to a specific Uri, such as a Uri affecting multiple rows or a match on TRACK-POINT_ID, java.lang.UnsupportedOperationException can be thrown to indicate this. In this example, though, trust is placed in the user of this content provider.

After calling the appropriate update() method, the system is notified of the change to the URI with a call to the notifyChange() method. This tells any observers of the URI that data has possibly changed. Finally, the affected number of rows is returned, which is information conveniently returned from the call to the update() method.

Implementing the delete() Method

Now it's time to clean up the database. The following is a sample implementation of the delete() method. It doesn't check to see whether the user might be deleting more data than they should. You also notice that this is similar to the update() method.

```
public int delete(Uri uri, String selection, String[] selectionArgs) {
    int match = sURIMatcher.match(uri);

    SQLiteDatabase sqlDB = mDB.getWritableDatabase();
    int rowsAffected = 0;
    switch (match) {

        case TRACKPOINTS:
            rowsAffected = sqlDB.delete(
                TrackPointDatabase.TRACKPOINTS_TABLE,
                selection, selectionArgs);
            break;

        case TRACKPOINT_ID:
            String id = uri.getLastPathSegment();
            if (TextUtils.isEmpty(selection)) {
            rowsAffected =
                sqlDB.delete(TrackPointDatabase.TRACKPOINTS_TABLE,
                _ID+"="+id, null);
            } else {
                rowsAffected =
                    sqlDB.delete(TrackPointDatabase.TRACKPOINTS_TABLE,
                    selection + " and " +_ID+"="+id, selectionArgs);
            }
```

```
            break;
        default:
            throw new IllegalArgumentException(
                "Unknown or Invalid URI " + uri);
    }
    getContext().getContentResolver().notifyChange(uri, null);

    return rowsAffected;
}
```

Again, a writable database instance is retrieved and the Uri type is determined using the match method of UriMatcher. If the result is a directory Uri, the delete is called with the selection the user passed in. However, if the result is a specific row, the row index is used to further limit the delete, with or without the selection. Allowing this without a specific selection enables deletion of a specified identifier without having to also know exactly where it came from.

As before, the system is then notified of this change with a call to the notifyChange() method of the ContentResolver class. Also as before, the number of affect rows is returned, which we stored after the call to the delete() method.

Implementing the getType() Method

The last method to implement is the getType() method. The purpose of this method is to return the MIME type for a particular Uri that is passed in. It does not need to return MIME types for specific columns of data.

```
public static final String CONTENT_ITEM_TYPE =
    ContentResolver.CURSOR_ITEM_BASE_TYPE +
    "/track-points";

public static final String CONTENT_TYPE =
    ContentResolver.CURSOR_DIR_BASE_TYPE +
    "/track-points";

public String getType(Uri uri) {
    int matchType = sURIMatcher.match(uri);
    switch (matchType) {

        case TRACKPOINTS:
            return CONTENT_TYPE;

        case TRACKPOINT_ID:
            return CONTENT_ITEM_TYPE;

        default:
            throw new
                IllegalArgumentException("Unknown or Invalid URI "
```

```
                    + uri);
    }
}
```

To start, a couple of MIME types are defined. The Android SDK provides some guideline values for single items and directories of items, which are used here. The corresponding string for each is vnd.android.cursor.item and vnd.android. cursor.dir, respectively. Finally, the match() method is used to determine the type of the provided Uri so that the appropriate MIME type can be returned.

Updating the Manifest File

Finally, you need to update your application's AndroidManifest.xml file so that it reflects that a content provider interface is exposed to the rest of the system. Here, the class name and the authorities, or what might be considered the domain of the content:// URI, need to be set. For instance, content://com.androidbook. TrackPointProvider is the base URI used in this content provider example, which means the authority is com.androidbook.TrackPointProvider. The following XML shows an example of this:

```
<provider
    android:authorities="com.androidbook.gpx.TrackPointProvider"
    android:multiprocess="true"
    android:name="com.androidbook.gpx.TrackPointProvider"
</provider>
```

The value of multiprocess is set to true because the data does not need to be synchronized between multiple running versions of this content provider. It's possible that two or more applications might access a content provider at the same time, so proper synchronization might be necessary.

Note

We frequently reference notifications that are sent to observers. In Chapter 6, "Working with Notifications," you learn about notifications that are sent to the device.

Enhancing Applications Using Content Providers

The concept of a content provider is complex and best understood by working through examples. The Pet Tracker applications from Chapter 3 are nice and all, but the application can use some graphics. Wouldn't it be great if we could include photos for each pet record? Well, let's do it! There's only one catch: We need to access pictures provided through another application on the Android system—the Media Store application.

Tip

The code examples provided in this section are taken from the PetTracker3 application. This source code for the PetTracker3 application is provided for download on the book's websites.

In Figure 4.1, you can see the results of extending the previous Pet Tracking projects using the Media Store content provider.

Figure 4.1   The main PetTracker3 application screens: Entry Screen (left, middle) and Pet Listing Screen (right).

Accessing Images on the Device

Now that you can visualize what adding photos looks like, let's break down the steps needed to achieve this feature. The PetTracker3 application has the same basic structure as our previous Pet Tracker projects, with several key differences:

- On the Pet Entry screen, you can choose a photo from a `Gallery` control, which displays all the images available on the SD card, or simulated SD card on the emulator, by accessing the `MediaStore` content provider (Figure 4.1, left).
- On the Pet Listing screen, each picture is displayed in the `ListView` control (Figure 4.1, right), again using the `MediaStore` content provider to access specific images.

- On the Pet Listing screen, each item in the `ListView` (Figure 4.1, right) is a custom layout. The new PetTracker3 sample application provides two methods to achieve this: by inflating a custom layout XML file and by generating the layout programmatically.

- Internally, we extend `BaseAdapter` on two different occasions to successfully bind pet data to the `ListView` and `Gallery` with our own custom requirements.

- Finally, we provide custom implementations of the methods for `SimpleCursorAdapter.CursorToStringConverter` and `FilterQueryProvider` to allow the `AutoCompleteTextView` to bind directly to the internal SQLite database table called `pet_types` (Figure 4.1, middle), and change the `AutoCompleteTextView` behavior to match all substrings, not only the beginning of the word. Although we won't go into detail about this in the subsequent text, check out the sample code for more information on the specific details of implementation.

First, we need to decide where we are going to get our photos. We can take pictures with the built-in camera and access those, but for simplicity's sake with the emulator (which can only take "fake pictures"), it is easier if we download those cute, fuzzy pictures from the browser onto the SD card and access them that way.

Tip

For the PetTracker3 sample application to work, you need to configure your emulator to use a virtual SD card. To keep the code simple and readable, we do not provide error handling for when this is not set up or where there are no images, nor do we check the content type of the media.

After you launch the browser on the emulator, browse to a website, and download some pictures, and then view these photographs in the Gallery application, you'll know you've set things up correctly. (Viewing them in the Gallery creates the thumbnails, so it's an important step.)

To download an image through the Browser application, select an image to download by long-pressing on the image (clicking and holding with the mouse works), and then selecting the Save Image option. Go ahead and download your own pet (or kid or whatever) images from whatever website you like and save them onto the SD card. If you don't have pets, kids, or whatever, you can borrow our personal bunny pictures that we use in our example from http://tinyurl.com/geekybuns.

Locating Content on the Android System Using URIs

Most access to content providers comes in the form of queries: a list of contacts, a list of bookmarks, a list of calls, a list of pictures, and a list of audio files. Applications make these requests much as they would access a database, and they get the same type of structured results. The results of a query are often iterated through the use of a cursor. However, instead of crafting queries, we use URIs.

You can think of a URI as an "address" to the location where content exists. URI addresses are hierarchical. Most content providers, such as the `Contacts` and the `MediaStore`, have URI addresses predefined. For example, to access thumbnails of the images on the External Media Device (sometimes an SD card, not always user removable), we use the following URI:

```
Uri thumbnailUri = MediaStore.Images.Thumbnails.EXTERNAL_CONTENT_URI;
```

Retrieving Content Provider Data with `CursorLoader`

We can query the Media Store content provider using the URI much like we would query a database. We use a `CursorLoader` to return a `Cursor` containing all image media available on the SD card. `CursorLoader` uses `AsyncTask` to load data in the background and not block the main thread. Loaders are handled by the `LoaderManager` object, of which there is an instance available to `Activity` classes.

```
Bundle args = new Bundle();
args.putString(GALLERY_CURSOR_URI_ARG, thumbnailUri.toString());
getLoaderManager().initLoader(GALLERY_CURSOR_LOADER_ID, args, this);
```

Then, you must implement `LoaderManager.LoaderCallbacks<Cursor>`. We did this as part of the `Activity` class. The three methods enable you to create the CursorLoader with the appropriate content provider query and set the `Cursor` on the adapter when the time is ready. (We create the adapter next.)

```
@Override
public Loader<Cursor> onCreateLoader(int id, Bundle args) {
    switch (id) {
    case GALLERY_CURSOR_LOADER_ID:
        String[] projection =
            new String[] { MediaStore.Images.Thumbnails._ID };
        Uri thumbnailUri = Uri
                .parse(args.getString(GALLERY_CURSOR_URI_ARG));
        CursorLoader loader = new CursorLoader(this, thumbnailUri,
                projection, null, null,
                MediaStore.Images.Thumbnails.DEFAULT_SORT_ORDER
                    );
        return loader;
    }
    return null;
}


@Override
public void onLoadFinished(Loader<Cursor> cursorLoader, Cursor cursor) {
    switch (cursorLoader.getId()) {
    case GALLERY_CURSOR_LOADER_ID:
        mGalleryAdapter.swapCursor(cursor);
        break;
```

```
    }
}

@Override
public void onLoaderReset(Loader<Cursor> cursorLoader) {
    switch (cursorLoader.getId()) {
    case GALLERY_CURSOR_LOADER_ID:
        mGalleryAdapter.swapCursor(null);
        break;
    }
}
```

We configured the `CursorLoader` to retrieve the records of thumbnail images for each piece of media available on the SD card and do so off the main thread.

Now we have this `Cursor`, but we still have some legwork to get our `Gallery` widget to display the individual images.

A Note on `CursorLoader`

Although `CursorLoader` was introduced in API Level 11, it is available for use in the Android support package. This means you can gain its benefits as far back as API Level 4.

Data-Binding to the Gallery Control

We need to extend the `CursorAdapter` class for a new type of data adapter called `ImageUriAdapter` to map the URI data we retrieved to the `Gallery` widget. Our custom `ImageUriAdapter` maps the `Cursor` results to the child items in the `Gallery` widget. Implementing a `CursorAdapter` means you implement two primary methods and a constructor. The methods are `bindView()`, which is called when an existing `View` object is reused with new data and `newView()`, which is called when a new `View` object must be created and data assigned to it. The constructor is a good place to cache anything that might be useful in each of these calls, such as column indexes. Here is our implementation of the `CursorAdapter`:

```
public class ImageUriAdapter extends CursorAdapter {
    private int colIndexMediaId;
    private final Uri baseUri;

    public ImageUriAdapter(Context context, Cursor c, boolean autoRequery,
            Uri baseUri) {
        super(context, c, autoRequery);
        if (c != null) {
            colIndexMediaId = c
                    .getColumnIndex(MediaStore.Images.Thumbnails._ID);
        }        this.baseUri = baseUri;
    }
```

```
@Override
public void bindView(View view, Context context, Cursor cursor) {
    long id = cursor.getLong(colIndexMediaId);

    Uri imageUri = Uri.withAppendedPath(baseUri, String.valueOf(id));
    ((ImageView) view).setImageURI(imageUri);
    view.setTag(imageUri);
}

@Override
public View newView(Context context, Cursor cursor,
    ViewGroup parent) {
    ImageView imageView = new ImageView(context);
    long id = cursor.getLong(colIndexMediaId);

    Uri imageUri = Uri.withAppendedPath(baseUri, String.valueOf(id));
    imageView.setImageURI(imageUri);

    imageView.setLayoutParams(new Gallery.LayoutParams(
            LayoutParams.WRAP_CONTENT, LayoutParams.WRAP_CONTENT));

    imageView.setTag(imageUri);

    return imageView;
}
}
```

After all this magic has been implemented, we can set our newly defined custom adapter to the adapter used by the `Gallery`. The `Cursor` is `null` here because it is set by the loader callbacks when the `Cursor` is finished loading in the background, as handled by the `CursorLoader`.

```
ImageUriAdapter iAdapter = new ImageUriAdapter(this,
        null, false, thumbnailUri);

final Gallery pictureGal =
    (Gallery) findViewById(R.id.GalleryOfPics);
pictureGal.setAdapter(iAdapter);
```

A Warning about `Bitmap.setImageURI()`

The `setImageURI()` method of the `Bitmap` object decodes the image from the URI on the main thread. As such, this should never be called on the main thread. Our example here does just that and you'll quickly find that without further work, `StrictMode` complains. Also interesting, though, is how `StrictMode` won't complain on an orientation change, showing the `CursorLoader` at work, caching the `Cursor` object across rotate operations.

Retrieving Gallery Images and Saving Them in the Database

Notice that we added two new columns to our SQLite database: the base URI for the image and the individual image id, which is the unique identifier tacked to the end of the URI. We do not save the image itself in the database, only the URI information to retrieve it.

When the user presses the Save button on the Pet Entry screen, we examine the Gallery item selected and extract the information we require from the Tag property of the selected View, like this:

```
final Gallery imagePickerGallery =
    (Gallery) findViewById(R.id.GalleryOfPics);
ImageView selectedImageView = (ImageView) imagePickerGallery
        .getSelectedView();
Uri imageUri = (Uri) selectedImageView.getTag();
String imageUriString = imageUri.toString();
```

We can then save our Pet Record as we have before.

Summary

Your application can leverage the data available in other Android applications, if they expose that data as a content provider. Applications can also share data among themselves by becoming content providers. Becoming a content provider involves implementing a set of methods that manage how and what data you expose for use in other applications. Content providers are usually backed by data in the form of a private application database.

References and More Information

Android Dev Guide: "Content Providers":
    http://d.android.com/guide/topics/providers/content-providers.html
Android Dev Guide: "Loaders":
    http://d.android.com/guide/topics/fundamentals/loaders.html

5

Broadcasting and Receiving Intents

The Android operating system enables applications to communicate with one another in a variety of ways. One way that information can be communicated across process or application boundaries is by using the broadcast event system built into the platform through the use of Intent objects. When an application has something it wants communicated, it can broadcast that information to the system at large. Applications that are interested in that sort of event can listen for and react to that broadcast by becoming a broadcast receiver. Although we develop numerous examples of broadcasts in the other chapters of this book, we felt it was worthwhile to cover some of the basics of broadcasting on the Android platform here in its own chapter, free of other lessons.

Sending Broadcasts

The Android operating system uses broadcasts to communicate information to applications. The system generates numerous broadcasts about the state of the device, such as when the device is docked, an SD card is ejected, or a call is about to be placed. Applications can also generate and send broadcasts. Some system broadcasts can be initiated by applications (with the appropriate permissions) or applications can create their own events and broadcast them.

The Android framework supports two kinds of broadcasts. Normal broadcasts are delivered to all receivers and completed asynchronously in an undefined order. Ordered broadcasts are delivered to each receiver in priority order; the receiver can pass the event on to the next appropriate receiver in the queue, or abort the broadcast before all receivers get it.

Broadcasts can also be sticky. This means that the Intent associated with the broadcast stays around after the broadcast has been completed, so that the broadcast receivers can retrieve valid Intent data from the registerReceiver() method return value. Both normal and ordered broadcasts can be sticky.

When dispatching a broadcast of any type, you have the option of specifying any permissions that the broadcast receiver must hold in order to receive your broadcast. These permissions are enforced by the Android operating system at runtime when matching occurs.

Tip

Many of the code examples provided in this chapter are taken from the SimpleBroadcasts application. This source code for the SimpleBroadcasts application is provided for download on the book's websites.

Sending Basic Broadcasts

Sending basic broadcasts is as simple as configuring the appropriate `Intent` object and dispatching it to the system using the `sendBroadcast()` method of the `Context` class. For example, the following code creates a simple intent with a custom action type:

```
Intent i = new Intent("ACTION_DO_A_LITTLE_DANCE");
sendBroadcast(i);
```

Intents may be much more specific, with data stored in the type, category, and extra data. The action, data, and category information are used by the Android operating system to match up the broadcast with the appropriate applications using intent filters. The intent extra and flag information is not used as part of intent resolution, but may be used by the broadcast receivers when handling a broadcast.

Tip

The intent action namespace is globally shared. When you broadcast "custom" intents, make sure you define unique action types. (It's common to tack them on to your application package namespace.) If you want other developers to listen for and react to your broadcasts, be sure to clearly document the broadcasts your application generates and the intent data stored in each type of broadcast.

To send a normal sticky broadcast, simply use the `sendStickyBroadcast()` method of the `Context` class instead of the `sendBroadcast()` method.

Sending Ordered Broadcasts

To send an ordered broadcast, simply create the appropriate `Intent` object as normal and then dispatch it to the system using the `sendOrderedBroadcast()` method of the `Context` class.

Tip

If multiple broadcast receivers that match a broadcast have the same priority, they will receive the broadcast in an arbitrary order.

To send an ordered sticky broadcast, simply use the
sendStickyOrderedBroadcast() method of the Context class instead of the
sendOrderedBroadcast() method.

Receiving Broadcasts

The Android operating system handles the transmission of broadcasts. Certain broadcasts
can be initiated by any application, whereas others are protected or require certain permissions. The Android operating system matches up a broadcast with suitable applica-
tion(s) using intent filters. Intent filters are criteria that the system uses as matching rules
when determining what should handle an intent. A simple intent filter might catch all
intents of a given action type (like our sample application). A more specific intent filter
might specify the intent action, data (URI and data type) and category details.

In order to become a broadcast receiver, your application must:

- Register to receive broadcasts, specifying a specific intent filter, which the Android
  operating system uses to match broadcasts to your receiver.
- Implement a broadcast receiver class.

After your application has received a broadcast, it is handled by your broadcast
receiver class—specifically by its onReceive() callback. The lifecycle of a
BroadcastReceiver is short; it is valid only for the duration of the onReceive()
method. This means that you should not perform lengthy synchronous operations within
this callback method. This also means that any asynchronous processing might be killed
off before it finishes. To perform an operation that goes beyond these limitations, create
and launch a Service instance instead. Android services are discussed in Chapter 2,
"Working with Services." For more information on the lifecycle of a broadcast receiver,
see the Android SDK documentation at http://developer.android.com/reference/
android/content/BroadcastReceiver.html#ReceiverLifecycle (http://goo.gl/Rdrjh).

Let's look at a simple example of a broadcast receiver that can react to the dancing
broadcast we sent earlier in this chapter. First, you must extend the BroadcastReceiver
class and implement your own event handling in the onReceive() callback method.
The following is an example implementation of a BroadcastReceiver called
MyDancingBroadcastReceiver:

```
class MyDancingBroadcastReceiver extends BroadcastReceiver
{
    @Override
    public void onReceive(Context context, Intent intent) {
        Toast.makeText(context, "Get Down and Boogie!",
            Toast.LENGTH_LONG).show();
    }
}
```

If this is an inner class, say of your `Activity` class, it must be declared as `public static` so it can be instantiated on its own. This is particularly important if the registration is done in the manifest file; see the later section, "Registering to Receive Broadcasts Statically."

Registering to Receive Broadcasts

To listen for and react to broadcast events, your application must register with the Android operating system as a broadcast receiver at runtime or in its Android manifest file. The type of events your application registers to listen for is dictated by what are called intent filters. You can filter on a variety of rules. For example, your application might want to listen only for broadcasts for specific intent action types or some other intent criteria.

Registering to Receive Broadcasts Dynamically

To register for specific broadcasts at runtime, use the `registerReceiver()` and `unregisterReceiver()` methods of the `Context` class. Registering dynamically enables your application to turn off receiving broadcasts of certain types when it can't handle them or doesn't need to. This can help improve performance compared to just ignoring broadcasts. It is fairly typical to register for broadcasts in the `onResume()` callback method of your `Activity` class, and unregister (stop listening for them) in the `onPause()` callback method. Here we have an example of how an `Activity` might manage its broadcast registration with a very simple intent filter that watches for a special intent action type:

```
public class SimpleBroadcastsActivity extends Activity {
    public static String ACTION_DANCE =
        "com.androidbook.simplebroadcasts.ACTION_DANCE";

    MyDancingBroadcastReceiver mReceiver;

    @Override
    public void onCreate(Bundle savedInstanceState) {
        super.onCreate(savedInstanceState);
        setContentView(R.layout.main);
        mReceiver = new MyDancingBroadcastReceiver();
    }

    @Override
    protected void onPause() {
        super.onPause();
        unregisterReceiver(mReceiver);
    }

    @Override
```

```
protected void onResume() {
    super.onResume();
    IntentFilter danceFilter =
        new IntentFilter(ACTION_DANCE);
    registerReceiver(mReceiver, danceFilter);
    }
}
```

Registering to Receive Broadcasts Statically

You can also register to receive broadcasts in your application's Android manifest file. This is useful when your application can always handle the broadcast. To recreate the same receiver configuration shown previously, where your broadcast receiver handles a specific intent action type, you use the following XML in your application's Android Manifest file inside the `<application>` tag:

```
<receiver android:name="com.androidbook.simplebroadcasts.
➥SimpleBroadcastsActivity$MyDancingBroadcastReceiver" >
    <intent-filter>
        <action
            android:name="com.androidbook.simplebroadcasts
➥.ACTION_DANCE" />
    </intent-filter>
</receiver>
```

You can also set numerous tag attributes, such as priority, on the intent filter.

Handling Incoming Broadcasts from the System

After you have registered your broadcast receiver and implemented its `onReceive()` callback method, you are ready to start processing broadcast events. In some cases, your application will send the broadcasts, but in many cases, you simply want to respond to broadcasts made by other applications or the Android operating system at large (the device). Some common broadcasts your application might want to listen for and react to are listed in Table 5.1:

Table 5.1   **Important System Broadcasts**

Broadcast Receiver Intent Action	Description
ACTION_AIRPLANE_MODE_CHANGED	A notification that the device has been switched into or out of Airplane Mode.
ACTION_BATTERY_CHANGED	The battery state has changed. Note: You must register for this broadcast dynamically.

Table 5.1   **Continued**

Broadcast Receiver Intent Action	Description
ACTION_BATTERY_LOW	A warning issued by the device that the battery is low. Applications may want to adjust background services or cancel lengthy operations in response. The ACTION_BATTERY_OKAY event may occur later if the battery gets a charge.
ACTION_BOOT_COMPLETED	The device has finished booting up. You need the RECEIVE_BOOT_COMPLETED permission to receive this broadcast.
ACTION_CAMERA_BUTTON ACTION_MEDIA_BUTTON	The user pressed a specific button.
ACTION_DATE_CHANGED ACTION_TIMEZONE_CHANGED	A notification issued by the device that the system date or time zone have changed. Applications that rely upon dates and times, such as alarm clock apps, may wish to take note.
ACTION_DEVICE_STORAGE_LOW	A warning issued by the device when there is a low memory condition. The ACTION_DEVICE_STORAGE_OKAY event may occur later if the storage gets freed up.
ACTION_DOCK_EVENT	A notification issued when the device has been attached to or detached from a dock.
ACTION_HEADSET_PLUG	A notification issued by the device that a headset has been plugged into the device or unplugged. Applications that leverage sound may wish to take note and adjust behavior.
ACTION_INPUT_METHOD_CHANGED	A notification that an input method has been changed.
ACTION_LOCALE_CHANGED	A notification issued by the device that the system locale has changed. Applications that have locale-sensitive code or use services that require locale information may want to take note.
ACTION_MEDIA_BAD_REMOVAL ACTION_MEDIA_CHECKING ACTION_MEDIA_EJECT ACTION_MEDIA_MOUNTED ACTION_MEDIA_NOFS ACTION_MEDIA_REMOVED ACTION_MEDIA_SHARED ACTION_MEDIA_UNMOUNTABLE ACTION_MEDIA_UNMOUNTED	Notifications related to external media availability and state. Applications that use external media, such as music, video or camera applications may want to pay special attention to these events. See the Android SDK documentation for details.

Broadcast Receiver Intent Action	Description

`ACTION_MEDIA_SCANNER_STARTED`
`ACTION_MEDIA_SCANNER_FINISHED`
`ACTION_MEDIA_SCANNER_SCAN_FILE`
	Events related to the media scanner. You can request to scan a specific file and add it to the media database using the action `ACTION_MEDIA_SCANNER_SCAN_FILE`.

`ACTION_MY_PACKAGE_REPLACED`	This notification is sent to the new version of an application when the old version is replaced.
`ACTION_NEW_OUTGOING_CALL`	A notification that a call is about to be placed. The application needs the permission `PROCESS_OUTGOING_CALLS` to receive this broadcast.

`ACTION_PACKAGE_ADDED`
`ACTION_PACKAGE_CHANGED`
`ACTION_PACKAGE_DATA_CLEARED`
`ACTION_PACKAGE_FIRST_LAUNCH`
`ACTION_PACKAGE_FULLY_REMOVED`
`ACTION_PACKAGE_NEEDS_`
`VERIFICATION`
`ACTION_PACKAGE_REMOVED`
`ACTION_PACKAGE_REPLACED`
`ACTION_PACKAGE_RESTARTED`
	Events related to application package installation, usage, and removal. Normally the package in question is not notified, but other related applications may react to such events.

`ACTION_POWER_CONNECTED` `ACTION_POWER_DISCONNECTED`	Notifications regarding device power state in terms of being plugged in or not (separate from battery events).
`ACTION_SCREEN_OFF` `ACTION_SCREEN_ON`	Notifications regarding device screen state.
`ACTION_SHUTDOWN`	A notification that the device will be shut down. Most applications shut down gracefully as part of the application lifecycle, but if your application needs to know that this is a full shut down (as opposed to a pause, and so on), this is the event to watch for.
`ACTION_TIME_TICK`	A notification that the system time has changed. This notification is sent every minute. You must register for this broadcast dynamically.
`ACTION_UID_REMOVED` `ACTION_USER_PRESENT`	Events related to users, including when user accounts are removed or when the user has woken up the device.
`ACTION_WALLPAPER_CHANGED`	A notification that the user has changed his device wallpaper.

Securing Application Broadcasts

Some broadcasts are meant to be "heard" by any application that is interested. Others are intended for specific recipients. For example, you might want to define a set of broadcasts that your suite of Android applications uses, but cannot be used by other applications. Here are some tips for securing the broadcasting and receiving ends of the broadcast system:

- Create unique `Intent` data for broadcast. If your application broadcasts only to specific target applications, create and enforce the permissions required for that broadcast when you send it.

- Send the most specific broadcasts you can and create the most specific intent filters possible. This helps avoid broadcasts accidentally making it to unintended receivers.

- As of API Level 14, you can specify the package limitations using the `setPackage()` method of the `Intent` class and these limitations will be enforced. This is good for cross-application broadcasts that need to target just one application, for whatever reason.

- You can set the target `Class` of the broadcast either through the appropriate constructor or the `setClass()` method. Use this for sending a broadcast directly to a particular receiver in your app. This avoids needing to set up and configure intent filters if you know exactly which receiver must handle each broadcast and you have full control over them within your app.

- You can use the `android:exported` attribute of the `<intent-filter>` tag in your application's Android manifest file to prevent other applications from sending broadcasts to your receiver.

Tip

Want to broadcast within the boundaries of your application but worried about privacy? Check out the Android Support package class called `LocalBroadcastManager` (`android.support.v4.content.LocalBroadcastManager`). It is basically an application-scoped broadcast that is more efficient than a system broadcast, and guarantees your `Intent` data never leaves your app—great for sending private data.

Summary

Broadcasts are a simple yet powerful way to communicate data across process boundaries. Broadcasts are sometimes used to communicate between services and their application user interfaces and between applications at large. Many broadcasts are initiated by the operating system to notify applications of events such as changes in device state. When an application sends a broadcast out, the Android operating system matches it up with all applications that have intent filters that match that request. For security purposes, there are some ways to lock down a broadcast such that it is handled by a specific application, and no other.

References and More Information

Android Dev Guide: "Application Fundamentals":
   http://d.android.com/guide/topics/fundamentals.html
Android SDK documentation regarding the `BroadcastReceiver` class:
   http://d.android.com/reference/android/content/BroadcastReceiver.html
Android Dev Guide: "Intent Resolution":
   http://d.android.com/guide/topics/intents/intents-filters.html#ires

## 6

Working with Notifications

Applications often need to communicate with the user, even when the application isn't actively running. Applications can alert users with text notifications, vibration, blinking lights, and even audio. In this chapter, you learn how to build different kinds of notifications into your Android applications.

Notifying the User

Applications can use notifications to greatly improve the user's experience. For example:

- An email application might notify a user when new messages arrive. A news reader application might notify a user when there are new articles to read.
- A game might notify a user when a friend has signed in, or sent an invitation to play, or beat a high score.
- A weather application might notify a user of special weather alerts.
- A stock market application might notify the user when certain stock price targets are met. (Sell now before it's too late!)

Users appreciate these notifications because they help drive application workflow, reminding the users when they need to launch the application. However, there is a fine line between just enough and too many notifications. Application designers need to consider carefully how they should employ the use of notifications so as not to annoy users or interrupt them without good reason. Each notification should be appropriate for the specific application and the event the user is being notified of. For example, an application should not put out an emergency style notification (think flashing lights, ringing noises, and generally making a "to-do") simply to notify the user that his picture has been uploaded to a website or that new content has been downloaded.

The Android platform provides a number of different ways of notifying the user. Notifications are often displayed on the status bar at the top of the screen. Notifications may involve

- Textual information
- Graphical indicators

- Sound indicators
- Vibration of the device
- Control over the indicator light

Warning

Although the Android SDK provides APIs for creating a variety of notifications, not all notifications are supported by all devices. For example, the indicator light and vibrate features are not available on all Android devices. There is also a degree of variation between how different devices handle notifications. Always test any notification implementations on target devices.

Now let's look at how to use these different kinds of notifications in your application. But, first, let's talk a little about compatibility.

A Word on Compatibility

Notifications have been around since the beginning of the Android platform. They've undergone some changes, but the basics have pretty much stayed the same. However, over time, there are some areas that have changed enough to no longer work the way they originally did. While we're not attempting to cover every single type of notification or option allowed for notifications in this book, even this overview covers at least one area that behaves differently on different versions of Android. We point out these areas as we come across them.

Additionally, a new method of creating notifications was introduced in API Level 11. As of this writing, API Level 11 and above covers just 3.9 percent of the market, so we feel most people will still want to know about the older method, which we introduce first. We go over the new method when we reach the changed notification mechanism.

Notifying with the Status Bar

The standard location for displaying notifications and indicators on an Android device is the status bar that runs along the top of the screen. Typically, the status bar shows information such as the current date and time. It also displays notifications (such as incoming SMS messages) as they arrive—in short form along the bar and in full if the user pulls down the status bar to see the notification list. The user can clear the notifications by pulling down the status bar and pressing the Clear button.

Developers can enhance their applications by using notifications from their applications to inform the user of important events. For example, an application might want to send a simple notification to the user whenever new content has been downloaded. A simple notification has a number of important components:

- An icon (appears on status bar and full notification)
- Ticker text (appears on status bar)
- Notification title text (appears in full notification)
- Notification body text (appears in full notification)
- An intent (launches if the user clicks on the full notification)

In this section, you learn how to create this basic kind of notification.

Tip

Many of the code examples provided in this chapter are taken from the SimpleNotifications application. The source code for this application is provided for download on the book's websites.

Using the `NotificationManager` Service

All notifications are created with the help of the `NotificationManager`. The `NotificationManager` (in the `android.app` package) is a system service that must be requested. The following code demonstrates how to obtain a valid `NotificationManager` object using the `getSystemService()` method:

```
NotificationManager notifier = (NotificationManager)
   getSystemService(Context.NOTIFICATION_SERVICE);
```

The `NotificationManager` is not useful without having a valid `Notification` object to use with the `notify()` method. The `Notification` object defines what information displays to the user when the `Notification` is triggered. This includes text that displays on the status bar, a couple of lines of text that display on the expanded status bar, an icon displayed in both places, a count of the number of times this `Notification` has been triggered, and a time for when the last event that caused this `Notification` took place.

Creating a Simple Text Notification with an Icon

You can set the icon and ticker text, both of which display on the status bar, through the constructor for the `Notification` object, as follows:

```
Notification notify = new Notification(
   R.drawable.ic_stat_notify, "Hello!", System.currentTimeMillis());
```

Additionally, you can set notification information through public member variable assignment, like this:

```
notify.icon = R.drawable.ic_stat_notify;
notify.tickerText = "Hello!";
notify.when = System.currentTimeMillis();
```

You need to set a couple more pieces of information before the call to the `notify()` method takes place. First, you need to make a call to the `setLatestEventInfo()` method, which configures a `View` that displays in the expanded status bar. Here is an example:

```
Intent toLaunch = new Intent
    (SimpleNotificationsActivity.this,
    SimpleNotificationsActivity.class);
PendingIntent intentBack = PendingIntent.getActivity
    (SimpleNotificationsActivity.this, 0, toLaunch, 0);

notify.setLatestEventInfo(SimpleNotificationsActivity.this,
    "Hi there!", "This is even more text.", intentBack);
```

Next, use the `notify()` method to supply the notification's title and body text as well as the `Intent` triggered when the user clicks on the notification. In this case, we're using our own `Activity` so that when the user clicks on the notification, our `Activity` launches again.

Note

When the expanded status bar is pulled down, the current `Activity` lifecycle is still treated as if it were the top (displayed) `Activity`. Triggering system notifications while running in the foreground, though, isn't particularly useful. An application that is in the foreground is better suited using a `Dialog` or `Toast` to notify the user, not by using notifications.

Working with the Notification Queue

Now the application is ready to actually notify the user of the event. All that is needed is a call to the `notify()` method of the `NotificationManager` with an identifier and the `Notification` we configured. This is demonstrated with the following code:

```
private static final int NOTIFY_1 = 0x1001;
// ...
notifier.notify(NOTIFY_1, notify);
```

The identifier matches up a `Notification` with any previous `Notification` instances of that type. When the identifiers match, the old `Notification` is updated instead of creating a new one. You might have a `Notification` that some file is being downloaded. You can update the `Notification` when the download is complete, instead of filling the notification queue with a separate `Notification`, which quickly becomes obsolete. This `Notification` identifier needs to be unique only in your application.

The notification displays as an icon and ticker text showing up on the status bar. This is shown at the top of Figure 6.1.

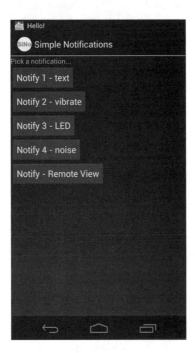

Figure 6.1   Status bar notification showing an icon and ticker text.

Shortly after the ticker text displays, the status bar returns to normal with each notification icon shown. If the users expand the status bar, they see something like what is shown in Figure 6.2.

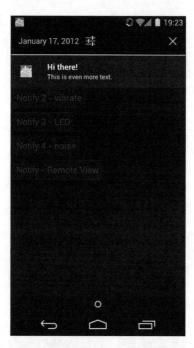

Figure 6.2   Expanded status bar showing the icon, both text fields, and
the time of the notification.

Updating Notifications

You don't want your application's notifications piling up in the notification bar.
Therefore, you might want to reuse or update notifications to keep the notification list
manageable. For example, there is no reason to keep a notification informing the user
that the application is downloading File X when you now want to send another notification saying File X has finished downloading. Instead, you can simply update the first
notification with new information.

When the notification identifiers match, the old notification is updated. When a notification with matching identifier is posted, the ticker text does not draw a second time.
To show the user that something has changed, you can use a counter. The value of the
number member variable of the Notification object tracks and displays this. For
instance, we can set it to the number 4, as shown here:

```
notify.number = 4;
```

This is displayed to the user as a small number over the icon. This is only displayed in the status bar and not in the expanded status bar, although an application can update the text to also display this information. Figure 6.3 (left) shows what this might look like in the status bar.

On API Level 11 and higher, simply setting the notify number does nothing. The look of the notification count has changed, too, and instead only displays when the whole notification tray is expanded (far right side). To show the notification count indicator, use the Notification.Builder class. Figure 6.3 (right) shows how this might look. Here's the code:

```
Intent toLaunch = new Intent(SimpleNotificationsActivity.this,
        SimpleNotificationsActivity.class);
Notification notify = new Notification.Builder(this)
        .setWhen(System.currentTimeMillis())
        .setSmallIcon(R.drawable.ic_stat_notify)
        .setAutoCancel(true)
        .setContentTitle("Hi there!")
        .setTicker("Hello!")
        .setNumber(4)
        .setContentIntent(
                PendingIntent.getActivity(
                        SimpleNotificationsActivity.this, 0,
                        toLaunch, 0))
        .setContentText("Hello from down here!").getNotification();
notifier.notify(NOTIFY_6, notify);
```

As you can see from the code, the idea is basically the same, just coded a little differently. This method works only on API Level 11 or later.

 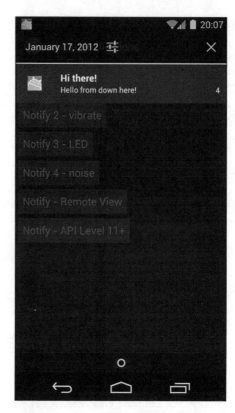

Figure 6.3   Status bar notification with the count of "4" showing over the icon on left; the count of "4" shows in the pull-down area on right.

Clearing Notifications

When a user clicks on the notification, the `Intent` assigned is triggered. At some point after this, the application might want to clear the notification from the system notifications queue. This is done through a call to the `cancel()` method of the `NotificationManager` object. For instance, the notification we created earlier can be canceled with the following call:

```
notifier.cancel(NOTIFY_1);
```

This cancels the notification that has the same identifier. However, if the application doesn't care what the user does after clicking on the notification, there is an easier way to cancel notifications. Simply set a flag to do so, as shown here:

```
notify.flags |= Notification.FLAG_AUTO_CANCEL;
```

Setting the `Notification.FLAG_AUTO_CANCEL` flag causes notifications to be canceled when the user clicks on them. This is convenient and easy for the application when just launching the intent is good enough.

The `Notification` object is a little different from other Android objects you might have encountered. Most of the interaction with it is through direct access to its public variables instead of through helper methods. This is useful for a background application or service, as discussed in Chapter 2, "Working with Services." The `Notification` object can be kept around and only the values that need to be changed can be modified. After any change, the `Notification` needs to be posted again by calling the `notify()` method.

Vibrating the Phone

Vibration is a great way to enable notifications to catch the attention of a user in noisy environments or alert the user when visible and audible alerts are not appropriate (though a vibrating phone is often noisy on a hard desktop surface). Android notifications give a fine level of control over how vibration is performed. However, before the application can use vibration with a notification, an explicit permission is needed. The following XML in your application's `AndroidManifest.xml` file is required to use vibration:

```
<uses-permission
    android:name="android.permission.VIBRATE" />
```

Warning

The vibrate feature must be tested on the device. The emulator does not indicate vibration in any way. Also, some Android devices do not support vibration.

Without this permission, the vibrate functionality does not work nor are there any errors. With this permission enabled, the application is free to vibrate the phone however it wants. This is accomplished by describing the `vibrate` member variable, which determines the vibration pattern. An array of `long` values describes the vibration duration. Thus, the following line of code enables a simple vibration pattern that occurs whenever the notification is triggered:

```
notify.vibrate = new long[] {0, 200, 200, 600, 600};
```

This vibration pattern vibrates for 200 milliseconds and then stops vibrating for 200 milliseconds. After that, it vibrates for 600 milliseconds and then stops for that long. To repeat the Notification alert, a notification flag can be set so it doesn't stop until the user clears the notification.

```
notify.flags |= Notification.FLAG_INSISTENT;
```

An application can use different patterns of vibrations to alert the user to different types of events or even present counts. For instance, think about a grandfather clock with which you can deduce the time based on the tones that are played.

Tip

Using short, unique patterns of vibration can be useful, and users become accustomed to them.

Blinking the Lights

Blinking lights are a great way to pass information silently to the user when other forms of alert are not appropriate. The Android SDK provides reasonable control over a multi-colored indicator light, when such a light is available on the device. Users might recognize this light as a service indicator or battery level warning. An application can also take advantage of this light, by changing the blinking rate or color of the light.

Warning

Indicator lights are not available on all Android devices. Also, the emulator does not display the light's state. This mandates testing on actual hardware.

You must set a flag on the Notification object to use the indicator light. Then, the color of the light must be set and information about how it should blink. The following block of code configures the indicator light to shine green and blink at rate of 1 second on and 1 second off:

```
notify.flags |= Notification.FLAG_SHOW_LIGHTS;


notify.ledARGB = Color.GREEN;
notify.ledOnMS = 1000;
notify.ledOffMS = 1000;
```

Although you can set arbitrary color values, a typical physical implementation of the indicator light has three small LEDs in red, green, and blue. Although the colors blend reasonably well, they won't be as accurate as the colors on the screen. For instance, on the T-Mobile G1, the color white looks a tad pink.

Warning

On some devices, certain notifications appear to take precedence when it comes to using the indicator light. For instance, the light on the T-Mobile G1 is always solid green when plugged in to a USB port, regardless of other applications trying to use the indicator light. Additionally, on the Nexus One, the color trackball is not lit unless the screen is off. You must unplug the phone from the USB port for the colors to change.

An application can use different colors and different blinking rates to indicate different information to the user. For instance, the more times an event occurs, the more urgent the indicator light could be. The following block of code shows changing the light based on the number of notifications that have been triggered:

```
notify.number++;
notify.flags |= Notification.FLAG_SHOW_LIGHTS;

if (notify.number < 2) {
    notify.ledARGB = Color.GREEN;
    notify.ledOnMS = 1000;
    notify.ledOffMS = 1000;
} else if (notify.number < 3) {
    notify.ledARGB = Color.BLUE;
    notify.ledOnMS = 750;
    notify.ledOffMS = 750;
} else if (notify.number < 4) {
    notify.ledARGB = Color.WHITE;
    notify.ledOnMS = 500;
    notify.ledOffMS = 500;
} else {
    notify.ledARGB = Color.RED;
    notify.ledOnMS = 50;
    notify.ledOffMS = 50;
}
```

The blinking light continues until the Notification is cleared by the user. The use of the Notification.FLAG_INSISTENT flag does not affect this as it does vibration effects.

Color and blinking rates can also be used to indicate other information. For instance, temperature from a weather service can be indicated with red and blue plus blink rate. Use of such colors for passive data indication can be useful even when other forms would work. It is far less intrusive than annoying, loud ringers or harsh, vibrating phone noises. For instance, a simple glance at the device can tell the user some useful piece of information without the need to launch any applications or change what he is doing.

Making Noise

Sometimes, the device has to make noise to get the user's attention. Luckily, the Android SDK provides a means for this using the Notification object. Begin by configuring the audio stream type to use when playing a sound. Generally, the most useful stream type is STREAM_NOTIFICATION. You can configure the audio stream type on your notification as follows:

```
notify.audioStreamType = AudioManager.STREAM_NOTIFICATION;
```

Now, assign a valid `Uri` object to the sound member variable and that sound plays when the notification is triggered. The following code demonstrates how to play a sound that is included as a project resource:

```
notify.sound = Uri.parse(
    ContentResolver.SCHEME_ANDROID_RESOURCE +
    "://com.androidbook.simplenotifications/" +
    R.raw.fallbackring);
```

By default, the audio file is played once. As with the vibration, the `Notification.FLAG_INSISTENT` flag can be used to repeat incessantly until the user clears the notification. No specific permissions are needed for this form of notification.

Note

The sound file used in this example is included in the project as a raw resource. However, you can use any sound file on the device. Keep in mind that the sound files available on a given Android device vary.

Customizing the Notification

Although the default notification behavior in the expanded status bar tray is sufficient for most purposes, developers can customize how notifications are displayed if they so choose. To do so, developers can use the `RemoteViews` object to customize the look and feel of a notification.

The following code demonstrates how to create a `RemoteViews` object and assign custom text to it:

```
RemoteViews remote =
    new RemoteViews(getPackageName(), R.layout.remote);

remote.setTextViewText(R.id.text1, "Big text here!");
remote.setTextViewText(R.id.text2, "Red text down here!");
notify.contentView = remote;
```

To better understand this, here is the layout file `remote.xml` referenced by the preceding code:

```
<LinearLayout
    xmlns:android="http://schemas.android.com/apk/res/android"
    android:orientation="vertical"
    android:layout_width="fill_parent"
    android:layout_height="fill_parent">
    <TextView
        android:id="@+id/text1"
        android:layout_width="fill_parent"
        android:layout_height="wrap_content"
        android:textSize="31dp"
```

```
            android:textColor="#ddd" />
    <TextView
            android:id="@+id/text2"
            android:layout_width="fill_parent"
            android:layout_height="wrap_content"
            android:textSize="18dp"
            android:textColor="#f00" />
</LinearLayout>
```

This particular example is similar to the default notification but does not contain an icon. The setLatestEventInfo() method is normally used to assign the text to the default layout. In this example, we use our custom layout instead. The Intent still needs to be assigned, though, as follows:

```
Intent toLaunch = new Intent
    (SimpleNotificationsActivity.this, SimpleNotificationsActivity.class);
PendingIntent intentBack = PendingIntent.getActivity
    (SimpleNotificationsActivity.this, 0, toLaunch, 0);

notify.contentIntent = intentBack;
notifier.notify(NOTIFY_5, notify);
```

The end result looks something like Figure 6.4.

Figure 6.4   Custom notification showing with just two lines of text.

Using a custom notification layout can provide better control over the information on the expanded status bar. Additionally, it can help differentiate your application's notifications from other applications by providing a themed or branded appearance.

Note

The size of the area that a layout can use on the expanded status bar is fixed for a given device. However, the exact details might change from device to device. Keep this in mind when designing a custom notification layout. Additionally, be sure to test the layout on all target devices in all modes of screen operation so that you can be sure the notification layout draws properly.

The default layout includes two fields of text: an icon and a time field for when the notification was triggered. Users are accustomed to this information. An application, where feasible and where it makes sense, should try to conform to at least this level of information when using custom notifications.

Designing Useful Notifications

As you can see, the notification capabilities on the Android platform are quite robust—so robust that it is easy to overdo it and make your application tiresome for the user. Here are some tips for designing useful notifications:

- Only use notifications when your application is not in the foreground. When in the foreground, use `Toast` or `Dialog` controls.
- Allow the user to determine what types (text, lights, sound, and vibration) and frequency of notifications she receives, as well as what events to trigger notifications for.
- Whenever possible, update and reuse an existing notification instead of creating a new one.
- Clear notifications regularly so as not to overwhelm the user with dated information.
- When in doubt, generate "polite" notifications (read as quiet).
- Make sure your notifications contain useful information in the ticker, title, and body text fields and launch sensible intents.

The notification framework is lightweight yet powerful. However, some applications such as alarm clocks or stock market monitors might also need to implement their own alert windows above and beyond the notification framework provided. In this case, they may use a background service and launch full `Activity` windows upon certain events. In Android 2.0 and later, developers can use the `WindowManager.LayoutParams` class to enable activity windows to display, even when the screen is locked with a keyguard.

Summary

Applications can interact with their users outside the normal activity boundaries by using notifications. Notifications can be visual, auditory, or use the vibrate feature of the device. Various methods can customize these notifications to provide rich information to the user. Special care must be taken to provide the right amount of appropriate information to the user without the application becoming a nuisance or the application being installed and forgotten about.

References and More Information

Android Dev Guide: "Notifying the User":
   http://d.android.com/guide/topics/ui/notifiers/index.html
Android Dev Guide: "Creating Status Bar Notifications":
   http://d.android.com/guide/topics/ui/notifiers/notifications.html
Android Reference for the NotificationManager class:
   http://d.android.com/reference/android/app/NotificationManager.html
Android Reference for the Nofitication.Builder class:
   http://d.android.com/reference/android/app/Notification.Builder.html

## 7

Designing Powerful User Interfaces

The Android platform has matured over time, especially when it comes to the user experience. We've already talked about many of the user interface controls you can leverage in your applications. Now we take a broader look at some of the user interface features available in the Android SDK, including various kinds of menus, action bars, styles, and themes. We also talk about the Android development team's new initiative to document a set of guidelines and best practices for Android application design.

Following Android User Interface Guidelines

When we wrote the first edition of this book several years ago, design was not the focus, and really it still isn't—not for us developers with little artistic sense whatsoever, anyway. That's what designers are for. As the platform has matured, design patterns have arisen. Some have succeeded, others have failed. It's hard to keep up and developers have expressed no small amount of frustration over the number of UI overhauls that have occurred with each new revision of the Android platform. In early 2011, the Android development team launched a new Android developer education initiative called Android Design. Android Design is a website where you can learn all about the user interface principles recommended by the platform designers. These are recommendations, not requirements, but they are generally sound. That doesn't mean you can't break the mold and do something innovative, but it provides a nice baseline that will help developers with or without design talent raise the bar in terms of application user interface design. Check out Android Design at http://d.android.com/design/.

Tip

We cover some of the most commonly used platform user interface features in this chapter, but there are many we do not have the space to cover. For more information, see the Resources listed at the end of this chapter.

One More Note… on Design

There's a famous quote by the late Steve Jobs that is appropriate here:

"People think it's this veneer—that the designers are handed this box and told, 'Make it look good!' That's not what we think design is. It's not just what it looks like and feels like. Design is how it works."

From the November 30, 2003, *New York Times* article, "The Guts of a Machine." http://goo.gl/6WiMe.

Working with Menus

You need to be aware of several types of application menus for use within your Android applications. The way menus have worked on the Android platform have changed over time, especially as we have seen devices move from hardware buttons to software buttons and action bars. The three main menu types available in Android are:

- The options menus (replaced by action bars as of API Level 11)
- The context menu (replaced by contextual action modes as of API Level 11)
- The popup menu (added in API Level 11)

Each type of menu has a special purpose, and each is used in different circumstances. It is best described in terms of scope. The scope of an options menu is the screen or the application at large—its actions apply in general. The scope of a context menu is the item for which the menu is attached to—for example, each item in a `ListView` might have a context menu for editing or deleting the item. Finally, popup menus are like secondary context menus—they are tied to a `View` control on the screen, but they should not provide actions that directly affect that item as a context menu would. Let's look at each of these menu types in more detail.

Using Options Menus

Options menus are an older style menu used primarily on devices running Android 2.3 and earlier. These devices normally have physical buttons for actions like Home and Menu. The Android SDK provides a method for users to bring up a menu in an `Activity` by pressing the Menu button, as shown in Figure 7.1. This is the traditional options menu behavior. Applications that target later versions of the Android SDK should use action bars instead, as discussed later in this chapter.

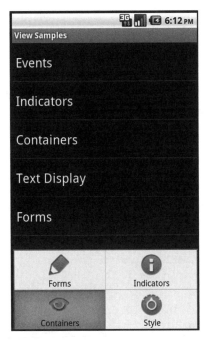

Figure 7.1   Traditional options menu behavior (up to Android 2.3).

You can use options menus in your application to bring up help, to navigate, to provide additional controls, or to configure options. The options menu items can contain icons, submenus, and keyboard shortcuts.

For an options menu to show when a user presses the Menu button on his device, you need to override the implementation of onCreateOptionsMenu() in your Activity. Here is a sample implementation that gives the user three menu items to choose from:

```
public boolean onCreateOptionsMenu( android.view.Menu menu) {
    super.onCreateOptionsMenu(menu);
    menu.add("Forms")
        .setIcon(android.R.drawable.ic_menu_edit)
        .setIntent(new Intent(this, FormsActivity.class));
    menu.add("Indicators")
        .setIntent(new Intent(this, IndicatorsActivity.class))
        .setIcon(android.R.drawable.ic_menu_info_details);
    menu.add("Containers")
        .setIcon(android.R.drawable.ic_menu_view)
        .setIntent(new Intent(this, ContainersActivity.class));
    return true;
}
```

For each of the items that are added, we also set a built-in icon resource and assign an `Intent` to each item. We give the item title with a regular text string, for clarity. You can also use a resource identifier. For this example, there is no other handling or code needed. When one of these menu items is selected, the `Activity` described by the `Intent` starts.

This type of options menu can be useful for navigating to important parts of an application, such as the help page, from anywhere within your application. Another great use for an options menu is to allow configuration options for a given screen. The user can configure these options in the form of checkable menu items. The initial menu that appears when the user presses the Menu button does not support checkable menu items. Instead, you must place these menu items on a `SubMenu` control, which is a type of `Menu` that can be configured in a menu. `SubMenu` objects support checkable items but do not support icons or other `SubMenu` items. Building on the preceding example, the following is code for programmatically adding a `SubMenu` control to the previous `Menu`:

```
SubMenu style_choice = menu.addSubMenu("Style")
    .setIcon(android.R.drawable.ic_menu_preferences);
style_choice.add(style_group, light_id, 1, "Light")
    .setChecked(isLight);
style_choice.add(style_group, dark_id, 2, "Dark")
    .setChecked(!isLight);
style_choice.setGroupCheckable(style_group, true, true);
```

This code would be inserted before the return statement in the implementation of the `onCreateOptionsMenu()` method. It adds a single menu item with an icon to the previous menu, called "Style." When the "Style" option is clicked, a menu with the two items of the `SubMenu` control is displayed. These items are grouped together and the checkable icon, by default, looks like the radio button icon. The checked state is assigned during creation time.

To handle the event when a menu option item is selected, we also implement the `onOptionsItemSelected()` method, as shown here:

```
public boolean onOptionsItemSelected(MenuItem item) {
    if (item.getItemId() == light_id) {
        item.setChecked(true);
        isLight = true;
        return true;
    } else if (item.getItemId() == dark_id) {
        item.setChecked(true);
        isLight = false;
        return true;
    }

    return super.onOptionsItemSelected(item);
}
```

This method must call the super class's `onOptionsItemSelected()` method for basic behavior to work. The actual `MenuItem` object is passed in, and we can use that to retrieve the identifier that we previously assigned to see which one is selected and performs an appropriate action. Here, we switch the values and return. By default, a `Menu` control goes away when any item is selected, including checkable items. This means it's useful for quick settings but not as useful for extensive settings where the user might want to change more than one item at a time.

As you add more menu items to your options menu, you might notice that a "More" item automatically appears. This happens whenever more than six items are visible. If the user selects this, the full menu is shown. The full, expanded menu doesn't show menu icons and although checkable items are possible, you should not use them here. Additionally, the full title of an item doesn't display. The initial menu, also known as the icon menu, shows only a portion of the title for each item. You can assign each item a `condensedTitle` attribute, which shows instead of a truncated version of the regular title. For example, instead of the title "Instant Message," you can set the `condensedTitle` attribute to "IM" as a common short form.

Using Context Menus

The `ContextMenu` class (`android.view.ContextMenu`) is a subtype of `Menu` that you can configure to display when a long press is performed on a `View`. As the name implies, the `ContextMenu` provides for contextual menus to display to the user for performing additional actions on selected items. This method of providing context-based actions is most appropriate for applications running API Level 10 or lower.

`ContextMenu` objects are slightly more complex than `OptionsMenu` objects. You need to implement the `onCreateContextMenu()` method of your `Activity` for one to display. However, before that is called, you must call the `registerForContextMenu()` method and pass in the `View` for which you want to have a context menu. This means each `View` on your screen can have a different context menu, which is appropriate as the menus are designed to be highly contextual.

Here we have an example of a `Chronometer` timer, which responds to a long click with a context menu:

```
registerForContextMenu(timer);
```

After the call to the `registerForContextMenu()` method has been executed, the user can then long click on the `View` to open the context menu. Each time this happens, your activity gets a call to the `onCreateContextMenu()` method, and your code creates the menu each time the user performs the long click.

The following is an example of a context menu for the `Chronometer` control, as previously used:

```
public void onCreateContextMenu(
    ContextMenu menu, View v, ContextMenuInfo menuInfo) {
    super.onCreateContextMenu(menu, v, menuInfo);
```

```
if (v.getId() == R.id.Chronometer01) {
    getMenuInflater().inflate(R.menu.timer_context, menu);
    menu.setHeaderIcon(android.R.drawable.ic_media_play)
        .setHeaderTitle("Timer controls");
}
```
}

Recall that any `View` control can register to trigger a call to the
`onCreateContextMenu()` method when the user performs a long press. This means we
have to check which `View` control it was for and which user tried to get a context
menu. Next, we inflate the appropriate menu from a menu resource that we defined
with XML. Because we can't define header information in the menu resource file, we set
a stock Android SDK resource to it and add a title. Here is the menu resource that is
inflated:

```
<menu
    xmlns:android="http://schemas.android.com/apk/res/android">
    <item
        android:id="@+id/start_timer"
        android:title="Start" />
    <item
        android:id="@+id/stop_timer"
        android:title="Stop" />
    <item
        android:id="@+id/reset_timer"
        android:title="Reset" />
</menu>
```

This defines three menu items. If this weren't a context menu, we could have assigned
icons. However, context menus do not support icons, submenus, or shortcuts.

Now we need to handle the `ContextMenu` clicks by implementing the
`onContextItemSelected()` method in our `Activity`. Here's an example:

```
public boolean onContextItemSelected(MenuItem item) {
    super.onContextItemSelected(item);
    boolean result = false;
    Chronometer timer = (Chronometer)findViewById(R.id.Chronometer01);
    switch (item.getItemId()){
        case R.id.stop_timer:
            timer.stop();
            result = true;
            break;
        case R.id.start_timer:
            timer.start();
            result = true;
            break;
        case R.id.reset_timer:
```

```
                timer.setBase(SystemClock.elapsedRealtime());
                result = true;
                break;
    }
    return result;
}
```

Because we have only one context menu in this example, we find the `Chronometer`
for use in this method. This method is called regardless of which context menu the
selected item is on, though, so you should take care to have unique resource identifiers
or keep track of which menu is shown. This can be accomplished because the context
menu is created each time it's shown.

Using Popup Menus

Introduced in API Level 11, the `PopupMenu` class (`android.widget.PopupMenu`) is a
modal window that pops up and floats near a `View` control. Touching outside the popup
dismisses it. Popup menus should be used when action bar options menus and context
menus are not appropriate. See the Android SDK documentation for more details.

Enabling Action Bars

Action bars are a relatively new navigational user interface mechanism introduced in
Android 3.0 (API Level 11). Action bars replace the traditional application title bar, but
provide a much richer set of features, allowing the user to traverse the screens and features of your applications more quickly, with fewer clicks, and with less confusion.
Action bars have also helped standardize application navigation as newer types of
Android devices like tablets have been moving away from having physical hardware buttons to software buttons.

> **Tip**
>
> Many of the code examples provided in this section are taken from the SimpleActionBars
> application. This source code for the SimpleActionBars application is provided for download
> on the book's websites.

The concept of the action bar is straightforward. If your application has an options
menu—that is, a menu of action items that comes up when the user presses the Menu
button—then your application can easily take advantage of the action bar features in
Android 3.0, which basically modify the application title bar to include those actions
previously shown in the options menu in an easy-to-use way, as shown in Figure 7.2.

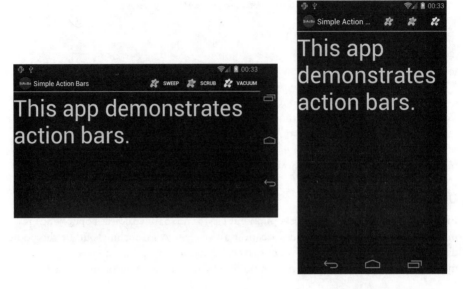

Figure 7.2   Action bar demonstration showing dynamic behavior.

One tricky thing about action bars is that they look and behave differently, depending on the Android platform version.

Building Basic Action Bars

Let's look at a simple example. Let's assume we have an application with four screens: a main `Activity` to launch into, and three other "cleaning" `Activity` classes for sweeping, scrubbing, and vacuuming. Now, we add an options menu to our main `Activity` that enables the user to jump to the three "cleaning" features easily, as shown in Figure 7.3.

Figure 7.3   A simple app with an options menu and four screens.

The two basic components of this application are the options menu resource file and the main `Activity` class. The other `Activity` classes simply display an `ImageView` and a `TextView` control. The options menu resource file simply defines the options menu items:

```xml
<?xml version="1.0" encoding="utf-8"?>
<menu
    xmlns:android="http://schemas.android.com/apk/res/android">
    <item
        android:id="@+id/sweep"
        android:icon="@drawable/ic_menu_sweep"
        android:title="@string/sweep"
        android:onClick="onOptionSweep" />
    <item
        android:id="@+id/scrub"
        android:icon="@drawable/ic_menu_scrub"
        android:title="@string/scrub"
        android:onClick="onOptionScrub" />
    <item
        android:id="@+id/vacuum"
        android:icon="@drawable/ic_menu_vac"
        android:title="@string/vacuum"
        android:onClick="onOptionVacuum" />
</menu>
```

The main `Activity` class loads this menu resource as an options menu, and defines the `onClick()` handlers for each options menu item, as follows:

```
public class SimpleActionBarsActivity extends Activity {
    @Override
    public void onCreate(Bundle savedInstanceState) {
        super.onCreate(savedInstanceState);
        setContentView(R.layout.main);
    }

    @Override
    public boolean onCreateOptionsMenu(Menu menu) {
        MenuInflater inflater = getMenuInflater();
        inflater.inflate(R.menu.cleaningoptions, menu);
        return true;
    }

    public void onOptionSweep(MenuItem i)
    {
        startActivity(new Intent(this, SweepActivity.class));
    }

    public void onOptionScrub(MenuItem i)
    {
        startActivity(new Intent(this, ScrubActivity.class));
    }

    public void onOptionVacuum(MenuItem i)
    {
        startActivity(new Intent(this, VacuumActivity.class));
    }
}
```

We aren't doing anything fancy here, so we technically do not need to set the application's Android manifest file to a high target API level. So let's say we simply set it to something older, such as API Level 9, as shown here:

```
<uses-sdk android:minSdkVersion="9" />
```

When we run this "legacy" application on a device running API Level 11 and later, the system bar shows a fourth icon that looks like a grid. This is the software button equivalent of the Menu button found on traditional Android phones. Clicking it displays the options menu, much as it would on an older smartphone, as shown in Figure 7.4. The title bar at the top of the screen is simply a skinny bar that shows the application's title.

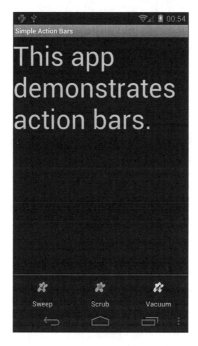

Figure 7.4   Legacy options menu application behavior on later SDKs.

If we modify the target API level of the application's Android manifest file and set it to API Level 11 (Honeycomb), then the action bar mechanism is automatically applied to the application.

```
<uses-sdk android:minSdkVersion="11" />
```

By default, the title bar is now thicker. It shows the application icon, the application name, and what is called the overflow menu icon. Clicking this icon results in a textual menu that lists the options menu items, as shown in Figure 7.5.

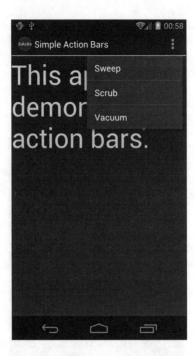

Figure 7.5   Action bar behavior on a device with API Level 11 and later.

Customizing Your Action Bar

When your application targets the Honeycomb platform or later, you can really start to take advantage of what the action bar widget has to offer by placing your option menu items right on the action bar to make things easier for the user. The primary menu item attribute that controls this behavior is the `android:showAsAction` attribute. This attribute can be any of the following values:

- `always`: This value causes the menu item to always be shown on the action bar.

- `ifRoom`: This value causes the menu item to be shown on the action bar if there is sufficient room.

- `never`: This value causes the menu item to never be shown on the action bar.

- `withText`: This value causes the menu item to be displayed with its icon and its menu text.

You can modify the options menu resource file to use this attribute in different ways. First, if you look back at Figure 7.2, this is what the action bar looks like if you set each menu item to display if there's room, along with its name. In other words, each menu item has the following attribute:

```
android:showAsAction="ifRoom|withText"
```

Another reasonable setting is to display each menu item on the action bar, provided there is space, but without the clutter of the text. In other words, each menu item has the following attribute:

```
android:showAsAction="ifRoom"
```

Figure 7.6 shows what this change achieves on your typical device with API Level 11 or later.

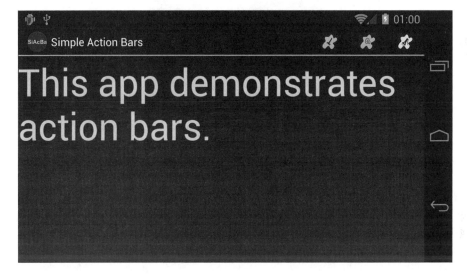

Figure 7.6   Showing menu items on the action bar when room is available, not including text.

Finally, let's say that we never want to see the Vacuum menu item on the action bar.

```
android:showAsAction="never"
```

This results in two menu items on the action bar: Sweep and Scrub. Then, in the far-right corner, you'll see the overflow menu again. Click it to see any menu items set to never (such as Vacuum) and any other menu items that might not have fit on the action bar, as shown in Figure 7.7.

Figure 7.7   Showing some menu items on the action bar while others never show (instead appear in the overflow menu).

Handling Application Icon Clicks on the Action Bar

Another feature of the action bar is that the user can click the application icon in the top-left corner. Although clicking does nothing by default, adding a custom "home" functionality, perhaps to your launch screen, is easy. Let's say you want to update the default action bar in the ScrubActivity class so that clicking the application icon causes the user to return to the main launch activity (clearing the activity stack at the same time).

To do this, you would simply implement the onOptionsItemSelected() method for the ScrubActivity class and handle the special menu item identifier called android.R.id.home, like this:

```
@Override
public boolean onOptionsItemSelected(MenuItem item)
{
    switch (item.getItemId())
    {
        case android.R.id.home:
            Intent intent = new Intent(this, ActOnThisActivity.class);
```

```
            intent.addFlags(Intent.FLAG_ACTIVITY_CLEAR_TOP);
            startActivity(intent);
            return true;
        default:
            return super.onOptionsItemSelected(item);
    }
}
```

That's all there is to it (refer to Figure 7.3, bottom center). You can also display a little arrow to the left of the application icon to identify that you are moving back up the screen hierarchy of your application by using the `setDisplayHomeAsUpEnabled()` method in your `onCreate()` method of the `Activity` in conjunction with implementing the special home menu item click handler.

```
ActionBar bar = getActionBar();
bar.setDisplayHomeAsUpEnabled(true);
```

The resulting action bar, if we were to enable it on the Sweep screen, is shown in Figure 7.8.

Figure 7.8   An action bar with a clickable Home button and an up indicator.

Working with Screens That Do Not Require Action Bars

Once you've set your application target to API 11 or higher, all your screens will have action bars by default. However, you can remove the action bar from a screen in several ways. Perhaps the simplest way is to turn it off programmatically from within your activity class. For example, we can turn off the action bar on the Vacuum screen with the following two lines of code added to the onCreate() method of the activity class:

```
ActionBar bar = getActionBar();
bar.hide();
```

This code removes the entire bar from the top of the screen (Figure 7.3, bottom, left). The application name is not shown at all. You can also hide the action bar easily in layout files by creating a special custom theme. See the Android SDK documentation about action bars for details.

Introducing Contextual Action Mode

In Android 3.0 and later, the design guidelines recommend developers use contextual action bars instead of the context menus you learned about in the previous section. Contextual action mode can be enabled for a single View in response to an action, such as a long click. An ActionMode.Callback instance is assigned to handle creation and click handling on the contextual action mode action bar. As with other menus, creation of the menu is usually handled through a MenuInflater. Clicks are handled through the onActionItemClicked() method and when the action is complete, the mode is returned to normal through a call to the finish() method of the ActionMode class.

With ListView and GridView controls, multiple items can be selected. Here you set the control to multiple choice mode and then register a MultiChoiceModeListener() instance on the view control. This combines the selection handling and the contextual action mode listening into one callback class.

Using Advanced Action Bar Features

There's a lot more you can do with action bars. Action bars can be styled, including change features such as the background graphic and other customizations. They also support several other more sophisticated view types and widgets, beyond those menu items found in the options menu, such as tabs and dropdowns. You can even add other types of view controls to create functional areas of the action bar. See the Android SDK documentation on action bars for details.

Working with Styles

Android user interface designers can group layout element attributes together in styles. A *style* is a group of common View attribute values that can be applied jointly to any user interface control. Styles can include such settings as the font to draw with or the color of text. The specific attributes depend on the View drawn. In essence, though, each style attribute can change the look and feel of the particular object drawn.

You can use a style to define your application's standard TextView attributes once and then reference to the style either in an XML layout file or programmatically from within Java. Styles are typically defined within the /res/values/styles.xml resource file using the <style> tag.

Building Simple Styles

Here's an example of a simple style resource file /res/values/styles.xml containing two styles: one for mandatory form fields and one for optional form fields on TextView and EditText objects:

```xml
<?xml version="1.0" encoding="utf-8"?>
<resources>
    <style name="mandatory_text_field_style">
        <item name="android:textColor">#000000</item>
        <item name="android:textSize">14pt</item>
        <item name="android:textStyle">bold</item>
    </style>
    <style name="optional_text_field_style">
        <item name="android:textColor">#0F0F0F</item>
        <item name="android:textSize">12pt</item>
        <item name="android:textStyle">italic</item>
    </style>
</resources>
```

Many useful style attributes are colors and dimensions. It is more appropriate to use references to resources. Here's the styles.xml file again; this time, the color and text size fields are available in the other resource files colors.xml and dimens.xml:

```xml
<?xml version="1.0" encoding="utf-8"?>
<resources>
    <style name="mandatory_text_field_style">
        <item name="android:textColor"
            >@color/mand_text_color</item>
        <item name="android:textSize"
            >@dimen/important_text</item>
        <item name="android:textStyle">bold</item>
    </style>
    <style name="optional_text_field_style">
        <item name="android:textColor"
            >@color/opt_text_color</item>
        <item name="android:textSize"
            >@dimen/unimportant_text</item>
        <item name="android:textStyle">italic</item>
    </style>
</resources>
```

Now, if you can create a new layout with a couple of `TextView` and `EditText` text controls, you can set each control's style attribute by referencing it as such:

```
style="@style/name_of_style"
```

Here we have a form layout called `/res/layout/form.xml` that does that:

```xml
<?xml version="1.0" encoding="utf-8"?>
<LinearLayout
    xmlns:android=
        "http://schemas.android.com/apk/res/android"
    android:orientation="vertical"
    android:layout_width="fill_parent"
    android:layout_height="fill_parent"
    android:background="@color/background_color">
    <TextView
        android:id="@+id/TextView01"
        style="@style/mandatory_text_field_style"
        android:layout_height="wrap_content"
        android:text="@string/mand_label"
        android:layout_width="wrap_content" />
    <EditText
        android:id="@+id/EditText01"
        style="@style/mandatory_text_field_style"
        android:layout_height="wrap_content"
        android:text="@string/mand_default"
        android:layout_width="fill_parent"
        android:singleLine="true" />
    <TextView
        android:id="@+id/TextView02"
        style="@style/optional_text_field_style"
        android:layout_width="wrap_content"
        android:layout_height="wrap_content"
        android:text="@string/opt_label" />
    <EditText
        android:id="@+id/EditText02"
        style="@style/optional_text_field_style"
        android:layout_height="wrap_content"
        android:text="@string/opt_default"
        android:singleLine="true"
        android:layout_width="fill_parent" />
    <TextView
        android:id="@+id/TextView03"
        style="@style/optional_text_field_style"
        android:layout_width="wrap_content"
        android:layout_height="wrap_content"
        android:text="@string/opt_label" />
    <EditText
```

```
        android:id="@+id/EditText03"
        style="@style/optional_text_field_style"
        android:layout_height="wrap_content"
        android:text="@string/opt_default"
        android:singleLine="true"
        android:layout_width="fill_parent" />
</LinearLayout>
```

The resulting layout has three fields, each made up of one TextView for the label and one EditText where the user can input text. The mandatory style is applied to the mandatory label and text entry. The other two fields use the optional style. The resulting layout looks something like Figure 7.9.

Figure 7.9   A layout using two styles, one for mandatory fields and another for optional fields.

Styles are applied to specific layout controls such as TextView and Button objects. Usually, you want to supply the style resource id when you call the control's constructor. For example, the style named myAppIsStyling would be referred to as R.style.myAppIsStyling.

Leveraging Style Inheritance

Styles support inheritance; therefore, styles can also reference another style as a parent. This way, they pick up the attributes of the parent style. Let's look at another example to illustrate how style inheritance works. Here we have two different styles:

```xml
<?xml version="1.0" encoding="utf-8"?>
<resources>
    <style name="padded_small">
        <item name="android:padding">2dp</item>
        <item name="android:textSize">8dp</item>
    </style>
    <style name="padded_large">
        <item name="android:padding">4dp</item>
        <item name="android:textSize">16dp</item>
    </style>
</resources>
```

When applied, the `padded_small` style sets the padding to 2 dp and the `textSize` to 8 dp. The following is an example of how it is applied to a `TextView` from within a layout resource file:

```xml
<TextView
    style="@style/padded_small"
    android:layout_width="fill_parent"
    android:layout_height="wrap_content"
    android:text="Small Padded" />
```

The following is an example of how you might use style inheritance:

```xml
<style name="red_padded">
    <item name="android:textColor">#F00</item>
    <item name="android:padding">3dp</item>
</style>

<style name="padded_normal" parent="red_padded">
    <item name="android:textSize">12dp</item>
</style>

<style name="padded_italics" parent="red_padded">
    <item name="android:textSize">14dp</item>
    <item name="android:textStyle">italic</item>
</style>
```

Here you find two common attributes in a single style and a reference to them from the other two styles that have different attributes. You can reference any style as a parent style; however, you can set only one style as the style attribute of a `View`. Applying the `padded_italics` style that is already defined makes the text 14 dp in size, italic, red, and padded. The following is an example of applying this style:

```xml
<TextView
    style="@style/padded_italics"
    android:layout_width="fill_parent"
    android:layout_height="wrap_content"
    android:text="Italic w/parent color" />
```

As you can see from this example, applying a style with a parent is no different than applying a regular style. In fact, a regular style can be used for applying to `View` controls and used as a parent in a different style.

```
<style name="padded_xlarge">
    <item name="android:padding">10dp</item>
    <item name="android:textSize">100dp</item>
</style>
<style name="green_glow" parent="padded_xlarge">
    <item name="android:shadowColor">#0F0</item>
    <item name="android:shadowDx">0</item>
    <item name="android:shadowDy">0</item>
    <item name="android:shadowRadius">10</item>
</style>
```

Here the `padded_xlarge` style is set as the parent for the `green_glow` style. All six attributes are then applied to any view that this style is set to.

Eclipse Tip

When in the Graphical Layout editor or the XML editor for layouts, you can use the Android Development Tools plug-in quick-fix capability to quickly make styles. When editing a view, simply add properties directly on it. Get them all correct. Then choose the quick fix option for Extract as Style. This displays a dialog for you to name the style and choose which properties go in it. The tool then creates the style, sets it on the control you chose to do the action on, and removes all of the properties that were included in the style.

Working with Themes

Themes are much like styles, but instead of being applied to one layout element at a time, they are applied to all elements of a given `Activity` or the application as a whole. Themes are defined in exactly the same way as styles. Themes use the `<style>` tag and should be stored in the `/res/values` directory. The only difference is that instead of applying that named style to a layout element, you define it as the `theme` attribute of an `Activity` in the Android manifest file.

A *theme* is a collection of one or more styles (as defined in the resources) but instead of applying the style to a specific control, the style is applied to all `View` objects in a specified `Activity`. Applying a theme to a set of `View` objects all at once simplifies making the user interface look consistent and can be a great way to define color schemes and other common control attribute settings.

You can specify the theme programmatically by calling the `Activity` method `setTheme()` with the style resource identifier. Each attribute of the style is applied to each `View` within that `Activity`, as applicable. Styles and attributes defined in the layout files explicitly override those in the theme.

For instance, consider the following style:

```
<style name="right">
    <item name="android:gravity">right</item>
</style>
```

You can apply this as a theme to the whole screen, which causes any view displayed within that `Activity` to have its `gravity` attribute right-justified. Applying this theme is as simple as making the method call to the `setTheme()` method from within the `Activity`, as shown here:

```
setTheme(R.style.right);
```

You can also apply themes to specific `Activity` instances by specifying them as an attribute within the `<activity>` element in the `AndroidManifest.xml` file, as follows:

```
<activity android:name=".myactivityname"
    android:label="@string/app_name"
    android:theme="@style/myAppIsStyling">
```

Unlike applying a style in an XML layout file, multiple themes can be applied to a screen. This gives you flexibility in defining style attributes in advance while applying different configurations of the attributes based on what might be displayed on the screen. This is demonstrated in the following code:

```
setTheme(R.style.right);
setTheme(R.style.green_glow);
setContentView(R.layout.style_samples);
```

In this example, both the `right` style and the `green_glow` style are applied as a theme to the entire screen. You can see the results of green glow and right-aligned gravity, applied to a variety of `TextView` controls on a screen, as shown in Figure 7.10. Finally, we set the layout to the `Activity`. You must do this after setting the themes. That is, you must apply all themes before calling the method `setContentView()` or the `inflate()` method so that the themes' attributes can take effect.

Figure 7.10   Packaging styles for glowing text, padding, and alignment into a theme.

A combination of well-designed and thought-out themes and styles can make the look of your application consistent and easy to maintain. Android comes with a number of built-in themes that can be a good starting point. These include such themes as `Theme_Black`, `Theme_Light`, and `Theme_NoTitleBar_Fullscreen`, as defined in the `android.R.style` class. They are all variations on the system theme, `Theme`, which built-in apps use.

Summary

The Android platform constantly changes as old user interface features are retired and new ones take their place. We are currently in a transitional period where most devices on the market still rely upon the legacy menu types, but more and more devices, especially tablets, use the new methods.

This chapter introduced you to the types of menus available in the Android SDK and what each menu's purpose is. You also learned about action bars and how they behave under different circumstances. Finally, you learned how to use styles and themes to provide a consistent user experience to your applications by "bottling up" groups of `View` attributes for reuse.

References and More Information

Android Design website:
   http://d.android.com/design/index.html
Article: "Add Horizontal Paging to Your Android Applications:"
   http://www.developer.com/ws/android/programming/add-horizontal-paging-to-your-android-applications.html (http://goo.gl/ujTwu)
Android Dev Guide: "Action Bar":
   http://d.android.com/guide/topics/ui/actionbar.html
Android Dev Guide: "Styles and Themes":
   http://d.android.com/guide/topics/ui/themes.html

## 8

Handling Advanced User Input

Users interact with Android devices in many ways, including using keyboards, track-balls, touch-screen gestures, and even voice. Different devices support different input methods and have different hardware. For example, certain devices have hardware keyboards, and others rely only on software keyboards. In this chapter, you learn about the different input methods available to developers and how you can use them to great effect within your applications.

Working with Textual Input Methods

The Android SDK includes input method framework classes that enable interested developers to use powerful input methods and create their own input methods, such as custom software keyboards and other Input Method Editors (IME). Users can download custom IMEs to use on their devices. For example, there's nothing stopping a developer from creating a custom keyboard with *Lord of the Rings*-style Elvish characters, smiley faces, or Greek symbols.

Tip

Most device settings related to input methods are available under the Settings, Language & Keyboard menu. Here, users can select the language, configure the custom user dictionary, and make changes to how their keyboards function. The user can change the input method on the device by press and holding an `EditText` control, for example. A context menu displays, allowing the user to change the input method (Android keyboard is usually the default).

The Android SDK also includes a number of other text input utilities that might benefit application users, such as text prediction and dictionaries and the clipboard framework, which can be used to enable sophisticated cut and paste features in your application for text and much more.

Working with Software Keyboards

Because text input methods are locale-based (different countries use different alphabets and keyboards) and situational (numeric versus alphabetic versus special keys), the

Android platform has trended toward software keyboards as opposed to relying on hard-ware manufacturers to deliver specialized hardware keyboards.

Choosing the Appropriate Software Keyboard

The Android platform has a number of software keyboards available for use. One of the easiest ways to enable your users to enter data efficiently is to specify the type of input expected in each text input field.

Tip

Many of the code examples provided in this section are taken from the SimpleTextInputTypes application. The source code for this application is provided for download on the book's websites.

For example, to specify an `EditText` control that should take only capitalized textual input, you can set the `inputType` attribute as follows:

```
<EditText android:layout_height="wrap_content"
    android:layout_width="fill_parent"
    android:inputType="text|textCapCharacters">
</EditText>
```

Figure 8.1 shows a number of `EditText` controls with different `inputType` configurations.

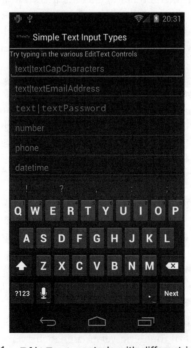

Figure 8.1   `EditText` controls with different input types.

The input type dictates which software keyboard is used by default and it enforces appropriate rules, such as limiting input to certain characters. Figure 8.2 (left) illustrates what the software keyboard looks like for an `EditText` control with its `inputType` attribute set to all capitalized text input. Note how the software keyboard keys are all capitalized. If you were to set the `inputType` to `textCapWords` instead, the keyboard switches to lowercase after the first letter of each word and then back to uppercase after a space. Figure 8.2 (middle) illustrates what the software keyboard looks like for an `EditText` control with its `inputType` attribute set to `number`. Figure 8.2 (right) illustrates what the software keyboard looks like for an `EditText` control with its `inputType` attribute set to textual input, where each sentence begins with a capital letter and the text can be multiple lines.

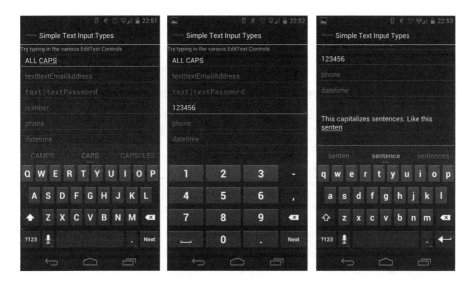

Figure 8.2   The software keyboards associated with specific input types.

Depending on the user's keyboard settings (specifically, if the user has enabled the Show Suggestions and Auto-complete options in the Android Keyboard settings of his device), the user might also see suggested words or spelling fixes while typing. For a complete list of `inputType` attribute values and their uses, see http://goo.gl/hr72U.

Tip

You can also have your `Activity` react to the display of software keyboards (to adjust where fields are displayed, for example) by requesting the `WindowManager` as a system service and modifying the layout parameters associated with the `softInputMode` field.

For more fine-tuned control over input methods, see the `android.view.inputmethod.InputMethodManager` class.

Providing Custom Software Keyboards

If you are interested in developing your own software keyboards, we highly recommend the following references:

- IMEs are implemented as an Android service. Begin by reviewing the Android packages called `android.inputmethodservice` and `android.view.inputmethod`, which can be used to implement custom input methods.

- The `SoftKeyboard` sample application in the Android SDK provides an implementation of a software keyboard.

- The Android Developer technical articles on onscreen input methods (http://d.android.com/resources/articles/on-screen-inputs.html) and creating an input method (http://d.android.com/resources/articles/creating-input-method.html). Don't forget to add voice typing to your input method (http://android-developers.blogspot.com/2011/12/add-voice-typing-to-your-ime.html).

Working with Text Prediction and User Dictionaries

Text prediction is a powerful and flexible feature available on Android devices. We've already talked about many of these technologies in other parts of this book, but they merit mentioning in this context as well.

- In *Android Wireless Application Development Volume I: Android Essentials*, you learned how to use `AutoCompleteTextView` and `MultiAutoCompleteTextView` controls to help users input common words and strings.

- In Chapter 3, "Leveraging SQLite Application Databases," you learned how to tie an `AutoCompleteTextView` control to an underlying SQLite database table.

- In *Android Wireless Application Development Volume I: Android Essentials*, you learned about the `UserDictionary` content provider (`android.provider.UserDictionary`), which can be used to add words to the user's custom dictionary of commonly used words.

Using the Clipboard Framework

On Android devices running Android 3.0 and higher (API Level 11), developers can access the clipboard to perform copy and paste actions. Previous to this, the clipboard had no public API. To leverage the clipboard in your applications, you need to use the clipboard framework of the Android SDK. You can copy and paste different data structures—everything from text to references to files, to application shortcuts as Intent objects. The clipboard holds only a single set of clipped data at a time, and the clipboard is shared across all applications, so you can easily copy and paste content between applications.

Copying Data to the System Clipboard

To save data to the system clipboard, call `getSystemService()` and request the clipboard service's `ClipboardManager` (`android.content.ClipboardManager`). Then, create a `ClipData` (`android.content.ClipData`) object and populate it with the data you want to save to the clipboard. Finally, commit the clip using the `ClipboardManager` class method `setPrimaryClip()`.

Pasting Data from the System Clipboard

To retrieve data from the system clipboard, call `getSystemService()` and request the clipboard service's `ClipboardManager` (`android.content.ClipboardManager`). You can determine whether the clipboard contains data using the `hasPrimaryClip()` method. After you have determined whether there is valid data in the system clipboard, you can inspect its description and type, and ultimately retrieve the `ClipData` object using the `getPrimaryClip()` method.

Handling User Events

You've seen how to do basic event handling in some of the previous control examples. For instance, you know how to handle when a user clicks on a button. There are a number of other events generated by various actions the user might take. This section briefly introduces you to some of these events. First, though, we need to talk about the input states in Android.

Listening for Touch Mode Changes

The Android screen can be in one of two states. The state determines how the focus on `View` controls is handled. When touch mode is on, typically only objects such as `EditText` get focus when selected. Other objects, because they can be selected directly by the user tapping on the screen, won't take focus but instead trigger their action, if any. When not in touch mode, however, the user can change focus between even more object types. These include buttons and other views that normally need only a click to trigger their action. In this case, the user uses the arrow keys, trackball, or wheel to navigate between items and select them with the Enter or select keys.

Knowing what mode the screen is in is useful if you want to handle certain events. If, for instance, your application relies on the focus or lack of focus on a particular control, your application might need to know whether the device is in touch mode because the focus behavior is likely different.

Your application can register to find out when the touch mode changes by using the `addOnTouchModeChangeListener()` method in the `android.view.ViewTreeObserver` class. Your application needs to implement the `ViewTreeObserver.OnTouchModeChangeListener` class to listen for these events. Here is a sample implementation:

```
View all = findViewById(R.id.events_screen);
ViewTreeObserver vto = all.getViewTreeObserver();
vto.addOnTouchModeChangeListener(
    new ViewTreeObserver.OnTouchModeChangeListener() {
        public void onTouchModeChanged(
            boolean isInTouchMode) {
            events.setText("Touch mode: " + isInTouchMode);
        }
});
```

In this example, the top-level View in the layout is retrieved. A ViewTreeObserver listens to a View and all its child View objects. Using the top-level View of the layout means the ViewTreeObserver listens to events in the entire layout. An implementation of the onTouchModeChanged() method provides the ViewTreeObserver with a method to call when the touch mode changes. It merely passes in which mode the View is now in.

In this example, the mode is written to a TextView named events. We use this same TextView in further event handling examples to visually show on the screen which events our application has been told about. The ViewTreeObserver can enable applications to listen to a few other events on an entire screen.

By running this sample code, we can demonstrate the touch mode changing to true immediately when the user taps on the touch screen. Conversely, when the user chooses to use any other input method, the application reports that touch mode is false immediately after the input event, such as a key being pressed or the trackball or scroll wheel moving.

Listening for Events on the Entire Screen

You saw in the last section how your application can watch for changes to the touch mode state for the screen using the ViewTreeObserver class. The ViewTreeObserver also provides three other events that can be watched for on a full screen or an entire View and all of its children. These are

- PreDraw: Get notified before the View and its children are drawn.
- GlobalLayout: Get notified when the layout of the View and its children might change, including visibility changes.
- GlobalFocusChange: Get notified when the focus in the View and its children changes.

Your application might want to perform some actions before the screen is drawn. You can do this by calling the method addOnPreDrawListener() with an implementation of the ViewTreeObserver.OnPreDrawListener class interface.

Similarly, your application can find out when the layout or visibility of a View has changed. This might be useful if your application dynamically changes the display contents of a View and you want to check to see whether a View still fits on the screen.

Your application needs to provide an implementation of the
`ViewTreeObserver.OnGlobalLayoutListener` class interface to the
`addGlobalLayoutListener()` method of the `ViewTreeObserver` object.

Finally, your application can register to find out when the focus changes between a
`View` control and any of its child `View` controls. Your application might want to do this
to monitor how a user moves about on the screen. When in touch mode, though, there
might be fewer focus changes than when the touch mode is not set. In this case, your
application needs to provide an implementation of the
`ViewTreeObserver.OnGlobalFocusChangeListener` class interface to the
`addGlobalFocusChangeListener()` method. Here is a sample implementation of this:

```
vto.addOnGlobalFocusChangeListener(new
    ViewTreeObserver.OnGlobalFocusChangeListener() {
        public void onGlobalFocusChanged(
            View oldFocus, View newFocus) {
                if (oldFocus != null && newFocus != null) {
                    events.setText("Focus \nfrom: " +
                        oldFocus.toString() + " \nto: " +
                        newFocus.toString());
                }
            }
    });
```

This example uses the same `ViewTreeObserver`, `vto` and `TextView` events as in the
previous example. This shows that both the currently focused `View` object and the previously focused `View` object are passed to the listener as method parameters. From here,
your application can perform needed actions.

If your application merely wants to check values after the user has modified a particular `View` object, though, you might need to only register to listen for focus changes of
that particular `View` object. This is discussed later in this chapter.

Listening for Long Clicks

You can add a context menu to a `View` that is activated when the user performs a long
click on that view. A long click is typically when a user presses on the touch screen and
holds his finger there until an action is performed. However, a long press event can also
be triggered if the user navigates there with a nontouch method, such as via a keyboard
or trackball, and then holds the Enter or Select key for a while. This action is also often
called a press-and-hold action.

Although the context menu is a great typical use case for the long-click event, you
can listen for the long-click event and perform any action you want. However, this is the
same event that triggers the context menu. If you've already added a context menu to a
`View`, you might not want to listen for the long-click event as other actions or side
effects might confuse the user or even prevent the context menu from showing. As
always with good user interface design, try to be consistent for usability sake.

Tip

Usually a long click is an alternative action to a standard click. If a left-click on a computer is the standard click, a long click can be compared to a right-click.

Your application can listen to the long-click event on any `View`. The following example demonstrates how to listen for a long-click event on a `Button` control:

```
Button long_press = (Button)findViewById(R.id.long_press);
long_press.setOnLongClickListener(new View.OnLongClickListener() {
    public boolean onLongClick(View v) {
        events.setText("Long click: " + v.toString());
        return true;
    }
});
```

First, the `Button` object is requested by providing its identifier. Then the `setOnLongClickListener()` method is called with our implementation of the `View.OnLongClickListener` class interface. The `View` that the user long-clicked on is passed in to the `onLongClick()` event handler. Here again we use the same `TextView` as before to display text saying that a long click occurred.

Listening for Focus Changes

We already discussed focus changes for listening for them on an entire screen. All `View` objects, though, can also trigger a call to listeners when their particular focus state changes. You do this by providing an implementation of the `View.OnFocusChangeListener` class to the `setOnFocusChangeListener()` method. The following is an example of how to listen for focus change events with an `EditText` control:

```
TextView focus = (TextView)findViewById(R.id.text_focus_change);
focus.setOnFocusChangeListener(new View.OnFocusChangeListener() {
    public void onFocusChange(View v, boolean hasFocus) {
        if (hasFocus) {
            if (mSaveText != null) {
                ((TextView)v).setText(mSaveText);
            }
        } else {
            mSaveText = ((TextView)v).getText().toString();
            ((TextView)v).setText("");
        }
    }
}
```

In this implementation, we also use a private member variable of type `String` for `mSaveText`. After retrieving the `EditText` control as a `TextView`, we do one of two things. If the user moves focus away from the control, we store off the text in `mSaveText` and set the `text` to empty. If the user changes focus to the control, though, we restore this text. This has the amusing effect of hiding the text the user entered when the control is not active. This can be useful on a form on which a user needs to make multiple, lengthy text entries but you want to provide the user with an easy way to see which one they edit. It is also useful for demonstrating a purpose for the focus listeners on a text entry. Other uses might include validating text a user enters after a user navigates away or prefilling the text entry the first time they navigate to it with something else entered.

Working with Gestures

Android devices often rely on touch screens for user input. Users are now quite comfortable using common finger gestures to operate their devices. Android applications can detect and react to one-finger (single-touch) and two-finger (multi-touch) gestures. Users can also use gestures with the drag/drop framework to enable the arrangement of `View` controls on a device screen.

Note

Even early Android devices supported simple single-touch gestures. Support for multi-touch gestures was added in the Android 2.2 SDK and is available only on devices with capacitive touch screen hardware. Some capacitive hardware is capable of tracking up to 10 different points at once.

One of the reasons that gestures can be a bit tricky is that a gesture can be made of multiple touch events or motions. Different sequences of motion add up to different gestures. For example, a fling gesture involves the user pressing his finger down on the screen, swiping across the screen, and lifting his finger up off the screen while the swipe is still in motion (that is, without slowing down to stop before lifting his finger). Each of these steps can trigger motion events that applications can react to.

Detecting User Motions Within a View

By now you've come to understand that Android application user interfaces are built using different types of `View` controls. Developers can handle gestures much like they do click events within a `View` control using the `setOnClickListener()` and `setOnLongClickListener()` methods. Instead, the `onTouchEvent()` callback method is used to detect that some motion has occurred within the `View` region.

The `onTouchEvent()` callback method has a single parameter, a `MotionEvent` object. The `MotionEvent` object contains all sorts of details about what kind of motion occurs in the `View`, enabling the developer to determine what sort of gesture is happening by collecting and analyzing many consecutive `MotionEvent` objects. You can use all of the `MotionEvent` data to recognize and detect every kind of gesture you can possibly imagine. Alternately, you can use built-in gesture detectors provided in the Android SDK to detect common user motions in a consistent fashion. Android currently has two different classes that can detect navigational gestures:

- The `GestureDetector` class can be used to detect common single-touch gestures.
- The `ScaleGestureDetector` can be used to detect multi-touch scale gestures.

It is likely that more gesture detectors will be added in future versions of the Android SDK. You can also implement your own gesture detectors to detect any gestures not supported by the built-in gesture detectors. For example, you might want to create a two-fingered rotate gesture to, say, rotate an image or a three-fingered swipe gesture that brings up an option menu.

In addition to common navigational gestures, you can use the `android.gesture` package with the `GestureOverlayView` to recognize command-like gestures. For instance, you can create an S-shaped gesture that brings up a search or a zig-zag gesture that clears a screen on a drawing app. Tools are available for recording and creating libraries of this style gesture. As it uses an overlay for detection, it isn't well suited for all types of applications. This package was introduced in API Level 4.

Warning

The type and sensitivity of the touch screen can vary by device. Different devices can detect different numbers of touch points simultaneously, which affects the complexity of gestures you can support.

Handling Common Single-Touch Gestures

Introduced in API Level 1, the `GestureDetector` class can be used to detect gestures made by a single finger. Some common single-finger gestures supported by the `GestureDetector` class include:

- `onDown`: Called when the user first presses on the touch screen.
- `onShowPress`: Called after the user first presses the touch screen but before he lifts his finger or moves it around on the screen; used to visually or audibly indicate that the press has been detected.
- `onSingleTapUp`: Called when the user lifts up (using the up `MotionEvent`) from the touch screen as part of a single-tap event.
- `onSingleTapConfirmed`: Called when a single-tap event occurs.
- `onDoubleTap`: Called when a double-tap event occurs.
- `onDoubleTapEvent`: Called when an event within a double-tap gesture occurs, including any down, move, or up `MotionEvent`.
- `onLongPress`: Similar to `onSingleTapUp`, but called if the user holds down his finger long enough to not be a standard click but also without any movement.

- `onScroll`: Called after the user presses and then moves his finger in a steady motion before lifting his finger. This is commonly called *dragging*.
- `onFling`: Called after the user presses and then moves his finger in an accelerating motion before lifting it. This is commonly called a *flick gesture* and usually results in some motion continuing after the user lifts his finger.

You can use the interfaces available with the `GestureDetector` class to listen for specific gestures such as single and double taps (see `GestureDetector.OnDoubleTapListener`), as well as scrolls and flings (see the documentation for `GestureDetector.OnGestureListener`). The scrolling gesture involves touching the screen and moving your finger around on it. The fling gesture, on the other hand, causes (though not automatically) the object to continue to move even after the finger has been lifted from the screen. This gives the user the impression of throwing or flicking the object around on the screen.

Tip

You can use the `GestureDetector.SimpleOnGestureListener` class to listen to any and all of the gestures recognized by the `GestureDetector`.

Let's look at a simple example. Let's assume you have a game screen that enables the user to perform gestures to interact with a graphic on the screen. We can create a custom `View` class called `GameAreaView` that can dictate how a bitmap graphic moves around within the game area based upon each gesture. The `GameAreaView` class can use the `onTouchEvent()` method to pass along `MotionEvent` objects to a `GestureDetector`. In this way, the `GameAreaView` can react to simple gestures, interpret them, and make the appropriate changes to the bitmap, including moving it from one location to another on the screen.

Tip

How the gestures are interpreted and what actions they cause is completely up to the developer. You can, for example, interpret a fling gesture and make the bitmap graphic disappear... but does that make sense? Not really. It's important to always make the gesture jive well with the resulting operation in the application so that users are not confused. Users are now accustomed to specific screen behavior based on certain gestures, so it's best to use the expected convention, too.

In this case, the `GameAreaView` class interprets gestures as follows:

- A double-tap gesture causes the bitmap graphic to return to its initial position.
- A scroll gesture causes the bitmap graphic to "follow" the motion of the finger.
- A fling gesture causes the bitmap graphic to "fly" in the direction of the fling.

Tip

Many of the code examples provided in this section are taken from the SimpleGestures application. The source code for this application is provided for download on the book's websites.

To make these gestures work, the `GameAreaView` class needs to include the appropriate gesture detector, which triggers any operations upon the bitmap graphic. Based upon the specific gestures detected, the `GameAreaView` class must perform all translation animations and other graphical operations applied to the bitmap. To wire up the `GameAreaView` class for gesture support, we need to implement several important methods:

- The class constructor must initialize any gesture detectors and bitmap graphics.
- The `onTouchEvent()` method must be overridden to pass the `MotionEvent` data to the gesture detector for processing.
- The `onDraw()` method must be overridden to draw the bitmap graphic in the appropriate position at any time.
- Various methods are needed to perform the graphics operations required to make a bitmap move around on the screen, fly across the screen, and reset its location based upon the data provided by the specific gesture.

All these tasks are handled by our `GameAreaView` class definition:

```
public class GameAreaView extends View {

    private static final String DEBUG_TAG =
        "SimpleGesture->GameAreaView";
    private GestureDetector gestures;
    private Matrix translate;
    private Bitmap droid;
    private Matrix animateStart;
    private Interpolator animateInterpolator;
    private long startTime;
    private long endTime;
    private float totalAnimDx;
    private float totalAnimDy;

    public GameAreaView(Context context, int iGraphicResourceId) {
        super(context);
        translate = new Matrix();
        GestureListener listener = new GestureListener(this);
        gestures = new GestureDetector(context, listener, null, true);
        droid = BitmapFactory.decodeResource(getResources(),
            iGraphicResourceId);
    }
```

```java
@Override
public boolean onTouchEvent(MotionEvent event) {
    boolean retVal = false;
    retVal = gestures.onTouchEvent(event);
    return retVal;
}

@Override
protected void onDraw(Canvas canvas) {
    Log.v(DEBUG_TAG, "onDraw");
    canvas.drawBitmap(droid, translate, null);
}

public void onResetLocation() {
    translate.reset();
    invalidate();
}

public void onMove(float dx, float dy) {
    translate.postTranslate(dx, dy);
    invalidate();
}

public void onAnimateMove(float dx, float dy, long duration) {
    animateStart = new Matrix(translate);
    animateInterpolator = new OvershootInterpolator();
    startTime = System.currentTimeMillis();
    endTime = startTime + duration;
    totalAnimDx = dx;
    totalAnimDy = dy;
    post(new Runnable() {
        @Override
        public void run() {
            onAnimateStep();
        }
    });
}

private void onAnimateStep() {
    long curTime = System.currentTimeMillis();
    float percentTime = (float) (curTime - startTime) /
        (float) (endTime - startTime);
    float percentDistance = animateInterpolator
        .getInterpolation(percentTime);
    float curDx = percentDistance * totalAnimDx;
    float curDy = percentDistance * totalAnimDy;
```

```
        translate.set(animateStart);
        onMove(curDx, curDy);

        if (percentTime < 1.0f) {
            post(new Runnable() {
                @Override
                public void run() {
                    onAnimateStep();
                }
            });
        }
    }
}
```

As you can see, the `GameAreaView` class keeps track of where the bitmap graphic should be drawn at any time. The `onTouchEvent()` method is used to capture motion events and pass them along to a gesture detector whose `GestureListener` we must implement as well (more on this in a moment). Typically, each method of the `GameAreaView` applies some operation to the bitmap graphic and then calls the `invalidate()` method, forcing the view to be redrawn. Now we turn our attention to the methods required to implement specific gestures:

- For double-tap gestures, we implement a method called `onResetLocation()` to draw the bitmap graphic in its original location.
- For scroll gestures, we implement a method called `onMove()` to draw the bitmap graphic in a new location. Note that scrolling can occur in any direction—it simply refers to a finger swipe on the screen.
- For fling gestures, things get a little tricky. To animate motion on the screen smoothly, we used a chain of asynchronous calls and a built-in Android interpolator to calculate the location to draw the graphic based upon how long it had been since the animation started. See the `onAnimateMove()` and `onAnimateStep()` methods for the full implementation of fling animation.

Now we need to implement our `GestureListener` class to interpret the appropriate gestures and call the `GameAreaView` methods we just implemented. Here's an implementation of the `GestureListener` class that our `GameAreaView` class can use:

```
private class GestureListener extends
    GestureDetector.SimpleOnGestureListener {

    GameAreaView view;

    public GestureListener(GameAreaView view) {
        this.view = view;
    }
```

```
    @Override
    public boolean onDown(MotionEvent e) {
        return true;
    }

    @Override
    public boolean onFling(MotionEvent e1, MotionEvent e2,
        final float velocityX, final float velocityY) {
        final float distanceTimeFactor = 0.4f;
        final float totalDx = (distanceTimeFactor * velocityX / 2);
        final float totalDy = (distanceTimeFactor * velocityY / 2);

        view.onAnimateMove(totalDx, totalDy,
            (long) (1000 * distanceTimeFactor));
        return true;
    }

    @Override
    public boolean onDoubleTap(MotionEvent e) {
        view.onResetLocation();
        return true;
    }

    @Override
    public boolean onScroll(MotionEvent e1, MotionEvent e2,
        float distanceX, float distanceY) {
        view.onMove(-distanceX, -distanceY);
        return true;
    }
}
```

Note that you must return true for any gesture or motion event that you want to detect. Therefore, you must return true in the onDown() method as it happens at the beginning of a scroll-type gesture. Most of the implementation of the GestureListener class methods involves our interpretation of the data for each gesture. For example:

- We react to double taps by resetting the bitmap to its original location using the onResetLocation() method of our GameAreaView class.

- We use the distance data provided in the onScroll() method to determine the direction to use in the movement to pass into the onMove() method of the GameAreaView class.

- We use the velocity data provided in the onFling() method to determine the direction and speed to use in the movement animation of the bitmap. The timeDistanceFactor variable with a value of 0.4 is subjective, but gives the resulting slide-to-a-stop animation enough time to be visible but is short enough to be controllable and responsive. You can think of it as a high-friction surface. This information is used by the animation sequence implemented in the `onAnimateMove()` method of the `GameAreaView` class.

Now that we have implemented the `GameAreaView` class in its entirety, you can display it on a screen. For example, you might create an `Activity` that has a user interface with a `FrameLayout` control and add an instance of a `GameAreaView` using the `addView()` method. The resulting scroll and fling gestures look something like Figure 8.3.

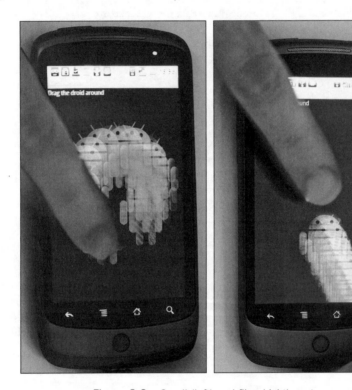

Figure 8.3   Scroll (left) and fling (right) gestures.

 Tip

To support the broadest range of devices, we recommend supporting simple, one-fingered gestures and providing alternate navigational items for devices that don't support multi-touch gestures. However, users are beginning to expect multi-touch gesture support now, so use them where you can and where they make sense. Resistive touch screens remain somewhat uncommon on lower-end devices.

Handling Common Multi-Touch Gestures

Introduced in API Level 8 (Android 2.2), the `ScaleGestureDetector` class can be used to detect two-fingered scale gestures. The scale gesture enables the user to move two fingers toward and away from each other. When the fingers are moving apart, this is considered scaling up; when the fingers are moving together, this is considered scaling down. This is the "pinch-to-zoom" style often employed by map and photo applications.

Tip

You can use the `ScaleGestureDetector.SimpleOnScaleGestureListener` class to detect scale gestures detected by the `ScaleGestureDetector`.

Let's look at another example. Again, we use the custom view class called `GameAreaView`, but this time we handle the multi-touch scale event. In this way, the `GameAreaView` can react to scale gestures, interpret them, and make the appropriate changes to the bitmap, including growing or shrinking it on the screen.

Tip

Many of the code examples provided in this section are taken from the SimpleMulti-TouchGesture application. The source code for this application is provided for download on the book's websites.

To handle scale gestures, the `GameAreaView` class needs to include the appropriate gesture detector, a `ScaleGestureDetector`. The `GameAreaView` class needs to be wired up for scale gesture support in a similar fashion as when we implemented single touch gestures earlier, including initializing the gesture detector in the class constructor, overriding the `onTouchEvent()` method to pass the `MotionEvent` objects to the gesture detector, and overriding the `onDraw()` method to draw the view appropriately as necessary. We also need to update the `GameAreaView` class to keep track of the bitmap graphic size (using a `Matrix`) and provide a helper method for growing or shrinking the graphic. Here is the new implementation of the `GameAreaView` class with scale gesture support:

```
public class GameAreaView extends View {
    private ScaleGestureDetector multiGestures;
    private Matrix scale;
    private Bitmap droid;

    public GameAreaView(Context context, int iGraphicResourceId) {
        super(context);
        scale = new Matrix();
        GestureListener listener = new GestureListener(this);
        multiGestures = new ScaleGestureDetector(context, listener);
```

```
        droid = BitmapFactory.decodeResource(getResources(),
            iGraphicResourceId);
    }

    public void onScale(float factor) {
        scale.preScale(factor, factor);
        invalidate();
    }

    @Override
    protected void onDraw(Canvas canvas) {
        Matrix transform = new Matrix(scale);
        float width = droid.getWidth() / 2;
        float height = droid.getHeight() / 2;
        transform.postTranslate(-width, -height);
        transform.postConcat(scale);
        transform.postTranslate(width, height);
        canvas.drawBitmap(droid, transform, null);
    }

    @Override
    public boolean onTouchEvent(MotionEvent event) {
        boolean retVal = false;
        retVal = multiGestures.onTouchEvent(event);
        return retVal;
    }
}
```

As you can see, the `GameAreaView` class keeps track of what size the bitmap should be at any time using the `Matrix` variable called `scale`. The `onTouchEvent()` method is used to capture motion events and pass them along to a `ScaleGestureDetector` gesture detector. As before, the `onScale()` helper method of the `GameAreaView` applies some scaling to the bitmap graphic and then calls the `invalidate()` method, forcing the `view` to be redrawn.

Now let's take a look at the `GestureListener` class implementation necessary to interpret the scale gestures and call the `GameAreaView` methods we just implemented. Here's the implementation of the `GestureListener` class:

```
private class GestureListener implements
    ScaleGestureDetector.OnScaleGestureListener {

    GameAreaView view;
```

```java
    public GestureListener(GameAreaView view) {
        this.view = view;
    }

    @Override
    public boolean onScale(ScaleGestureDetector detector) {
        float scale = detector.getScaleFactor();
        view.onScale(scale);
        return true;
    }

    @Override
    public boolean onScaleBegin(ScaleGestureDetector detector) {
        return true;
    }

    @Override
    public void onScaleEnd(ScaleGestureDetector detector) {
    }
}
```

Remember that you must return true for any gesture or motion event that you want to detect. Therefore, you must return true in the onScaleBegin() method as it happens at the beginning of a scale-type gesture. Most of the implementation of the GestureListener methods involves our interpretation of the data for the scale gesture. Specifically, we use the scale factor (provided by the getScaleFactor() method) to calculate whether we should shrink or grow the bitmap graphic, and by how much. We pass this information to the onScale() helper method we just implemented in the GameAreaView class.

Now, if you were to use the GameAreaView classin your application, scale gestures might look something like Figure 8.4.

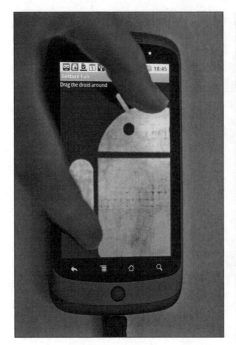

Figure 8.4   Scale up (left) and scale down (right) gestures.

Note

The Android emulator does not currently support multi-touch input. You will have to run and test multi-touch support such as the scale gesture using a device running Android 2.2 or higher.

Making Gestures Look Natural

Gestures can enhance your Android application user interfaces in new, interesting, and intuitive ways. Closely mapping the operations being performed on the screen to the user's finger motion makes a gesture feel natural and intuitive. Making application operations look natural requires some experimentation on the part of the developer. Keep in mind that devices vary in processing power, and this might be a factor in making things seem natural. Minimal processing, even on fast devices, will help keep gestures and the reaction to them smooth and responsive, and thus natural feeling.

Using the Drag and Drop Framework

On Android devices running Android 3.0 and higher (API Level 11), developers can access the drag and drop framework to perform drag and drop actions. You can drag and drop view controls within the scope of a screen or `Activity` class.

The drag-and-drop process basically works like this:

- The user triggers a drag operation. How this is done depends on the application, but long clicks are a reasonable option for selecting a `View` for a drag under the appropriate conditions.

- The data for the selected `View` control is packaged in a `ClipData` object (also used by the clipboard framework), and the `View.DragShadowBuilder` class is used to generate a little visual representation of the item being dragged. For example, if you were dragging a filename into a directory bucket, you might include a little icon of a file.

- You call the `startDrag()` method on the `View` control to be dragged. This starts a drag event. The system signals a drag event with `ACTION_DRAG_STARTED`, which listeners can catch.

- There are a number of events that occur during a drag that your application can react to. The `ACTION_DRAG_ENTERED` event can be used to adjust the screen controls to highlight other View controls that the dragged `View` control might want to be dragged over to. The `ACTION_DRAG_LOCATION` event can be used to determine where the dragged `View` is on the screen. The `ACTION_DRAG_EXITED` event can be used to reset any screen controls that were adjusted in the `ACTION_DRAG_ENTERED` event.

- When the user ends the drag operation by releasing the shadow item over a specific target `View` on the screen, the system signals a drop event with `ACTION_DROP`, which listeners can catch. Any data can be retrieved using the `getClipData()` method.

For more information about the drag and drop framework, see the Android SDK documentation. You can also find a great example of using the drag and drop framework called `DragAndDropDemo.java`.

Working with the Trackball

Some Android devices have hardware trackballs, but not all. Developers can handle trackball events in a `View` control in a similar fashion to click events or gestures. To handle trackball events, you can leverage the `View` class method called `onTrackballEvent()`. This method, like a gesture, has a single parameter, a `MotionEvent` object. You can use the `getX()` and `getY()` methods of the `MotionEvent` class to determine the relative movement of the trackball. Optical track-pads such as those available on the DROID Incredible can be supported in the same way.

Tip

If your application requires the device to have a trackball, you should set the
`<uses-configuration>` tag to specify that a trackball is required within your
application's Android manifest file.

Handling Screen Orientation Changes

Many Android devices on the market today have landscape and portrait modes and can
seamlessly transition between these orientations. The Android operating system automatically handles these changes for your application, if you so choose. You can also provide
alternative resources, such as different layouts, for portrait and landscape modes. Also, you
can directly access device sensors such as the accelerometer, which we talk about in
Chapter 16, "Accessing Android's Hardware Sensors," to capture device orientation along
three axes.

However, if you want to listen for simple screen orientation changes programmatically
and have your application react to them, you can use the `OrientationEventListener`
class to do this within your activity.

Tip

Many of the code examples provided in this section are taken from the SimpleOrientation
application. The source code for this application is provided for download on the book websites. Orientation changes are best tested on devices, not the emulator.

Implementing orientation event handling in your `Activity` is simple. Simply instantiate an `OrientationEventListener` and provide its implementation. For example, the
following activity class called `SimpleOrientationActivity` logs orientation information to LogCat:

```
public class SimpleOrientationActivity extends Activity {

    OrientationEventListener mOrientationListener;

    @Override
    public void onCreate(Bundle savedInstanceState) {
        super.onCreate(savedInstanceState);
        setContentView(R.layout.main);

        mOrientationListener = new OrientationEventListener(this,
            SensorManager.SENSOR_DELAY_NORMAL) {

            @Override
            public void onOrientationChanged(int orientation) {
                Log.v(DEBUG_TAG,
```

```
                     "Orientation changed to " + orientation);
            }
        };

        if (mOrientationListener.canDetectOrientation() == true) {
            Log.v(DEBUG_TAG, "Can detect orientation");
            mOrientationListener.enable();
        } else {
            Log.v(DEBUG_TAG, "Cannot detect orientation");
            mOrientationListener.disable();
        }
    }

    @Override
    protected void onDestroy() {
        super.onDestroy();
        mOrientationListener.disable();
    }
}
```

You can set the rate to check for orientation changes to a variety of different values. There are other rate values appropriate for game use and other purposes. The default rate, SENSOR_DELAY_NORMAL, is most appropriate for simple orientation changes. Other values, such as SENSOR_DELAY_UI and SENSOR_DELAY_GAME, might make sense for your application.

After you have a valid OrientationEventListener object, you can check if it can detect orientation changes using the canDetectOrientation() method, and enable and disable the listener using its enable() and disable() methods.

The OrientationEventListener has a single callback method, which enables you to listen for orientation transitions, the onOrientationChanged() method. This method has a single parameter, an integer. This integer normally represents the device tilt as a number between 0 and 359:

- A result of ORIENTATION_UNKNOWN (-1) means the device is flat (perhaps on a table) and the orientation is unknown.
- A result of 0 means the device is in its "normal" orientation, with the top of the device facing in the up direction. (What "normal" means is defined by the manufacturer. You need to test on the device to find out for sure what it means.)
- A result of 90 means the device is tilted at 90 degrees, with the left side of the device facing in the up direction.
- A result of 180 means the device is tilted at 180 degrees, with the bottom side of the device facing in the up direction (upside down).
- A result of 270 means the device is tilted at 270 degrees, with the right side of the device facing in the up direction.

Figure 8.5 shows an example of how the device orientation might read when the device is tilted to the right by 90 degrees.

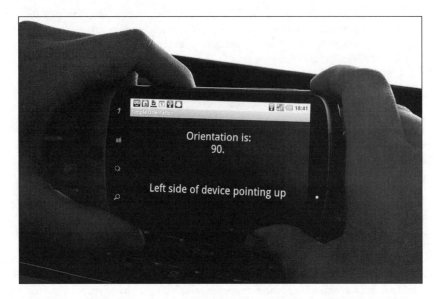

Figure 8.5   Orientation of the device as reported by an
`OrientationEventListener`.

Warning

Early versions of the Android SDK included a class called `OrientationListener`, which many early developers of the platform used to handle screen orientation transitions. This class is now deprecated and you should not use it.

Summary

The Android platform enables great flexibility when it comes to ways that users can provide input to the device. Developers benefit from the fact that many powerful input methods are built into the view controls themselves, just waiting to be leveraged. Applications can take advantage of built-in input methods, such as software keyboards, or can customize them for special purposes. The Android framework also includes powerful features, such as a clipboard service, gesture support and a drag and drop framework that your applications can use. It is important to support a variety of input methods in your applications, as users often have distinct preferences and not all methods are available on all devices.

References and More Information

Android Dev Guide: "Copy and Paste":
  http://d.android.com/guide/topics/clipboard/copy-paste.html
Android SDK Documentation regarding the `ClipboardManager` class:
  http://d.android.com/reference/android/content/ClipboardManager.html
Android SDK Documentation regarding the `ClipData` class:
  http://d.android.com/reference/android/content/ClipData.html
Android Dev Guide: "Drag and Drop":
  http://d.android.com/guide/topics/ui/drag-drop.html
Android SDK Documentation regarding the `android.gesture` package:
  http://d.android.com/reference/android/gesture/package-summary.html
Android Reference on faster orientation changes:
  http://d.android.com/resources/articles/faster-screen-orientation-change.html
(http://goo.gl/JSIsa)
Android Reference on screen orientation and direction:
  http://android-developers.blogspot.com/2010/09/one-screen-turn-deserves-another.html (http://goo.gl/XENJN)

9

Designing Accessible Applications

Android devices are as varied as their users. As the platform has matured and grown, its audience has become more diverse. The Android SDK includes numerous features and services for the benefit of users with physical impairments. Those users without impairments can also benefit from improved accessibility features such as speech recognition and text-to-speech services, especially when they are not paying complete attention to the device (such as when driving). In this chapter, we explore some of the accessibility features of Android devices and discuss how to make your applications accessible to as many different kinds of users as possible.

Exploring the Accessibility Framework

Accessibility is a commonly overlooked aspect of application development, but one that is becoming increasingly more important as time goes on. Many of the newest Android devices are well suited for new user audiences, and the addition of the Android Accessory Development Kit (ADK) for building hardware accessories makes the issue that much more relevant.

Perhaps it would surprise you to know that the same sort of technology that drives Apple's Siri speech-recognizing assistant has been available on the Android platform for quite some time, if developers want to leverage it. Because speech recognition and Text-To-Speech applications are all the rage and their technologies are often used for navigation applications (especially because many states are passing laws making driving while using a mobile device without hands-free operation illegal), we look at these two technologies in a little more detail.

Android applications can leverage speech input and output. Speech input can be achieved using speech recognition services and speech output can be achieved using Text-To-Speech services. Not all devices support these services. However, certain types of applications—most notably hands-free applications such as directional navigation—often benefit from the use of these types of input.

Some of the accessibility features available in the Android SDK include the following:

- The Speech Recognition Framework.
- The Text-To-Speech (TTS) Framework.
- The ability to create and extend accessibility applications in conjunction with the Android Accessibility Framework. See the following packages to get started writing accessibility applications: `android.accessibilityservice` and `android.view.accessibility`. There are also a number of accessibility applications, such as KickBack, SoundBack, and TalkBack, that ship with the platform. For more information, see the device settings under Settings, Accessibility.

There are a number of subtle things you can do to greatly improve how users with disabilities can navigate your applications. For example, you can:

- Enable haptic feedback (that vibration you feel when you press a button, rather like a rumble pack game controller) on any `View` object (API Level 3 and higher). See the `setHapticFeedbackEnabled()` method of the `View` class.
- Specify rich descriptions of visual controls, such as providing a text description for an `ImageView` control. This can be performed on any `View` control (API Level 4 and higher) and makes audio-driven screen navigation (for the visually impaired) much more effective. This feature is often helpful for the visually impaired. See the `setContentDescription()` method of the `View` class.
- Review and enforce the focus order of screen controls. You can finely control screen navigation and control focus, overriding default behavior as necessary. See the focus-oriented methods of the `View` class for details on how to explicitly set focus order of controls on the screen.
- If you implement custom `View` controls, it is your responsibility to send appropriate events to the accessibility service. To do this, your custom `View` control must implement the `AccessibilityEventSource` interface (`android.view.Accessibility.AccessibilityEventSource`) and fire off `AccessibilityEvent` events (`android.view.Accessibility.AccessibilityEvent`) that let accessibility tools know what your control has done. The behavior of these changed with API Level 14. The Android 4.0 platform overview document, available at http://developer.android.com/sdk/android-4.0.html (http://goo.gl/Epxq4), discusses some of these changes in behavior.

- Assume users may configure their devices for larger font sizes, and similar settings, and do not design screens that are overly cluttered or "break" under these conditions.

- Support alternative input methods, such as directional pads and trackballs, and do not assume your users will rely solely on touch screen navigation.

Warning

Many of the most powerful accessibility features were added in later versions of the Android SDK, so check the API level for a specific class or method before using it in your application.

Using Android Lint to Detect Common Accessibility Issues

The Android Lint Tool is used to detect common coding and configuration mistakes. It has a section for accessibility. Enabling this in your Android Link Preferences will help catch known accessibility issues. Currently, this will only detect missing `contentDescription` fields on `ImageViews`, but may eventually detect more accessibility issues.

Leveraging Speech Recognition Services

Speech services are available in the Android SDK in the `android.speech` package. The underlying services that make these technologies work might vary from device to device; some services might require a network connection to function properly.

Let's begin with speech recognition. You can enhance an application with speech recognition support by using the speech recognition framework provided in the Android SDK. Speech recognition involves speaking into the device microphone and enabling the software to detect and interpret that speech and translate it into a string.

There are several different methods of leveraging speech recognition in your application. First, the default Android keyboard (available in API Level 7+, as shown in Figure 9.1) and many third-party input methods have a microphone that can be used by users whenever they are presented with an input opportunity, such as on an `EditText` field. Second, applications can start a built-in speech recognition activity that will return text results (API Level 3+). Finally, applications can directly leverage the `SpeechRecognizer` class (API Level 8+) to more closely control the recognition and results.

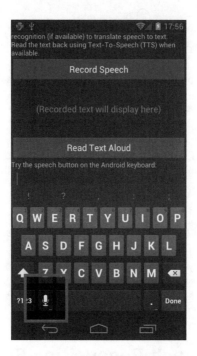

Figure 9.1   The Speech Recording option is available on many software keyboards.

Using the built-in recognition activity has some advantages. First, your application needs no permissions, such as record audio and network access. (Although it does currently require network access, it does not require the permission because it's a different application handling the request.) Second, it's simple to use for developers and familiar to users (see Figure 9.2). However, the disadvantage is that you can't easily enable long-form dictation with it. For that, the SpeechRecognizer class should be used. That said, the default input method for EditText fields may already allow for long-form, such as the continuous voice type available in Android 4.0.

Tip

Many of the code examples provided in this section are taken from the SimpleSpeech application. The source code for this application is provided for download on the book's websites. Speech services are best tested on a real Android device. We used a Galaxy Nexus running API Level 14 in our testing.

You can use the android.speech.RecognizerIntent intent to launch the built-in speech recorder. This launches the recorder (shown in Figure 9.2), allowing the user to record speech.

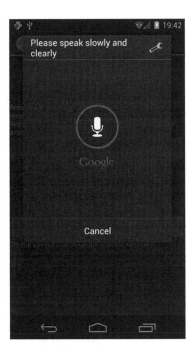

Figure 9.2   Recording speech with the `RecognizerIntent`.

The sound file is sent to an underlying recognition server for processing, so this feature is not practical for devices that don't have a reasonable network connection. You can then retrieve the results of the speech recognition processing and use them in your application. Note that you might receive multiple results for a given speech segment.

Note

Speech recognition technology is continually evolving and improving. Be sure to enunciate clearly when speaking to your device. Sometimes it might take several tries before the speech recognition engine interprets your speech correctly.

The following code demonstrates how an application can be enabled to record speech using the `RecognizerIntent` intent:

```
public class SimpleSpeechActivity extends Activity
{
    private static final int VOICE_RECOGNITION_REQUEST = 1;

    @Override
    public void onCreate(Bundle savedInstanceState) {
        super.onCreate(savedInstanceState);
```

```
        setContentView(R.layout.main);
    }
    public void recordSpeech(View view) {
        Intent intent =
            new Intent(RecognizerIntent.ACTION_RECOGNIZE_SPEECH);
        intent.putExtra(RecognizerIntent.EXTRA_LANGUAGE_MODEL,
            RecognizerIntent.LANGUAGE_MODEL_FREE_FORM);
        intent.putExtra(RecognizerIntent.EXTRA_PROMPT,
            "Please speak slowly and clearly");
        startActivityForResult(intent, VOICE_RECOGNITION_REQUEST);
    }

    @Override
    protected void onActivityResult(int requestCode,
        int resultCode, Intent data) {
        if (requestCode == VOICE_RECOGNITION_REQUEST &&
            resultCode == RESULT_OK) {
            ArrayList<String> matches = data.getStringArrayListExtra(
                RecognizerIntent.EXTRA_RESULTS);
            TextView textSaid = (TextView) findViewById(R.id.TextSaid);
            textSaid.setText(matches.get(0));
        }
        super.onActivityResult(requestCode, resultCode, data);
    }
}
```

In this case, the intent is initiated through the click of a Button control, which causes the recordSpeech() method to be called. The RecognizerIntent is configured as follows:

- The Intent action is set to ACTION_RECOGNIZE_SPEECH to prompt the user to speak and send that sound file in for speech recognition.

- An Intent extra called EXTRA_LANGUAGE_MODEL is set to LANGUAGE_MODEL_FREE_FORM to simply perform standard speech recognition. There is also another language model especially for web searches called LAN-GUAGE_MODEL_WEB_SEARCH.

- An Intent extra called EXTRA_PROMPT is set to a string to display to the user during speech input.

After the RecognizerIntent object is configured, the intent can be started using the startActivityForResult() method, and then the result is captured in the onActivityResult() method. The resulting text is then displayed in the TextView control called TextSaid. In this case, only the first result provided in the results is displayed to the user. So, for example, the user can press the button initiating the recordSpeech() method, say "We're going to need a bigger boat," and that text is then displayed in the application's TextView control, as shown in Figure 9.3.

Figure 9.3   The text string resulting from the `RecognizerIntent`.

Leveraging Text-To-Speech Services

The Android platform includes a TTS engine (`android.speech.tts`) that enables
devices to perform speech synthesis. You can use the TTS engine to have your applications "read" text to the user. You might have seen this feature used frequently with
location-based service (LBS) applications that allow hands-free directions. Other applications use this feature for users who have reading or sight problems. The synthesized
speech can be played immediately or saved to an audio file, which can be treated like
any other audio file.

Note

To provide TTS services to users, an Android device must have both the TTS engine (available in Android SDK 1.6 and higher) and the appropriate language resource files. In some
cases, the user must install the appropriate language resource files (assuming that the
user has space for them) from a remote location. The users can install the language
resource files by going to Settings, Voice Input & Output Settings, Text-to-Speech, Install
Voice Data. Unlike some other settings pages, this one doesn't have a specific intent
action defined under `android.provider.Settings`. You might also need to do this on
your devices. Additionally, the application can verify that the data is installed correctly or
trigger the installation if it's not.

For a simple example, let's have the device read back the text recognized in our earlier speech recognition example. First, we must modify the activity to implement the TextToSpeech.OnInitListener interface, as follows:

```
public class SimpleSpeechActivity extends Activity
    implements TextToSpeech.OnInitListener
{
    // class implementation
}
```

Next, we need to initialize TTS services in your Activity:

```
TextToSpeech mTts = new TextToSpeech(this, this);
```

Initializing the TTS engine happens asynchronously. The TextToSpeech.OnInitListener interface has only one method, onInit(), that is called when the TTS engine has finished initializing successfully or unsuccessfully. Here is an implementation of the onInit() method:

```
@Override
public void onInit(int status) {
    Button readButton = (Button) findViewById(R.id.ButtonRead);
    if (status == TextToSpeech.SUCCESS) {
        int result = mTts.setLanguage(Locale.US);
        if (result == TextToSpeech.LANG_MISSING_DATA
            || result == TextToSpeech.LANG_NOT_SUPPORTED) {
            Log.e(DEBUG_TAG, "TTS Language not available.");
            readButton.setEnabled(false);
        } else {
            readButton.setEnabled(true);
        }
    } else {
        Log.e(DEBUG_TAG, "Could not initialize TTS Engine.");
        readButton.setEnabled(false);
    }
}
```

We use the onInit() method to check the status of the TTS engine. If it is initialized successfully, the Button control called readButton is enabled; otherwise, it is disabled. The onInit() method is also the appropriate time to configure the TTS engine. For example, you should set the language used by the engine using the setLanguage() method. In this case, the language is set to American English. The voice used by the TTS engine uses American pronunciation.

Note

The Android TTS engine supports a variety of languages, including English (in American or British accents), French, German, Italian, and Spanish. You can just as easily have enabled British English pronunciation using the following language setting in the `onInit()` method implementation instead:

```
int result = mTts.setLanguage(Locale.UK);
```

We amused ourselves trying to come up with phrases that illustrate how the American and British English TTS services differ. The best phrase we came up with was: "*We adjusted our schedule to search for a vase of herbs in our garage.*"

Feel free to send us your favorite locale-based phrases, and we will post them on the book's websites. Also, any amusing misinterpretations of the voice recognition are also welcome (for example, we often had "our garage" come out as "nerd haha").

Finally, you are ready to actually convert some text into a sound file. In this case, we grab the text string currently stored in the `TextView` control (where we set using speech recognition in the previous section) and pass it to TTS using the `speak()` method:

```
public void readText(View view) {
    TextView textSaid = (TextView) findViewById(R.id.TextSaid);
    mTts.speak((String) textSaid.getText(),
        TextToSpeech.QUEUE_FLUSH, null);
}
```

The `speak()` method takes three parameters: the string of text to say, the queuing strategy, and the speech parameters. The queuing strategy can either add some text to speak to the queue or flush the queue—in this case, we use the `QUEUE_FLUSH` strategy, so it is the only speech spoken. No special speech parameters are set, so we simply pass in null for the third parameter. Finally, when you are done with the `TextToSpeech` engine (such as in your `Activity` class's `onDestroy()` method), make sure to release its resources using the `shutdown()` method:

```
mTts.shutdown();
```

Now, if you wire up a `Button` control to call the `readText()` method when clicked, you have a complete implementation of TTS. When combined with the speech recognition example discussed earlier, you can develop an application that can record a user's speech, translate it into a string, display that string on the screen, and then read that string back to the user. In fact, that is exactly what the sample project called `SimpleSpeech` does.

Summary

The Android platform includes extensive accessibility features, including speech recognition, text-to-speech support, and many subtle accessibility features peppered throughout the user interface classes of the Android SDK. All Android applications should be reviewed for basic accessibility features, such as providing text labels to graphical controls for eyes-free app navigation purposes. Other applications might benefit from more comprehensive accessibility controls.

Give some thought to providing accessibility features, such as providing View metadata, in your applications. There's no excuse for not doing so. Your users appreciate these small details, which make all the difference in terms of whether or not certain users can use your application at all. Also, make sure your quality assurance team verifies accessibility features as part of its testing process.

References and More Information

Android Dev Guide: "Designing for Accessibility":
   http://d.android.com/guide/practices/design/accessibility.html
The Eyes-Free Project:
   http://code.google.com/p/eyes-free/
YouTube: Leveraging Android Accessibility APIs to Create an Accessible Experience:
   http://www.youtube.com/watch?v=BPXqsPeCneA
Android SDK Documentation regarding the android.speech.tts package:
   http://d.android.com/reference/android/speech/tts/package-summary.html
Android SDK Documentation regarding the android.speech package:
   http://d.android.com/reference/android/speech/package-summary.html

## 10

Best Practices for Tablet and Google TV Development

The Android platform may have started as a smartphone platform, but it has quickly moved into other device form factors. Android tablets and eBook readers such as the Amazon Kindle Fire have been especially popular lately. At the same time, Google released its Google TV, a highly interactive and connected television experience that runs on Android. Designing and developing for these different types of devices involves maximizing where the devices are similar, and handling the differences as necessary. In this chapter, we talk about some of the best practices for developing for different types of devices such as tablets and Google TV.

Understanding Device Diversity

These new types of Android devices do not require a special Android SDK; they use the same SDKs that the other Android devices use. Many application developers want to publish their applications to as many users (and therefore devices) as possible. This was relatively straightforward when Android was almost exclusively a smartphone platform. Developers can assume that the device screen size is within a certain reasonably small range. They can assume the device had telephony features, a camera, a numeric keypad, and the like.

These days, with the Android platform making its way onto tablets, TVs, toasters, eBook readers, net books, watches, and even car rearview mirrors (no joke: http://goo.gl/lUhuh) application developers cannot make these assumptions, which brings us to our first tip.

Don't Make Assumptions about Device Characteristics

Don't make assumptions about the device your application runs on, because tomorrow (or the day after), there will be yet another new type of Android device that users are trying to download your app onto that breaks your assumptions. Instead, ensure that your application runs smoothly by configuring your application's Android manifest file appropriately to reflect what your application does and does not need to run correctly. Does it require a certain version of the Android SDK? If so, specify it. Does the application require a camera or telephony features? Declare those features using the `<uses-feature>` tag. Do you want your application to display correctly on a variety of device screens, whether they are large or small, portrait or landscape, high definition, or otherwise? Start by using flexible user interface design that can attempt to smooth over and accommodate the differences between devices.

Designing Flexible User Interfaces

Regardless of what devices your application targets, there's no substitute for good application design. In many ways, all Android devices are created equal—they use the same operating system, the same SDKs, the same platform targets, the same tools for development. Designing for all device sizes, shapes, and form factors enables your application to look, behave, and run smoothly across the widest range of devices, regardless of type. Here are some things to consider with any Android project:

- Use flexible layout designs and controls such as `RelativeLayout`.
- Use dimension values such as `dp` instead of `px` to enable better scaling and support of multiple screen attributes with less work.
- Make your graphics stretchable using graphic formats (nine-patch, XML-defined drawables) where possible.
- Provide alternative resources for various screen sizes and densities.
- Don't limit alternative resources to just images and layouts. Styles and values also make great alternate resources; they can sometimes be effective enough to reduce the need for some layouts.
- Adjust your user interface when hardware features aren't available. For instance, instead of requiring a camera, make it optional and present only that option when the camera is available. If it's not available, present an option to pick an image from the gallery instead. Perhaps the user has a device with a camera that is syncing to the gallery on the device without the camera.
- Be aware that not all devices have touch screens and that keyboards are a primary input mechanism on many devices, including Google TV, tablets and phones with docks, and so on. Even the mouse gets used on several popular devices. Handle the Enter key and arrow keys appropriately.
- Use a `Fragment`-based application design from the start, as this new technology is supported in both smartphones and tablets and makes for flexible screen workflows and more code reuse.

Following these guidelines enables your application to display and function well on a variety of different devices. However, when working with devices that are often substantially larger that smartphones, scaling gracefully is not usually enough; you need to provide alternative resources for different resolutions and orientations.

Attracting New Types of Users

When you add new types of devices, different types of users buy them. This expands the user base—a good thing for developers who make a living from downloads. The audience for smartphones is different from that of tablets and TVs and other devices such as eBook readers. The Kindle Fire is a great example of a device that introduced many new people to the Android platform—many without even knowing the device runs Android. Understanding these new audiences can have an impact on your application design and development process.

Tablets can be used by individuals with special needs who are incapable of using smaller smartphones. This is especially true of the visually impaired, but certainly not limited to this crowd. Leverage the accessibility APIs available in the Android SDK to make your application as accessible as possible to these audiences, regardless of your device targets. The same design principles hold true for another audience—very young users—who generally require larger button controls, high contrast colorations, and other such design features. Televisions are used by the whole family, not just the tech-savvy users or those who can afford (or are old enough to have) smartphones.

Tablets aren't phones and can sometimes be purchased outright without a wireless data plan for use on Wi-Fi networks. This enables new classes of Android users—those who live outside the current wireless coverage maps of the world. This makes localization even more important for applications that support tablets.

Leveraging Alternative Resources

You can achieve a lot by simply using alternative resources. The Android SDK enables you to supply project resources such as graphics and layout designs for different target device characteristics such as screen sizes, resolutions, orientations, and other device features. Used well, each class of device can have its own distinct look and feel while the underlying code remains unchanged. For more information on alternative resources, see the Android SDK documentation at http://d.android.com/guide/topics/resources/providing-resources.html#AlternativeResources (http://goo.gl/1YTdc).

Using Screen Space Effectively on Big Landscape Screens

Most tablets and televisions have screens that are seven inches or larger. In terms of resources, tablets are usually defined as having large or extra large screens. A *large screen* is defined as 5 inches to around 7 inches and extra large as 7–10 inches. There is some overlap in the definition and the one a device uses is manufacturer-dependent. When using the resource qualifier, you're looking at the `large` and `xlarge` values. Although `xlarge` was introduced at API Level 9, it will be quietly ignored on earlier devices.

Tablets are most frequently held and used in landscape mode and televisions are exclusively used in landscape mode. Although supporting both orientations is ideal, if you're going to focus on only one orientation for a tablets and televisions, we recommend landscape mode. Keep in mind that you can use alternative resources to design a landscape layout that differs substantially from the portrait layout. You'll want to consider different layouts using the `port` and `land` qualifiers.

Just scaling graphics up for these big screens is often not enough. Take, for example, a smartphone layout that has four buttons across, sized so even big fingers will have no trouble tapping them. Enlarge that to a 10-inch tablet screen—which might be over 8 inches wide—and you now have buttons on the order of 2 inches wide. That might work for a toddler-friendly interface, but for most people, those big buttons will look silly—and on television interfaces without touch screens, a complete waste of space. Reduce the size of the buttons and find something else useful to put in the newly gained space.

A Note on Game Design

One kind of application that may pose special challenges when it comes to design is games. Today's games use a lot of custom user interface, are fully 3D, and naturally scale by virtue of their rendering systems. These apps can transition easily to tablets and other larger devices, but they are not immune to problems—especially when a game has been designed as a "handheld" game.

Let's look at a simple example. You have a great game that is normally played while held in landscape mode with side thumb controls. On a typical Android smartphone, this generally means that the player can reach most of the screen with his thumbs. However, on a tablet, your thumbs only go so far. Entire areas of the screen are unreachable using thumb controls; if the user is required to tap in the middle of the screen, the tablet cannot be "held" or "cradled" as easily either.

Going even farther, on a Google TV, there is no touch screen. If you can, implement alternative controls with a keyboard or mouse. If you can't, possibly look into using another device, such as a phone, which you can use as a controller connected via Wi-Fi to the Google TV. Keep in mind, though, that if a touch screen is used as a controller and the user isn't looking at it, he'll need some sort of cues about what buttons he's pressing. Another option is to use one of the many wireless controllers that can hook up directly to the device and be used as an alternative input method.

Developing Applications for Tablets

Some say that 2011 was the year of the tablet (see Figure 10.1), the year they went mainstream (the way was paved by the success of the iPad—thanks Apple!). Samsung, Motorola, ASUS, HTC, ARCHOS, and many others shipped some fantastic tablet devices in various sizes and orientations. Amazon shipped the Kindle Fire to great fanfare. This new niche poses new challenges for Android developers creating apps, so let's look at what it means to design, develop, test, and publish Android applications for tablet devices.

Figure 10.1   Tablets everywhere! (Google image search result.)

- From a developer perspective, tablets can be considered just another device, provided you haven't made any unfortunate development assumptions.
- Tablets run different versions of the Android platform, as far back as Android 1.0, although official tablet support by Google did not occur until Android 3.0.
- Tablets are not smartphones. This means that if your applications include telephony features, you will have to provide graceful alterative features for devices without these features, or effectively exclude these devices through Android Manifest file configuration.
- Unlike smartphones, most tablets default to landscape, not portrait mode. Tablet users are more likely to change orientations than smartphone users.
- Tablets tend to have fewer hardware sensors than high-end smartphones.
- Fragments help separate user interface functionality from application logic. Using the `Fragment` class from the start greatly simplifies any shuffling of the user interface later on, speeds up development of tablet-centric user interfaces, and makes your app ready for the Android devices of the future.
- The Android Market has no specific way to target or disable publication to specific types of devices such as tablets. You can, of course, use market filters to restrict your application to users with devices of certain screen sizes, libraries, and other device features, but there is no tablet "flag," per se.

Tip

We do not recommend naming your app for its device target (for example, "The ACME App for Tablets").

Developing Applications for Google TV

Google announced a new platform initiative in early 2010—Google TV. The vision: a highly interactive and connected television experience leveraging the Android platform. Google wasn't going to do it alone, but partner with some of the top manufacturers in the television and set-top box business, including Sony (see Figure 10.2), Vizio, LG, Samsung, and others.

Figure 10.2   Google TV devices are often set-top boxes. This one, from Sony, was announced at CES 2012.

Just as smartphones put apps in your pocket, Google TV brings them to your living room. The sky's the limit when it comes to the types of apps and content you might want to provide to Google TV users. Let's talk for a moment about what types of applications are suitable for Google TV users.

There are two ways to bring your applications to Google TV devices: Chrome web apps and native Android apps. The Google TV website lists all supported Google TV devices you can purchase at http://www.google.com/tv/get.html. You have the option of purchasing a complete package (TV screen and all) or a set-top box that works with existing HDTV systems.

Suitability may be less of an issue for web-based applications. However, many Android applications rely upon hardware assumptions that are not applicable to Google TV users, including the existence of cameras, location-based services, sensors, telephony, and such. In terms of user interface design, you don't have to worry so much about state changes like orientation changes or frequent network drops because your user is always connected. Therefore, only certain classes of existing Android applications are appropriate for the Google TV platform. Only you, the developer, can determine whether your app is suitable. There's nothing stopping you from developing interesting apps that fuse the power of existing smartphones and tablets (that have cameras, hardware sensors, and such) with the power of Google TVs.

Optimizing Web Applications for Google TV

Your existing website and web applications, including those using HTML5 and Flash, can target the Google TV. At this time, Google TVs run Chrome and support Adobe Flash. Optimizing your websites for display on a high definition television screen involves many common sense tweaks. You'll hear a lot of Google TV developers talk about "the 10-foot experience." This simply acknowledges the fact that Google TV users sit at some distance from the screen, and developers need to adjust their application's user experience to suit this typical use case.

Screen designs should be simple and elegant, using extra-large, readable fonts, and graphics. There's quite a bit more wide-screen real estate to work with, but scrolling is less appealing and navigation, typically by D-pad, should be simple and straightforward. Some color schemes need to be adjusted for the high contrast and saturation levels typical of televisions. Finally, you'll want to come up with a high-resolution favicon so that your website looks slick in the Chrome bookmarks and other references.

Tip

When it comes to Flash, you'll want to check out Adobe's recommendations for optimizing Flash apps for televisions.

Developing Native Android Applications for Google TV

Native Google TV apps are written using the Android SDK and can be published through the Android Market. At this time, Google TVs are running the Honeycomb SDK (Android 3.1) and must be developed using the latest Android tools and the GoogleTV add-on from the Android SDK Manager.

Developing native applications for Google TV is basically like developing for a large tablet without a touch screen, camera, and so on. Most of the challenges of porting an Android app to Google TV revolve around:

- Setting the appropriate manifest file settings to allow for, market filter for, and not accidentally exclude Google TV devices.

- Using appropriate alternative resources for large, high-definition television displays (at 10 feet).
- Avoiding certain methods and API calls that assume telephony device features.
- Adjusting user interface controls to be large and readable for television viewing.
- Adjusting layout navigation to support D-pad as the primary input. Add handling for the media keys for play, pause, and so on. Consider fast ways to get out of long lists; don't make a user traverse a long list just to get to a button at the bottom of the screen.
- Avoid using methods and APIs that assume telephony device features and other features unsupported by the Google TV, such as the Android NDK. For more information, see the Google TV documentation for feature support at https://developers.google.com/tv/android/docs/gtv_android_features.

Tip

Once you have installed the Google TV add-on, you can use it to create compatible AVDs to run in the Google TV Emulator. Find out more in the Google TV Emulator documentation at https://developers.google.com/tv/android/docs/gtv_emulator.

Developing Apps for the Amazon Kindle Fire

The Amazon Kindle Fire, shown in Figure 10.3, is another type of new Android device in the hands of today's users. Although the device itself is simply a basic tablet, it runs a modified version of the Android platform that centers around the Amazon Appstore, instead of the Google experience many users associate with the platform—and there is no Android Market. The home screen is customized and, as such, doesn't present such opportunities as app widgets or live wallpapers. To learn more about app development for the Amazon Kindle Fire, check out the Amazon Appstore Developer Portal at https://developer.amazon.com/welcome.html or check out our book, *Learning Android Application Programming for the Kindle Fire* (Addison-Wesley, August 2012, ISBN 9780321833976).

Figure 10.3   The Amazon Kindle Fire, a 7-inch Android device with
Amazon Appstore and a custom home screen.

Summary

Tablets, Google TVs, and other new types of devices that run mobile operating systems
are a new and popular category of Android device. As you have learned, designing and
developing for these new niche devices is fairly simple when you keep your assumptions
about device characteristics at a minimum and specify which device features and permissions your application requires in the Android manifest file. With planning, careful use of
resources, and good development techniques, supporting these exciting new devices need
not be a trial.

References and More Information

Android Dev Guide: "Supporting Tablets and Handsets":
   http://d.android.com/guide/practices/tablets-and-handsets.html
Google TV Developers website:
   https://developers.google.com/tv/
Google TV Web Developer's Guide:
   https://developers.google.com/tv/web/
Google TV Native Android Application Developer's Guide:
   https://developers.google.com/tv/android/

## 11

Using Android Networking APIs

Applications written with networking components are far more dynamic and content-rich than those that are not. Applications leverage the network for a variety of reasons: to deliver fresh and updated content, to enable social networking features of an otherwise standalone application, to offload heavy processing to high-powered servers, and to enable data storage beyond what the user can achieve on the device.

Those accustomed to Java networking will find the `java.net` package familiar. There are also some helpful Android utility classes for various types of network operations and protocols. This chapter focuses on Hypertext Transfer Protocol (HTTP), the most common protocol for networked mobile applications.

Understanding Mobile Networking Fundamentals

Networking on the Android platform is standardized, using a combination of powerful yet familiar technologies and libraries such as `java.net`. Network implementation is generally straightforward, but mobile application developers need to plan for less stable connectivity than one might expect in a home or office network setting—connectivity depends on the location of the users and their devices. Users demand stable, responsive applications. This means that you must take extra care when designing network-enabled applications. Luckily, the Android SDK provides a number of tools and classes for ensuring just that.

Warning

Recall that developers must agree to a number of network best practices as part of the Android Software Development Kit License Agreement. If you plan to use network support in your application, you might want to review these contractual points to ensure that your application complies with the agreement.

Understanding Strict Mode with Networking

As discussed in Chapter 1, "Threading and Asynchronous Processing," strict mode is a method that developers can use to detect operations performed on the main thread that should not be there. API Level 11 expanded upon strict mode in ways that impact networking code. By default, if you perform network operations on the main thread, your application throws an exception, specifically `android.os.NetworkOnMainThreadException`. The way to avoid this is to use proper coding techniques and put all networking operations on a thread other than the main thread. We show you how later in this chapter, or you can review Chapter 1 for the basics.

If you're not writing a production application and want to run some quick network code without wiring up a full thread, you can disable the crashing and simply flash the screen instead (on API Level 11) or log the mistakes. You can also call the `permitAll()` method to skip strict mode entirely. This is not recommended for production applications.

On Android 4 and later devices, a Developer options setting screen is available to turn on and off the screen flashing with strict mode. However, this will not disable exceptions for networking activity.

Accessing the Internet (HTTP)

The most common way to transfer data to and from the network is to use HTTP. You can use HTTP to encapsulate almost any type of data and to secure the data with Secure Sockets Layer (SSL), which can be important when you transmit data that falls under privacy requirements. Also, most common ports used by HTTP are typically open from the device networks.

Tip

Many of the code examples provided in this chapter are taken from the SimpleNetworking application. This source code for the SimpleNetworking application is provided for download on the book's websites.

Reading Data from the Web

Reading data from the Web can be simple. For example, if all you need to do is read some data from a website and you have the web address of that data, you can leverage the URL class (available as part of the `java.net` package) to read a fixed amount of text from a file on a web server, like this:

```
import java.io.InputStream;
import java.net.URL;
```

```
// ...

URL text = new URL(
    "http://api.flickr.com/services/feeds/photos_public.gne" +
    "?id=26648248@N04&lang=en-us&format=atom");

InputStream isText = text.openStream();
byte[] bText = new byte[250];
int readSize = isText.read(bText);
Log.i("Net", "readSize = " + readSize);
Log.i("Net", "bText = "+ new String(bText));
isText.close();
```

First, a new URL object is created with the URL to the data we want to read. A stream is then opened to the URL resource. From there, we read the data and close the InputStream. Reading data from a server can be that simple.

Note

As we state in the book's introduction, exception handling has been stripped from book code examples for readability. However, when it comes to networking code, you often need to add this handling for the code examples to compile. See the sample code provided on the book's websites for examples of how to implement exception handling properly.

However, remember that because we work with a network resource, errors can be more common. Our device might not have network coverage; the server might be down for maintenance or disappear entirely; the URL might be invalid; and network users might experience long waits and timeouts.

This method might work in some instances—for example, when your application has lightweight, noncritical network features—but it's not particularly elegant. In many cases, you might want to know more about the data before reading from it from the URL. For instance, you might want to know how big it is.

Finally, for networking to work in any Android application, permission is required. Your application needs to have the following statement in its AndroidManifest.xml file:

```
<uses-permission
    android:name="android.permission.INTERNET"/>
```

Using `HttpURLConnection`

We can use the `HttpURLConnection` object to do a little reconnaissance on our URL before we transfer too much data. `HttpURLConnection` retrieves some information about the resource referenced by the URL object, including HTTP status and header information.

Some of the information you can retrieve from the `HttpURLConnection` includes the length of the content, content type, and date-time information so that you can check to see whether the data changed since the last time you accessed the URL.

Here is a short example of how to use `HttpURLConnection` to query the same URL previously used:

```
import java.io.InputStream;
import java.net.HttpURLConnection;
import java.net.URL;

// ...

URL text = new URL(
    "http://api.flickr.com/services/feeds/photos_public.gne?
➥id=26648248@N04&lang=en-us&format=atom");
HttpURLConnection http =
    (HttpURLConnection)text.openConnection();
Log.i("Net", "length = " + http.getContentLength());
Log.i("Net", "respCode = " + http.getResponseCode());
Log.i("Net", "contentType = "+ http.getContentType());
Log.i("Net", "content = " + http.getContent());
```

The log lines demonstrate a few useful methods with the `HttpURLConnection` class. If the URL content is deemed appropriate, you can then call `http.getInputStream()` to get the same `InputStream` object as before. From there, reading from the network resource is the same, but more is known about the resource.

Parsing XML from the Network

A large portion of data transmitted among network resources is stored in a structured fashion in Extensible Markup Language (XML). In particular, RSS feeds are provided in a standardized XML format, and many web services provide data using these feeds. Android SDK provides a variety of XML utilities. Parsing XML from the network is similar to parsing an XML resource file or a raw file on the file system. Android provides a fast and efficient XML Pull Parser, which is a parser of choice for networked applications.

The following code demonstrates how to use the XML Pull Parser to read an XML file from flickr.com and extract specific data from within it. A `TextView` called `status` is assigned before this block of code is executed and displays the status of the parsing operation.

```
import java.net.URL;

import org.xmlpull.v1.XmlPullParser;
import org.xmlpull.v1.XmlPullParserFactory;
```

```
// ...

URL text = new URL(
    "http://api.flickr.com/services/feeds/photos_public.gne
➥?id=26648248@N04&lang=en-us&format=atom");

XmlPullParserFactory parserCreator =
    XmlPullParserFactory.newInstance();
XmlPullParser parser = parserCreator.newPullParser();

parser.setInput(text.openStream(), null);

status.setText("Parsing...");
int parserEvent = parser.getEventType();
while (parserEvent != XmlPullParser.END_DOCUMENT) {
    switch(parserEvent) {
        case XmlPullParser.START_TAG:
            String tag = parser.getName();

            if (tag.compareTo("link") == 0) {
                String relType =
                    parser.getAttributeValue(null, "rel");

                if (relType.compareTo("enclosure") == 0 ) {
                    String encType =
                        parser.getAttributeValue(null, "type");

                    if (encType.startsWith("image/")) {
                        String imageSrc =
                            parser.getAttributeValue(null, "href");
                        Log.i("Net",
                            "image source = " + imageSrc);
                    }
                }
            }
            break;
    }
    parserEvent = parser.next();
}
status.setText("Done...");
```

After the URL is created, the next step is to retrieve an XmlPullParser instance from the XmlPullParserFactory. A Pull Parser has a main method that returns the next event. The events returned by a Pull Parser are similar to methods used in the implementation of a SAX parser handler class. Instead, though, the code is handled iteratively. This method is more efficient for mobile use.

In this example, the only event that we check for is the `START_TAG` event, signifying the beginning of an XML tag. Attribute values are queried and compared. This example looks specifically for image URLs in the XML from a flickr feed query. When found, a log entry is made.

You can check for the following XML Pull Parser events:

- `START_TAG`: Returned when a new tag is found (that is, `<tag>`)
- `TEXT`: Returned when text is found (that is, `<tag>text</tag>` where text has been found)
- `END_TAG`: Returned when the end of tag is found (that is, `</tag>`)
- `END_DOCUMENT`: Returned when the end of the XML file is reached

Additionally, the parser can be set to validate the input. Typically, parsing without validation is used when under constrained memory environments, such as a mobile environment. Compliant, non-validating parsing is the default for this XML Pull Parser.

Handling Network Operations Asynchronously

Networking operations can take an indefinite amount of time to complete and should not block the main UI thread. The style of networking presented so far causes the UI thread it runs on to block until the operation finishes. You must move network operations off of the main UI thread.

Offloading networking operations is straightforward using the `AsyncTask` class and the standard Java `Thread` class. You can find out more about both methods in Chapter 1.

Handling Network Operations with the `AsyncTask` class

The simplest way to handle asynchronous processing is with the `AsyncTask` class. The following code demonstrates an example implementation of `AsyncTask` to perform the same functionality as the code earlier off the UI thread:

```
private class ImageLoader extends
    AsyncTask<URL, String, String> {

@Override
protected String doInBackground(
    URL... params) {
    // just one param
    try {
        URL text = params[0];

        // ... parsing code {

        publishProgress(
            "imgCount = " + curImageCount);
```

```
            // ... end parsing code }

      }
      catch (Exception e ) {
          Log.e("Net",
              "Failed in parsing XML", e);
          return "Finished with failure.";
      }

      return "Done...";
}


protected void onCancelled() {
   Log.e("Net", "Async task Cancelled");
}

protected void onPostExecute(String result) {
    mStatus.setText(result);
}


protected void onPreExecute() {
    mStatus.setText("About to load URL");
}

protected void onProgressUpdate(
    String... values) {
    // just one value, please
    mStatus.setText(values[0]);
}}
```

When launched with the `AsyncTask.execute()` method, `doInBackground()` runs
in a background thread while the other methods run on the UI thread. There is no need
to manage a `Handler` or post a `Runnable` object to it. This simplifies coding and debugging.

Handling Network Operations with the `Thread` class

If you're more comfortable working with traditional Java threads, you can use the
`Thread` class instead. The following code demonstrates how to launch a new `Thread`
that connects to a remote server, retrieves and parses some XML, and posts a response
back to the UI thread to change a `TextView`:

```
import java.net.URL;

import org.xmlpull.v1.XmlPullParser;
import org.xmlpull.v1.XmlPullParserFactory;
```

```
// ...

new Thread() {
    public void run() {
        try {
            URL text = new URL(
                "http://api.flickr.com/services/feeds/photos_public.gne?
➥id=26648248@N04&lang=en-us&format=atom");

            XmlPullParserFactory parserCreator =
                XmlPullParserFactory.newInstance();
            XmlPullParser parser =
                parserCreator.newPullParser();

            parser.setInput(text.openStream(), null);

            mHandler.post(new Runnable() {
                public void run() {
                    status.setText("Parsing...");
                }
            });

            int parserEvent = parser.getEventType();
            while (parserEvent !=
                XmlPullParser.END_DOCUMENT) {

                // Parsing code here ...

                parserEvent = parser.next();
            }

            mHandler.post(new Runnable() {
                public void run() {
                    status.setText("Done...");
                }
            });

        } catch (Exception e) {
            Log.e("Net", "Error in network call", e);
        }
    }
}.start();
```

For this example, an anonymous `Thread` object is reasonable. We create it and call its `start()` method immediately. However, now that the code runs on a separate thread, the user interface updates must be posted back to the main thread. This is done by using a `Handler` object on the main thread and creating `Runnable` objects that execute to call `setText()` on the `TextView` widget named status.

The rest of the code remains the same as in the previous examples. Executing both the parsing code and the networking code on a separate thread allows the user interface to continue to behave in a responsive fashion while the network and parsing operations are done behind the scenes, resulting in a smooth and friendly user experience. This also allows for handling of interim actions by the user, such as canceling the transfer. You can accomplish this by implementing the `Thread` to listen for certain events and check for certain flags.

Displaying Images from a Network Resource

Now that we have covered how you can use a separate thread to parse XML, let's take our example a bit deeper and talk about working with non-primitive data types.

Continuing with the previous example of parsing for image locations from a flickr feed, let's display some images from the feed. The following example reads the image data and displays it on the screen, demonstrating another way you can use network resources:

```java
import java.io.InputStream;
import java.net.URL;

import org.xmlpull.v1.XmlPullParser;
import org.xmlpull.v1.XmlPullParserFactory;
import android.os.Handler;

// ...

final String imageSrc =
    parser.getAttributeValue(null, "href");

final String currentTitle = new String(title);
imageThread.queueEvent(new Runnable() {
    public void run() {
        InputStream bmis;
        try {
            bmis = new URL(imageSrc).openStream();
            final Drawable image = new BitmapDrawable(
                BitmapFactory.decodeStream(bmis));
            mHandler.post(new Runnable() {
                public void run() {
                    imageSwitcher.setImageDrawable(image);
                    info.setText(currentTitle);
                }
            });
        } catch (Exception e) {
            Log.e("Net", "Failed to grab image", e);
        }
    }
});
```

You can find this block of code in the parser thread, as previously described. After the image source and title of the image have been determined, a new `Runnable` object is queued for execution on a separate image-handling thread. The thread is merely a queue that receives the anonymous `Runnable` object created here and executes it at least 10 seconds after the last one, resulting in a slideshow of the images from the feed.

Warning

Although the preceding code is sound for local resources and URLs, for sources over slow connections, it might not work properly. This is a known issue with the Android SDK and is caused by a buffering issue with loading large bitmaps over slow connections. There is a relatively straightforward workaround that you can find in the code provided for this chapter.

As with the first networking example, a new `URL` object is created and an `InputStream` retrieved from it. You need a `Drawable` object to assign to the `ImageSwitcher`. Then you use the `BitmapFactory.decodeStream()` method, which takes an `InputStream`.

Finally, from this `Runnable` object, which runs on a separate queuing thread, spacing out image drawing, another anonymous `Runnable` object posts back to the main thread to actually update the `ImageSwitcher` with the new image. Figure 11.1 shows what the screen might look like showing decoding status and displaying the current image.

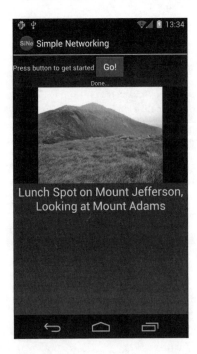

Figure 11.1   Screen showing a flickr image and decoding status of feed.

Although all this continues to happen while the feed from flickr is decoded, certain operations are slower than others. For instance, while the image is decoded or drawn on the screen, you can notice a distinct hesitation in the progress of the decoding. This is to be expected on current mobile devices because most have only a single thread of execution available for applications. You need to use careful design to provide a reasonably smooth and responsive experience to the user.

Retrieving Android Network Status

The Android SDK provides utilities for gathering information about the current state of the network. This is useful to determine whether a network connection is even available before trying to use a network resource. The ConnectivityManager class provides a number of methods to do this. The following code determines whether the mobile (cellular) network is available and connected. In addition, it determines the same for the Wi-Fi network:

```
import android.net.ConnectivityManager;
import android.net.NetworkInfo;

// ...

ConnectivityManager cm = (ConnectivityManager)
    getSystemService(Context.CONNECTIVITY_SERVICE);
NetworkInfo ni =
    cm.getNetworkInfo(ConnectivityManager.TYPE_WIFI);
boolean isWifiAvail = ni.isAvailable();
boolean isWifiConn = ni.isConnected();
ni = cm.getNetworkInfo(ConnectivityManager.TYPE_MOBILE);
boolean isMobileAvail = ni.isAvailable();
boolean isMobileConn = ni.isConnected();

status.setText("WiFi\nAvail = "+ isWifiAvail +
    "\nConn = " + isWifiConn +
    "\nMobile\nAvail = "+ isMobileAvail +
    "\nConn = " + isMobileConn);
```

First, an instance of the ConnectivityManager object is retrieved with a call to the getSystemService() method, available as part of your application Context. Then this instance retrieves NetworkInfo objects for both TYPE_WIFI and TYPE_MOBILE (for the cellular network). These objects are queried for their availability but can also be queried at a more detailed status level to learn exactly what state of connection (or disconnection) the network is in. Figure 11.2 shows the typical output for the emulator in which the mobile network is simulated but Wi-Fi isn't available.

If the network is available, this does not necessarily mean the server that the network resource is on is available. However, a call to the ConnectivityManager method `requestRouteToHost()` can answer this question. This way, the application can give the user better feedback when there are network problems.

For your application to read the status of the network, it needs explicit permission. The following statement is required to be in its `AndroidManifest.xml` file:

```
<uses-permission
    android:name="android.permission.ACCESS_NETWORK_STATE"/>
```

Figure 11.2   Network status with Wi-Fi turned off by the user.

Tip

Use the emulator networking settings to simulate various types of cellular networks, from GSM to HSDPA (and unlimited) data rates. Additionally, you can control the latency of the network to be similar to that of the cellular networks. Although this is useful for testing how your application behaves in good conditions for the chosen network type, it can't simulate the real behavior of the network out in the field when the user is in bad coverage, goes on an elevator, or is on a train rapidly losing and reacquiring network coverage. Only physical device testing can truly reveal these results.

Summary

Many applications use networking to enhance and improve the features they can provide to the user. However, a user's network connectivity is not a guaranteed, always-available service. Application developers need to design and implement networking features carefully to ensure a stable and responsive application. Integrating networking features into your mobile application needs to be considered at the design level. Deciding how much networking support your application should contain is part of the application design process.

References and More Information

Android SDK documentation on `java.net` package:
  http://d.android.com/reference/java/net/package-summary.html
Android SDK documentation on `android.net` package:
  http://d.android.com/reference/android/net/package-summary.html
Android SDK documentation on `Strict Mode` class:
  http://d.android.com/reference/android/os/StrictMode.html
XML pull parsing:
  http://www.xmlpull.org/
Android SDK documentation on Android XML Pull Parser:
  http://d.android.com/reference/org/xmlpull/v1/XmlPullParser.html

## 12

Using Android Web APIs

Mobile developers often rely on web technologies to enrich their applications, provide fresh content, and integrate with popular web services such as social networks. Android application can harness the power of the Internet in a variety of ways, including adding browser functionality to applications, using the special `WebView` control and ext, and ending web-based functionality using standard WebKit libraries. Android devices can also run Flash applications. In this chapter, we discuss the web technologies available on the Android platform.

Browsing the Web with `WebView`

Applications that retrieve and display content from the Web often end up displaying that data on the screen. Instead of customizing various screens with custom controls, Android applications can simply use the `WebView` control to display web content to the screen. You can think of the `WebView` control as a browser-like view.

The `WebView` control uses the WebKit rendering engine to draw HTML content on the screen. This content can be HTML pages on the Web or it can be locally sourced. WebKit is an open source browser engine. You can read more about it on its official website at http://webkit.org.

Tip

Many of the code examples provided in this section are taken from the SimpleWeb application. The source code for this application is provided for download on the book's websites.

Using the `WebView` control requires the `android.permission.INTERNET` permission. You can add this permission to your application's Android manifest file as follows:

```
<uses-permission android:name="android.permission.INTERNET" />
```

When deciding whether the `WebView` control is right for your application, consider that you can always launch the Browser application using an `Intent` object. When you want the user to have full access to all Browser features, such as bookmarking and browsing, you're better off launching into the Browser application to a specific website, letting users do their browsing and having them return to your application when they're done. You can do this as follows:

```
Uri uriUrl = Uri.parse("http://androidbook.blogspot.com/");
Intent launchBrowser = new Intent(Intent.ACTION_VIEW, uriUrl);
startActivity(launchBrowser);
```

Launching the Browser via an `Intent` does not require any special permissions. This means that your application is not required to have the `android.permission.INTER-NET` permission. In addition, because Android transitions from your application's current activity to a specific Browser application's `Activity`, and then returns when the user presses the Back key, the experience is nearly as seamless as implementing your own `Activity` class with an embedded `WebView` object.

Designing a Layout with a `WebView` Control

The `WebView` control can be added to a layout resource file like any other view. It can take up the entire screen or just a portion of it. A typical `WebView` definition in a layout resource might look like this:

```
<WebView
    android:id="@+id/web_holder"
    android:layout_height="match_parent"
    android:layout_width="match_parent"
/>
```

Generally speaking, you should give your `WebView` controls ample room to display text and graphics. Keep this in mind when designing layouts using the `WebView` control.

Warning

The Eclipse Layout Resource Editor does not display the `WebView` control properly. You need to run either the Android emulator or a device to make sure the layout displays properly.

Loading Content into a `WebView` Control

You can load content into a `WebView` control in a variety of ways. For example, a `WebView` control can load a specific website or render raw HTML content. Web pages can be stored on a remote web server or stored on the device.

Here is an example of how to use a `WebView` control to load content from a specific website:

```
final WebView wv = (WebView) findViewById(R.id.web_holder);
wv.loadUrl("http://www.perlgurl.org/");
```

You do not need to add any additional code to load the referenced web page on the screen. Similarly, you can load an HTML file called `webby.html` stored in the application's assets directory like this:

```
wv.loadUrl("file:///android_asset/webby.html");
```

If, instead, you want to render raw HTML, you can use the `loadData()` method:

```
String strPageTitle = "The Last Words of Oscar Wilde";
String strPageContent = "<h1>" + strPageTitle +
    ": </h1>\"Either that wallpaper goes, or I do.\"";
String myHTML = "<html><title>" + strPageTitle
    +"</title><body>"+ strPageContent +"</body></html>";
wv.loadData(myHTML, "text/html", "utf-8");
```

The resulting `WebView` control is shown in Figure 12.1.

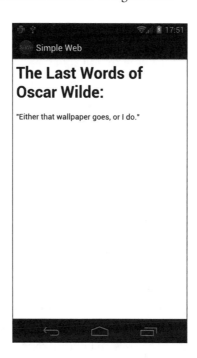

Figure 12.1   A `WebView` control used to display HTML.

Unfortunately, not all websites are designed for mobile devices. It can be handy to change the scale of the web content to fit comfortably in the `WebView` control. You can achieve this by setting the initial scale of the control, like this:

```
wv.setInitialScale(30);
```

The call to the `setInitialScale()` method scales the view to 30 percent of the original size. For pages that specify absolute sizes, scaling the view is necessary to see the entire page on the screen. Some text might become too small to read, though, so you might need to test and make page design changes (if the web content is under your control) for a good user experience.

Tip

If you want an entire screen to be a `WebView` control, you can simply create a `WebView` programmatically and pass it into the `setContentView()` method in the `onCreate()` method of your `Activity`.

Adding Features to the `WebView` Control

You might have noticed that the `WebView` control does not have all the features of a full browser. For example, it does not display the title of a webpage or provide buttons for reloading pages. In fact, if the user clicks on a link in the `WebView` control, that action does not load the new page in the view. Instead, it fires up the Browser application.

By default, all the `WebView` control does is display the web content provided by the developer using its internal rendering engine, WebKit. You can enhance the `WebView` control in a variety of ways, though. You can use three classes, in particular, to help modify the behavior of the control: the `WebSettings` class, the `WebViewClient` class, and the `WebChromeClient` class.

Modifying `WebView` Settings with `WebSettings`

By default, a `WebView` control has various default settings: no zoom controls, JavaScript disabled, default font sizes, user-agent string, and so on. You can change the settings of a `WebView` control using the `getSettings()` method. The `getSettings()` method returns a `WebSettings` object that can be used to configure the desired `WebView` settings. Some useful settings include the following:

- Enabling and disabling zoom controls using the `setSupportZoom()` and `setBuiltInZoomControls()` methods
- Enabling and disabling JavaScript using the `setJavaScriptEnabled()` method
- Enabling and disabling mouseovers using the `setLightTouchEnabled()` method
- Configuring font families, text sizes, and other display characteristics

You can also use the `WebSettings` class to configure `WebView` plug-ins and allow for multiple windows.

Handling `WebView` Events with `WebViewClient`

The `WebViewClient` class enables the application to listen for certain `WebView` events, such as when a page is loading, when a form is submitted, and when a new URL is about to be loaded. You can also use the WebViewClient class to determine and handle any errors that occur with page loading. You can tie a valid WebViewClient object to a WebView using the setWebViewClient() method.

The following is an example of how to use WebViewClient to handle the onPageFinished() method to draw the title of the page on the screen:

```
WebViewClient webClient = new WebViewClient() {


    public void onPageFinished(WebView view, String url) {
        super.onPageFinished(view, url);
        String title = wv.getTitle();
        pageTitle.setText(title);
    }};


wv.setWebViewClient(webClient);
```

When the page finishes loading, as indicated by the call to onPageFinished(), a call to the getTitle() method of the WebView object retrieves the title for use. The result of this call is shown in Figure 12.2.

Figure 12.2   A WebView control showing page title.

Adding Browser Chrome with `WebChromeClient`

You can use the `WebChromeClient` class in a similar way to the `WebViewClient`. However, `WebChromeClient` is specialized for the sorts of items that are drawn outside the region in which the web content is drawn, typically known as *browser chrome*. The `WebChromeClient` class also includes callbacks for certain JavaScript calls, such as `onJsBeforeUnload()`, to confirm navigation away from a page. A valid `WebChromeClient` object can be tied to a `WebView` using the `setWebChromeClient()` method.

The following code demonstrates using `WebView` features to enable interactivity with the user. An `EditText` and a `Button` control are added below the `WebView` control, and a `Button` handler is implemented as follows:

```
Button go = (Button) findViewById(R.id.go_button);
go.setOnClickListener(new View.OnClickListener() {
    public void onClick(View v) {
        wv.loadUrl(et.getText().toString());
    }
});
```

Calling the `loadUrl()` method again, as shown, is all that is needed to cause the `WebView` control to download another HTML page for display, as shown in Figure 12.3. From here, you can build a generic web browser in to any application, but you can apply restrictions so that the user is restricted to browsing relevant materials.

Figure 12.3   `WebView` with `EditText` allowing entry of arbitrary URLs.

Using `WebChromeClient` can help add some typical chrome on the screen. For instance, you can use it to listen for changes to the title of the page, various JavaScript dialogs that might be requested, and even for developer-oriented pieces, such as the console messages.

```
WebChromeClient webChrome = new WebChromeClient() {
    @Override
    public void onReceivedTitle
        (WebView view, String title) {
        Log.v(DEBUG_TAG, "Got new title");
        super.onReceivedTitle(view, title);
        pageTitle.setText(title);
    }
};
wv.setWebChromeClient(webChrome);
```

Here, the default `WebChromeClient` object is overridden to receive changes to the title of the page. This title of the web page is then set to a `TextView` visible on the screen.

Whether you use `WebView` to display the main user interface of your application or use it sparingly to draw such things as help pages, there are circumstances where it might be the ideal control for the job to save coding time, especially when compared to a custom screen design. Leveraging the power of the open source engine, `WebKit`, `WebView` can provide a powerful, standards-based HTML viewer for applications. Support for WebKit is widespread because it is used in various desktop browsers, including Apple Safari and Google Chrome; a variety of mobile browsers, including those on the Apple iOS, Nokia, Palm WebOS, and BlackBerry handsets; and various other platforms, such as Adobe AIR.

Managing `WebView` State

On API Level 11 and higher, be sure to make the appropriate calls to the `onPause()` and `onResume()` methods of the `WebView` object. The `onPause()` call reduces or stops unnecessary processing activity, such as those from plug-ins and JavaScript. Without making these calls, or in previous API versions, processing would continue in the background. These methods should be called from your `Activity` class's `onPause()` and `onResume()` methods, at minimum.

When running on older versions of the platform, you can terminate the `WebView` instance entirely. If that's too much, you can make a call to `pauseTimers()`, which stops some processing but also affects all `WebView` instances. Keep in mind that the rest of the device performance might be adversely affected if you don't do what you can to reduce processing. If your `WebView` doesn't allow plug-ins or JavaScript, then only layout and parsing would continue.

You can have code such as the following in your `onPause()` method:

```
WebView wv = (WebView) findViewById(R.id.web_holder);
if (Build.VERSION.SDK_INT >= Build.VERSION_CODES.HONEYCOMB) {
    wv.onPause();
} else {
    wv.pauseTimers();
}
```

During testing, you must recognize that the behavior is not identical and should be tested as such.

Building Web Extensions Using WebKit

All HTML rendering on the Android platform is done using the WebKit rendering engine. The `android.webkit` package provides a number of APIs for browsing the Internet using the powerful `WebView` control. You should be aware of the WebKit interfaces and classes available, as you are likely to need them to enhance the `WebView` user experience.

These are not classes and interfaces to the Browser app (although you can interact with the Browser data using contact providers). Instead, these are the classes and interfaces that you must use to control the browsing abilities of `WebView` controls you implement in your applications.

Browsing the WebKit APIs

Some of the most helpful classes of the `android.webkit` package are

- The `CacheManager` class gives you some control over cache items of a `WebView`.
- The `ConsoleMessage` class can be used to retrieve JavaScript console output from a `WebView`.
- The `CookieManager` class is used to set and retrieve user cookies for a `WebView`.
- The `URLUtil` class is handy for validating web addresses of different types.
- The `WebBackForwardList` and `WebHistoryItem` classes can be used to inspect the web history of the `WebView`.

Now let's take a quick look at how you might use some of these classes to enhance a `WebView`.

Extending Web Application Functionality to Android

Let's take some of the WebKit features we have discussed so far in this chapter and work through an example. It is fairly common for mobile developers to design their applications as web applications to reach users across a variety of platforms. This minimizes the amount of platform-specific code to develop and maintain. However, on its own, a web application cannot call into native platform code and take advantage of the features that native apps (such as those written in Java for the Android platform) can, such as using a built-in camera or accessing some other underlying Android feature.

Developers can enhance web applications by designing a lightweight shell application in Java and using a `WebView` control as a portal to the web application content. Two-way communication between the web application and the native Java application is possible through scripting languages such as JavaScript.

Tip

Many of the code examples provided in this section are taken from the SimpleWebExtension application. The source code for this application is provided for download on the book's websites.

Let's create a simple Android application that illustrates communication between web content and native Android code. This example requires that you understand JavaScript. To create this application, take the following steps:

1. Create a new Android application.

2. Create a layout with a `WebView` control called `html_viewer` and a `Button` control called `call_js`. Set the `onClick` attribute of the `Button` control to a method called `setHTMLText`.

3. In the `onCreate()` method of your application activity, retrieve the `WebView` control using the `findViewById()` method.

4. Enable JavaScript in the `WebView` by retrieving its `WebSettings` and calling the `setJavaScriptEnabled()` method.

5. Create a `WebChromeClient` object and implement its `onConsoleMessage()` method to monitor the JavaScript console messages.

6. Add the `WebChromeClient` object to the `WebView` using the `setWebChromeClient()` method.

7. Allow the JavaScript interface to control your application by calling the `addJavascriptInterface()` method of the `WebView` control. You need to define the functionality that you want the JavaScript interface to control and in what namespace the calls will be available. In this case, we allow the JavaScript to initiate `Toast` messages.

8. Load your content into the `WebView` control using one of the standard methods, such as the `loadUrl()` method. In this case, we load an HTML asset we defined within the application package.

If you followed these steps, you should end up with your activity's `onCreate()` method looking something like this:

```
@Override
public void onCreate(Bundle savedInstanceState) {
    super.onCreate(savedInstanceState);
    setContentView(R.layout.main);
```

```
final WebView wv = (WebView) findViewById(R.id.html_viewer);
WebSettings settings = wv.getSettings();
settings.setJavaScriptEnabled(true);
WebChromeClient webChrome = new WebChromeClient() {
    @Override
    public boolean onConsoleMessage(ConsoleMessage consoleMessage) {
        Log.v(DEBUG_TAG, consoleMessage.lineNumber()
            + ": " + consoleMessage.message());
        return true;
    }
};

wv.setWebChromeClient(webChrome);
wv.addJavascriptInterface(new JavaScriptExtensions(), "jse");
wv.loadUrl("file:///android_asset/sample.html");
}
```

A custom `WebChromeClient` class is set so that any JavaScript `console.log` messages go out to LogCat output, using a custom debug tag as usual to enable easy tracking of log output specific to the application. Next, a new JavaScript interface is defined with the namespace called `jse`—the namespace is up to you. To call from JavaScript to this Java class, the JavaScript calls must all start with namespace `jse.`, followed by the appropriate exposed method—for instance, `jse.javaMethod()`.

You can define the `JavaScriptExtensions` class as a subclass in the activity as a subclass with a single method that can trigger Android `Toast` messages, as follows:

```
class JavaScriptExtensions {
    public static final int TOAST_LONG = Toast.LENGTH_LONG;
    public static final int TOAST_SHORT = Toast.LENGTH_SHORT;
    public void toast(String message, int length) {
        Toast.makeText(SimpleWebExtension.this, message, length).show();
    }
}
```

The JavaScript code has access to everything in the `JavaScriptExtensions` class, including the member variables as well as the methods. Return values work as expected from the methods, too.

Now switch your attention to defining the web page to load in the `WebView` control. For this example, simply create a file called `sample.html` in the /assets directory of the application. The contents of the `sample.html` file are shown here:

```
<html>
<head>
<script type="text/javascript">

function doToast() {
    jse.toast("'"+document.getElementById('form_text').value +
```

```
        "' -From Java!", jse.TOAST_LONG);
}

function doConsoleLog() {
    console.log("Console logging.");
}

function doAlert() {
    alert("This is an alert.");
}

function doSetFormText(update) {
    document.getElementById('form_text').value = update;
}

</script>
</head>
<body>
<h2>This is a test.</h2>
<input type="text" id="form_text" value="Enter something here..." />
<input type="button" value="Toast" onclick="doToast();" /><br />
<input type="button" value="Log" onclick="doConsoleLog();" /><br />
<input type="button" value="Alert" onclick="doAlert();" />
</body>
</html>
```

The sample.html file defines four JavaScript functions and displays the form shown in the WebView:

- The doToast() function calls into the Android application using the jse object defined earlier with the call to the addJavaScriptInterface() method. The addJavaScriptInterface() method, for all practical intents and purposes, can be treated literally as the JavaScriptExtensions class as if that class had been written in JavaScript. If the doToast() function had returned a value, we could assign it to a variable here.

- The doConsoleLog() function writes into the JavaScript console log, which is picked up by the onConsoleMessage() callback of the WebChromeClient.

- The doAlert() function illustrates how alerts work within the WebView control by launching a dialog. If you want to override what the alert looks like, you can override the WebChromeClient.onJSAlert() method.

- The doSetFormText() function illustrates how native Java code can communicate back through the JavaScript interface and provide data to the web application.

Finally, to demonstrate making a call from Java back to JavaScript, you need to define the click handler for the Button control within your Activity class. Here, the onClick handler, called setHTMLText(), executes some JavaScript on the currently loaded page by calling a JavaScript function called `doSetFormText()`, which we defined earlier in the web page. Here is an implementation of the `setHTMLText()` method:

```
public void setHTMLText(View view) {
    WebView wv = (WebView) findViewById(R.id.html_viewer);
    wv.loadUrl("javascript:doSetFormText('Java->JS call');");
}
```

This method of making a call to the JavaScript on the currently loaded page does not allow for return values. There are ways, however, to structure your design to allow checking of results, generally by treating the call as asynchronous and implementing another method for determining the response.

Warning

Keep in mind that opening up the Android application to a JavaScript control using the `addJavascriptInterface()` method must be done securely. Make sure your `WebView` loads only the content under your control—not just any content on the Web. Also, the JavaScript interface does not run on the UI thread, so you need to employ normal cross-thread communication techniques, such as using a handler to post messages back to the other thread in order to communicate.

Figure 12.4 shows how this application might behave on an Android device.

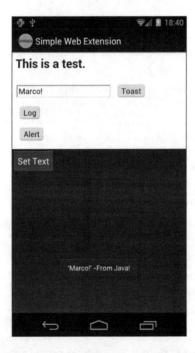

Figure 12.4   A simple Android application with a JavaScript interface.

This style of development has been popularized by the open source PhoneGap project, which aims to provide a set of standard JavaScript interfaces to native code across a variety of platforms, including iOS, Android, BlackBerry, Symbian, and Palm. Learn more about PhoneGap at http://phonegap.com.

Working with Flash

For those web developers wanting to bring their Flash applications to mobile, Android supports Adobe Flash 11 (as opposed to Flash Lite, a common mobile variant of Flash that's limited). However, there are both benefits and drawbacks to including Flash technology on the platform. Let's look at some of the facts:

- Flash might not be the future, but it's the status quo in some web circles. There are millions of Flash applications and websites out there that can now be accessed from Android devices. This makes users happy, which should make the rest of us happy.
- Flash on mobile browsers is most definitely not the future. Adobe has decided that they will not continue to create new mobile browser plug-ins. Instead, developers can use their tools to create HTML5 websites that work on mobile. Developers who use Adobe AIR to create packaged applications using Flash are not affected by this. See http://blogs.adobe.com/conversations/2011/11/flash-focus.html (http://goo.gl/grIct) for more information.
- Native Android applications are always going to perform better, use fewer resources (read: drain the battery slower), provide tighter platform integration, have fewer platform prerequisites, and support more Android devices than Flash applications.
- Deciding to build Flash applications for the Android platform instead of native Java applications is a design decision that should not be taken lightly. There are performance and security tradeoffs as well as limited device support (and no backward compatibility) for Flash.
- You can't expect all Flash applications to just load up and work. All the usual mobile constraints and UI paradigms apply. This includes designing around such constraints as a touch interface on a small screen, a relatively slow processor, and interruptions (such as phone calls) being the norm.

Still, there are those millions of great Flash applications out there. Let's look at how you can bring these applications to the Android platform.

Enabling Flash Applications

Android devices with Android 2.2 and higher can run Flash applications (currently Flash 11). In order to run Flash, the Android device must have Adobe's Flash Player for Android installed.

Users can download the Adobe Flash Player for Android application from the Android Market. Android handsets might also ship with the Adobe application pre-loaded. Keep in mind that only the faster, more powerful Android devices are likely to run Flash smoothly and provide a positive user experience. After it's installed, the Flash Player for Android application behaves like a typical browser plug-in. Users can enable or disable it, and you can control whether plug-ins are enabled or not within your screens that use the `WebView` control.

Building AIR Applications for Android

Adobe has created tools for developing cross-platform applications using its AIR tool suite in ActionScript 3, which is Adobe's web scripting language for web and Flash applications. The company recently announced Adobe AIR for Android, which enables developers to create AIR applications that can be compiled into native Android APK files that can then be published like any other Android application. Developers use Adobe's Flash Professional CS5 tools with a special extension to develop AIR applications that can be compiled into Android package files and distributed like native Android applications.

Summary

Android developers can add browser support to their applications using the versatile `WebView` control. Applications that require more control can enhance their applications with web features using powerful yet familiar technologies such as WebKit. In Android 2.2 and later, Flash support is available on the Android platform in the form of an Adobe application. Adobe has also developed a tool suite that allows ActionScript applications to be compiled into Android APK files and distributed as native Android applications.

References and More Information

WebKit Open Source Project:
    http://www.webkit.org
W3School's JavaScript tutorial:
    http://www.w3schools.com/js/js_intro.asp
Adobe AIR tool suite:
    http://www.adobe.com/products/air/tools/

13

Using Location-Based Services APIs

Whether for safety or for convenience, location-based features on cell phones are mostly standard these days. As such, incorporating location information, navigation, and mapping features into your project can make your application much more robust.

In this chapter, you learn how to leverage location-based services available in the Android SDK. You learn how to determine the location of the device using a particular device hardware provider, such as a built-in Global Positioning Systems (GPS) unit. You also learn how to translate raw location coordinates into descriptive location names— and how to do the reverse. Finally, we explore a couple of different methods for mapping and utilities that work with the maps.

Using Global Positioning Services (GPS)

The Android SDK provides the means for accessing location via a built-in GPS hardware, when it's available. Generally speaking, just about every Android phone has some LBS capabilities. For example, in the United States, emergency services use mobile phone location information. That said, not all Android devices are phones, nor do all phones enable consumer-usage of LBS services. If GPS features are disabled, or an Android device does not have LBS hardware, the Android SDK provides additional APIs for determining alternate location providers. These other providers might have advantages and disadvantages in terms of power use, speed, and accuracy of reporting.

Tip

Many of the code examples provided in this chapter are taken from the SimpleLocation application. The source code for this application is provided for download on the book's websites.

Using GPS Features in Your Applications

LBS services and hardware such as a built-in precision GPS are optional features for Android devices. In addition to requiring the appropriate permissions, you can specify which optional features your application requires in the Android Manifest file. You can declare that your application uses or requires specific LBS services using the `<uses-feature>` tag of the Android Manifest file. Although this tag is not enforced by the Android operating system, it enables popular publication mechanisms such as the Android Market to filter your app and provide it only to users with appropriate devices. If your application functions well only on devices with some sort of method for determining the current location, you can use the following `<uses-feature>` tag in your application's manifest file:

```
<uses-feature android:name="android.hardware.location" />
```

If your application requires a precise location fix (that is, the device has functional GPS hardware, not just cell tower triangulation or other such mechanisms), use the following `<uses-feature>` tag instead:

```
<uses-feature android:name="android.hardware.location.gps" />
```

Determining the Location of the Device

To determine device location, you need to perform a few steps and make some choices. The following list summarizes this process:

1. Retrieve an instance of the `LocationManager` using a call to the `getSystemService()` method using the `LOCATION_SERVICE`.
2. Add an appropriate permission to the `AndroidManifest.xml` file, depending on what type of location information the application needs.
3. Choose a provider using either the `getAllProviders()` method or the `getBestProvider()` method.
4. Implement a `LocationListener` class.
5. Call the `requestLocationUpdates()` method with the chosen provider and the `LocationListener` object to start receiving location information.

Specific permissions are not needed to retrieve an instance of the `LocationManager` object. Instead, the permissions determine the available providers. The following code retrieves an instance of the `LocationManager` object:

```
import android.location.*;
...
LocationManager location =
    (LocationManager)getSystemService(Context.LOCATION_SERVICE);
```

The following block of XML provides the application with both coarse and fine location permissions when added within the `AndroidManifest.xml` permissions file:

```
<uses-permission
    android:name="android.permission.ACCESS_FINE_LOCATION" />
<uses-permission
    android:name="android.permission.ACCESS_COARSE_LOCATION" />
```

Requesting fine permission implies coarse support as well, but it's helpful to be explicit. Now that the application has permissions to use location information and the `LocationManager` object is valid, we must determine what provider to use for location information. The following code configures a `Criteria` object and requests the provider based on this information:

```
Criteria criteria = new Criteria();
criteria.setAccuracy(Criteria.NO_REQUIREMENT);
criteria.setPowerRequirement(Criteria.NO_REQUIREMENT);

String bestProvider = location.getBestProvider(criteria, true);
```

The `setAccuracy()` method can take values for `ACCURACY_COARSE` and `ACCURACY_FINE` that can be used (along with the appropriate permissions) to request a provider that the application has permissions to use. You can use the `setPowerRequirement()` method to find a provider that fits certain power use requirements, such as `POWER_HIGH` or `POWER_LOW`. The `Criteria` object also enables us to specify whether the provider can incur a monetary cost to the user, whether altitude is needed, and some other details. If the application has specific requirements, this is where you set them. However, setting these criteria doesn't imply that the provider is available to the user. Some flexibility might be required to allow use on a broad range of devices. A `Boolean` parameter of the `getBestProvider()` method enables the application to ask for only enabled providers.

Using the provider returned by the `getBestProvider()` method, the application can request the location. Before doing so, however, the application needs to provide an implementation of `LocationListener`. The `LocationListener` implementation consists of several methods: to tell the application whether the provider has been disabled or enabled; to give the status about the provider (such as the number of satellites the GPS receiver can see); and to tell the application location information. The following is a sample implementation for the last method, the `onLocationChanged()` method:

```
public void onLocationChanged(Location location) {
    String locInfo = String.
        format("Current loc = (%f, %f) @ (%f meters up)",
        location.getLatitude(), location.getLongitude(),
        location.getAltitude() );
    if (lastLocation != null) {
        float distance = location.distanceTo(lastLocation);
```

```
        locInfo += String.
            format("\n Distance from last = %f meters", distance);
    }
    lastLocation = location;
    status.setText(locInfo);
}
```

The `onLocationChanged()` method receives a `Location` object with the most recent location information from the chosen provider. In this example, the application merely prints out the location, including the altitude, which might be returned by the provider. Then, it uses a utility method of the `Location` object, `distanceTo()`, to calculate how far the device has moved since the last time `onLocationChanged()` was called.

It is up to the application to determine how to use this location information. The application might want to turn the location information into an address, display the location on an embedded map, or launch the built-in Maps application (if the Google applications are installed) centered at the location.

Tip

To use many LBS services, you should use Android Virtual Device (AVD) configurations that target the Android SDK with the Google APIs. Using the Google APIs target puts applications like the Maps on the emulator. Other times, LBS design and testing are best done on a real Android device.

Locating Your Emulator

The Android emulator can simulate location-based services, but as you would expect, it does not have any "underlying hardware" to get a real satellite fix. The Android SDK provides a means to simulate location data with the use of a single location point, GPX file, or KML file. This works only with the emulator, not the physical device, but it can be useful for testing your location-based application.

Geocoding Locations

Determining the latitude and longitude is useful for precise location, tracking, and measurements; however, it's not usually descriptive to users. The Android SDK provides some helper methods to turn raw location data into addresses and descriptive place names. These methods can also work in reverse, turning place names or addresses into raw location coordinates.

Warning

According to the Android documentation, AVDs that target the Google APIs enable developers to test on emulator instances with the "Google experience." The Google APIs provide the capability to use Google Maps as well as a backend geocoder service. Although it is not documented, not all AVD API Levels support these geocoder services. For example, AVDs for API Level 6 with the Google APIs provide geocoder services, whereas AVDs with API Levels 7 and 8 with the Google APIs do not (as of this writing). When you use an AVD without backend geocoder services, you simply get an exception stating there is no backend service. The code in this chapter is best run in an emulator running an AVD with API Level 6 plus the Google APIs, or on a real device with true geocoder backend services.

The Geocoder object can be used without any special permissions. The following block of code demonstrates using the Geocoder object to get the location names of a Location object passed into the onLocationChanged() method of a LocationListener:

```
if (Geocoder.isPresent()) {
    Geocoder coder = new Geocoder(this);
    try {
        List<Address> addresses = coder.getFromLocation(
                location.getLatitude(), location.getLongitude(), 3);
        if (addresses != null) {
            for (Address namedLoc : addresses) {
                String placeName = namedLoc.getLocality();
                String featureName = namedLoc.getFeatureName();
                String country = namedLoc.getCountryName();
                String road = namedLoc.getThoroughfare();
                locInfo.append(String.format("[%s] [%s] [%s] [%s]\n",
                        placeName, featureName, road, country));
                int addIdx = namedLoc.getMaxAddressLineIndex();
                for (int idx = 0; idx <= addIdx; idx++) {
                    String addLine = namedLoc.getAddressLine(idx);
                    locInfo.append(String.format("Line %d: %s\n", idx,
                            addLine));
                }
            }
        }
    } catch (IOException e) {
        Log.e("GPS", "Failed to get address", e);
    }
} else {
    Toast.makeText(GPSActivity.this, "No geocoding available",
            Toast.LENGTH_LONG).show();
}
```

You can extract information from the results of the call to the `getFromLocation()` method in two ways, both of which are demonstrated. Note that a particular location might have multiple `Address` results in the form of a `List<Address>` object. Typically, the first `Address` is the most detailed, and the subsequent `Address` objects have less detail and describe a broader region.

The first method is to query for specific information, such as by using the `getFeatureName()` method or the `getLocality()` method. These methods are not guaranteed to return useful information for all locations. They are useful, though, when you know you need only a specific piece of general information, such as the country.

The second method for querying information is by "address lines." This is generally used for displaying the "address" of a location to the user. It might also be useful to use the location in directions and in other cases where a street address is desired. That said, the addresses returned might not be complete. Simply use the `getMaxAddressLineIndex()` and `getAddressLine()` methods to iterate through the addresses. Figure 13.1 shows a sample location with three resulting addresses.

Figure 13.1   Image showing location geocoded to three "addresses."

The Geocoder object also supports using named locations or address lines to generate latitude and longitude information. The input is forgiving and returns reasonable results in most cases. For instance, all the following returns valid and correct results: "Eiffel Tower," "London, UK," "Iceland," "BOS," "Yellowstone," and "1600 Pennsylvania Ave, DC."

The following code demonstrates a button handler for computing location data based on user input of this kind:

```
public void onClick(View v) {
    if (Geocoder.isPresent()) {
        String placeName = name.getText().toString();

        try {
            // coder initialized elsewhere
            List<Address> geocodeResults = coder
                    .getFromLocationName(placeName, 3);

            StringBuilder locInfo = new StringBuilder("Results:\n");
            double lat = 0f;
            double lon = 0f;

            for (Address loc : geocodeResults) {
                lat = loc.getLatitude();
                lon = loc.getLongitude();
                locInfo.append("Location: ").append(lat)
                        .append(", ").append(lon).append("\n");
            }

            results.setText(locInfo);
        } catch (IOException e) {
            Log.e("GeoAddress", "Failed to get location info", e);
        }
    } else {
        Toast.makeText(GeoAddressActivity.this,
                "No geocoding available", Toast.LENGTH_LONG).show();
    }
}
```

The result of the call to the getFromLocationName() method is a List of Address objects, much like the previous example. Figure 13.2 shows the results for entering Eiffel Tower.

Figure 13.2   The results for geocoding the term "Eiffel Tower."

Always assume that you will get more than one result. It is good form to provide a picker for the user to select from the results and choose the most appropriate location. Another good way to confirm with the user that they entered the correct location is to map it. We now discuss a couple of different methods for mapping locations using Google Maps.

Warning

Geocoding operations typically require a network connection and therefore should not be run on the main UI thread. Instead, perform geocoding tasks in a separate thread so as not to cause your application responsiveness to degrade.

Mapping Locations

The Android SDK provides two different methods to show a location with Google Maps. The first method is to use a location `Uri` to launch the built-in Google Maps application with the specified location. The second method is to use a `MapView` embedded within your application to display the map location.

Mapping Intents

In the previous section, we demonstrated how to determine the latitude and longitude for a place name. Now we map the location using the built-in maps application. The following block of code demonstrates how to perform this:

```
String geoURI = String.format("geo:%f,%f", lat, lon);
Uri geo = Uri.parse(geoURI);
Intent geoMap = new Intent(Intent.ACTION_VIEW, geo);
startActivity(geoMap);
```

The first task is to create a `String` that conforms to the `URI` handled by the mapping application. In this case, it's `geo:` followed by the latitude and longitude. This `URI` is then used to create a new `Uri` object for creating a new `ACTION_VIEW` `Intent`. Finally, we call the `startActivity()` method. If the latitude and longitude are valid, such as the location for the Hoover Dam, the screen would look like Figure 13.3.

Figure 13.3   The resulting map for geocoding the term "Hoover Dam"
and launching a geo URI.

Using this method of mapping launches the user into a built-in mapping application—in this case, Google Maps. If the application does not want to bother with the details of a full mapping application or does not need to provide any further control over the map, this is a fast-and-easy method to use. Users are typically accustomed to the controls of the mapping application on their device, too.

Mapping Views

Sometimes, though, we want to have the map integrated into our application for a more seamless user experience. Let's add a small map to our geocoding example to show the location immediately to the users when they enter a place name.

The following block of XML shows the change needed in the layout file to include a widget called the `MapView`:

```
<com.google.android.maps.MapView
    android:id="@+id/map"
    android:apiKey="yourMapKey"
    android:layout_width="fill_parent"
    android:layout_height="wrap_content" />
```

As you might have already noticed, the `MapView` XML is a little different. First, the tag name is the fully qualified name. And second, an `apiKey` attribute is needed. We get to the key in a moment.

The `AndroidManifest.xml` file also needs to be modified to allow the use of the `MapView` with Google Maps. Here are the two changes needed:

```
<application
...
    <uses-library
        android:name="com.google.android.maps" />
</application>
<uses-permission
    android:name="android.permission.INTERNET" />
```

Both of these permission lines are required. The `MapView` object specifically requires the `INTERNET` permission and its library must be referenced explicitly. Otherwise, an error occurs.

Finally, you can use a `MapView` only within a `MapActivity`. Accessing a `MapView` from outside a `MapActivity` results in an error. The `MapActivity` is similar to a normal `Activity`, but it requires implementing the `isRouteDisplayed()` method. This method must return true if a route will be displayed. Otherwise, false must be returned. Here is the default implementation for when no route is displayed:

```
@Override
protected boolean isRouteDisplayed() {
    // we do not display routes
    return false;
}
```

Now the application can use the `MapView` to display locations to the user. The following block of code demonstrates retrieval of a `MapController` object, which is used to control the location that the `MapView` displays:

```
MapView map = (MapView) findViewById(R.id.map);
map.setSatellite(true);
final MapController mapControl = map.getController();
mapControl.setZoom(17);
```

These lines of code set the display to show the satellite view, which is visually interesting. The `MapController` object then sets the zoom level of the map. Larger values are zoomed in farther, with `1` zoomed all the way out. The given value, `17`, usually shows a few city blocks, but there are some areas where even this is too close for the data available. In a moment, we talk about how to easily give control of this to the user.

Building on the previous example, the following lines of code are added to the button handler for geocoding a place name:

```
GeoPoint newPoint = new
    GeoPoint((int)(lat * 1E6), (int)(lon * 1E6));
mapControl.animateTo(newPoint);
```

In this case, we create a new `GeoPoint` to use with the `animateTo()` method. A `GeoPoint` object uses microdegrees, so we must multiply the result of the geocoding by 1E6 (1,000,000 or one million). The `animateTo()` method smoothly animates the `MapView` to the new location. How much of the interim mapping data displays depends on the speed of the Internet connection and what mode the `MapView` is in. The `setCenter()` method can set the center of the map.

Finally, this is almost enough to test the results. However, there is one last thing you need to take care of. You need to get a Google Maps API Key from Google to use its API and mapping services.

Getting Your Debug API Key

To use a `MapView` in your applications, you must obtain a Google Maps API Key from Google. The key is generated from an MD5 fingerprint of a certificate that you use to sign your applications.

For production distribution, you need to follow these steps, substituting your release distribution signing certificate. For testing purposes, you can use the debug certificate that is created by the Android SDK.

You need to do the following to generate the appropriate API key:

1. Generate an MD5 fingerprint for your debug certificate.
2. Sign in to http://code.google.com/android/maps-api-signup.html with a Google account.
3. Accept the Terms of Service.
4. Paste in the fingerprint from Step 1.
5. Save the Android Maps API key presented on the next screen.

The first step is performed on your development machine. Locate the debug certificate used by the Android SDK. On all platforms, the filename is debug.keystore by default. If you use Eclipse, the location of the file is listed under the Android Build preferences. Using this file, you then need to execute the following command (make sure the Java tools are in your path):

```
keytool -list -keystore /path/to/debug.keystore -storepass android
```

The result is the fingerprint that you must paste into the form on step 4. Read the Terms of Service carefully before proceeding. Although the terms allow many types of applications, you need to make sure your application is allowed and that your anticipated usage is acceptable to Google.

Tip

The default debug keystore on the Android SDK lasts for only one year and is unique to a developer's computer. We highly recommend making a debug key that lasts longer and can be shared among team members. This enables your Google Maps API key to last much longer. In addition, you won't have to uninstall apps from a shared device before you can install one with someone else's debug key. Luckily, it's easy to do this using the keytool command-line tool with the following command:

```
keytool -genkey -keypass android -keystore debug.keystore
  alias androiddebugkey -storepass android
  -validity 10000
  -dname "CN=Android Debug,O=Android,C=US"
```

This command generates a valid debug keystore that can be shared among team members and lasts for 10,000 days. After creating it, make sure you reference it from Eclipse if it's not in the default location.

When you have successfully completed the steps to get your key, you can then reference your map key in the Layout file definition for the MapView you use. Now, when you execute the code, you should be presented with a screen that looks like Figure 13.4.

Tip

If you work on multiple development machines or work as part of a team, you need to have an API key for everyone's debug certificate. Alternatively, you can copy the debug certificate from one machine to other machines so that the signing and check against the Android Maps API key is successful. This can save you time because you don't have to modify the code or layout files for each developer on the team.

Figure 13.4   `MapView` results for geocoding the term "Pentagon."

Panning the Map View

Sometimes the locations returned either do not show the exact location that the user wants or the user might want to determine where in the world they are by exploring the map a bit. One way to do this is through panning the map. Luckily, this is as easy as enabling clicking from within the layout file:

```
<com.google.android.maps.MapView
    android:id="@+id/map"
    android:clickable="true"
    android:apiKey="mapApiKey"
    android:layout_width="fill_parent"
    android:layout_height="wrap_content" />
```

Now, if the user searches for "Giza Pyramids," panning east will find a recognizable statue, as shown in Figure 13.5.

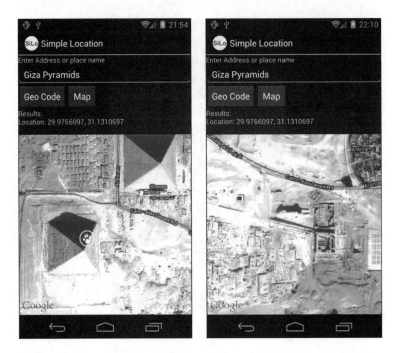

Figure 13.5   Results for "Giza Pyramids" on the left, panned east to the Sphinx on the right.

Zooming the Map View

Other times, panning won't help users. They might want to zoom in or out from the same location. Our application does not have to again implement the zoom controls, though. Instead, simply enable the built-in zoom controls as follows:

```
map.setBuiltInZoomControls(true);
```

When the user clicks on the map, the zoom controls fade in to view and are functional, as shown in Figure 13.6.

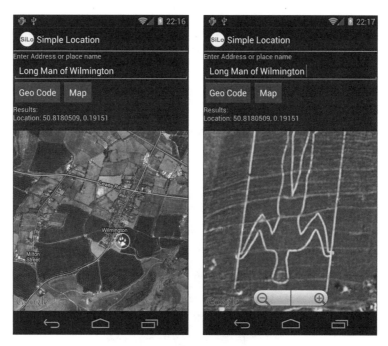

Figure 13.6   On the left, you see a bird's eye view of the town of Wilmington, but zoom in to the south and you see "The Long Man of Wilmington," as shown on the right.

Marking the Spot

Now that panning and zooming works, users might lose track of their position. Sure, they could just search again, but wouldn't it be more helpful if we marked the point of interest directly on the map? The Android SDK provides a few different ways to do this. One way is to use the `MapView` as a container for an arbitrary `View` object that can be assigned using a `GeoPoint` instead of typical screen or `View` coordinates. Another way is to use `ItemizedOverlay`, which is especially useful if you have more than one place to mark. Finally, you can manually draw items over the map using the `Overlay` and implement the `onDraw()` method.

For the place name finder example, we use the first method. Assuming you have a suitable map marker as a drawable resource, the following code demonstrates how to do this:

```
GeoPoint newPoint = new GeoPoint((int)(lat * 1E6), (int)(lon*1E6));

// add a view at this point
MapView.LayoutParams mapMarkerParams = new
```

```
MapView.LayoutParams(LayoutParams.WRAP_CONTENT,
LayoutParams.WRAP_CONTENT,
newPoint, MapView.LayoutParams.TOP_LEFT );

ImageView mapMarker = new ImageView(getApplicationContext());
mapMarker.setImageResource(R.drawable.paw);
map.addView(mapMarker, mapMarkerParams);
```

The `MapView` layout parameters enable you to set a `GeoPoint`. Doing this enables the added View to stay put at a geographic location and pan with the map, as shown in Figure 13.7.

Figure 13.7   "The Kremlin" at the top right of the marker
(paw print in a circle).

Keep in mind that the added View sticks around as long as the `MapView` does. If the application needs to present multiple locations to the user, though, there is a simpler way. Just use the `ItemizedOverlay` object.

In this example, a static `ItemizedOverlay` is created to represent the chain of backpacker huts in the White Mountains along the Appalachian Trail:

```
private class HutsItemizedOverlay
    extends ItemizedOverlay<OverlayItem> {

    public HutsItemizedOverlay(Drawable defaultMarker) {}

    protected OverlayItem createItem(int i) {}
    public int size() {}
}
```

To do this, we provide implementations for each of the required methods of
`ItemizedOverlay<OverlayItem>`. First, we define the constructor:

```
public HutsItemizedOverlay(Drawable defaultMarker) {
    super(defaultMarker);

    boundCenterBottom(defaultMarker);

    populate();
}
```

The `Drawable` passed in is one that we define later in the `onCreate()` method of
`MapActivity`. The system does not provide a default marker. The call to the
`boundCenterBottom()` method is made so that the map coordinates are at the center
bottom and the shadow is cast from the bottom of the marker, which is a more natural
look. The default shadow is from the top. If, however, we'd rather turn off the shadow
completely, you can override the `draw()` method, as follows:

```
@Override
public void draw(Canvas canvas, MapView mapView, boolean shadow) {
    super.draw(canvas, mapView, false);
}
```

Finally, in the constructor, we call the `populate()` method. This should be done as
soon as the location data is available. Because we have it statically compiled into the
application, we call it before returning. The `populate()` method calls our implementation of the `createItem()` method for as many items as we defined in our implementation of the `size()` method. Here is the implementation of our `createItem()` method,
along with a small array of hut locations, in no particular order:

```
public GeoPoint hutPoints[] = new GeoPoint[] {
    // Lakes of the Clouds
    new GeoPoint(44258793, -71318940),
    // Zealand Falls
    new GeoPoint(44195798, -71494402),
    // Greanleaf
    new GeoPoint(44160372, -71660385),
    // Galehead
    new GeoPoint(44187866, -71568734),
```

```
    // Carter Notch
    new GeoPoint(44259224, -71195633),
    // Mizpah Spring
    new GeoPoint(44219362, -71369473),
    // Lonesome Lake
    new GeoPoint(44138452, -71703064),
    // Madison Spring
    new GeoPoint(44327751, -71283283)
};

@Override
protected OverlayItem createItem(int i) {

    OverlayItem item = new OverlayItem(hutPoints[i], null, null);
    return item;
}
```

In the array, we've multiplied all the location values by one million so that they are in microdegrees, as required by the GeoPoint object. Within the createItem() method, the location array is indexed with the passed-in value. Neither of the two text fields, Title and Snippet, are used at this time, so they are set to null. The maximum index value is determined by the size() method, which, in this case, merely has to return the length of the array:

```
@Override
public int size() {
    return hutPoints.length;
}
```

The necessary ItemizedOverlay<OverlayItem> class is now implemented. Next, the application needs to tell the MapView about it. The following code demonstrates how to do this in the onCreate() method of our MapActivity:

```
@Override
protected void onCreate(Bundle data) {
    super.onCreate(data);
    setContentView(R.layout.huts);

    Drawable marker = getResources().getDrawable(R.drawable.paw);

    HutsItemizedOverlay huts = new HutsItemizedOverlay(marker);

    MapView map = (MapView)findViewById(R.id.map);
    map.setSatellite(true);

    List<Overlay> overlays = map.getOverlays();
    overlays.add(huts);
```

```
FrameLayout zoomFrame = (FrameLayout)
    findViewById(R.id.map_zoom_holder);
zoomFrame.addView(map.getZoomControls());
}
```

First, the `Drawable` is retrieved from the resources. Next, we instantiate the `HutsItemizedOverlay` object. The `OverlayItems` in it need to be added to the ones that might already exist within the `MapView`. The `getOverlays()` method of `MapView` returns a list of the current `Overlay` objects. Calling the `add()` method on this list inserts our new ones for each hut. Finally, the zoom controls are added to the `MapView` so that the user can zoom in and out. After launching this application and zooming in on New Hampshire, the user should see a screen like Figure 13.8.

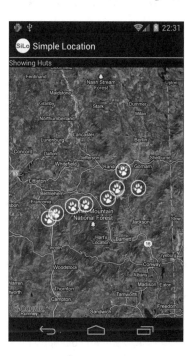

Figure 13.8   A map with markers at each of the Appalachian Mountain Huts of New Hampshire.

Forcing the user to pan and zoom to the location of the huts is not user-friendly. Two utility methods that the `ItemizedOverlay<OverlayItem>` class provides return values for the span of the location of the items. Combining this functionality with an override to the default behavior of the `getCenter()` method, which normally returns the location of the first item, enables the map to start to draw at a convenient zoom level covering all the huts. You can add this block of code to the `onCreate()` method to do just that:

```
MapController mapControl = map.getController();

mapControl.setCenter(huts.getCenter());
mapControl.zoomToSpan(
    huts.getLatSpanE6(), huts.getLonSpanE6());
```

The `getCenter()` method computes the average latitude and the average longitude across all the given hut locations. You can provide a central point or you can place the first item near the center of all the points requiring no override of the `getCenter()` method.

Doing More with Location-Based Services

You have been introduced to a number of different location tools provided on Android; however, you should be aware of several more.

The `LocationManager` supports proximity alerts, which are alerts that trigger a `PendingIntent` when the device comes within some distance of a location. This can be useful for warning the user of an upcoming turn in directions, for scavenger hunts, or help in geocaching.

You saw how to do `ItemizedOverlays`. In general, you can assign your own `Overlays` to draw custom objects and `Views` on the given `Canvas`. This is useful for drawing pop-up information for locations, putting logos over the map that don't move with the map, or putting hints for scavenger hunts over the map. This functionality is similar to displaying photos at a given location, which are often provided on Google Maps at famous locations.

The `GpsStatus`, `GpsStatus.Listener`, and `GpsSatellite` classes provide more detailed information about the GPS satellites used by the GPS engine. The `GpsStatus` and its `Listener` subclass monitor the GPS engine and get a list of the satellites used. The `GpsSatellite` class represents the current state of an individual satellite used by the GPS engine with state information such as satellite elevation and whether the particular satellite was used in the most recent GPS fix.

Tip

LBS applications are a popular category of Android applications. LBS services are like networking services: sometimes unreliable or unresponsive. Make sure to consider application responsiveness when designing LBS applications. This means completing LBS-related tasks asynchronously using threads or `AsyncTask` as well as considering Android services.

Summary

The Android SDK with Google Maps support is available to developers who register for a key, and it can be used to enhance Android applications with location-rich information. Some applications want to build in seamless map support, whereas others might just launch the built-in map application for the user to leverage. Developers can add to the information provided on the map by using various types of overlays to include even more information to the user. The opportunities for using location-based services to improve Android applications are only just beginning to be explored.

References and More Information

Android Dev Guide: "Location and Maps":
   http://d.android.com/guide/topics/location/index.html
Get your own Google Maps API key:
   http://code.google.com/android/add-ons/google-apis/mapkey.html

## 14

Using Android Multimedia APIs

Multimedia—whether we're talking about images, videos, or audio—has become a key driver of mobile device sales. Many modern "smart-devices" have built-in cameras to capture and display still images, video, and sophisticated music playback abilities. Your basic smartphone has at least one camera, sometimes two if you count the front-facing cameras used for video chat and self portraits. In this chapter, you learn how to capture still images using the camera, and you learn how to record and play back audio and video files.

Working with Multimedia

The Android SDK provides a variety of methods for applications to incorporate audio and visual media, including support for many different media types and formats. Individual Android devices and developers can extend the list of supported media to other formats. Not every Android device has the same multimedia capabilities. Always verify the capabilities of target devices before publication.

The multimedia features of the Android platform generally fall into three categories:

- Still images (recorded with the camera)
- Audio (recorded with the microphone, played back with speakers or audio output)
- Video (recorded with the camera and microphone, played back with speakers or video output)

Multimedia hardware such as a built-in camera, speakers, and audio or video output ports are optional features for Android devices.

In addition to requiring the appropriate permissions, you can specify which optional features your application requires within the Android Manifest file. You can do this using the `<uses-feature>` tag of the Android Manifest file to declare that your application uses the camera. Remember, though, that the `<uses-feature>` tag is not enforced by the Android platform. Instead, application stores such as the Android Market use this data to filter which applications to sell to certain devices.

Any application that requests the CAMERA permission is assumed to use all camera features. If your application accesses the camera, but can function properly without it, you can also set the android:required field of <uses-feature> to false. However, if your application requires a microphone and a camera with autofocus but not a flash to be present on the device, you can set the camera features your application requires specifically, like this:

```
<uses-feature android:name="android.hardware.microphone" />
<uses-feature android:name="android.hardware.camera" />
<uses-feature android:name="android.hardware.camera.autofocus" />
```

Tip

Many of the code examples provided in this chapter are taken from the SimpleMultimedia application. The source code for this application is provided for download on the book websites.

Working with the Camera

Many Android devices have at least one camera for capturing images and video. If the user's device has built-in camera hardware, the user can capture still images using the Camera object (android.hardware.Camera) of the Android SDK. You can use these images in a variety of ways, such as by customizing the home screen wallpaper using the WallpaperManager class.

Tip

Beginning in Android 4.0 (API Level 14), the system broadcasts when a new picture or video has been taken with the camera. Your applications can listen for these events and react to them.

Capturing Still Images Using the Camera

The Camera object controls the camera on devices that have camera support enabled. The preview feature of the camera relies on the assignment of a SurfaceHolder of an appropriate type. This enables applications to control the placement and size of the preview area that the camera can use.

Follow these steps to add camera capture capability to an application without having to draw preview frames (the CameraSurfaceView displays the camera view):

1. Create a new class extending SurfaceView and implement SurfaceHolder.Callback. For this example, we name this class CameraSurfaceView.

2. In the surfaceCreated() method, get an instance of the Camera object.

3. In the surfaceChanged() method, configure and apply the Camera.Parameters; then call the startPreview() method.

4. Add a method in CameraSurfaceView for capturing images.

5. Add the CameraSurfaceView to an appropriate layout.

6. Include some way, such as a button, for the user to trigger the capturing of images.

7. Implement a PictureCallback class to handle the storing of the captured image.

8. Add the android.permission.CAMERA permission to the AndroidManifest.xml file.

9. Release the Camera object in the surfaceDestroyed() method.

Let's start by looking at the CameraSurfaceView class:

```
import android.hardware.Camera;
import android.view.SurfaceHolder;
import android.view.SurfaceView;

private class CameraSurfaceView extends SurfaceView
    implements SurfaceHolder.Callback {

    private SurfaceHolder mHolder;
    private Camera camera = null;

    public CameraSurfaceView(Context context) {
        super(context);
        mHolder = getHolder();
        mHolder.addCallback(this);
        mHolder.setType(
            SurfaceHolder.SURFACE_TYPE_PUSH_BUFFERS);
    }

    public void surfaceChanged(SurfaceHolder holder,
        int format, int width, int height) {
    }

    public void surfaceCreated(SurfaceHolder holder) {
    }

    public void surfaceDestroyed(SurfaceHolder holder) {
    }

    public boolean capture(Camera.PictureCallback
        jpegHandler) {
    }
}
```

The constructor for the CameraSurfaceView configures the SurfaceHolder, including setting the SurfaceHolder type to SURFACE_TYPE_PUSH_BUFFERS, which is used by the camera internals. The constructor is appropriate for calling from an Activity's onCreate() method. When the display is ready, the surfaceCreated() method is called. Here we instantiate the Camera object:

```
public void surfaceCreated(SurfaceHolder holder) {
    camera = Camera.open();
    camera.setPreviewDisplay(mHolder);
}
```

The Camera object has a static method to retrieve a usable instance. Because the Surface is now available, the configured holder can now be assigned to it. Information about the Surface might not yet be available, but at the next call to the surfaceChanged() method, the camera parameters will be assigned and the preview will start, as shown here:

```
public void surfaceChanged(SurfaceHolder holder,
    int format, int width, int height) {
    List<Camera.Size> sizes = params.getSupportedPreviewSizes();

    Camera.Size pickedSize = getBestFit(sizes, width, height);
    if (pickedSize != null) {
        params.setPreviewSize(pickedSize.width, pickedSize.height);
        camera.setParameters(params);
    }
    camera.startPreview();
}
```

The surfaceChanged() method provides the application with the proper width and height for use with the camera preview. After assigning this to the Camera object, the preview starts. At this point, the users see whatever is in front of the camera on their device. If, however, you debug this within the emulator, you see a black-and-white checkerboard with an animated square on it, as shown in Figure 14.1. This is the simulated camera preview, so camera testing can take place, to some extent, on the emulator.

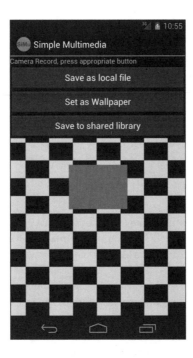

Figure 14.1   Emulator screen showing simulated camera view.

Note

The format parameter passed in to the surfaceChanged() method is not related to the format parameter of the setPreviewFormat() method of the Camera object.

When the Surface is no longer displayed, the surfaceDestroyed() method is called. Here is an implementation of the surfaceDestroyed() method suitable for this example:

```
public void surfaceDestroyed(SurfaceHolder holder) {
    camera.stopPreview();
    camera.release();
    camera = null;
}
```

In the surfaceDestroyed() method, the application stops the preview and releases the Camera object. If the CameraSurfaceView is used again, the surfaceCreated() method is called again, so this is the appropriate place to perform this operation.

The final step required to capture a still image is to add some way to call the `takePicture()` method of the `Camera` object. `CameraSurfaceView` can provide public access to the `Camera` object, but in this example, we provide a method to perform this within the `CameraSurfaceView` class:

```
public boolean capture(Camera.PictureCallback jpegHandler) {
    if (camera != null) {
        camera.takePicture(null, null, jpegHandler);
        return true;
    } else {
        return false;
    }
}
```

You can also use the `takePicture()` method to assign a callback suitable to play a shutter sound, or any other action just before the image is collected from the sensor. In addition, you can assign a `PictureCallback` to get raw data from the camera.

Note

The format of the raw camera data can vary from device to device.

The `CameraSurfaceView` object is now ready for use in an `Activity`. For this example, an `Activity` with a layout that contains a `FrameLayout` widget for positioning the preview is used. Here is a sample implementation of assigning the `cameraView` to the layout:

```
final CameraSurfaceView cameraView = new
    CameraSurfaceView(getApplicationContext());
FrameLayout frame = (FrameLayout) findViewById(R.id.frame);
frame.addView(cameraView);
```

Next, a `Button` click handler calls the `capture()` method of the `CameraSurfaceView` object. A sample implementation is shown here:

```
public void onClick(View v) {
    cameraView.capture(new Camera.PictureCallback() {

        public void onPictureTaken(byte[] data,
            Camera camera) {
            FileOutputStream fos;

            try {
                String filename = "capture.jpg";
                fos = openFileOutput(filename,
                    MODE_WORLD_READABLE);

                fos.write(data);
```

```
                fos.close();

        } catch (Exception e) {
            Log.e("Still", "Error writing file", e);
        }
    }
    });
}
```

The data that comes back from the callback can be written out directly to a JPEG file in the application file directory. If written as shown, though, the captured image is usable only by the application. In some cases, this might be suitable. However, the application might want to share the image with the rest of the device, for example, by including it within the Pictures application, which uses the `MediaStore` content provider. You do this by using the `ContentResolver` object to place an entry for the image in the media library.

Warning

As with all lengthy operations, you should perform large file system writes from a separate thread to keep the application interface as responsive as possible.

Configuring Camera Mode Settings

You can use the `Camera` class to configure the specific capture settings for a picture. Many of the capture settings are stored in the `Camera.Parameters` class, and set in the `Camera` class using the `setParameters()` method.

Working with Common Camera Parameters

Let's take a closer look at the `Camera.Parameters` class. Some of the most interesting camera parameters are:

- Flash modes (where flash hardware is available)
- Focus types (fixed point, depth of field, infinity, and so on)
- White balance settings (fluorescent, incandescent, and so on)
- Scene modes (snow, beach, fireworks, and so on)
- Effects (photo negative, sepia, and so on)
- Anti-banding settings (noise reduction)

Different parameters are supported by different devices, so always check for support before trying to enable parameters. Use the `Camera.Parameters` class to determine what camera features are supported. For example, you can use the set of methods called `getSupportedFlashModes()`, `getSupportedFocusModes()`, and so on. Also, the `Camera.Parameters` class contains methods to access more technical camera settings, such as exposure compensation and EXIF information.

Tip

The `Camera` class received a major upgrade in Android 4.0. Application developers now have much finer camera control, including the ability to set focus or metering areas, enable continuous auto-focusing, and more. See the `Camera` class documentation for details.

Zooming the Camera

The camera zoom setting is controlled using the `startSmoothZoom()` and `stopSmoothZoom()` methods of the `Camera` class. As you might expect, you can set zoom parameters using the `Camera.Parameters` class. Useful zoom methods in the `Camera.Parameters` class include

- Determining whether zooming is supported with `isZoomSupported()`
- Determining whether smooth zooming is supported with `isSmoothZoomSupported()`
- Determining the maximum zoom value with `getMaxZoom()`
- Retrieving the current zoom value with `getZoom()`
- Setting the current zoom value with `setZoom()`
- Calculating the zoom increments (for example, 1x, 2x, and 10x) with `getZoomRatios()`

Depending on the features available for a specific camera, zoom might be digital, optical, or some combination of the two.

Sharing Images

Storing an image in the local application directory, as demonstrated, might work for some applications; however, other applications might find it useful if the image goes in the shared image library on the device. The `ContentResolver` can be used in conjunction with the `MediaStore` object to push the image into the shared image library. The following example demonstrates storing the still image taken by the camera as an image file in the `MediaStore` content provider, using the same camera image callback:

```
public void onPictureTaken(byte[] data, Camera camera) {
    Log.v("Still", "Image data received from camera");
    try {
        Bitmap bm = BitmapFactory.decodeByteArray(
            data, 0, data.length);
        String fileUrl = MediaStore.Images.Media.
            insertImage(getContentResolver(), bm,
            "Camera Still Image",
            "Camera Pic Sample App Took");

        if (fileUrl == null) {
            Log.d("Still", "Image Insert failed");
```

```
        return;
    } else {
        Uri picUri = Uri.parse(fileUrl);
        sendBroadcast(new Intent(
            Intent.ACTION_MEDIA_SCANNER_SCAN_FILE,
            picUri));
    }
} catch (Exception e) {
    Log.e("Still", "Error writing file", e);
}
}
```

The image is turned into a `Bitmap` object, which is passed into the `insertImage()` method. This method creates an entry in the shared image library. After the image is inserted, we use the returned URL to create a `Uri` object representing the new image's location, which we instruct the media scanner to pick up by broadcasting a specialized intent. To determine whether the scan completed successfully, you can make a call to the static `MediaScannerConnection.scanFile()` method, and provide a `MediaScannerConnection.OnScanCompletedListener` class implementation.

Now the image is available to all applications that use the `MediaStore` content provider, such as the Pictures application.

Warning

To use the `MediaStore` with the emulator, you must have a mounted SD card image.

Additionally, although it's technically not necessary to force the media scanner to scan for new images, we've found that the Pictures application on the emulator and device might crash if the `MediaStore` does not perform a scan before trying to access the image. It's a good idea to send the `Intent` or use the `MediaScannerConnection` class.

Assigning Images as Wallpapers

Wallpapers are a great way for users to personalize their phones with interesting and fun images. The `WallpaperManager` class is used for all wallpaper interaction. You learn more about it in Chapter 22, "Extending Android Application Reach," when you create Live Wallpaper. For now, use it to set still image wallpapers.

The current wallpaper can be retrieved with a call to the `getDrawable()` or `peekDrawable()` methods. The methods `getDesiredMinimumHeight()` and `getDesiredMinimumWidth()` enable the application to programmatically determine the size that a wallpaper should be on the particular device. Finally, you can assign wallpaper through the `setResource()`, `setBitmap()`, and `setStream()` methods.

The following callback of the `Camera` object sets the wallpaper:

```
public void onPictureTaken(byte[] data, Camera camera) {
    Bitmap recordedImage =
        BitmapFactory.decodeByteArray(data, 0, data.length);
```

```
    try {
        WallpaperManager wpManager = WallpaperManager
            .getInstance(StillImageActivity.this);
        wpManager.setBitmap(recordedImage);
    } catch (Exception e) {
        Log.e("Still", "Setting wallpaper failed.", e);
    }
}
```

The image is copied locally for the wallpaper, so the original doesn't need to be kept, which is good in this case because it was never written to disk. You can remove the wallpaper completely with a call to the `clear()` method.

Finally, your application needs the `android.permission.SET_WALLPAPER` permission in the `AndroidManifest.xml` file.

> **Note**
>
> Prior to API Level 5 (Android 2.0), simple wallpaper commands were handled directly through the `Context` object. See the Android SDK documentation on the `Context.setWallpaper()` and `Context.getWallpaper()` methods for further information.

Choosing from Various Device Cameras

Many of the newer Android devices, especially the newer smartphones, have front-facing cameras and the main camera. Since API Level 9, the Android SDK has provided a method for accessing multiple cameras on devices. Leveraging the front-facing camera lends itself to all kinds of interesting application features in the realm of self portraiture and video chat.

All device cameras are accessed using the `Camera` class. To determine which camera is the front-facing camera, you need to iterate through the available cameras on the device and look for those with the front-facing attribute, as follows:

```
private int findFirstFrontFacingCamera() {
    int foundId = -1;
    int numCams = Camera.getNumberOfCameras();
    for (int camId = 0; camId < numCams; camId++) {
        CameraInfo info = new CameraInfo();
        Camera.getCameraInfo(camId, info);
        if (info.facing == CameraInfo.CAMERA_FACING_FRONT) {
            foundId = camId;
            break;
        }
    }
    return foundId;
}
```

Here, we use the `getNumberOfCameras()` method of the `Camera` class to iterate over each camera instance and retrieve its `CameraInfo`. We then check the facing field to determine whether the camera is a `CAMERA_FACING_FRONT` (or `CAMERA_FACING_BACK` if we were looking for other cameras besides the default). If so, we have found a front-facing camera to use. After you've detected an appropriate camera, you can use it as you would the normal device camera, as discussed earlier in this chapter.

Working with Video

In recent years, video has become commonplace on devices. Most devices on the market now can record and play back video, and this is no different with Android, although the specific video features might vary from device to device.

Recording Video

Android applications can record video using the `MediaRecorder` class. Using `MediaRecorder` is a matter of following a few simple steps:

1. Instantiate a new `MediaRecorder` object.
2. Set the video source.
3. Set the video output format.
4. Set the video size to record (optional).
5. Set the video frame rate (optional).
6. Set the video encoder.
7. Set the file to record to. (The extension must match output format.)
8. Set the preview surface.
9. Prepare the object for recording.
10. Start the recording.
11. Stop and release the recording object when finished.

Using some standard button controls, you can create an `Activity` to record and play back video using the preceding steps. The `onClick()` method for a record button might look like this:

```
public void onClick(View v) {
    if (videoRecorder == null) {
        videoRecorder = new MediaRecorder();
    }
    String pathForAppFiles =
        getFilesDir().getAbsolutePath();
    pathForAppFiles += RECORDED_FILE;

    videoRecorder.setVideoSource(
        MediaRecorder.VideoSource.CAMERA);
```

```
videoRecorder.setOutputFormat(
    MediaRecorder.OutputFormat.MPEG4 );

videoRecorder.setVideoSize(640, 480);
videoRecorder.setVideoFrameRate(30);
videoRecorder.setVideoEncoder(
    MediaRecorder.VideoEncoder.H264);

videoRecorder.setOutputFile(pathForAppFiles);
videoRecorder.setPreviewDisplay(surface);

videoRecorder.prepare();
videoRecorder.start();

// button handling and other behavior here
}
```

The `videoRecorder` object is instantiated and given some video configuration values for the recording source. There are several values for each video configuration setting; however, supported values can vary by device.

A Stop button configured with an `onClick()` handler might look like this:

```
public void onClick(View v) {
    if (videoRecorder!= null) {
        videoRecorder.stop();
        videoRecorder.release();
        videoRecorder = null;
    }
    // button handling and other behavior here
}
```

Finally, applications wanting to record video require the explicit permission `android.permission.CAMERA` set in the `AndroidManifest.xml` file.

Tip

Beginning in Android 4.0 (API Level 14), you can take still photos during video sessions if the device supports this feature. To do this, first check that the device supports this feature using the `isVideoSnapshotSupported()` method, and then call the `takePicture()` method of the `Camera` class.

Playing Video

The simplest way to play back video with the Android SDK is to use the `VideoView` control along with the `MediaController` widget to provide basic video controls. The following is an implementation of an `onCreate()` method in an `Activity` that demonstrates a workable video playback solution:

```
@Override
protected void onCreate(Bundle savedInstanceState) {
    super.onCreate(savedInstanceState);
    setContentView(R.layout.moving);

    VideoView vv = (VideoView) findViewById(R.id.video);
    MediaController mc = new MediaController(this);
    Uri video = Uri.parse(MOVIE_URL);

    vv.setMediaController(mc);
    vv.setVideoURI(video);
}
```

Note

The Android emulator doesn't play video files particularly well in all screen resolutions. Instead, it's best to test video code on the device.

A simple layout file with these controls might look like Figure 14.2. The `MediaController` presents a nice `ProgressBar` that shows download completion and the current location. The use of the `setAnchorView()` method of the `MediaController` is not needed when used with the `setMediaController()` method of the `VideoView` class—it's automatically set to the `VideoView`.

Figure 14.2   Screen showing video playback with default media
controller displayed.

The call to the setVideoURI() method automatically starts playback. You can create
a listener for when playback finishes using the setOnCompletionListener() method
of the ViewView. The VideoView object has several other helpful methods, such as
getDuration() and direct control over playback through methods such as pause().
For finer control over the media, or for an alternate way to play back media, you can use
the MediaPlayer object. Use of it is similar to using the Camera class—you need a
SurfaceHolder.

Warning

The MediaController can't be retrieved from a layout file XML definition by a call to
findViewById(). It must be instantiated programmatically and uses the Context of
the Activity class, not the application Context.

Note

When the URI to the video points to an Internet resource, your application will require the
android.permission.INTERNET permission in the manifest file.

Working with Face Detection

Beginning in Android 4.0 (API Level 14), the `Camera` class supports face detection. To detect faces, you can register a `Camera.FaceDetectionListener`. Then start the `Camera` and call the `startFaceDetection()` method to begin detecting faces. When a face is detected, you'll get an `onFaceDetection()` callback event, which returns an array of `Camera.Face` objects you can inspect. The `Camera.Face` class encapsulates a plethora of information about the face, including a bounded rectangle representing the facial area, a number of `Point` objects where the eyes and mouth of the face are thought to be located, as well as a numeric score for how confident the face detection engine is that you've detected a human face. When you're done, call `stopFaceDetection()`. For more information about face detection, see the most recent `Camera` class documentation.

Working with Audio

Much like video, the Android SDK provides methods for audio playback and recording. Audio files can be resources, local files, or `Uri` objects to shared or network resources. Audio recording takes place through the built-in microphone on the device, if one is present (typically a requirement for a phone because one speaks into it quite often).

Recording Audio

The `MediaRecorder` object of the Android SDK provides audio recording functionality. Using it is a matter of following a few simple steps you should now find familiar:

1. Instantiate a new `MediaRecorder` object.
2. Set the audio source.
3. Set the audio format to record with.
4. Set the file format to store the audio in.
5. Set the file to record to.
6. Prepare the object for recording.
7. Start the recording.
8. Stop and release the recording object when finished.

Using a couple simple buttons, you can create a simple `Activity` to record and play back audio using the preceding steps. The `onClick()` method for a record button might look like this:

```
public void onClick(View v) {
    if (audioRecorder == null) {
        audioRecorder = new MediaRecorder();
    }
    String pathForAppFiles =
```

```
            getFilesDir().getAbsolutePath();
        pathForAppFiles += RECORDED_FILE;

        audioRecorder.setAudioSource(
            MediaRecorder.AudioSource.MIC);
        audioRecorder.setOutputFormat(
            MediaRecorder.OutputFormat.DEFAULT);
        audioRecorder.setAudioEncoder(
            MediaRecorder.AudioEncoder.DEFAULT);

        audioRecorder.setOutputFile(pathForAppFiles);

        audioRecorder.prepare();
        audioRecorder.start();

        // button handling and other behavior here
}
```

The `audioRecorder` object is instantiated, if necessary. The default values for the recording source and output file work fine for our purposes. Of note are the values for `CAMCORDER`, which uses a microphone in the direction of the camera, and various voice values that can be used to record calls (beware of local laws) and choose the proper microphone for voice recognition uses.

Warning

If you find that recording does not start, check the file extension used. For instance, when using the MPEG4 container, the Android SDK requires that the file extension is `.mp4`; otherwise, the recording does not start.

A stop button is configured with an `onClick()` handler that looks like this:

```
public void onClick(View v) {
    if (audioRecorder != null) {
        audioRecorder.stop();
        audioRecorder.release();
        audioRecorder = null;
    }
    // button handling and other behavior here
}
```

Finally, applications that want to record audio require the explicit permission `android.permission.RECORD_AUDIO` set within the `AndroidManifest.xml` file.

Now it is time to add the playback functionality, so we can listen to the audio we just recorded.

Playing Audio

The `MediaPlayer` object can be used to play audio. The following steps are required to prepare a file for playback:

1. Instantiate a new `MediaPlayer` object.
2. Set the path to the file using the `setDataSource()` method.
3. Call the `prepare()` method of the `MediaPlayer` object.
4. Call the `start()` method to begin playback.
5. Playback can then be stopped with a call to the `stop()` method.

The `onClick()` handler for a button to play the recorded audio from the previous example might look like the following:

```
public void onClick(View v) {
    if (player == null) {
        player = new MediaPlayer ();
    }
    try {
        String audioFilePath =
            getFilesDir().getAbsolutePath();
        audioFilePath += RECORDED_FILE;

        player.setDataSource(audioFilePath);

        player.prepare();
        player.start();
    } catch (Exception e) {
        Log.e("Audio", "Playback failed.", e);
    }
}
```

The audio data source can be a local file path, valid file object, or valid `Uri` to an audio resource. You can programmatically stop the sound playback by a call to the `stop()` method. You can set a `MediaPlayer.OnCompletionListener` object to get a callback when the playback finishes. When done with the `MediaPlayer` object, you should use a call to the `release()` method to free up any resources it might be using, much like the releasing of the `MediaRecorder` object.

Tip

The `AudioManager` (`android.media.AudioManager`) is a system service. You can request the `AudioManager` by calling the `getSystemService(Context.AUDIO_SERVICE)` method. You can use the `AudioManager` to inspect, manage, and modify device-wide audio settings. A number of new APIs were added to the `AudioManager` in the Android 2.2 SDK for managing audio focus—that is, how multiple audio sources playing at the same time give one another "right of way," and so forth. This functionality can be crucial for audio-streaming applications like podcast and music players.

Sharing Audio

Audio can be shared with the rest of the system. The `ContentResolver` can send the file to the `MediaStore` content provider. The following code snippet shows how to configure an audio entry in the audio library on the device:

```
ContentValues values = new ContentValues(9);
values.put(MediaStore.MediaColumns.TITLE, "RecordedAudio");
values.put(MediaStore.Audio.Media.ALBUM,
    "Your Groundbreaking Album");
values.put(MediaStore.Audio.Media.ARTIST, "Your Name");
values.put(MediaStore.Audio.Media.DISPLAY_NAME,
    "The Audio File You Recorded In Media App");
values.put(MediaStore.Audio.Media.IS_RINGTONE, 1);
values.put(MediaStore.Audio.Media.IS_MUSIC, 1);
values.put(MediaStore.MediaColumns.DATE_ADDED,
    System.currentTimeMillis() / 1000);
values.put(MediaStore.MediaColumns.MIME_TYPE, "audio/mp4");
values.put(MediaStore.Audio.Media.DATA, pathForAppFiles);

Uri audioUri = getContentResolver().insert(
    MediaStore.Audio.Media.EXTERNAL_CONTENT_URI, values);
if (audioUri == null) {
    Log.d("Audio", "Content resolver failed");
    return;
}
```

Setting these values enables the recorded audio to be used by different audio-oriented applications on the device. For example, setting the `IS_MUSIC` flag enables the audio file to appear in the various sections of the music player and be sorted by its album information. Setting the `IS_RINGTONE` flag enables the audio file to appear in the list of ringtones for the device.

Periodically, the device scans for new media files. However, to speed up this process, a `BroadcastIntent` can be sent telling the system about new audio files. The following code demonstrates this for the audio added to the content library:

```
sendBroadcast(new Intent(
    Intent.ACTION_MEDIA_SCANNER_SCAN_FILE,audioUri));
```

After this intent is broadcast is handled, the audio file immediately appears in the designated applications.

Searching for Multimedia

You can use the search intent called `android.intent.action.MEDIA_SEARCH` to search for multimedia on a given device. You can also register an intent filter with your application to show up as a source for multimedia with this action. For example, you can perform a search for a specific artist and song like this:

```
Intent searchMusic = new Intent(
    android.provider.MediaStore.INTENT_ACTION_MEDIA_SEARCH);
searchMusic.putExtra(android.provider.MediaStore.EXTRA_MEDIA_ARTIST,
    "Cyndi Lauper");
searchMusic.putExtra(android.provider.MediaStore.EXTRA_MEDIA_TITLE,
    "I Drove All Night");
searchMusic.putExtra(android.provider.MediaStore.EXTRA_MEDIA_FOCUS,
    "audio/*");
startActivity(searchMusic);
```

If you load up a bunch of music on your device (such as Cyndi Lauper's "I Drove All Night") and launch this intent, you are then directed straight to the song you requested. Note that if you have many music apps installed, you might need to select an appropriate one (such as the Music application) the first time you send the Intent.

If you don't have any music on your device, but have several music apps, you may be prompted to pick the app that you want to perform this search. For example, Figure 14.3 shows what happens on one of our devices.

Figure 14.3   Screen showing video playback with default media
controller displayed.

Working with Ringtones

Much like wallpapers, ringtones are a popular way to personalize a device. The Android SDK provides a variety of ways to manage ringtones through the `RingtoneManager` object. You can assign the recorded audio from the previous example as the current ringtone with the following static method call:

```
RingtoneManager.setActualDefaultRingtoneUri(
    getApplicationContext(),
    RingtoneManager.TYPE_RINGTONE, audioUri);
```

The type can also be `TYPE_ALARM` or `TYPE_NOTIFICATION` to configure sounds of other system events that use audio tones. To successfully perform this operation, though, the application must have the `android.permission.WRITE_SETTINGS` permission set in the `AndroidManifest.xml` file. You can also query the default ringtone with a call to the static `RingtoneManager.getActualDefaultRingtoneUri()` method. You can use the resulting `Uri` to play the ringtone, which might be useful in applications that want to alert the user.

Summary

Use of multimedia in many applications can dramatically increase their appeal, usefulness, and even usability. The Android SDK provides a variety of APIs for recording audio, video, and images using the camera and microphone hardware; it also provides the capability to play audio and video and display still images. Newer devices support more fine-tuned camera usage, including application-level access to front-facing cameras and face-detection capabilities. Multimedia can be private to a specific application or shared among all applications using the `MediaStore` content provider.

References and More Information

Android Dev Guide: "Audio and Video":
    http://d.android.com/guide/topics/media/index.html
Android supported media formats:
    http://d.android.com/guide/appendix/media-formats.html
Android SDK documentation on the `Camera` class:
    http://d.android.com/reference/android/hardware/Camera.html
Android SDK documentation on the `android.media` package:
    http://d.android.com/reference/android/media/package-summary.html
Android SDK documentation on the `MediaPlayer` class:
    http://d.android.com/reference/android/media/MediaPlayer.html

15

Using Android Telephony APIs

Although the Android platform has been designed to run on almost any type of device, many of the Android devices currently available on the market are smartphones. Applications can take advantage of this fact by integrating phone or telephony features into their feature set. This chapter introduces you to the telephony-related APIs available in the Android SDK.

Working with Telephony Utilities

The Android SDK provides a number of useful utilities for applications to integrate phone features available on the device. Although devices run applications, phone operations generally take precedence on smartphones. Your application should not interrupt a phone conversation, for example. To avoid this kind of behavior, your application should know something about what the user is doing, so that it can react differently. For instance, an application might query the state of the phone and determine that the user is talking on the phone, and then choose to vibrate instead of play an alarm.

Tip

There are many different types of Android devices now available to consumers. If your application uses telephony features, make sure you set the `<uses-feature>` tag with the `android.hardware.telephony` feature (or one of its sub-features) in your application's manifest file to ensure your application is installed only on compatible devices. See the Android SDK documentation for more details.

In other cases, applications might need to place a call or send a text message. Phones typically support a Short Message Service (SMS), which is popular for texting (text messaging). Enabling the capability to leverage this feature from an application can enhance the appeal of the application and add features that can't be easily replicated on a desktop environment. Because many Android devices are phones, applications frequently deal with phone numbers and the contacts database; some might want to access the phone dialer to place calls or check phone status information. Adding telephony features to an application enables a more integrated user experience and enhances the overall value of the application to the users.

Tip

Many of the code examples provided in this chapter are taken from the SimpleTelephony application. The source code for this application is provided for download on the book's websites.

Gaining Permission to Access Phone State Information

Let's begin by looking at how to determine the telephony state of the device, including the capability to request the hook state of the phone, information of the phone service, and utilities for handling and verifying phone numbers. The TelephonyManager object in the android.telephony package is a great place to start.

Many of the method calls in this section require explicit permission set with the Android application manifest file. The READ_PHONE_STATE permission is required to retrieve information such as the call state, handset phone number, and device identifiers or serial numbers. The ACCESS_COARSE_LOCATION permission is required for cellular location information. Recall that we cover location-based services in detail in Chapter 13, "Using Location-Based Services APIs."

The following block of XML is typically needed in your application's AndroidManifest.xml file to access basic phone state information:

```
<uses-permission
    android:name="android.permission.READ_PHONE_STATE" />
```

Requesting Call State

You can use the TelephonyManager object to retrieve the state of the phone and some information about the phone service itself, such as the phone number of the handset.

You can request an instance of TelephonyManager using the getSystemService() method, like this:

```
TelephonyManager telManager = (TelephonyManager)
    getSystemService(Context.TELEPHONY_SERVICE);
```

With a valid TelephonyManager instance, an application can now make several queries. One important method is getCallState(). This method can determine the voice call status of the handset. The following block of code shows how to query for the call state and all the possible return values:

```
int callStatus = telManager.getCallState();
String callState = null;

switch (callStatus) {
        case TelephonyManager.CALL_STATE_IDLE:
            callState = "Phone is idle.";
            break;
```

```
        case TelephonyManager.CALL_STATE_OFFHOOK:
            callState = "Phone is in use.";
            break;
        case TelephonyManager.CALL_STATE_RINGING:
            callState = "Phone is ringing!";
            break;
    }
Log.i("telephony", callState);
```

The three call states can be simulated with the emulator through the Dalvik Debug Monitor Service (DDMS) tool. Querying for the call state can be useful in certain circumstances. However, listening for changes in the call state can enable an application to react appropriately to something the user might be doing. For instance, a game might automatically pause and save state information when the phone rings so that the user can safely answer the call. An application can register to listen for changes in the call state by making a call to the `listen()` method of `TelephonyManager`.

```
telManager.listen(new PhoneStateListener() {
    public void onCallStateChanged(
        int state, String incomingNumber) {

        String newState = getCallStateString(state);
        if (state == TelephonyManager.CALL_STATE_RINGING) {
            Log.i("telephony", newState +
                " number = " + incomingNumber);
        } else {
            Log.i("telephony", newState);
        }
    }
}, PhoneStateListener.LISTEN_CALL_STATE);
```

The listener is called, in this case, whenever the phone starts ringing, the user makes a call, the user answers a call, or a call is disconnected. The listener is also called right after it is assigned so an application can get the initial state.

Another useful piece of information is determining the state of the telephony service. This information can tell an application if the phone has coverage at all, if it can make emergency calls only, or if the radio for phone calls is turned off as it might be when in airplane mode. To do this, an application can add the `PhoneStateListener.LISTEN_SERVICE_STATE` flag to the listener described earlier and implement the `onServiceStateChanged` method, which receives an instance of the `ServiceState` object. Alternatively, an application can check the state by constructing a `ServiceState` object and querying it directly, as shown here:

```
int serviceStatus = serviceState.getState();
String serviceStateString = null;
switch (serviceStatus) {
```

```
    case ServiceState.STATE_EMERGENCY_ONLY:
        serviceStateString = "Emergency calls only";
        break;

    case ServiceState.STATE_IN_SERVICE:
        serviceStateString = "Normal service";
        break;

    case ServiceState.STATE_OUT_OF_SERVICE:
        serviceStateString = "No service available";
        break;

    case ServiceState.STATE_POWER_OFF:
        serviceStateString = "Telephony radio is off";
        break;
    }
Log.i("telephony", serviceStateString);
```

A status such as whether the handset is roaming can be determined by a call to the getRoaming() method. A friendly and frugal application can use this method to warn the user before performing any costly roaming operations such as data transfers within the application.

Requesting Service Information

In addition to call and service state information, your application can retrieve other information about the device. This information is less useful for the typical application but can diagnose problems or provide specialized services available only from certain provider networks. The following code retrieves several pieces of service information:

```
String opName = telManager.getNetworkOperatorName();
Log.i("telephony", "operator name = " + opName);

String phoneNumber = telManager.getLine1Number();
Log.i("telephony", "phone number = " + phoneNumber);

String providerName = telManager.getSimOperatorName();
Log.i("telephony", "provider name = " + providerName);
```

The network operator name is the descriptive name of the current provider that the handset connects to. This is typically the current tower operator. The SIM operator name is typically the name of the provider that the user is subscribed to for service. The phone number is defined as the MSISDN, typically the directory number of a GSM handset (that is, the number someone would dial to reach that particular phone).

Monitoring Signal Strength and Data Connection Speed

Sometimes an application might want to alter its behavior based on the signal strength or service type of the device. For example, a high-bandwidth application might alter stream quality or buffer size based on whether the device has a low-speed connection (such as 1xRTT or EDGE) or a high-speed connection (such as EVDO or HSDPA). The `TelephonyManager` class can be used to determine such information.

If your application needs to react to changes in telephony state, you can use the `listen()` method of `TelephonyManager` and implement a `PhoneStateListener` to receive changes in service, data connectivity, call state, signal strength, and other phone state information.

Working with Phone Numbers

Applications that deal with telephony, or even just contacts, frequently have to deal with the input, verification, and usage of phone numbers. The Android SDK includes a set of helpful utility functions that simplify handling of phone number strings. Applications can have phone numbers formatted based on the current locale setting. For example, the following code uses the `formatNumber()` method:

```
String formattedNumber =
    PhoneNumberUtils.formatNumber("9995551212");
Log.i("telephony", formattedNumber);
```

The resulting output to the log would be the string "999-555-1212" in my locale. Phone numbers can also be compared using a call to the `PhoneNumberUtils.compare()` method. An application can also check to see whether a given phone number is an emergency phone number by calling `PhoneNumberUtils.isEmergencyNumber()`, which enables your application to warn users before they call an emergency number. This method is useful when the source of the phone number data might be questionable.

> **Tip**
>
> There are a number of formatting utilities for formatting phone numbers based upon locale. Keep in mind that different countries format their numbers in different ways. For example, there is a utility method called `formatJapaneseNumber()` for formatting numbers with special prefixes in the Japanese style.

The `formatNumber()` method can also take an `Editable` as a parameter to format a number in place. The useful feature here is that you can assign the `PhoneNumberFormattingTextWatcher` object to watch a `TextView` (or `EditText` for user input) and format phone numbers as they are entered. The following code demonstrates the ease of configuring an `EditText` to format phone numbers that are entered:

```
EditText numberEntry = (EditText) findViewById(R.id.number_entry);
numberEntry.addTextChangedListener(
    new PhoneNumberFormattingTextWatcher());
```

While the user is typing in a valid phone number, the number is formatted in a way suitable for the current locale. Just the numbers for 19995551212 were entered on the `EditText` shown in Figure 15.1.

Figure 15.1   Screen showing formatting results after entering only digits.

Using SMS

SMS usage has become ubiquitous in the last several years. Integrating messaging services, even if only outbound, to an application can provide familiar social functionality to the user. SMS functionality is provided to applications through the `android.telephony` package.

Gaining Permission to Send and Receive SMS Messages

SMS functionality requires two different permissions, depending on whether the application sends or receives messages. The following XML, to be placed with `AndroidManifest.xml`, shows the permissions needed for both actions:

```
<uses-permission
    android:name="android.permission.SEND_SMS" />
<uses-permission
    android:name="android.permission.RECEIVE_SMS" />
```

Sending an SMS

To send an SMS, an application first needs to get an instance of the `SmsManager`. Unlike other system services, this is achieved by calling the static method `getDefault()` of `SmsManager`:

```
final SmsManager sms = SmsManager.getDefault();
```

Now that the application has an `SmsManager` instance, sending an SMS is as simple as a single call:

```
sms.sendTextMessage(
    "9995551212", null, "Hello!", null, null);
```

The application does not know whether the actual sending of the SMS was successful without providing a `PendingIntent` to receive the broadcast of this information. The following code demonstrates configuring a `PendingIntent` to listen for the status of the SMS:

```
Intent msgSent = new Intent("ACTION_MSG_SENT");


final PendingIntent pendingMsgSent =
    PendingIntent.getBroadcast(this, 0, msgSent, 0);
registerReceiver(new BroadcastReceiver() {
    public void onReceive(Context context, Intent intent) {
        int result = getResultCode();
        if (result != Activity.RESULT_OK) {
            Log.e("telephony",
                "SMS send failed code = " + result);
            pendingMsgReceipt.cancel();
        } else {
            messageEntry.setText("");
        }
    }
}, new IntentFilter("ACTION_MSG_SENT"));
```

The `PendingIntent pendingMsgSent` can be used with the call to the `sendTextMessage()`. The code for the message-received receipt is similar but is called when the sending handset receives acknowledgment from the network that the destination handset received the message.

If we put all this together with the preceding phone number formatting `EditText`, a new entry field for the message, and a button, we can create a simple form for sending an SMS message. The code for the button handling looks like the following:

```
Button sendSMS = (Button) findViewById(R.id.send_sms);
sendSMS.setOnClickListener(new View.OnClickListener() {
    public void onClick(View v) {
        String destination =
```

```
            numberEntry.getText().toString();

        String message =
            messageEntry.getText().toString();

        sms.sendTextMessage(destination, null, message,
            pendingMsgSent, pendingMsgReceipt);

        registerReceiver(...);
    }
}
```

After this code is hooked in, the result should look something like Figure 15.2. In this application, we used the emulator "phone number" trick (its port number). This is a great way to test sending SMS messages without using hardware or without incurring charges by the handset operator.

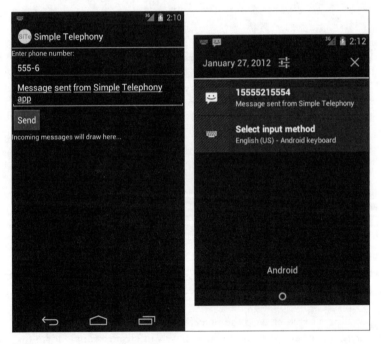

Figure 15.2   Two emulators, one sending an SMS from an application
and one receiving an SMS.

A great way to extend this is to set the sent receiver to modify a graphic on the screen until the sent notification is received. Further, you could use another graphic to indicate when the recipient has received the message. Alternatively, you can use ProgressBar widgets to track the progress to the user.

Receiving an SMS

Applications can also receive SMS messages. To do so, your application must register a
BroadcastReceiver to listen for the Intent action associated with receiving an SMS.
An application listening to SMS in this way doesn't prevent the message from getting to
other applications.

Expanding on the previous example, the following code shows how any incoming
text message can be placed within a TextView on the screen:

```
final TextView receivedMessage = (TextView)findViewById(
    R.id.received_message);

rcvIncoming = new BroadcastReceiver() {

    public void onReceive(Context context, Intent intent) {
        Log.i("telephony", "SMS received");
        Bundle data = intent.getExtras();
        if (data != null) {
            Object pdus[] =
                (Object[]) data.get("pdus");

            String message = "New message:\n";
            String sender = null;

            for (Object pdu : pdus) {
                SmsMessage part = SmsMessage.
                    createFromPdu((byte[])pdu);

                message += part.
                    getDisplayMessageBody();

                if (sender == null) {
                    sender = part.
                        getDisplayOriginatingAddress();
                }
            }
            receivedMessage.setText(
                message + "\nFrom: "+sender);
            numberEntry.setText(sender);
        }
    }
};

registerReceiver(rcvIncoming, new IntentFilter(
    "android.provider.Telephony.SMS_RECEIVED"));
```

This block of code is placed in the onCreate() method of the Activity. First, the
message Bundle is retrieved. In it, an array of Objects holds several byte arrays that

contain PDU data—the data format that is customarily used by wireless messaging protocols. Luckily, the Android SDK can decode these with a call to the static `SmsMessage.createFromPdu()` utility method. From here, we can retrieve the body of the SMS message by calling `getDisplayMessageBody()`.

The message that comes in might be longer than the limitations for an SMS. If it is, it will have been broken up in to a multipart message on the sending side. To handle this, we loop through each of the received `Object` parts and take the corresponding body from each, while only taking the sender address from the first.

Tip

When dealing with multipart text messages, it's important to know that the user might be charged the full texting charge for each part of the message. This can add up quickly. Care should be taken to warn users that applications that use any text messaging, sending, or receiving might incur charges by their operator.

An application can send a similar multipart message by taking advantage of the `SmsManager.divideMessage()` method. This method breaks up a `String` into parts no larger than the maximum size allowed by the SMS specification. The application could then use the method called `sendMultipartTextMessage()`, passing in the result of the call to `divideMessage()`.

Next, the code updates the text string in the `TextView` to show the user the received message. The sender address is also updated so that the recipient can respond with less typing. Finally, we register the `BroadcastReceiver` with the system. The `IntentFilter` used here, `android.provider.Telephony.SMS_RECEIVED`, is a well-known but undocumented `IntentFilter` used for this. As such, we have to use the string literal for it.

Warning

We strongly recommend watching for updates to the Android SDK in relation to this functionality. Future versions of the SDK might either add this string officially or remove the feature entirely. While it has continued to work for several versions of the platform, that is no guarantee of future functionality because it isn't publicly documented.

Making and Receiving Phone Calls

It might come as a surprise to the younger generation (they usually just text), but phones are often still used for making and receiving phone calls. Any application can be made to initiate calls and answer incoming calls; however, these abilities should be used judiciously so as not to unnecessarily disrupt the calling functionality of the user's device.

Tip

You can also use two emulator instances to test calling to another handset. As with the SMS sending, the port number of the emulator is the phone number that can be called.

Making Phone Calls

You've seen how to find out if the handset is ringing. Now let's look at how to enable your application to make phone calls as well.

Building on the previous example, which sent and received SMS messages, we now walk through similar functionality that adds a call button to the screen to call the phone number instead of messaging it.

The Android SDK enables phone numbers to be passed to the dialer in two different ways. The first way is to launch the dialer with a phone number already entered. The user then needs to press the Send button to actually initiate the call. This method does not require any specific permissions. The second way is to actually place the call. This method requires the `android.permission.CALL_PHONE` permission to be added to the application's `AndroidManifest.xml` file.

Let's look at an example of how to enable an application to take input in the form of a phone number and launch the Phone dialer after the user presses a button, as shown in Figure 15.3.

Figure 15.3   The user can enter a phone number in the `EditText` control and press the Call button to initiate a phone call from within the application.

We extract the phone number the user entered in the `EditText` field (or the most recently received SMS when continuing with the previous example). The following code demonstrates how to launch the dialer after the user presses the Call button:

```
Button call = (Button) findViewById(R.id.call_button);
call.setOnClickListener(new View.OnClickListener() {
    public void onClick(View v) {
        Uri number = Uri.parse("tel:" +
            numberEntry.getText().toString());
        Intent dial = new Intent(
            Intent.ACTION_DIAL, number);
        startActivity(dial);
    }
});
```

First, the phone number is requested from the `EditText` and `tel:` is prepended to it, making it a valid `Uri` for the `Intent`. Then, a new `Intent` is created with `Intent.ACTION_DIAL` to launch in to the dialer with the number dialed in already. You can also use `Intent.ACTION_VIEW`, which functions the same. Replacing it with `Intent.ACTION_CALL`, however, immediately calls the number entered. This is generally not recommended; otherwise, calls might be made by mistake. Finally, the `startActivity()` method is called to launch the dialer, as shown in Figure 15.4.

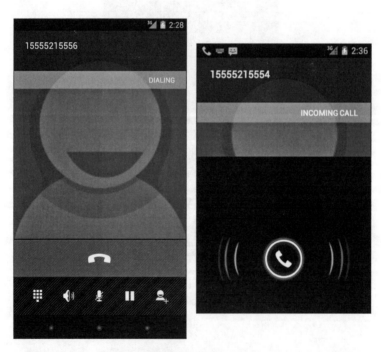

Figure 15.4   One emulator calling the other after the Call button is pressed in the application.

Receiving Phone Calls

Much like applications can receive and process incoming SMS messages, an application can register to answer incoming phone calls. To enable this in an application, you must implement a broadcast receiver to process intents with the action `Intent.ACTION_ANSWER`.

Remember, too, that if you're not interested in the call itself, but information about the incoming call, you might want to consider using the `CallLog.Calls` content provider (`android.provider.CallLog`) instead. You can use the `CallLog.calls` class to determine recent call information, such as

- Who called
- When they called
- Whether it was an incoming or outgoing call
- Whether or not anyone answered
- The duration of the call

Working with SIP

Session Initiated Protocol (SIP) is a protocol for controlling communication sessions. SIP is at the same networking protocol level as HTTP or SMTP. The Android SDK addded support for SIP in API Level 9. The SIP APIs can be found in the `android.net.sip` package. Although the SIP APIs support generic sessions, the only type of session that is handled automatically is a VOIP session.

Using SIP requires that you have a SIP account with a SIP service provider. Using SIP also requires the `android.permission.USE_SIP` permission to be set in your application's Android manifest file. Additionally, for market filtering, the `<uses-feature>` tag should be set with `android.software.sip` and `android.software.sip.voip` features.

For more information about creating an application that uses SIP, including a fully working sample application that comes with the Android SDK, please see the links provided in the "References and More Information" section at the end of this chapter.

What can you use SIP for? After all, aren't most Android devices still phones? In-app voice communication can be useful. Perhaps your service provides a custom SIP server where users can make voice connections with each other.

Summary

The Android SDK provides many helpful telephony utilities to handle making and receiving phone calls and SMS messages (with appropriate permissions) and tools to help with formatting phone numbers entered by the user or from other sources.

These telephony utilities enable applications to work seamlessly with the device's core phone features. Developers might also integrate voice calls and messaging features into their own applications, resulting in compelling new features. Messaging is more popular than ever, so integrating text messaging into an application can add a familiar and exciting social feature that users will likely enjoy.

References and More Information

3GPP specifications (SMS):
   http://www.3gpp.org/specifications
Wikipedia's writeup on SMS:
   http://en.wikipedia.org/wiki/SMS
Android samples: "SipDemo":
   http://developer.android.com/resources/samples/SipDemo/index.html
Android Dev Guide: "Session Initiated Protocol":
   http://d.android.com/guide/topics/network/sip.html

16

Accessing Android's Hardware Sensors

The Android Software Development Kit provides a variety of application programming interfaces for accessing low-level hardware features on the device. In addition to the camera, Android devices might have a number of other sensors and hardware. Some popular device sensors include the magnetic and orientation sensors, light sensors, and temperature sensors. Applications can also access battery state information. In this chapter, you explore the optional hardware APIs provided as part of the Android SDK.

Interacting with Device Hardware

The Android platform allows unprecedented access to the device's underlying hardware in a secure and robust manner. Because not all Android devices support or contain all hardware options, it is important to follow these guidelines when accessing underlying device hardware:

- Make no assumptions about the existence or availability of underlying hardware in code or otherwise.
- Always check and verify optional features before trying to access hardware programmatically.
- Pay special attention to exception handling and error and return value checking when working with hardware APIs.
- Understand that hardware features are device resources. Acquire them late, and release them as soon as you're done. In other words, play nice with the other apps. Don't hog the hardware or drain the device battery by misusing hardware resources.

Warning

The Android emulator has limited to no support for simulating hardware sensors and the device battery. These are cases when testing on real devices is crucial. Much of the code and APIs discussed in this chapter work only on Android hardware and do little or nothing in the Android emulator.

The optional hardware features of different Android devices are key market differentiators to consumers. For example, some might want a device that can act as a Wi-Fi hotspot. Others might require Bluetooth, which we talk about in Chapter 17, "Using Android's Optional Hardware APIs." Still others might be interested in the data that can be collected from various sensors on the device. Finally, applications can access data about the battery and the power management state. Also recall that we talked about other hardware-related features, such as the camera and location-based services, in Chapter 13, "Using Location-Based Services APIs," and Chapter 14, "Using Android Multimedia APIs," respectively.

Tip

Many of the code examples provided in this chapter are taken from the SimpleHardware application. The source code for this application is provided for download on the book's websites.

Using the Device Sensors

The Android SDK provides access to raw data from sensors on the device. The sensors, and their precision and features, vary from device to device. Some of the sensors that applications can interact with include the magnetic sensor, which can be used as a compass, and the accelerometer sensor that can detect motion.

You can access the device sensors through the `SensorManager` object (`android.hardware.SensorManager`). The `SensorManager` object listens for data from the sensors. It is a system service, and you can retrieve an instance retrieved with the `getSystemService()` method, as shown here:

```
SensorManager sensors =
    (SensorManager) getSystemService(Context.SENSOR_SERVICE);
```

Working with Different Sensors

The `Sensor` class (`android.hardware.Sensor`) defines a number of identifiers for the various sensors that you might find on a device. Not all sensors are available on each device. Some interesting sensors are listed here:

- `TYPE_ACCELEROMETER`: Measures acceleration in three directions; values are in SI units (m/s^2).

- `TYPE_GYROSCOPE`: Measures angular orientation in three directions; values are angles in degrees.

- `TYPE_LIGHT`: Measures ambient light; values are in SI lux units.

- `TYPE_MAGNETIC_FIELD`: Measures magnetism in three directions; the compass values are in micro-Tesla (uT).

- `TYPE_PRESSURE`: Measures barometric pressure.

- `TYPE_PROXIMITY`: Measures the distance to an object; values are in centimeters, or "near" versus "far."

- `TYPE_RELATIVE_HUMIDITY`: Measures the relative humidity.

- `TYPE_AMBIENT_TEMPERATURE`: Measures temperature.

The `SensorManager` class also has a number of constants that can be useful with certain sensors. For instance, you can use the `STANDARD_GRAVITY` constant with the accelerometer and the `LIGHT_SUNLIGHT` constant with the light sensor.

Tip

Not all sensors are available on all devices. For instance, the Galaxy Nexus Android device has a gravity, linear acceleration, magnetic sensor, pressure sensor, proximity sensor, and more, but no temperature sensors or humidity sensors.

Unfortunately, the emulator does not provide any sensor data. All sensor testing must be done on a physical device. Alternatively, OpenIntents.org also provides a handy Sensor Simulator (http://code.google.com/p/openintents/wiki/SensorSimulator). This tool simulates accelerometer, compass, and temperature sensors, and it transmits data to the emulator.

Configuring the Android Manifest File for Sensors

The `<uses-feature>` tag in the Android manifest file is used to indicate which sensors are required by your application. For example, to declare that your application requires the barometer, but can optionally use the gyroscope, you add the following to your application's manifest file:

```
<uses-feature android:name="android.hardware.sensor.barometer" />
<uses-feature
    android:name="android.hardware.sensor.gyroscope"
    android:required="false" />
```

A full list of sensor declarations can be found in the Android SDK documentation at http://developer.android.com/guide/topics/manifest/uses-feature-element.html#hw-features (http://goo.gl/CG1Va).

Acquiring a Reference to a Sensor

You can acquire a reference to a specific sensor using the `SensorManager` class method called `getDefaultSensor()`. This method takes a sensor type parameter. For example, you can acquire the default accelerometer sensor as follows:

```
Sensor accelSensor = sensors.getDefaultSensor(Sensor.TYPE_ACCELEROMETER);
```

Reading Sensor Data

After you have a valid `Sensor` object, you can read the sensor data periodically. Sensor values are sent back to an application using a `SensorEventListener` object that the application must implement and register using the `registerListener()` method.

```
boolean isAvailable = sensors.registerListener(SensorsActivity.this,
    accelSensor, SensorManager.SENSOR_DELAY_NORMAL);
```

In this case, the accelerometer sensor is watched. The `onSensorChanged()` method is called at particular intervals defined by the delay value in `registerListener()`, which is the default value in this case.

The `SensorEventListener` interface has two required methods you must implement: `onAccuracyChanged()` and `onSensorChanged()`. The `onAccuracyChanged()` method is called whenever the accuracy of a given sensor changes. The `onSensorChanged()` method is called whenever the values of the sensor change. The `onSensorChanged()` method is generally used to inspect sensor information.

Here is a sample implementation of `onSensorChanged()` that works for displaying various types of sensor data (not just the accelerometer):

```java
@Override
public void onSensorChanged(SensorEvent event) {
    StringBuilder sensorMessage =
        new StringBuilder(event.sensor.getName()).append(" new values: ");

    for (float value : event.values) {
        sensorMessage.append("[").append(value).append("]");
    }

    sensorMessage.append(" with accuracy ").append(event.accuracy);
    sensorMessage.append(" at timestamp ").append(event.timestamp);

    sensorMessage.append(".");

    Log.i(DEBUG_TAG, sensorMessage);
}
```

The onSensorChanged() method has a single parameter, a SensorEvent object. The SensorEvent class contains all the data about the sensor, including which sensor caused the event, the accuracy of the sensor, the sensor's current readings, and a timestamp. For details about what data to expect for each type of sensor, see the SensorEvent class documentation provided with the Android SDK.

The accelerometer sensor provides three values corresponding to the acceleration currently felt by the device on the x, y, and z axes. The barometer provides the atmospheric pressure in millibars, and fills only one of the value fields, as shown in Figure 16.1.

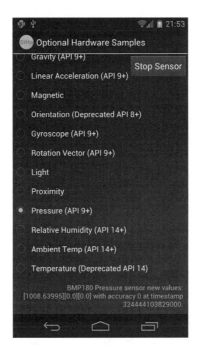

Figure 16.1   Sensor sample application showing barometric values.

Warning

Depending on the sensor in use, the rate of sensor data might be high. Be aware that your application should do as little as possible in the onSensorChanged() method. Do not make blocking calls. If you must process the data, pass the data on to a different thread, as described in Chapter 1, "Threading and Asynchronous Processing." Some devices modify the rate in other ways, such as slowing the rate down if the information is not changing quickly. Do not rely on the flow of sensor data for performing unrelated processing.

Calibrating Sensors

The sensor values won't be useful to the application until they are calibrated. One way to calibrate is to ask the user to click a button to calibrate the sensor. The application can then store the current values. Then new values can be compared against the original values to see how they have changed from their original values (delta). Although the phone sensors have a specific orientation, this enables the user to use the app in either portrait or landscape mode, regardless of how the user holds the device.

When registering a sensor, the `registerListener()` method returns `true` if the sensor is available and can be activated. It returns `false` if the sensor isn't available or cannot be activated.

The sensor values are typically quite sensitive. For most uses, an application probably wants to provide some smoothing of the values to reduce the effects of any noise or shaking. How this is done depends on the purpose of the application. For instance, a simulated bubble level might need less smoothing than a game where too much sensitivity can be frustrating. The orientation values might be appropriate in cases where only the device's orientation is needed but not the rate at which it is changed (accelerometer) or specific direction it's pointing (compass).

Determining Device Orientation

You can use the `SensorManager` class to determine the orientation of the device. Although the `Sensor.TYPE_ORIENTATION` sensor value is deprecated, it is still valid on most popular devices. However, the recommended way is to use the `getOrientation()` method of the `SensorManager` class instead.

The `getOrientation()` method takes two parameters: a rotation matrix and an array of three float values (azimuth [z], pitch [x], and roll [y]).

Finding True North

In addition to the `SensorManager`, there is a helpful class called `GeomagneticField` available in the `android.hardware` package. The `GeomagneticField` class uses the World Magnetic Model to estimate the magnetic field anywhere on the planet, which is typically used to determine magnetic variation between compass north and true north. This model, developed by the United States National Geospatial-Intelligence Agency (NGA), is updated for precision every five years. This model expires in 2015, although results are accurate enough for most purposes for some time after that date, at which point the Android `GeomagneticField` class will be likely updated to the latest model.

Monitoring the Battery

Mobile devices operate with the use of the battery. Although many applications do not need to know the state of the battery, some types of applications might want to change their behavior based on the battery level, charging state or power management settings.

For instance, a monitoring application can reduce the monitoring frequency when the battery is low and can increase it if the device is powered by an external power source. The battery levels can also help indicate the efficiency of an application, allowing developers to find areas where behavior can be modified to improve battery life, which would be appreciated by users.

To monitor the battery, the application must have the BATTERY_STATS permission. The following XML added to the AndroidManifest.xml file is sufficient:

```
<uses-permission
    android:name="android.permission.BATTERY_STATS" />
```

Then the application needs to register for a particular BroadcastIntent. In this case, it must be Intent.ACTION_BATTERY_CHANGED. The following code demonstrates this:

```
registerReceiver(batteryRcv,
    new IntentFilter(Intent.ACTION_BATTERY_CHANGED));
```

Next, the application needs to provide an implementation of the BroadcastReceiver. The following is an example of a battery monitoring BroadcastReceiver:

```
batteryRcv = new BroadcastReceiver() {

    public void onReceive(Context context, Intent intent) {
        int level =
            intent.getIntExtra(BatteryManager.EXTRA_LEVEL, -1);
        int maxValue =
            intent.getIntExtra(BatteryManager.EXTRA_SCALE, -1);
        int batteryStatus =
            intent.getIntExtra(BatteryManager.EXTRA_STATUS, -1);
        int batteryHealth =
            intent.getIntExtra(BatteryManager.EXTRA_HEALTH, -1);
        int batteryPlugged =
            intent.getIntExtra(BatteryManager.EXTRA_PLUGGED, -1);
        String batteryTech =
            intent.getStringExtra(BatteryManager.EXTRA_TECHNOLOGY);
        int batteryIcon =
            intent.getIntExtra(BatteryManager.EXTRA_ICON_SMALL, -1);
        float batteryVoltage =
            (float) intent.getIntExtra(BatteryManager.EXTRA_VOLTAGE,
                -1) / 1000;
        boolean battery =
            intent.getBooleanExtra(BatteryManager.EXTRA_PRESENT,
                false);
        float batteryTemp =
            (float) intent.getIntExtra(
```

```
        BatteryManager.EXTRA_TEMPERATURE, -1) / 10;
    int chargedPct = (level * 100)/maxValue ;

    String batteryInfo = "Battery Info:\nHealth=" +
        (String)healthValueMap.get(batteryHealth)+"\n" +
        "Status="+(String)statusValueMap.get(batteryStatus)+"\n" +
        "Charged % = "+chargedPct+"%\n"+
        "Plugged = " + pluggedValueMap.get(batteryPlugged) + "\n" +
        "Type = " + batteryTech + "\n"         +
        "Voltage = " + batteryVoltage + " volts\n" +
        "Temperature = " + batteryTemp + "°C\n"+
        "Battery present = " + battery + "\n";

    status.setText(batteryInfo);
    icon.setImageResource(batteryIcon);

    Toast.makeText(Battery.this, "Battery state changed",
        Toast.LENGTH_LONG).show();
    }

};
```

There are a couple of interesting items here. First, notice that the battery level isn't used directly. Instead, it's used with the scale, or maximum value, to find the percentage charged. The raw value wouldn't have much meaning to the user. The next property is the status. The values and what they mean are defined in the android.os.BatteryManager object. This is typically the charging state of the battery. Next, the health of the battery, also defined in the android.os.BatteryManager object, is an indication of how worn out the battery is. It can also indicate other issues, such as overheating. Additionally, the plugged value indicates whether the device is plugged in and, if it is, whether it uses AC or USB power. For more information about broadcast receivers, see Chapter 5, "Broadcasting and Receiving Intents."

Warning

On specific devices, not all this information is available or accurate. For instance, even though we see good data for most fields, we have noted in several instances that devices, including the Galaxy Nexus, return false for the present field or aren't including it at all. Proper testing might be required before relying on battery data for a particular device.

Some other information is returned as well, including an icon identifier that can visually display the state of the battery and some technical details, such as the type of battery, current voltage, and temperature. All displayed, this information looks something like what is shown in Figure 16.2.

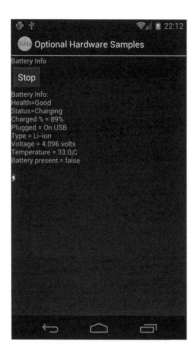

Figure 16.2   Screen capture showing values from the battery monitor
from a physical device.

Summary

Unlike many other mobile platforms, Android allows complete access to the underlying
hardware on the device, including the capability to read raw device sensor data and
monitor battery usage. It is important to remember that different devices have different
underlying hardware and sensors. Always verify the functionality available on each target
phone platform during the planning stage of your Android project.

References and More Information

Android API Reference: "Sensor Data Details":
    http://d.android.com/reference/android/hardware/SensorEvent.html#values
NOAA: "World Magnetic Model":
    http://www.ngdc.noaa.gov/geomag/WMM/DoDWMM.shtml

## 17

Using Android's Optional Hardware APIs

The Android Software Development Kit provides a variety of application programming interfaces for accessing low-level hardware features on the device. In addition to the camera, Android devices have other hardware resources that developers can take advantage of in their applications, such as Wi-Fi, NFC, Bluetooth radios, and a variety of USB connectivity options. In this chapter, you explore the optional hardware APIs provided as part of the Android SDK.

Working with Bluetooth

Bluetooth APIs have been available since API Level 5, though not all Android devices have Bluetooth hardware. However, this is a popular consumer feature that Android developers can use to their advantage. When Bluetooth hardware is present, Android applications can

- Scan for and discover Bluetooth devices and interact with the Bluetooth adapter.
- Establish RFCOMM connections and transfer data to and from devices via data streams.
- Maintain point-to-point and multipoint connections with Bluetooth devices and manage multiple connections.

The Bluetooth APIs are part of the `android.bluetooth` package. As you might expect, the application must have permission to use the Bluetooth services. The `android.permission.BLUETOOTH` permission is required to connect to Bluetooth devices. Similarly, Android applications must have the `android.permission.BLUETOOTH_ADMIN` permission to administer Bluetooth hardware and related services, which includes managing tasks, enabling or disabling the hardware, and performing discovery scans.

The Bluetooth APIs are divided into several useful classes, including the following:

- The `BluetoothAdapter` class represents the Bluetooth radio hardware on the local device.
- The `BluetoothDevice` class represents a remote Bluetooth device.
- The `BluetoothServerSocket` class is used to open a socket to listen for incoming connections and provides a `BluetoothSocket` object when a connection is made.
- The `BluetoothSocket` class is used by the client to establish a connection to a remote device. After the device is connected, the `BluetoothSocket` object is used by both sides to handle the connection and retrieve the input and output streams.

Tip

Many of the code examples provided in this section are taken from the SimpleWireless application. This source code for the SimpleWireless application is provided for download on the book's websites.

Checking for the Existence of Bluetooth Hardware

The first thing to do when trying to enable Bluetooth functionality in your application is to establish whether or not the device has a Bluetooth radio. You can do this by calling and checking the return value of the `BluetoothAdapter` class's static method called `getDefaultAdapter()`.

```
BluetoothAdapter btAdapter = BluetoothAdapter.getDefaultAdapter();
if (btAdapter == null) {
    Log.d(DEBUG_TAG, "No bluetooth available.");
    // ...
} else {
    // bt available
}
```

Tip

Applications that use Bluetooth should declare as such in the Android manifest file to ensure installation only on compatible devices. You can use the `<uses-feature>` manifest tag to indicate this application requirement, such as this: `<uses-feature android:name="android.hardware.bluetooth" />`.

Enabling Bluetooth

After you have determined that the device has a Bluetooth radio, you need to check to see whether it is enabled using the `BluetoothAdapter` class method called `isEnabled()`. If the Bluetooth adapter is enabled, you can proceed. Otherwise, you need to request that it is turned on. This can be done in several ways:

- Fire off the `BluetoothAdapter.ACTION_REQUEST_ENABLE` intent using the `startActivityForResult()` method. This launches an `Activity` that enables the user to choose to turn on the Bluetooth adapter. If the result is `RESULT_OK`, then Bluetooth has been enabled; otherwise, the user canceled the Bluetooth-enabling process.

- Call the `BluetoothAdapter enable()` method. This method should be used only by applications that need to explicitly enable the Bluetooth radio. It requires the `BLUETOOTH_ADMIN` permission. In addition, it should be performed only as the result of a direct request from the user, such as through a button, menu item, or query dialog.

- The process of making an Android device discoverable also automatically enables Bluetooth. This can be achieved by firing off the `BluetoothAdapter.ACTION_REQUEST_DISCOVERABLE` intent using the `startActivityForResult()` method. This launches an `Activity` that presents the user with a choice to make the device discoverable for a set amount of time.

Querying for Paired Devices

You can use the `BluetoothAdapter` to query for available Bluetooth devices to connect to. The `getBondedDevices()` method returns a set of `BluetoothDevice` objects that represent the devices paired to the Bluetooth adapter.

```
Set<BluetoothDevice> pairedBtDevices = btAdapt.getBondedDevices();
```

Discovering Devices

Bluetooth devices must be discovered and paired to the adapter before use. You can use the `BluetoothAdapter` to start and stop the discovery process for available Bluetooth devices to connect to. The `startDiscovery()` method starts the discovery process asynchronously. This method requires the `android.permission.BLUETOOTH_ADMIN` permission.

After you have initiated the discovery process, your application needs to register to receive broadcasts for the following `Intent` actions:

- `ACTION_DISCOVERY_STARTED`: Occurs when the discovery process initiates
- `ACTION_FOUND`: Occurs each time a remote Bluetooth device is found
- `ACTION_DISCOVERY_FINISHED`: Occurs when the discovery process completes

The discovery process is resource and time-intensive. You can use the `isDiscovering()` method to test whether the discovery process is currently underway. The `cancelDiscovery()` method can be used to stop the discovery process. This method should also be used any time a connection is about to be established with a remote Bluetooth device.

Establishing Connections Between Devices

The general idea behind connecting two devices via Bluetooth is for one device to find the other device via whatever means necessary, depending upon whether it be a previously paired device or found through discovery. After it's found, the device calls the connect() method. Both devices then have a valid BluetoothSocket object that can be used to retrieve the InputStream and OutputStream objects for initiating data communications between the two devices.

Now, that's where the theory ends and reality sets in. If it's the same application running on both devices, as it usually is, this means both devices should find a remote device and both should be discoverable so they can also be found, as well as open a listening socket via the BluetoothServerSocket object so they can receive incoming connection requests, and be able to connect to the other device. Add to that the fact that both the calls to the accept() method of the BluetoothServerSocket class and to the connect() method of the BluetoothSocket class are blocking synchronous calls, and you can quickly see you need to use some threads here. Discovery also uses a fair amount of the Bluetooth hardware resources, so you need to cancel and then later restart this process as appropriate. Performing discovery during a connection or even while attempting a connection likely leads to negative device performance.

Tip

The short code listings provided in the Bluetooth section are taken from the SimpleWireless application. The full source code for this application is provided for download on the book's websites. The code required to establish and maintain connections between two devices is lengthy. Therefore, we have chosen to discuss it broadly here and not to include full Bluetooth code listings in this section. Instead, please consult the sample project for a complete implementation of Bluetooth, including the ability to cause one device to make a "ping" sound (sonar style) on the other device.

Figure 17.1 shows a reasonable layout for a Bluetooth implementation and the threads used in the SimpleWireless project.

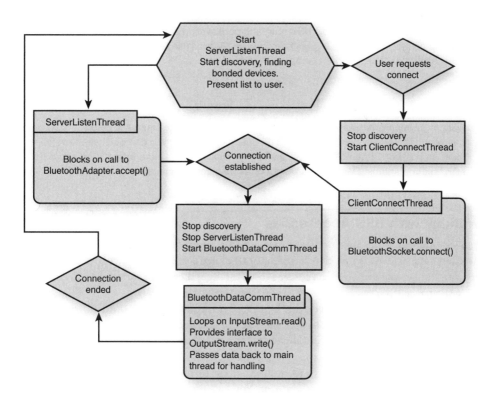

Figure 17.1   Diagram showing behavior flow for a Bluetooth application
on Android.

Working with USB

The Android platform supports a variety of flexible USB-related features. Android
devices can act as both USB peripherals (client devices) or USB hosts, depending on the
circumstances. This expands the opportunities available for developers to extend the
reach of their applications to a variety of situations. Android devices can act as remote
controllers or be controlled by accessories. You can even use the Android Open
Accessory Development Kit (ADK) to create new Android hardware accessories.

Tip

To debug on devices while they are connected to USB hardware, you can use adb over a
network connection.

Warning

Not all Android devices support USB host and accessory modes, so make sure you declare the appropriate `<uses-feature>` tags in your Android manifest file to make sure your application is installed only on compatible Android devices.

Developing Android Accessories with the ADK

Want to develop your own Android accessories? Check out the Open Accessory Development Kit, available in Android 3.1. Based on Arduino, you can purchase development boards from a number of suppliers and get hacking. For more information about the ADK, see the Android Dev Guide at http://d.android.com/guide/topics/usb/adk.html.

Working with USB Accessories

In accessory mode, the approved accessory acts as a controller, providing power to the Android device. Data can be transferred in both directions. The USB accessory APIs can be found under the `android.hardware.usb` package; they were introduced in Android 3.1 (API Level 12).

Your application can interface with USB accessories by accessing the USB system service using the `Context.getSystemService()` method. You can use the `UsbManager` class (`android.hardware.usb.UsbManager`) to discover and communicate with any USB accessories connected to the device.

The `UsbManager` class has a `getAccessoryList()` method, which lists all connected USB accessories available to the application. You can also set up a broadcast receiver to be notified when specific USB accessories are connected. Each USB accessory is represented as an `UsbAccessory` (`android.hardware.usb.UsbAccessory`) object. In order to connect to a USB accessory, you need to request permission from the user. When your application has received permission to communicate with the accessory, it can open a connection to the accessory and communicate using streams; this communication should be handled off the main UI thread. When it is complete, you can terminate your application's connection to the accessory.

Applications that rely on USB accessories have numerous Android Manifest file configuration details to consider. At minimum, applications should declare a `<uses-feature>` tag with the `android.hardware.usb.accessory` feature and set their minimum SDK to API Level 12 or higher. See the Android SDK class documentation for more details.

Tip

The USB accessory APIs were back-ported to Android 2.3.4 (API Level 10, though not Android 2.3.3, which is also API Level 10) as part of the third-party Google Add-on library so many more devices now support this functionality. There are subtle differences when working with the add-on version of the USB accessory APIs. This add-on is available for download in the Android SDK Manager.

Working as a USB Host

In host mode, the Android device acts as a controller, providing power to the connected USB device. Data can be transferred in both directions. The USB hosts APIs, and it can be found under the `android.hardware.usb` package. It was introduced in Android 3.1 (API Level 12).

Your application can interface with USB devices by accessing the USB system service using the `Context.getSystemService()` method. You can use the `UsbManager` class (`android.hardware.usb.UsbManager`) to discover and communicate with any USB devices available. You can also set up a broadcast receiver to be notified when specific USB devices are connected.

The `UsbManager` class has a `getDeviceList()` method that lists all connected USB devices available to the application. Each USB device is represented as a `UsbDevice` (`android.hardware.usb.UsbDevice`) object. To connect to a USB device, you need to request permission from the user. After your application has received permission to communicate with the device, it can open a connection to the device; this communication should be handled off the main UI thread. The Android SDK includes a number of classes for facilitating communication, including the `UsbInterface`, `UsbEndpoint`, `UsbDeviceConnection`, and `UsbRequest` classes (see the `android.hardware.usb` package for class details). After it is complete, you can terminate your application's connection to the device.

Applications that act as USB hosts have numerous Android Manifest file configuration details to consider. At minimum, applications should declare a `<uses-feature>` tag with the `android.hardware.usb.host` feature and set their minimum SDK to API Level 12 or higher. See the Android SDK class documentation for more details.

Working with Android Beam

Near Field Communications (NFC) isn't a new technology, but lately it's been gaining traction with Google's introduction of NFC in Android handsets starting with API Level 9, expanded in API Level 10, and simplified in API Level 14. Previously, you'd be lucky to find it in anything but Nokia devices. The most recent incarnation of NFC technology from Google is called Android Beam, which is an easy-to-market name for NDEF (NFC Data Exchange Format) Push over NFC, and is available in API Level 14 and later.

Read on for a brief introduction to using Android Beam in your applications.

Tip

The code listings in this section are taken from the SimpleWireless application. The full source code for this application is provided for download on the book's websites.

Enabling Android Beam Sending

In fact, sending is enabled by default and triggers automatically. When another NFC device is in range, the system shrinks the current screen of the foreground application and displays a message, "Touch to beam" (see Figure 17.2). If your application has no data to send, nothing happens.

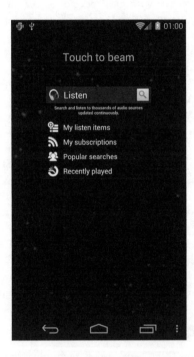

Figure 17.2   An app (Listen) in "Touch to beam" mode when near another NFC device.

What you want to know about is sending data with this tap. That's easy; just get an instance of the NfcAdapter class and call the setNdefPushMessageCallback() method with a valid CreateNdefMessageCallback instance. For example:

```
mNfcAdapter.setNdefPushMessageCallback(new CreateNdefMessageCallback() {
    @Override
    public NdefMessage createNdefMessage(NfcEvent event) {
        Time time = new Time();
        time.setToNow();
        String message = messageToBeam.getText().toString();
        String text = (message + " \n[Sent @ "
                + time.format("%H:%M:%S") + "]");
        byte[] mime = MIMETYPE.getBytes(Charset.forName("US-ASCII"));
        NdefRecord mimeMessage = new NdefRecord(
```

```
        NdefRecord.TNF_MIME_MEDIA, mime,
        new byte[0], text.getBytes());
    NdefMessage msg = new NdefMessage(
        new NdefRecord[] { mimeMessage,NdefRecord.
        createApplicationRecord("com.androidbook.simplewireless") });
    return msg;
    }
}, this);
```

The implementation of the `createNdefMessage()` method gets a `String` from an `EditText` control (`messageToBeam`), adds the time to it, and encapsulates it inside an `NdefRecord` object that is, itself, encapsulated in an `NdefMessage`. This message is returned and the system pushes it to the other device. You can register to be informed when the message has been successfully sent using the `setOnNdefPushCompleteCallback()` method of the `NfcAdapter`.

Receiving Android Beam Messages

Receiving messages is even more straightforward. Your `Activity` needs a new intent filter. Conveniently, NDEF messages come in as normal `Intent` objects.

```
<intent-filter>
    <action android:name="android.nfc.action.NDEF_DISCOVERED" />
    <category android:name="android.intent.category.DEFAULT" />
    <data android:mimeType="application/com.androidbook.simplewireless" />
</intent-filter>
```

Then you need to check the `Intent` contents to see whether it has an NDEF message. If so, extract the data you're looking for out of it (see Figure 17.3). This is just reversing the `NdefMessage` and `NdefRecord` creation from previously.

```
@Override
public void onResume() {
    super.onResume();
    // Did we receive an NDEF message?

    Intent intent = getIntent();
    if (NfcAdapter.ACTION_NDEF_DISCOVERED.equals(intent.getAction())) {
        try {
            Parcelable[] rawMsgs = intent
                .getParcelableArrayExtra(NfcAdapter.EXTRA_NDEF_MESSAGES);

            // we created the message, so we know the format
            NdefMessage msg = (NdefMessage) rawMsgs[0];
            NdefRecord[] records = msg.getRecords();
            byte[] firstPayload = records[0].getPayload();
            String message = new String(firstPayload);
            mStatusText.setText(message);
```

```
    } catch (Exception e) {
        Log.e(DEBUG_TAG, "Error retrieving beam message.", e);
    }
  }
}
```

Figure 17.3   Sending the message (left) and receiving it (right).

Incorporating Android Beam into your applications can be that easy. Looking to do something more complex? Check out the resources at the end of this chapter for further reading on NFC topics.

Configuring the Manifest File for Android Beam

Android Beam requires API Level 14. Using NFC requires the `android.permission.NFC` permission to be added to the application's Android manifest file. Additionally, `android.hardware.nfc` should be added as a `<uses-feature>` value to help app stores filter your application correctly to devices that have NFC hardware.

```
<uses-sdk
    android:minSdkVersion="14"
    android:targetSdkVersion="14" />
```

```
<uses-permission android:name="android.permission.NFC" />
<uses-feature
    android:name="android.hardware.nfc"
    android:required="true" />
```

Working with Wi-Fi

Developers can also integrate Wi-Fi features into their applications in two main ways; they can work with the Wi-Fi system service to find and connect to various Wi-Fi networks. Newer versions of the Android SDK also support Wi-Fi Direct, which helps facilitate connections.

Introducing Wi-Fi Direct

Wi-Fi Direct is a relatively new standard that attempts to solve the problems and difficulties with ad-hoc Wi-Fi—namely configuration and connection management. In doing so, a host Wi-Fi direct device basically becomes an access point and variation of the Protected Setup protocol is used to connect the two devices. With the longer range, faster data communications and simpler networking than Bluetooth, some think Wi-Fi Direct will ultimately replace Bluetooth for certain kinds of connections.

Wi-Fi Direct functionality first appeared in the Android SDK in the Android 4.0 (API Level 14). In fact, the Galaxy Nexus, the flagship Android 4.0 smartphone that shipped in late 2011, was one of the first Android devices to support Wi-Fi Direct for use by developers. The first certified Wi-Fi Direct smartphone was actually the Samsung Galaxy S Android device, back in November 2010, but no Android API was available at that time.

Using Wi-Fi Direct on Android is fairly straightforward; start by checking out the peer-to-peer Wi-Fi package `android.net.wifi.p2p`. Using the `WifiP2pManager` class (`android.net.wifi.p2p.WifiP2pManager`), you configure several callback classes that are used to asynchronously get the status of requests you make. You can also configure a broadcast receiver to handle various notifications as the state of Wi-Fi Direct changes, both in response to your requests and in changing availability of devices.

In terms of permissions, there is no distinction between regular Wi-Fi and Internet access and Wi-Fi Direct and peer-to-peer networking access. Thus, you need permissions for `INTERNET`, `ACCESS_WIFI_STATE`, `ACCESS_NETWORK_STATE`, `CHANGE_WIFI_STATE`, and `CHANGE_NETWORK_STATE`. Wi-Fi Direct requires API Level 14.

The fastest way to get started with exploring Wi-Fi Direct in code is using the WifiDirectDemo sample application that ships with the Android SDK. To create this project in Eclipse, simply choose New Android Project, Create project from existing sample, choose AOSP API 14, and then choose WiFiDirectDemo from the list of samples. Alternately, the source for the sample can be browsed online at http://developer.android.com/resources/samples/WiFiDirectDemo/index.html (http://goo.gl/2iJrX).

Monitoring Wi-Fi State

The Wi-Fi sensor can read network status and determine nearby wireless access points. The Android SDK provides a set of APIs for retrieving information about the Wi-Fi networks available to the device and Wi-Fi network connection details. This information can be used for tracking signal strength, finding access points of interest, or performing actions when connected to specific access points. This section describes how to get Wi-Fi information. However, if you are looking for information on networking, it is more thoroughly discussed as part of Chapter 11, "Using Android Networking APIs."

The following samples require two explicit permissions in the `AndroidManifest.xml` file. The `CHANGE_WIFI_STATE` permission is needed when an application is accessing information about Wi-Fi networks that can turn on the Wi-Fi radio, thus changing its state. The `ACCESS_WIFI_STATE` permission is also needed to request any information from the Wi-Fi device. You can add these to the `AndroidManifest.xml` file as follows:

```
<uses-permission
    android:name="android.permission.CHANGE_WIFI_STATE" />
<uses-permission
    android:name="android.permission.ACCESS_WIFI_STATE" />
```

The next thing the application needs is an instance of the `WifiManager` object. It is a system service, so the `getSystemService()` method works.

```
WifiManager wifi =
    (WifiManager) getSystemService(Context.WIFI_SERVICE);
```

Now that the `WifiManager` object is available, the application can do something interesting or useful with it. First, the application performs a Wi-Fi scan to see what access points are available in the local area. You need to complete a few steps to perform a scan:

1. Start the scan with the `startScan()` method of the `WifiManager` object.
2. Register a `BroadcastReceiver` for the `SCAN_RESULTS_AVAILABLE` intent.
3. Call `getScanResults()` to get a list of `ScanResult` objects.
4. Iterate over the results and do something with them.

You can perform the first two steps with the following code:

```
wifi.startScan();

registerReceiver(rcvWifiScan,
    new IntentFilter(WifiManager.SCAN_RESULTS_AVAILABLE_ACTION));
```

The sample `BroadcastReceiver` object, shown here, performs the last two steps. It is called regularly until the `stopScan()` method is called on the `WifiManager` object.

```
rcvWifiScan = new BroadcastReceiver() {

    public void onReceive(Context context, Intent intent) {
        List<ScanResult> resultList = wifi.getScanResults();
        int foundCount = resultList.size();

        Toast.makeText(WiFi.this,
            "Scan done, " + foundCount + " found",
            Toast.LENGTH_SHORT).show();
        ListIterator<ScanResult> results = resultList.listIterator();
        String fullInfo = "Scan Results : \n";
        while (results.hasNext()) {
            ScanResult info = results.next();
            String wifiInfo = "Name: " + info.SSID +
                "; capabilities = " + info.capabilities +
                "; sig str = " + info.level + "dBm";

            Log.v("WiFi", wifiInfo);

            fullInfo += wifiInfo + "\n";
        }

        status.setText(fullInfo);
    }
};
```

The ScanResult object contains a few more fields than demonstrated here. However, the SSID, or name, property is probably the most recognizable to users. The capabilities property lists such things as what security model can be used (such as "WEP"). The signal strength (level), as given, isn't all that descriptive for most users.

However, the WifiManager object provides a couple of helper methods for dealing with signal levels. The first is the calculateSignalLevel() that effectively turns the number into a particular number of "bars" of strength. You can use the second, compareSignalLevel(), to compare the relative signal strengths of two results.

Note

The emulator does not provide Wi-Fi emulation but the WifiManager APIs do work. However, there are not any results when you use them. Perform testing of Wi-Fi APIs on actual hardware that has a functional Wi-Fi radio.

You can use the WifiManager object to list known access points. These are typically access points that the user has configured or connected to in the past. The following code demonstrates the use of the getConfiguredNetworks() method:

```
ListIterator<WifiConfiguration> configs =
    wifi.getConfiguredNetworks().listIterator();

String allConfigs = "Configs: \n";
while (configs.hasNext()) {
    WifiConfiguration config = configs.next();
    String configInfo = "Name: " + config.SSID +
        "; priority = " + config.priority;

    Log.v("WiFi", configInfo);

    allConfigs += configInfo + "\n";
}

status.setText(allConfigs);
```

The returned `WifiConfiguration` object does not include all the fields that it could. For instance, it does not fill any network key fields. It does, however, fill in similar fields to those found in the `ScanResults` object. This can be used, for instance, to notify the users when they are in range of known Wi-Fi networks if their devices are set to not automatically connect.

You can use the `WifiManager` object to configure Wi-Fi networks, get the state of the Wi-Fi radio, and more. See the `android.net.wifi` package for more information.

Summary

Unlike many other mobile platforms, Android allows substantial access to the underlying hardware as well as devices attached via USB. Application developers can create new and exciting applications that leverage the Bluetooth, Wi-Fi, and Wi-Fi Direct technologies. They can also create applications that enable the device to act as a USB host or accessory. Developers can even use the ADK to develop their own Android USB accessories. It is important to remember that different devices have different underlying hardware. Always verify the functionality available on each target platform during the planning stage of your Android project.

References and More Information

Android Dev Guide: "Bluetooth":
    http://d.android.com/guide/topics/wireless/bluetooth.html
Android sample application, Bluetooth Chat:
    http://d.android.com/resources/samples/BluetoothChat/index.html
Android SDK documentation on the `android.net.wifi.p2p` package:
    http://d.android.com/reference/android/net/wifi/p2p/package-summary.html
Android Dev Guide: "Wi-Fi Direct":
    http://d.android.com/guide/topics/wireless/wifip2p.html

Wikipedia entry on Wi-Fi Direct:
  http://en.wikipedia.org/wiki/Wi-Fi_Direct
Android Dev Guide: "Near Field Communication":
  http://d.android.com/guide/topics/nfc/index.html
Android SDK documentation on the `android.nfc` package:
  http://d.android.com/reference/android/nfc/package-summary.html
Android Dev Guide: "USB Host and Accessory":
  http://d.android.com/guide/topics/usb/index.html
Android Dev Guide: "Android Open Accessory Development Kit":
  http://d.android.com/guide/topics/usb/adk.html

## 18

Developing Android 2D Graphics Applications

I n *Android Wireless Application Development Volume I: Android Essentials*, we talked about layouts and the various `View` classes available in Android to make screen design simple and efficient. Now we must think at a slightly lower level and talk about drawing objects on the screen. This chapter talks about the two dimensional drawing features built into the Android platform, including creating custom `View` classes and working with `Canvas` and `Paint` to draw shapes and text. You also learn about the hardware acceleration features of the Android platform and how to use them.

Drawing on the Screen

With Android, we can display images such as PNG and JPG graphics, as well as text and primitive shapes to the screen. We can paint these items with various colors, styles, or gradients and modify them using standard image transforms. We can even animate objects to give the illusion of motion.

Tip

Many of the code examples provided in this chapter are taken from the SimpleDrawing application. This source code for the SimpleDrawing application is provided for download on the book's websites.

Working with Canvases and Paints

To draw to the screen, you need a valid `Canvas` object. Typically, we get a valid `Canvas` object by extending the `View` class for our own purposes and implementing the `onDraw()` method.

For example, here's a simple `View` subclass called `ViewWithRedDot`. We override the `onDraw()` method to dictate what the `View` looks like; in this case, it draws a red circle on a black background.

```
private static class ViewWithRedDot extends View {
    public ViewWithRedDot(Context context) {
        super(context);
    }

    @Override
    protected void onDraw(Canvas canvas) {
        canvas.drawColor(Color.BLACK);
        Paint circlePaint = new Paint();
        circlePaint.setColor(Color.RED);
        canvas.drawCircle(canvas.getWidth()/2,
            canvas.getHeight()/2,
            canvas.getWidth()/3, circlePaint);
    }
}
```

We can then use this View like any other layout. For example, we might override the onCreate() method in our Activity with the following:

```
setContentView(new ViewWithRedDot(this));
```

The resulting screen looks something like Figure 18.1.

Figure 18.1   The ViewWithRedDot view draws a red circle on a black canvas background.

Understanding the `Canvas`

The `Canvas` (`android.graphics.Canvas`) object holds the draw calls, in order, for a rectangle of space. There are methods available for drawing images, text, shapes, and support for clipping regions.

The dimensions of the `Canvas` are bound by the container view. You can retrieve the size of the `Canvas` using the `getHeight()` and `getWidth()` methods.

Understanding the `Paint`

In Android, the `Paint` (`android.graphics.Paint`) object stores far more than a color. The `Paint` class encapsulates the style and complex color and rendering information, which can be applied to a drawable such as a graphic, shape, or piece of text in a given `Typeface`.

Working with `Paint` Colors

You can set the color of the `Paint` using the `setColor()` method. Standard colors are predefined in the `android.graphics.Color` class, an integer value can be used, and a helper method called `setARGB()` can be used to when you don't have the integer value for the color. For example, the following code sets the paint color to red:

```
Paint redPaint = new Paint();
redPaint.setColor(Color.RED);
```

Working with `Paint` Antialiasing

Anti-aliasing makes many graphics—whether they are shapes or typefaces—look smoother on the screen. This property is set in the `Paint` of an object.

For example, the following code instantiates a `Paint` object with anti-aliasing enabled:

```
Paint aliasedPaint = new Paint(Paint.ANTI_ALIAS_FLAG);
```

Working with `Paint` Styles

Paint style controls how an object is filled with color. For example, the following code instantiates a `Paint` object and sets the `Style` to `STROKE`, which signifies that the object should be painted as a line drawing and not filled (the default):

```
Paint linePaint = new Paint();
linePaint.setStyle(Paint.Style.STROKE);
```

Working with `Paint` Gradients

You can create a gradient of colors using one of the gradient subclasses. The different gradient classes (see Figure 18.2), including `LinearGradient`, `RadialGradient`, and `SweepGradient`, are available under the superclass `android.graphics.Shader`.

All gradients need at least two colors—a start color and an end color—but might contain any number of colors in an array. The different types of gradients are differentiated by the direction in which the gradient "flows." Gradients can be set to mirror and repeat as necessary.

You can set the Paint gradient using the setShader() method.

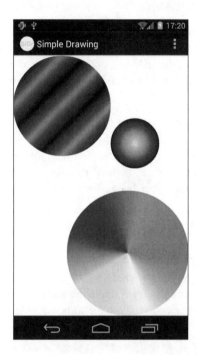

Figure 18.2　An example of a LinearGradient (top), a RadialGradient (right), and a SweepGradient (bottom).

Working with Linear Gradients

A *linear gradient* is one that changes colors along a single straight line. The top-left circle in Figure 18.2 is a linear gradient between black and red, which is mirrored.

You can achieve this by creating a LinearGradient and setting the Paint method setShader() before drawing on a Canvas, as follows:

```
import android.graphics.Canvas;
import android.graphics.Color;
import android.graphics.LinearGradient;
import android.graphics.Paint;
import android.graphics.Shader;
...
Paint circlePaint = new Paint(Paint.ANTI_ALIAS_FLAG);
```

```
LinearGradient linGrad = new LinearGradient(0, 0, 25, 25,
    Color.RED, Color.BLACK,
    Shader.TileMode.MIRROR);
circlePaint.setShader(linGrad);
canvas.drawCircle(100, 100, 100, circlePaint);
```

Working with Radial Gradients

A *radial gradient* is one that changes colors starting at a single point and radiating outward in a circle. The smaller circle on the right in Figure 18.2 is a radial gradient between green and black.

You can achieve this by creating a `RadialGradient` and setting the `Paint` method `setShader()` before drawing on a `Canvas`, as follows:

```
import android.graphics.Canvas;
import android.graphics.Color;
import android.graphics.RadialGradient;
import android.graphics.Paint;
import android.graphics.Shader;
...
Paint circlePaint = new Paint(Paint.ANTI_ALIAS_FLAG);
RadialGradient radGrad = new RadialGradient(250,
    175, 50, Color.GREEN, Color.BLACK,
    Shader.TileMode.MIRROR);
circlePaint.setShader(radGrad);
canvas.drawCircle(250, 175, 50, circlePaint);
```

Working with Sweep Gradients

A *sweep gradient* is one that changes colors using slices of a pie. This type of gradient is often used for a color chooser. The large circle at the bottom of Figure 18.2 is a sweep gradient between red, yellow, green, blue, and magenta.

You can achieve this by creating a `SweepGradient` and setting the `Paint` method `setShader()` before drawing on a `Canvas`, as follows:

```
import android.graphics.Canvas;
import android.graphics.Color;
import android.graphics.SweepGradient;
import android.graphics.Paint;
import android.graphics.Shader;
...
Paint circlePaint = new Paint(Paint.ANTI_ALIAS_FLAG);
SweepGradient sweepGrad = new
    SweepGradient(canvas.getWidth()-125,
    canvas.getHeight()-125,
    new int[] { Color.RED, Color.YELLOW, Color.GREEN,
    Color.BLUE, Color.MAGENTA, Color.RED }, null);
```

```
circlePaint.setShader(sweepGrad);
canvas.drawCircle(canvas.getWidth()-125,
    canvas.getHeight()-125, 125,
    circlePaint);
```

Working with Paint Utilities for Drawing Text

The `Paint` class includes a number of utilities and features for rendering text to the screen in different typefaces and styles. Now is a great time to start drawing some text to the screen.

Working with Text

Android provides several default font typefaces and styles. Applications can also use custom fonts by including font files as application assets and loading them using the `AssetManager`, much as one would use resources.

Using Default Fonts and Typefaces

By default, Android uses the Sans Serif typeface, but Monospace and Serif typefaces are also available. The following code excerpt draws some anti-aliased text in the default typeface (Sans Serif) to a `Canvas`:

```
import android.graphics.Canvas;
import android.graphics.Color;
import android.graphics.Paint;
import android.graphics.Typeface;
...
Paint mPaint = new Paint(Paint.ANTI_ALIAS_FLAG);
Typeface mType;

mPaint.setTextSize(16);
mPaint.setTypeface(null);

canvas.drawText("Default Typeface", 20, 20, mPaint);
```

You can instead load a different typeface, such as Monospace:

```
Typeface mType = Typeface.create(Typeface.MONOSPACE,
    Typeface.NORMAL);
```

Perhaps you would prefer *italic* text, in which case you can simply set the style of the typeface and the font family:

```
Typeface mType = Typeface.create(Typeface.SERIF,
    Typeface.ITALIC);
```

Warning

Not all typeface styles are supported by all typeface families. You need to test to make sure the typeface and style desired exists on the device.

You can set certain properties of a typeface such as antialiasing, underlining, and strike-through using the `setFlags()` method of the `Paint` object:

```
mPaint.setFlags(Paint.UNDERLINE_TEXT_FLAG);
```

Figure 18.3 shows some of the typeface families and styles available by default on Android.

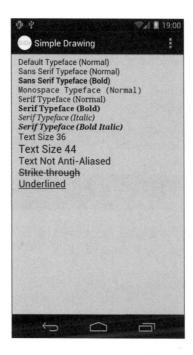

Figure 18.3   Some typefaces and typeface styles available on Android.

Using Custom Typefaces

You can easily use custom typefaces with your application by including the font file as an application asset and loading it on demand. Fonts might be used for a custom look-and-feel, for implementing language symbols that are not supported natively, or for custom symbols.

For example, you might want to use a handy chess font to implement a simple, scalable chess game. A chess font includes every symbol needed to implement a chessboard, including the board and the pieces. Hans Bodlaender has kindly provided a free chess font called Chess Utrecht. Using the Chess Utrecht font, the letter Q draws a black queen on a white square, whereas a q draws a white queen on a white square, and so on. This nifty font is available at http://www.chessvariants.com/d.font/utrecht.html as chess1.ttf.

To use a custom font, such as Chess Utrecht, simply download the font from the website and copy the `chess1.ttf` file from your hard drive to the project directory `/assets/fonts/chess1.ttf`.

Now you can load the `Typeface` object programmatically much as you would any resource:

```
import android.graphics.Typeface;
import android.graphics.Color;
import android.graphics.Paint;
...
Paint mPaint = new Paint(Paint.ANTI_ALIAS_FLAG);
Typeface mType =
    Typeface.createFromAsset(getContext().getAssets(),
    "fonts/chess1.ttf");
```

You can then use the Chess Utrecht typeface to "draw" a chessboard (see Figure 18.4) using the appropriate character sequences.

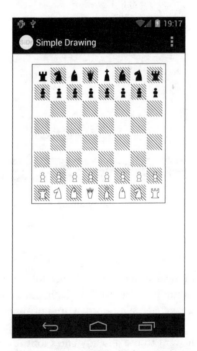

Figure 18.4   Using the Chess Utrecht font to draw a chessboard.

Measuring Text Screen Requirements

You can measure how large text with a given `Paint` is and how big of a rectangle you need to encompass it using the `measureText()` and `getTextBounds()` methods.

Working with Bitmaps

You can find lots of goodies for working with graphics such as bitmaps (including `NinePatch`) in the `android.graphics` package. The core class for bitmaps is `android.graphics.Bitmap`.

Drawing Bitmap Graphics on a Canvas

You can draw bitmaps onto a valid `Canvas`, such as in the `onDraw()` method of a `View`, using one of the `drawBitmap()` methods. For example, the following code loads a `Bitmap` resource and draws it on a canvas:

```
import android.graphics.Bitmap;
import android.graphics.BitmapFactory;
...
Bitmap pic = BitmapFactory.decodeResource(getResources(),
    R.drawable.bluejay);
canvas.drawBitmap(pic, 0, 0, null);
```

Scaling Bitmap Graphics

Perhaps you want to scale your graphic to a smaller size. In this case, you can use the `createScaledBitmap()` method, like this:

```
Bitmap sm = Bitmap.createScaledBitmap(pic, 50, 75, false);
```

You can preserve the aspect ratio of the `Bitmap` by checking the `getWidth()` and `getHeight()` methods and scaling appropriately.

Transforming Bitmaps Using Matrixes

You can use the helpful `Matrix` class to perform transformations on a `Bitmap` graphic (see Figure 18.5). Use the `Matrix` class to perform tasks such as mirroring and rotating graphics, among other actions.

The following code uses the `createBitmap()` method to generate a new `Bitmap` that is a mirror of an existing `Bitmap` called `pic`:

```
import android.graphics.Bitmap;
import android.graphics.Matrix;
...
Matrix mirrorMatrix = new Matrix();
mirrorMatrix.preScale(-1, 1);
```

```
Bitmap mirrorPic = Bitmap.createBitmap(pic, 0, 0,
    pic.getWidth(), pic.getHeight(), mirrorMatrix, false);
```

You can perform a 30-degree rotation in addition to mirroring by using this `Matrix` instead:

```
Matrix mirrorAndTilt30 = new Matrix();
mirrorAndTilt30.preRotate(30);
mirrorAndTilt30.preScale(-1, 1);
```

You can see the results of different combinations of tilt and mirror `Matrix` transforms in Figure 18.5. When you're no longer using a `Bitmap`, you can free its memory using the `recycle()` method:

```
pic.recycle();
```

Figure 18.5   A single-source bitmap: scaled, tilted, and mirrored using Android `Bitmap` classes.

There are a variety of other `Bitmap` effects and utilities available as part of the Android SDK, but they are numerous and beyond the scope of this book. See the `android.graphics` package for more details.

Working with Shapes

You can define and draw primitive shapes such as rectangles and ovals using the ShapeDrawable class in conjunction with a variety of specialized Shape classes. You can define Paintable drawables as XML resource files, but more often, especially with more complex shapes, this is done programmatically.

Tip

Many of the code examples provided in this section are taken from the SimpleShapes application. This source code for the SimpleShapes application is provided for download on the book's websites.

Defining Shape Drawables as XML Resources

You can define primitive shapes such as rectangles using specially formatted XML files in the /res/drawable/ resource directory, as discussed in *Android Wireless Application Development Volume I: Android Essentials*. The following resource file called /res/drawable/green_rect.xml describes a simple, green rectangle shape Drawable:

```
<?xml version="1.0" encoding="utf-8"?>
<shape xmlns:android=
    "http://schemas.android.com/apk/res/android"
    android:shape="rectangle">
    <solid android:color="#0f0"/>
</shape>
```

You can then load the shape resource and set it as the Drawable as follows:

```
ImageView iView = (ImageView)findViewById(R.id.ImageView1);
iView.setImageResource(R.drawable.green_rect);
```

You should note that many Paint properties can be set via XML as part of the Shape definition. For example, the following Oval shape is defined with a linear gradient (red to white) and stroke style information:

```
<?xml version="1.0" encoding="utf-8"?>
<shape xmlns:android="http://schemas.android.com/apk/res/android"
    android:shape="oval">
    <solid android:color="#f00"/>
    <gradient android:startColor="#f00"
        android:endColor="#fff"
        android:angle="180"/>
    <stroke android:width="3dp" android:color="#00f"
        android:dashWidth="5dp" android:dashGap="3dp"/>
</shape>
```

Defining Shape Drawables Programmatically

You can also define these `ShapeDrawable` instances programmatically. The different shapes are available as classes in the `android.graphics.drawable.shapes` package. For example, you can programmatically define the aforementioned green rectangle as follows:

```
import android.graphics.drawable.ShapeDrawable;
import android.graphics.drawable.shapes.RectShape;
...
ShapeDrawable rect = new ShapeDrawable(new RectShape());
rect.getPaint().setColor(Color.GREEN);
```

You can then set the `Drawable` for the `ImageView` directly:

```
ImageView iView = (ImageView)findViewById(R.id.ImageView1);
iView.setImageDrawable(rect);
```

The resulting green rectangle is shown in Figure 18.6.

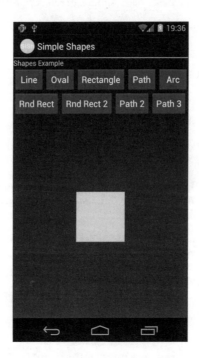

Figure 18.6   A green rectangle.

Drawing Different Shapes

Some of the different shapes available in the `android.graphics.drawable.shapes` package include the following:

- Rectangles (and squares)
- Rectangles with rounded corners
- Ovals (and circles)
- Arcs and lines
- Other shapes defined as paths

You can create and use these shapes as `Drawable` resources directly in `ImageView` views, or you can find corresponding methods for creating these primitive shapes in a `Canvas`.

Drawing Rectangles and Squares

Drawing rectangles and squares (rectangles with equal height/width values) is simply a matter of creating a `ShapeDrawable` from a `RectShape` object. The `RectShape` object has no dimensions but is bound by the container object—in this case, the `ShapeDrawable`. You can set some basic properties of the `ShapeDrawable`, such as the Paint color and the default size.

For example, here we create a magenta-colored rectangle that is 100 pixels long and 2 pixels wide, which looks like a straight, horizontal line. We then set the shape as the drawable for an `ImageView` so the shape can be displayed:

```
import android.graphics.drawable.ShapeDrawable;
import android.graphics.drawable.shapes.RectShape;
...
ShapeDrawable rect = new ShapeDrawable(new RectShape());
rect.setIntrinsicHeight(2);
rect.setIntrinsicWidth(100);
rect.getPaint().setColor(Color.MAGENTA);

ImageView iView = (ImageView)findViewById(R.id.ImageView1);
iView.setImageDrawable(rect);
```

Drawing Rectangles with Rounded Corners

You can create rectangles with rounded corners, which can be nice for making custom buttons. Simply create a `ShapeDrawable` from a `RoundRectShape` object. The `RoundRectShape` requires an array of eight float values, which signify the radii of the rounded corners. For example, the following creates a simple cyan-colored, rounded-corner rectangle:

```
import android.graphics.drawable.ShapeDrawable;
import android.graphics.drawable.shapes.RoundRectShape;
```

```
...
ShapeDrawable rndrect = new ShapeDrawable(
    new RoundRectShape( new float[] { 5, 5, 5, 5, 5, 5, 5, 5 },
    null, null));
rndrect.setIntrinsicHeight(50);
rndrect.setIntrinsicWidth(100);
rndrect.getPaint().setColor(Color.CYAN);
ImageView iView = (ImageView)findViewById(R.id.ImageView1);
iView.setImageDrawable(rndrect);
```

The resulting round-corner rectangle is shown in Figure 18.7.

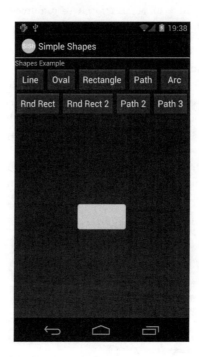

Figure 18.7   A cyan rectangle with rounded corners.

You can also specify an inner-rounded rectangle within the outer rectangle, if you choose. The following creates an inner rectangle with rounded edges within the outer white rectangle with rounded edges:

```
import android.graphics.drawable.ShapeDrawable;
import android.graphics.drawable.shapes.RoundRectShape;
...
float[] outerRadii = new float[]{ 6, 6, 6, 6, 6, 6, 6, 6 };
RectF insetRectangle = new RectF(8, 8, 8, 8);
float[] innerRadii = new float[]{ 6, 6, 6, 6, 6, 6, 6, 6 };
```

```
ShapeDrawable rndrect = new ShapeDrawable(
    new RoundRectShape(
    outerRadii,insetRectangle , innerRadii));

rndrect.setIntrinsicHeight(50);
rndrect.setIntrinsicWidth(100);
rndrect.getPaint().setColor(Color.WHITE);
ImageView iView = (ImageView)findViewById(R.id.ImageView1);
iView.setImageDrawable(rndrect);
```

The resulting round rectangle with an inset rectangle is shown in Figure 18.8.

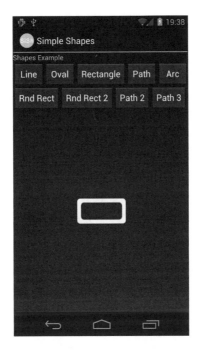

Figure 18.8   A white rectangle with rounded corners, with an inset
rounded rectangle.

Drawing Ovals and Circles

You can create ovals and circles (which are ovals with equal height/width values) by creating a ShapeDrawable using an OvalShape object. The OvalShape object has no
dimensions but is bound by the container object—in this case, the ShapeDrawable. You
can set some basic properties of the ShapeDrawable, such as the Paint color and the
default size. For example, here we create a red oval that is 40 pixels high and 100 pixels
wide, which looks like a Frisbee:

```
import android.graphics.drawable.ShapeDrawable;
import android.graphics.drawable.shapes.OvalShape;
...
ShapeDrawable oval = new ShapeDrawable(new OvalShape());
oval.setIntrinsicHeight(40);
oval.setIntrinsicWidth(100);
oval.getPaint().setColor(Color.RED);
ImageView iView = (ImageView)findViewById(R.id.ImageView1);
iView.setImageDrawable(oval);
```

The resulting red oval is shown in Figure 18.9.

Figure 18.9   A red oval.

Drawing Arcs

You can draw arcs, which look like pie charts or Pac-Man, depending on the sweep angle you specify. You can create arcs by creating a `ShapeDrawable` by using an `ArcShape` object. The `ArcShape` object requires two parameters: a `startAngle` and a `sweepAngle`. The `startAngle` begins at 3 o'clock. Positive `sweepAngle` values sweep clockwise; negative values sweep counterclockwise. You can create a circle by using the values 0 and 360.

The following code creates an arc that looks like a magenta Pac-Man:

```
import android.graphics.drawable.ShapeDrawable;
import android.graphics.drawable.shapes.ArcShape;
...
ShapeDrawable pacMan =
    new ShapeDrawable(new ArcShape(45, 270));
pacMan.setIntrinsicHeight(100);
pacMan.setIntrinsicWidth(100);
pacMan.getPaint().setColor(Color.MAGENTA);
ImageView iView = (ImageView)findViewById(R.id.ImageView1);
iView.setImageDrawable(pacMan);
```

The resulting arc is shown in Figure 18.10.

Figure 18.10   A magenta arc of 270 degrees, starting at 45 degrees
(resembling Pac-Man or a pie chart with 75 percent showing).

Drawing Paths

You can specify any shape you want by breaking it down into a series of points along a
path. The android.graphics.Path class encapsulates a series of lines and curves that
make up some larger shape.

For example, the following Path defines a rough five-point star shape:

```
import android.graphics.Path;
...
```

```
Path p = new Path();
p.moveTo(50, 0);
p.lineTo(25,100);
p.lineTo(100,50);
p.lineTo(0,50);
p.lineTo(75,100);
p.lineTo(50,0);
```

You can then encapsulate this star `Path` in a `PathShape`, create a `ShapeDrawable`, and paint it yellow.

```
import android.graphics.drawable.ShapeDrawable;
import android.graphics.drawable.shapes.PathShape;
...
ShapeDrawable star =
    new ShapeDrawable(new PathShape(p, 100, 100));
star.setIntrinsicHeight(100);
star.setIntrinsicWidth(100);
star.getPaint().setColor(Color.YELLOW);
```

By default, this generates a star shape filled with the `Paint` color yellow (see Figure 18.11).

Figure 18.11   A yellow star.

Or, you can set the `Paint` style to `Stroke` for a line drawing of a star.

```
star.getPaint().setStyle(Paint.Style.STROKE);
```

The resulting star would look something like Figure 18.12.

Figure 18.12   A yellow star using the stroke style of Paint.

Tip

The graphics support available in the Android SDK could be the subject of an entire book. After you have familiarized yourself with the basics, we recommend that you check out the APIDemos sample application provided with the Android SDK.

Leveraging Hardware Acceleration Features

Just about every Android application draws on the screen in some form or another. Whether you're using standard `View` controls or custom drawing, 2D hardware acceleration can improve your application. Android developers can easily harness the built-in hardware acceleration features added to the Android platform in Android 3.0 from within their applications. These newer versions of the Android platform boast an improved OpenGL rendering pipeline for common 2D graphics operations.

There's little reason not to leverage hardware acceleration for a smoother, more responsive experience for your users. You can simply take advantage of the default features, or you can fine-tune your application graphics acceleration at the application, `Activity`, `Window` or `View` level, if required.

Controlling Hardware Acceleration

Hardware acceleration is available on devices running Android 3.0 and higher. In fact, if your application has a `minSdkVersion` or `targetSdkVersion` set to API level 14 or greater, hardware acceleration is enabled for all windows. You may still want to control acceleration in your application, though. This can be done directly in the manifest file in the `<application>` and `<activity>` tags. Set the `android:hardwareAccelerated` attribute to `true` or `false`, depending on your needs. To control acceleration at the window or even for a specific `View` instance, you need to do this programmatically. For the window, use the `setFlags()` method with `WindowManager.LayoutParams.FLAG_HARDWARE_ACCELERATED` to enable acceleration. There is no programmatic way to disable acceleration. For a `View` control, use the `setLayerType()` method with the appropriate layer type, such as `View.LAYER_TYPE_HARDWARE`. For more information on layers, see the Android documentation at http://developer.android.com/guide/topics/graphics/hardware-accel.html#layers (http://goo.gl/6SWjd).

Fine-Tuning Hardware Acceleration

If you've got custom drawing operations or work with the `Canvas` and `Paint` classes in your application, you need to pay attention to which features are available in the Android hardware acceleration at this time. Certain `Canvas` and `Paint` operations are not currently supported, whereas others behave differently depending on hardware versus software acceleration. Notably, the methods `clipPath()`, `clipRegion()`, `drawPicture()`, `drawVertices()`, `drawPosText()`, and `drawTextOnPath()` are not supported in the `Canvas` class. In the `Paint` class, `setLinearText()`, `setMaskFilter()`, and `setRasterizer()` are not supported. The Android documentation has a list of specific drawing operations not fully supported by hardware acceleration at this time, available at http://developer.android.com/guide/topics/graphics/hardware-accel.html#unsupported (http://goo.gl/Zm73k).

Test your app thoroughly, and if you run into problems, you have a couple of options. You can work around any problems by re-implementing your drawing code using supported functionality. You can also turn off hardware acceleration on that `Activity`, `Window`, or specific `View` control and rely on the default software acceleration instead.

Tip

You can determine whether a `View` is leveraging hardware acceleration at runtime using the `View.isHardwareAccelerated()` method. You can disable hardware acceleration on a specific `View` control at runtime using the following method call:

```
setLayerType(View.LAYER_TYPE_SOFTWARE, null);
```

For more details about hardware acceleration on the Android platform, see the "References and More Information" at the end of this chapter.

Summary

The Android SDK comes with the `android.graphics` package, which includes powerful classes for drawing graphics and text to the screen in a variety of different ways. Some features of the graphics library include `Bitmap` graphics utilities, `Typeface` and font style support, `Paint` colors and styles, different types of gradients, and a variety of primitive and not-so-primitive shapes that can be drawn to the screen. Hardware acceleration is now enabled on the platform and may affect drawing operations.

References and More Information

Android SDK Documentation for the `android.graphics` package:
http://d.android.com/reference/android/graphics/package-summary.html
Android SDK Documentation for the `Bitmap` class:
http://d.android.com/reference/android/graphics/Bitmap.html
Android Dev Guide: "Hardware Acceleration":
http://d.android.com/guide/topics/graphics/hardware-accel.html

## 19

Working with Animation

This chapter talks about the different animation features built into Android. Here, we cover everything from using animated GIF and frame-by-frame animation to using the two animation frameworks that the Android SDK has to offer: tweened or view animation and the more robust property animation features that were added in later versions of the Android SDK.

Exploring Android's Animation Abilities

The Android platform supports several types of graphics animation:

- Animated GIF images
- Frame-by-frame animation
- Tweened animation (also known as view animation)
- Property animation

Animated GIFs store the animation frames in the image, and you simply include these GIFs like any other graphic-drawable resource. For frame-by-frame animation, the developer must provide all graphic frames of the animation. However, with tweened animation (or view animation), only a single graphic is needed, upon which transforms can be programmatically applied. Property animation, or the modification of any object property over a certain time duration, was added in Android 3.0. The Android animation framework also supports numerous interpolators for different animation effects.

Tip

Many of the code examples provided in this chapter are taken from the ShapeShifter application. This source code for the ShapeShifter application is provided for download on the book's websites.

Working with Frame-by-Frame Animation

You can think of frame-by-frame animation as a digital flipbook in which a series of similar images display on the screen in a sequence, each subtly different from the last. When you display these images quickly, they give the illusion of movement. This technique is called frame-by-frame animation and is often used on the Web in the form of animated GIF images.

Frame-by-frame animation is best used for complicated graphics transformations that are not easily implemented programmatically.

For example, we can create the illusion of a genie juggling gifts using a sequence of three images, as shown in Figure 19.1.

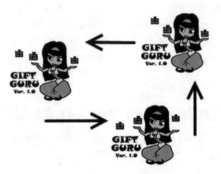

Figure 19.1   Three frames for an animation of a genie juggling.

In each frame, the genie remains fixed, but the gifts are repositioned slightly. The smoothness of the animation is controlled by providing an adequate number of frames and choosing the appropriate speed on which to swap them.

The following code demonstrates how to load three `Bitmap` resources (our three genie frames) and create an `AnimationDrawable`. We then set the `AnimationDrawable` as the background resource of an `ImageView` and start the animation:

```
ImageView img = (ImageView)findViewById(R.id.ImageView1);


BitmapDrawable frame1 = (BitmapDrawable)getResources().
    getDrawable(R.drawable.f1);
BitmapDrawable frame2 = (BitmapDrawable)getResources().
    getDrawable(R.drawable.f2);
BitmapDrawable frame3 = (BitmapDrawable)getResources().
    getDrawable(R.drawable.f3);


int reasonableDuration = 250;
AnimationDrawable mAnimation = new AnimationDrawable();
```

```
mAnimation.addFrame(frame1, reasonableDuration);
mAnimation.addFrame(frame2, reasonableDuration);
mAnimation.addFrame(frame3, reasonableDuration);

img.setBackgroundDrawable(mAnimation);
```

To name the animation loop continuously, we can call the `setOneShot()` method:

```
mAnimation.setOneShot(false);
```

To begin the animation, we call the `start()` method:

```
mAnimation.start();
```

We can end our animation at any time using the `stop()` method:

```
mAnimation.stop();
```

Although we used an `ImageView` background in this example, you can use a variety of different `View` controls for animations. For example, you can instead use the `ImageSwitcher` view and change the displayed `Drawable` resource using a timer. This sort of operation is best done on a separate thread. The resulting animation might look something like Figure 19.2—you just have to imagine it moving.

Figure 19.2   The genie animation in the Android emulator.

Working with Tweened Animations

With tweened animation (also called view animation), you can provide a single
Drawable resource—it is a Bitmap graphic (see Figure 19.3, left), a ShapeDrawable, a
TextView (see Figure 19.3, right), or any other type of View object—and the intermediate frames of the animation are rendered by the system. Android provides tweening
support for several common image transformations, including alpha, rotate, scale, and
translate animations. You can apply tweened animation transformations to any View,
whether it is an ImageView with a Bitmap, a shape Drawable, or a layout such as a
TableLayout.

Defining Tweening Transformations

You can define tweening transformations as XML resource files or programmatically. All
tweened animations share some common properties, including when to start, how long
to animate, and whether to return to the starting state upon completion.

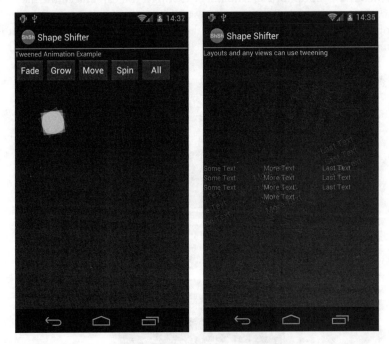

Figure 19.3   Rotating a green rectangle shape drawable (left) and a
TableLayout (right).

Defining Tweened Animations as XML Resources

You can store animation sequences as specially formatted XML files in the /res/anim/
resource directory. For example, the following resource file called /res/anim/spin.xml
describes a simple five-second rotation:

```
<?xml version="1.0" encoding="utf-8" ?>
<set xmlns:android
    = "http://schemas.android.com/apk/res/android"
    android:shareInterpolator="false">
    <rotate
        android:fromDegrees="0"
        android:toDegrees="360"
        android:pivotX="50%"
        android:pivotY="50%"
        android:duration="5000" />
</set>
```

Defining Tweened Animations Programmatically

You can programmatically define these animations. The different types of transformations are available as classes in the `android.view.animation` package. For example, you can define the aforementioned rotation animation as follows:

```
import android.view.animation.RotateAnimation;
...
RotateAnimation rotate = new RotateAnimation(
    0, 360, RotateAnimation.RELATIVE_TO_SELF, 0.5f,
    RotateAnimation.RELATIVE_TO_SELF, 0.5f);

rotate.setDuration(5000);
```

Defining Simultaneous and Sequential Tweened Animations

Animation transformations can happen simultaneously or sequentially when you set the `startOffset` and `duration` properties, which control when and for how long an animation takes to complete. You can combine animations into the `<set>` tag (programmatically, using `AnimationSet`) to share properties.

For example, the following animation resource file `/res/anim/grow.xml` includes a set of two scale animations: First, we take 2.5 seconds to double in size, and then at 2.5 seconds, we start a second animation to shrink back to our starting size:

```
<?xml version="1.0" encoding="utf-8" ?>
<set xmlns:android=
    http://schemas.android.com/apk/res/android
    android:shareInterpolator="false">
    <scale
        android:pivotX="50%"
        android:pivotY="50%"
        android:fromXScale="1.0"
        android:fromYScale="1.0"
        android:toXScale="2.0"
        android:toYScale="2.0"
        android:duration="2500" />
```

```
    <scale
        android:startOffset="2500"
        android:duration="2500"
        android:pivotX="50%"
        android:pivotY="50%"
        android:fromXScale="1.0"
        android:fromYScale="1.0"
        android:toXScale="0.5"
        android:toYScale="0.5" />
</set>
```

Loading Animations

Loading animations is made simple using the `AnimationUtils` helper class. The following code loads an animation XML resource file called `/res/anim/grow.xml` and applies it to an `ImageView` whose source resource is a green rectangle shape `drawable`:

```
import android.view.animation.Animation;
import android.view.animation.AnimationUtils;
...
ImageView iView = (ImageView)findViewById(R.id.ImageView1);
iView.setImageResource(R.drawable.green_rect);
Animation an =
    AnimationUtils.loadAnimation(this, R.anim.grow);
iView.startAnimation(an);
```

We can listen for `Animation` events, including the animation start, end, and repeat events, by implementing an `AnimationListener` class, such as the `MyListener` class shown here:

```
class MyListener implements Animation.AnimationListener {

    public void onAnimationEnd(Animation animation) {
        // Do at end of animation
    }

    public void onAnimationRepeat(Animation animation) {
        // Do each time the animation loops
    }

    public void onAnimationStart(Animation animation) {
        // Do at start of animation
    }
}
```

You can then register your `AnimationListener` as follows:

```
an.setAnimationListener(new MyListener());
```

Exploring the Four Different Tweening Transformations

Now let's look at each of the four types of tweening transformations individually. These types are

- Transparency changes (Alpha)
- Rotations (Rotate)
- Scaling (Scale)
- Movement (Translate)

Working with Alpha Transparency Transformations

Transparency is controlled using Alpha transformations. Alpha transformations can be used to fade objects in and out of view or to layer them on the screen.

Alpha values range from 0.0 (fully transparent or invisible) to 1.0 (fully opaque or visible). Alpha animations involve a starting transparency (fromAlpha) and an ending transparency (toAlpha).

The following XML resource file excerpt defines a transparency-change animation, taking five seconds to fade in from fully transparent to fully opaque:

```
<alpha
    android:fromAlpha="0.0"
    android:toAlpha="1.0"
    android:duration="5000">
</alpha>
```

Programmatically, you can create this same animation using the AlphaAnimation class within the android.view.animation package.

Working with Rotating Transformations

You can use rotation operations to spin objects clockwise or counterclockwise around a pivot point in the object's boundaries.

Rotations are defined in terms of degrees. For example, you might want an object to make one complete clockwise rotation. To do this, you set the fromDegrees property to 0 and the toDegrees property to 360. To rotate the object counterclockwise instead, you set the toDegrees property to −360.

By default, the object pivots around the (0,0) coordinate, or the top-left corner of the object. This is great for rotations such as those of a clock's hands, but much of the time, you want to pivot from the center of the object. You can do this easily by setting the pivot point, which can be a fixed coordinate or a percentage.

The following XML resource file excerpt defines a rotation animation, taking five seconds to make one full clockwise rotation, pivoting from the center of the object:

```
<rotate
    android:fromDegrees="0"
    android:toDegrees="360"
```

```
android:pivotX="50%"
android:pivotY="50%"
android:duration="5000" />
```

Programmatically, you can create this same animation using the `RotateAnimation` class in the `android.view.animation` package.

Working with Scaling Transformations

You can use scaling operations to stretch objects vertically and horizontally. Scaling operations are defined as relative scales. Think of the scale value of 1.0 as 100 percent, or full-size. To scale to half-size, or 50 percent, set the target scale value of 0.5.

You can scale horizontally and vertically on different scales or on the same scale (to preserve aspect ratio). You need to set four values for proper scaling: starting scale (`fromXScale`, `fromYScale`) and target scale (`toXScale`, `toYScale`). Again, you can use a pivot point to stretch your object from a specific (x,y) coordinate such as the center or another coordinate.

The following XML resource file excerpt defines a scaling animation, taking five seconds to double an object's size, pivoting from the center of the object:

```
<scale
    android:pivotX="50%"
    android:pivotY="50%"
    android:fromXScale="1.0"
    android:fromYScale="1.0"
    android:toXScale="2.0"
    android:toYScale="2.0"
    android:duration="5000" />
```

Programmatically, you can create this same animation using the `ScaleAnimation` class within the `android.view.animation` package.

Working with Moving Transformations

You can move objects around using translate operations. Translate operations move an object from one position on the (x,y) coordinate to another coordinate.

To perform a translate operation, you must specify the change, or delta, in the object's coordinates. You can set four values for translations: starting position (`fromXDelta`, `fromYDelta`) and relative target location (`toXDelta`, `toYDelta`).

The following XML resource file excerpt defines a translate animation, taking 5 seconds to move an object up (negative) by 100 on the y-axis. We also set the `fillAfter` property to be true, so the object doesn't "jump" back to its starting position when the animation finishes:

```
<translate android:toYDelta="-100"
    android:fillAfter="true"
    android:duration="2500" />
```

Programmatically, you can create this same animation using the `TranslateAnimation` class in the `android.view.animation` package.

Working with Property Animation

Introduced in Android API Level 11 and refined in Android API Level 12, property animation is the capability to animate any object property over time. The property animation system is much more flexible and robust than the features available in the tweened view animation framework. Unlike the view animation framework, when property animation is used, the properties of the objects (such as a `View` control) are actually modified over the course of time, as opposed to just drawn with the underlying object remaining unchanged.

Property animation can be configured in the following ways:

- Animations can be applied to value or object types.

- Animations can use the various interpolators available on the platform.

- Animations can be defined in sets, with multiple attributes changing simultaneously or in sequence.

- Animations are created separate from the target objects they are applied to, and can be reused.

- Animation duration, repeat count (a number or infinite), repeat behavior (repeat from the beginning or reverse), and other animation characteristics can be set as needed.

Tip

The code examples provided in this section are taken from the SimplePropertyAnimation application. This source code for the SimplePropertyAnimation application is provided for download on the book websites.

There are several important classes you'll want to be aware of for property animation:

- The `ValueAnimator` class (`android.animation.ValueAnimator`) is the base class for all property animations.

- The `ObjectAnimator` class (`android.animation.ObjectAnimator`) is the convenience class for animating a specific target object and property. This is the class you will use most frequently for animating properties on objects like `View` controls.

- The `ViewPropertyAnimator` class (`android.animation.ViewPropertyAnimator`) enables optimized and easy animation for `View` objects. The `animate()` method of `View` objects provides access to this class and its performance may be better than alternate methods. In fact, the results may be hardware accelerated.

- There are a number of evaluator classes (`android.animation.*`), such as `IntEvaluator`, `FloatEvaluator`, `ArgbEvaluator`, and `TypeEvaluator`. These enable you to animate any type of property an object can have by defining how to calculate changes in the property over time.

In addition to these classes, which are specific to property animation, you also use the standard `AnimationSet` and interpolator classes.

Defining Property Animations as XML Resources

Property animation sets can be configured via XML, much like view animations. You can store property animation sequences as specially formatted XML files in the `/res/animator/` resource directory.

> **Tip**
>
> Although you can save your animation resources wherever you like, it is recommended in Android 3.1+ that property animation resources be stored in the `/res/animator/` resource directory instead of the `/res/anim` directory so that the Eclipse ADT plug-in can find them.

A property animation has a number of attributes, including:

- A duration—the amount of time it takes, in milliseconds, for the animation to complete. This value is set with the `android:duration` attribute.

- A property name—the name of the property to be modified in the animation. This value is set with the `android:propertyName` attribute; drop the `android:` from the property name. Only properties with getter/setter methods that return int or float should be used.

- The repeat count—the number of times this animation should take place. This value is set with the `android:repeatCount` attribute. If you want the animation to repeat without stopping, use −1.

- The repeat mode—the way the animation repeats. This value is set with the `android:repeatMode` attribute. If you want the animation to repeat by resetting and starting from the beginning, use repeat. If you want the animation to reverse and go back to the way it started, use reverse.

- The value start and stop points—the range of values between which to animate the value of the property. These values are set with the `android:valueFrom` and `android:valueTo` attributes. If you want to animate from the current value of the property, you need not specify it with the `android:valueFrom` attribute.

- The value type—this is the datatype of the property being animated on. This value is set with the `android:valueType` attribute. XML files support both `intType` and `floatType`. Other types, such as color values, can be set programmatically.

For example, the following resource file called `/res/animator/blinky_anim.xml` describes a simple property animation set that modifies the `alpha` and `backgroundColor` properties of an object over time:

```
<?xml version="1.0" encoding="utf-8" ?>
<set xmlns:android="http://schemas.android.com/apk/res/android"
```

```
        android:ordering="together" >
    <objectAnimator
        android:duration="2500"
        android:propertyName="alpha"
        android:repeatCount="-1"
        android:repeatMode="reverse"
        android:valueFrom="0"
        android:valueTo="1"
        android:valueType="floatType" />
    <objectAnimator
        android:duration="7500"
        android:propertyName="backgroundColor"
        android:repeatCount="-1"
        android:repeatMode="reverse"
        android:valueFrom="#2E0854"
        android:valueTo="#BF5FFF" />
</set>
```

This animation set contains two animations that are performed simultaneously. The first animates the `alpha` property, causing the object to fade in and out of view over the course of 5 seconds, indefinitely, because a `repeatCount` of −1 means to animate continuously and the `repeatMode` causes the animation to reverse itself each time. The second animation happens more slowly in duration, changing the `backgroundColor` attribute of the object between two purple colors, as specified in the `valueFrom` and `valueTo` attributes of the animation configuration.

Defining and Modifying Property Animations Programmatically

You can also programmatically define property animations. The property animation classes are available in the `android.animation` package. There are also times when you may need to modify an animation defined in XML. For example, here we load the animation set that was defined earlier in XML and set the value type of the `objectAnimator` for the `backgroundColor` attribute to an `ArgbEvaluator`, which can't be defined via XML:

```
AnimatorSet set = (AnimatorSet) AnimatorInflater.loadAnimator(this,
            R.animator.blinky_anim);

ArrayList<Animator> animations = set.getChildAnimations();
for (Animator animator : animations)
{
    if (animator instanceof ObjectAnimator)
    {
        ObjectAnimator anim = (ObjectAnimator) animator;
        if (anim.getPropertyName().compareTo("backgroundColor") == 0)
        {
            anim.setEvaluator(new ArgbEvaluator());
```

```
        }
    }
}
set.setInterpolator(new LinearInterpolator());
```

Starting Property Animations Programmatically

To use a property animation, you must attach it to an object of your choice. For example, we can attach the property animation we just created to a `TextView` control (defined in the layout) and start the animation as follows:

```
TextView   tv = (TextView) findViewById(R.id.myText);
set.setTarget(tv);
set.start();
```

Here, we attach the property animation to a view using the `setTarget()` method and then begin animating with the `start()` method.

When you are just animating properties of a `View` control, it is often more efficient and usually easier to use the `animate()` method. Starting with API Level 12, all `View` objects have an `animate()` method that returns a `ViewPropertyAnimator` object. Through this object, a subset of properties can be animated easily and efficiently. For example:

```
tv.animate().translationXBy(75f).rotationXBy(720).setDuration(1250);
layout.animate().scaleX(0.5f).scaleY(0.5f)
        .setInterpolator(new BounceInterpolator())
        .setDuration(1500);
```

The first one shows a `TextView` being moved horizontally by 75 pixels and rotated around the X axis, both of which take place over 1250 ms. The rotation around the X-axis is, indeed, a three-dimensional rotation. The second example shows an entire layout—including all buttons, images, text, indeed, all children—being scaled to 50 percent of its original size with a bounce interpolator, over a duration of 1500ms.

For more examples of programmatic property animation, see the sample application provided. We recommend running it so you can see what the animations do; print does not treat animations well (see Figure 19.4). You can also find numerous property animation examples in the Android SDK samples, such as API Demos.

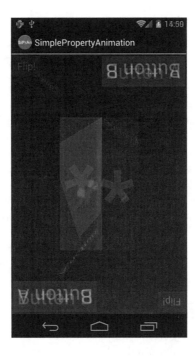

Figure 19.4   Example of a `ViewPropertyAnimator` in action.

Working with Different Interpolators

The interpolator determines the rate at which an animation happens in time. Interpolators apply to both view and property animation. There are a number of different interpolators provided as part of the Android SDK framework. Some of these interpolators include:

- `AccelerateDecelerateInterpolator`: Animation starts slowly, speeds up, and ends slowly.
- `AccelerateInterpolator`: Animation starts slowly and then accelerates.
- `AnticipateInterpolator`: Animation starts backward, and then flings forward.
- `AnticipateOvershootInterpolator`: Animation starts backward, flings forward, overshoots its destination, and then settles at the destination.
- `BounceInterpolator`: Animation "bounces" into place at its destination.
- `CycleInterpolator`: Animation is repeated a certain number of times, smoothly transitioning from one cycle to the next.
- `DecelerateInterpolator`: Animation begins quickly and then decelerates.

- LinearInterpolator: Animation speed is constant throughout.
- OvershootInterpolator: Animation overshoots its destination, and then settles at the destination.

You can specify the interpolator used by an animation programmatically using the setInterpolator() method or in the animation XML resource using the android:interpolator attribute. For more information, check out the Interpolator class (android.view.animation.Interpolator) and its subclasses.

Summary

The Android SDK supports several different types of animation. All versions of the Android SDK support frame-by-frame animation, animated GIF files, and tweened (view) animation. Android 3.0 added a much more robust animation framework that supports property animation that leverages the hardware acceleration features built into newer versions of the Android platform. Property animation allows developers to animate any object attribute over time, be it a View control or something else.

References and More Information

Android SDK Documentation on the android.animation package:
   http://d.android.com/reference/android/animation/package-summary.html
Android SDK Documentation on the android.view.animation package:
   http://d.android.com/reference/android/view/animation/package-summary.html
Android Dev Guide: "Animation":
   http://d.android.com/guide/topics/graphics/animation.html
Android Dev Guide: "Property Animation":
   http://d.android.com/guide/topics/graphics/prop-animation.html
Android Dev Guide: "View Animation":
   http://d.android.com/guide/topics/graphics/view-animation.html
Android Developer Blog: Animation in Honeycomb:
   http://android-developers.blogspot.com/2011/02/animation-in-honeycomb.html

## 20

Developing Android 3D Graphics Applications

The world around us is not two-dimensional but rich with depth. Although Android device displays are flat surfaces, presenting games and applications with visual depth has long been a way to enhance and add realism to them. For this purpose, developers can use the OpenGL ES and RenderScript 3D graphic frameworks provided in the Android SDK.

Working with OpenGL ES

Before 1992, Silicon Graphics (SGI) had a proprietary graphics standard called Integrated Raster Imaging System Graphics Library (IRIS GL) and was known typically as just GL. In 1992, to clean up the code and make GL more maintainable, SGI created OpenGL and set up a consortium of companies to maintain the open standard form of GL. Today, this consortium is known as the nonprofit Khronos Group, with more than 100 member companies. OpenGL ES was developed in the early 2000s to extend this open library to embedded devices. OpenGL ES is a subset of OpenGL. EGL was developed shortly thereafter to provide a common interface layer to native platform graphics.

In the interfaces, OpenGL is simply referred to as GL. This is true for OpenGL ES, as well. In the text of this chapter, GL typically refers to the underlying objects and interfaces in OpenGL to be consistent with the naming conventions in the code. OpenGL ES typically refers to the Android implementation of the OpenGL ES subset of OpenGL. Finally, OpenGL is used in a more generic fashion to refer to the generic concept or library.

Note

This chapter discusses how to use OpenGL ES in the Android SDK. Familiarity with OpenGL concepts can be helpful. This chapter does not teach you OpenGL, but it shows you how to perform a variety of common tasks with OpenGL ES on Android devices. These include configuring EGL (Embedded-System Graphics Library) and GL (Graphics Libraries), drawing objects, animating objects and scenes, lighting a scene, and texturing objects.

Leveraging OpenGL ES in Android

OpenGL ES is a graphics application programming interface (API) for embedded systems based on the OpenGL desktop standard. It is popular on wireless platforms and is supported on all major mobile phone platforms, including Windows Mobile, Symbian, MeeGo, BREW, Apple iOS, Palm WebOS, and now Android. Android devices support different versions of OpenGL ES depending on the platform version.

Android developers can implement 3D graphics applications that leverage OpenGL ES in two ways:

- The Android SDK provides OpenGL ES functionality in the `android.opengl` package in conjunction with the Khronos `javax.microedition.khronos.opengles` and `javax.microedition.khronos.egl` packages.
- The Android Native Development Kit (NDK) can be used to leverage OpenGL ES 1.1 and 2.0 native libraries for optimum performance.

Note

In this chapter, we focus on how to use the Android SDK to develop OpenGL ES applications. We discuss the Android Native Development Kit in Chapter 21, "Using the Android NDK."

·   The Android SDK has support for different versions of OpenGL ES, depending on the API Level or platform version:

- OpenGL ES 1.0 functionality (`android.opengl`) is fully supported on devices running Android 1.0 (API Level 1) and higher.
- OpenGL ES 1.1 (`android.opengl.GLES11`) is fully supported by devices running Android 1.6 (API Level 4) and higher.
- OpenGL ES 2.0 (`android.opengl.GLES20`) is fully supported by devices running Android 2.2 (API Level 8) and higher.

Ensuring Device Compatibility

Applications that require OpenGL functionality should declare this fact in the Android manifest file using the `<uses-feature>` tag with the `android:glEsVersion` attribute. This enables stores like the Android Market to filter the application and provide it only to devices that support the OpenGL version required by the application. The `android:glEsVersion` attribute is a 32-bit number where the high bits specify the major version and the low bits specify the minor version.

- If the application requires OpenGL ES 1.0, then you do not need to declare any `<uses-feature>` tag, as this is the default for all applications. All Android devices support OpenGL ES 1.0.

- If the application requires OpenGL ES 1.1, then you should declare a `<uses-feature>` tag as follows: `<uses-feature android:glEsVersion= "0x00010001" />`.

- If the application requires OpenGL ES 2.0, then you should declare a `<uses-feature>` tag as follows: `<uses-feature android:glEsVersion= "0x00020000" />`.

Only one OpenGL ES version should be listed in the Android manifest file. Applications that can function using different versions of OpenGL ES by checking for the supported graphics libraries at runtime should specify the lowest version supported by their application. It's also safe to assume that if a platform supports a newer version of OpenGL ES, such as 2.0, then it also supports all older versions (such as 1.1 and 1.0).

Using OpenGL ES APIs in the Android SDK

Using OpenGL ES on Android is a mix of using Android `View` object concepts and regular OpenGL ES concepts. There are a number of different ways to initialize and use the OpenGL ES functionality provided as part of the Android SDK.

- Developers can implement their own OpenGL ES solutions, handling the initialization of EGL and GL, managing a separate worker thread for OpenGL ES calls, and drawing on a `SurfaceView` control.

- As of Android API Level 3, developers can take advantage of the `GLSurfaceView` and `GLSurfaceView.Renderer` classes to help handle EGL initialization and threading. Calls are made into a user-defined `Renderer` class. The `Renderer` class handles the drawing and GL initialization and is run outside of the UI thread.

In this chapter, we give examples of both of these methods. Although the second method (using `GLSurfaceView`) is indeed simpler, you gain a more complete understanding of the fundamentals of Android OpenGL ES by following along as we describe the "manual" way first. In addition, many developers port their code over from a platform where they normally go through this configuration and might have the need to customize many pieces. Therefore, we start with the "manual" method so that we can review the steps necessary to set up, draw, and tear down OpenGL ES correctly. The concepts and classes used for both methods are similar, though, making this discussion useful even if you choose to use only the included `GLSurfaceView` method for your projects.

Tip

Many of the code examples provided in this chapter are taken from the SimpleOpenGL application. The source code for this application is provided for download on the book's websites.

Handling OpenGL ES Tasks Manually

We have provided a custom implementation leveraging OpenGL without using
`GLSurfaceView` for users who need to develop for Android versions previous to
Android 1.5 or who have a need for tighter control of the rendering pipeline and initialization. The following steps to initialize OpenGL ES enable you to start drawing on the
screen via the OpenGL interface:

1. Initialize `SurfaceView` with a surface of type `SURFACE_TYPE_GPU`.
2. Start a thread for OpenGL; all OpenGL calls are performed on this thread.
3. Initialize EGL.
4. Initialize GL.
5. Start drawing!

Warning

When OpenGL ES is initialized on a particular thread of your application, all subsequent
calls must be on this same thread; otherwise, they will fail. You should not use your application's main thread for OpenGL ES calls, as the extra processing and loops can cause
your application to become less responsive. This does introduce some thread synchronization consequences that you must handle, and we discuss those later in this chapter.

Creating a `SurfaceView`

The first step to drawing fancy 3D graphics on the screen is to create your
`SurfaceView`. This involves extending `SurfaceView` and implementing callbacks for
`SurfaceHolder.Callback`. The following is an empty implementation that we com-
plete shortly:

```
private class BasicGLSurfaceView
    extends SurfaceView
    implements SurfaceHolder.Callback {

    SurfaceHolder mAndroidHolder;

    BasicGLSurfaceView(Context context) {
        super(context);
        mAndroidHolder = getHolder();
        mAndroidHolder.addCallback(this);
        mAndroidHolder.setType(
            SurfaceHolder.SURFACE_TYPE_GPU);
    }

    public void surfaceChanged(SurfaceHolder holder,
        int format, int width, int height) {}
```

```
    public void surfaceCreated(SurfaceHolder holder) {}

    public void surfaceDestroyed(SurfaceHolder holder) {}
}
```

First, in the constructor, the `getHolder()` method is called to get and store the `SurfaceHolder`. Because the `SurfaceView` implements the `SurfaceHolder.Callback` interface, this `SurfaceView` is assigned for receiving callbacks for those events. Finally, you must set the surface type to `SURFACE_TYPE_GPU` for OpenGL ES calls to work on it. This class is initialized and set as the content `View` for the activity as follows:

```
protected void onCreate(Bundle savedInstanceState) {
    super.onCreate(savedInstanceState);
    mAndroidSurface = new BasicGLSurfaceView(this);
    setContentView(mAndroidSurface);
}
```

Although setting the `SurfaceView` as the entire content `View` works fine, it isn't flexible if you want other functionality on the screen besides the 3D area. One way to place the `SurfaceView` on your screen and still have the benefits of using an XML layout file is to use one of the container widgets, such as `FrameLayout`, and add this `View` to it. For instance, consider this `FrameLayout` definition, which can exist anywhere in a layout:

```
<FrameLayout
    android:id="@+id/gl_container"
    android:layout_height="100px"
    android:layout_width="100px" />
```

This puts a 100x100-pixel square container somewhere on the screen, depending on the rest of the layout. Now, the following code uses the identifier for this `FrameLayout` to place the child `SurfaceView` in the `FrameLayout`:

```
mAndroidSurface = new TextureGLSurfaceView(this);
setContentView(R.layout.constrained);
FrameLayout v = (FrameLayout) findViewById(R.id.gl_container);
v.addView(mAndroidSurface);
```

In this example, `R.layout.constrained` is our layout resource, which contains the `FrameLayout` with the particular identifier we used. You see why this works regardless of what is drawn in the OpenGL surface as we continue through the initialization of OpenGL ES on Android.

Starting Your OpenGL ES Thread

In Android, you can update only the screen from the main thread of your application, sometimes referred to as the UI thread. The `SurfaceView` widget, however, is used so that we can offload graphics processing to a secondary thread, which can update this part of the screen. This is our OpenGL thread. Like updating the screen from the UI thread, all OpenGL calls must be in the same thread.

Recall that the SurfaceView presented also implemented the SurfaceHolder.Callback interface. You can access the underlying surface of the SurfaceView only after calling surfaceCreated() and before calling surfaceDestroyed(). Between these two calls is the only time that we have a valid surface for our OpenGL instance to draw to.

As such, we won't bother creating the OpenGL thread until surfaceCreated() is called. The following is an example implementation of surfaceCreated(), which starts up the OpenGL thread:

```
public void surfaceCreated(SurfaceHolder holder) {
    mGLThread = new BasicGLThread(this);
    mGLThread.start();
}
```

As promised, little more than launching the thread takes place here. The SurfaceView is passed to the thread. This is done because the OpenGL calls need to know which SurfaceView to draw upon.

The BasicGLThread class is an implementation of a Thread that contains the code we run in the OpenGL thread described. The following code block shows which functionality is placed where. The BasicGLThread is placed as a private member of the Activity class.

```
private class BasicGLThread extends Thread {
    SurfaceView sv;
    BasicGLThread(SurfaceView view) {
        sv = view;
    }

    private boolean mDone = false;
    public void run() {
        initEGL();
        initGL();
        while (!mDone) {
            // drawing code
        }
    }

    public void requestStop() {
        mDone = true;
        try {
            join();
        } catch (InterruptedException e) {
            Log.e("GL", "failed to stop gl thread", e);
        }
```

```
        cleanupGL();
    }

    public void cleanupGL() {}
    public void initGL() {}
    public void initEGL() {}

    // main OpenGL variables
}
```

During creation, the `SurfaceView` is saved for later use. In the `run()` method, EGL and GL are initialized, which we describe later in this chapter. Then, the drawing code is executed either once or, as shown here, in a loop. Finally, the thread can safely be stopped from outside the thread with a call to the `requestStop()` method. This also cleans up the OpenGL resources. More on this is found in the "Cleaning Up OpenGL ES" section later in this chapter.

Initializing EGL

Up to this point, the application has a `SurfaceView` with a valid `Surface` and an OpenGL thread that has just been launched. The first step with most OpenGL implementations is to initialize EGL, or the native hardware. You do this in basically the same way each time, and this is a good block of code to write once and reuse. The following steps must be performed to initialize EGL on Android:

1. Get the EGL object.
2. Initialize the display.
3. Get a configuration.
4. Link the `EGLSurface` to an Android `SurfaceView`.
5. Create the EGL context.
6. Tell EGL which display, surface, and context to use.
7. Get our GL object for use in rendering.

The Android SDK provides some utility classes for use with OpenGL ES. The first of these is the `GLDebugHelper` class. OpenGL calls don't directly return errors. Instead, they set an error internally that can be queried. You can use the `GLDebugHelper` class to wrap all EGL and GL calls and have the wrapper check for errors and throw an exception. The first call for getting the EGL object uses this wrapper, as shown here:

```
mEGL = (EGL10) GLDebugHelper.wrap(
    EGLContext.getEGL(),
    GLDebugHelper.CONFIG_CHECK_GL_ERROR |
    GLDebugHelper.CONFIG_CHECK_THREAD,
    null);
```

Here, the `EGL10` object is retrieved and wrapped. Turning on the `CONFIG_CHECK_GL_ERROR` flag checks for all `GL Errors`. In addition, the wrapper makes sure all our `GL` and `EGL` calls are made from the correct thread because `CONFIG_CHECK_THREAD` is enabled.

Now we can proceed with initializing the display, as shown here:

```
mGLDisplay = mEGL.eglGetDisplay(EGL10.EGL_DEFAULT_DISPLAY);
```

The default display, `EGL10.EGL_DEFAULT_DISPLAY`, is configured by the internals of the Android implementation of OpenGL ES. Now that we have the display, we can initialize EGL and get the version of the implementation:

```
int[] curGLVersion = new int[2];
mEGL.eglInitialize(mGLDisplay, curGLVersion);
```

The current GL version varies by device. With the display initialized, we can request which configuration is closest to the one we require:

```
int[] mConfigSpec = { EGL10.EGL_RED_SIZE, 5,
                      EGL10.EGL_GREEN_SIZE, 6,
                      EGL10.EGL_BLUE_SIZE, 5,
                      EGL10.EGL_DEPTH_SIZE, 16,
                      EGL10.EGL_NONE };
EGLConfig[] configs = new EGLConfig[1];
int[] num_config = new int[1];
mEGL.eglChooseConfig(mGLDisplay, mConfigSpec,
                     configs, 1, num_config);
mGLConfig = configs[0];
```

The preceding configuration works on the emulator and the current hardware. If you are unsure that the configuration you've chosen works with your application's target platforms, this is a good way to check the resulting list of configurations.

Now we can create the EGL surface based on this configuration:

```
mGLSurface = mEGL.eglCreateWindowSurface
   (mGLDisplay, mGLConfig, sv.getHolder(), null);
```

Recall that we stored our `SurfaceView` for use later. Here, we use it to pass the native Android surface to EGL so they can be linked correctly. We still need to get the EGL context before we can finalize and get our instance of the `GL` object.

```
mGLContext = mEGL.eglCreateContext(
   mGLDisplay, mGLConfig, EGL10.EGL_NO_CONTEXT, null);
```

Now that we have our display, surface, and context, we can get our GL object.

```
mEGL.eglMakeCurrent(mGLDisplay, mGLSurface,
   mGLSurface, mGLContext);
mGL = (GL10) GLDebugHelper.wrap(
   mGLContext.getGL(),
```

```
GLDebugHelper.CONFIG_CHECK_GL_ERROR |
GLDebugHelper.CONFIG_CHECK_THREAD, null);
```

Once again, we use `GLDebugHelper` to wrap the `GL` object so that it checks errors and confirms the thread for us. This completes the initialization of EGL on Android. Next, we can initialize `GL` to set up our projection and other rendering options.

Initializing GL

Now the fun begins. We have EGL fully initialized, and we have a valid GL object, so we can initialize our drawing space. For this example, we won't be drawing anything complex. We leave most options at their default values.

Typically, one of the first calls made to initialize GL is to set the viewport. Here is an example of how to set the viewport to the same dimensions as our `SurfaceView`:

```
int width = sv.getWidth();
int height = sv.getHeight();
mGL.glViewport(0, 0, width, height);
```

The location of the surface on the screen is determined internally by EGL. We also use the following width and height of the `SurfaceView` to determine the aspect ratio for `GL` to render in. In the following code, we complete the configuration of a basic `GL` projection setup:

```
mGL.glMatrixMode(GL10.GL_PROJECTION);
mGL.glLoadIdentity();
float aspect = (float) width/height;
GLU.gluPerspective(mGL, 45.0f, aspect, 1.0f, 30.0f);
mGL.glClearColor(0.5f, 0.5f, 0.5f, 1);
```

The Android SDK provides a few helpers similar to those found in GLUT (OpenGL Utility Toolkit). Here, we use one of them to define a perspective in terms of the vertical angle of view, aspect ratio, and near and far clipping planes. The `gluPerspective()` method is useful for configuring the projection matrix, which transforms the 3D scene into a flat surface. Finally, we clear the screen to gray.

Drawing on the Screen

Now that EGL and GL are initialized, objects can be drawn to the screen. For this example, to demonstrate that we've set up everything to actually draw, we put a simple three-vertex flat surface (in layman's terms, a triangle) on the screen. Here is some sample code to do this:

```
mGL.glMatrixMode(GL10.GL_MODELVIEW);
mGL.glLoadIdentity();
GLU.gluLookAt(mGL, 0, 0, 10f, 0, 0, 0, 0, 1, 0f);
mGL.glColor4f(1f, 0f, 0f, 1f);
while (!mDone) {
```

```
mGL.glClear(GL10.GL_COLOR_BUFFER_BIT |
    GL10.GL_DEPTH_BUFFER_BIT);
mGL.glRotatef(1f, 0, 0, 1f);
triangle.draw(mGL);
mEGL.eglSwapBuffers(mGLDisplay, mGLSurface);
}
```

If it looks like something is missing, you are correct. This code doesn't actually show
the draw command for the triangle. However, it does use an Android SDK utility
method to transform the model view matrix with the intuitive `gluLookAt()` method.
Here, it sets the eye point 10 units away from the origin and looks toward the origin.
The up value is, as usual, set to the positive y-axis. In the loop, notice that the identity
matrix is not assigned. This gives the `glRotatef()` method a compounding effect, causing the triangle to rotate in a counter-clockwise direction. In the next section, "Drawing
3D Objects," we discuss the details of drawing with OpenGL ES in Android.

When launched, a screen similar to that in Figure 20.1 should display.

Figure 20.1   A red triangle rendered using OpenGL ES on the Android
emulator.

You now have a working OpenGL ES environment in the Android SDK. We continue from this point to talk more about drawing in the environment.

Drawing 3D Objects

Now that you have the OpenGL ES environment working within Android, it's time to do some actual drawing. This section leads you through a number of examples, each building upon the previous. In doing so, these examples introduce new Android-specific concepts with OpenGL ES.

Drawing Your Vertices

OpenGL ES supports two primary drawing calls, `glDrawArrays()` and `glDrawElements()`. Both of these methods require the use of a vertex buffer assigned through a call to `glVertexPointer`. Because Android runs on top of Java, though, an arbitrary array cannot be passed in as the array contents might move around in memory. Instead, we have to use a `ByteBuffer`, `FloatBuffer`, or `IntBuffer` so the data stays at the same location in memory. Converting various arrays to buffers is common, so we have implemented some helper methods. Here is one for converting a float array into a `FloatBuffer`:

```
FloatBuffer getFloatBufferFromFloatArray(float array[]) {
    ByteBuffer tempBuffer =
        ByteBuffer.allocateDirect(array.length * 4);
    tempBuffer.order(ByteOrder.nativeOrder());
    FloatBuffer buffer = tempBuffer.asFloatBuffer();
    buffer.put(array);
    buffer.position(0);
    return buffer;
}
```

This creates a buffer of 32-bit float values with a stride of 0. You can then store the resulting `FloatBuffer` and assign it to OpenGL calls. Here is an example of doing this, using the triangle we showed previously in this chapter:

```
float[] vertices = {
    -0.559016994f, 0, 0,
    0.25f, 0.5f, 0f,
    0.25f, -0.5f, 0f
};
mVertexBuffer = getFloatBufferFromFloatArray(vertices);
```

With the buffer assigned, we can now draw the triangle, as shown here:

```
void drawTriangle(GL10 gl) {
    gl.glEnableClientState(GL10.GL_VERTEX_ARRAY);
    gl.glVertexPointer(3, GL10.GL_FLOAT, 0, mVertexBuffer);
    gl.glDrawArrays(GL10.GL_TRIANGLES, 0, 3);
}
```

We have to enable the GL_VERTEX_ARRAY state, though you can do this in GL configuration, as it is required to draw anything with OpenGL ES. We then assign the vertex buffer through a call to glVertexPointer(), also telling GL that we're using float values. Fixed point values, through GL_FIXED, can also be used and might be faster with some Android implementations. Finally, a call to glDrawArrays() is made to draw the triangles using three vertices from the vertex buffer. The result of this can be seen in Figure 20.1.

Coloring Your Vertices

In OpenGL ES, you can use an array of colors to individually assign colors to each vertex that is drawn. This is accomplished by calling the glColorPointer() method with a buffer of colors. The following code sets up a small buffer of colors for three vertices:

```
float[] colors = {
    1f, 0, 0, 1f,
    0, 1f, 0, 1f,
    0, 0, 1f, 1f
    };
mColorBuffer = getFloatBufferFromFloatArray(colors);
```

With the buffer available, we can now use it to color our triangle, as shown in the following code:

```
void drawColorful(GL10 gl) {
    gl.glEnableClientState(GL10.GL_COLOR_ARRAY);
    gl.glColorPointer(4, GL10.GL_FLOAT, 0, mColorBuffer);
    draw(gl);
    gl.glDisableClientState(GL10.GL_COLOR_ARRAY);
}
```

First, the client state for GL_COLOR_ARRAY is enabled. Then, calling the glColorPointer method sets the preceding color buffer created. The call to draw() draws the triangle like the colorful one shown in Figure 20.2.

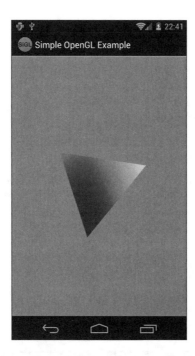

Figure 20.2   A triangle with red, green, and blue vertices smoothly blended.

Drawing More Complex Objects

A standard cube has eight vertices. However, in OpenGL ES, each of the six faces needs to be drawn with two triangles. Each of these triangles needs three vertices. That's a total of 36 vertices to draw an object with just 8 of its own vertices. There must be a better way.

OpenGL ES supports index arrays. An index array is a list of vertex indexes from the current vertex array. The index array must be a buffer, and in this example, we use a `ByteBuffer` because we don't have many vertices to indicate. The index array lists the order that the vertices should be drawn when used with `glDrawElements()`. Note that the color arrays (and normal arrays that we get to shortly) are still relative to the vertex array and not the index array. Here is some code that draws an OpenGL cube using just eight defined vertices:

```
float vertices[] = {
    -1,1,1,  1,1,1,  1,-1,1,  -1,-1,1,
    1,1,-1,  -1,1,-1,  -1,-1,-1,  1,-1,-1
};
byte indices[] = {
```

```
    0,1,2, 2,3,0,  1,4,7, 7,2,1,  0,3,6, 6,5,0,
    3,2,7, 7,6,3,  0,1,4, 4,5,0,  5,6,7, 7,4,5
};
FloatBuffer vertexBuffer =
    getFloatBufferFromFloatArray(vertices);
ByteBuffer indexBuffer =
    getByteBufferFromByteArray(indices);
gl.glVertexPointer(3, GL10.GL_FLOAT, 0, vertexBuffer);
gl.glDrawElements(GL10.GL_TRIANGLES, indices.length,
    GL10.GL_UNSIGNED_BYTE, indexBuffer);
```

The vertices define the typical shape for a cube. Then, however, we use the index array to define in what order the vertices are drawn to create the cube out of the 12 triangles that we need (recalling that OpenGL ES does not support quads). Now you have a red shape on your screen that looks like Figure 20.3 (left). It doesn't actually look much like a cube, though, does it? Without some shading, it looks too much like a random polygon. If, however, you switch the glDrawElements() to GL_LINE_LOOP instead of GL_TRIANGLES, you see a line-drawing version of the shape, such as Figure 20.3 (right). Now you can see that it is a cube. You can reuse the vertices buffer with different index buffers, too. This is useful if you can define multiple shapes using the same set of vertices and then draw them in their own locations with transformations.

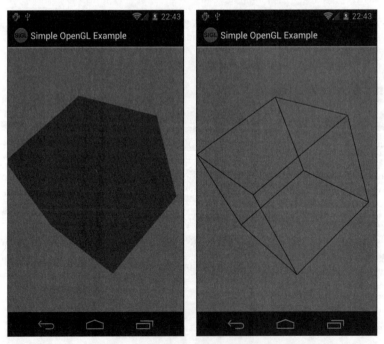

Figure 20.3   A solid cube with no shading (left) and the same cube with only lines (right). (Colors modified for print.)

Lighting Your Scene

The last 3D object that we drew was a cube that looked like some strange polygon on your flat 2D screen. The colors of each face could be made different by applying coloring between each call to draw a face. However, that still produces a fairly flat-looking cube. Instead, why not shine some light on the scene and let the lighting give the cube some additional depth?

Before you can provide lighting on a scene, each vertex of each surface needs a vector applied to it to define how the light reflects and, thus, how it is rendered. Although this vector can be anything, most often it is perpendicular to the surface defined by the vertices; this is called the normal of a surface. Recalling our cube from the preceding example, we see now that a cube can't actually be created out of eight vertices as each vertex can carry only one normal array, and we would need three per vertex because each vertex belongs to three faces. Instead, we have to use a cube that does, in fact, contain the entire lot of 24 vertices. (Technically, you can define a bunch of index arrays and change the normal array between calls to each face, but it's more commonly done with a large list of vertices and a single list of normal vectors.)

Like the color array, the normal array is applied to each vertex in the vertex array in order. Lighting is a fairly complex topic and if it's unfamiliar, you need to check out the "References and More Information" section at the end of this chapter where you can learn more. For now, we just give an example of how to use the lighting features of Open GL ES in Android.

Here is some code for enabling simple lighting:

```
mGL.glEnable(GL10.GL_LIGHTING);
mGL.glEnable(GL10.GL_LIGHT0);
mGL.glLightfv(GL10.GL_LIGHT0, GL10.GL_AMBIENT,
    new float[] {0.1f, 0.1f, 0.1f, 1f}, 0);
mGL.glLightfv(GL10.GL_LIGHT0, GL10.GL_DIFFUSE,
    new float[] {1f, 1f, 1f, 1f}, 0);
mGL.glLightfv(GL10.GL_LIGHT0, GL10.GL_POSITION,
    new float[] {10f, 0f, 10f, 1f}, 0);
mGL.glEnable(GL10.GL_COLOR_MATERIAL);
mGL.glShadeModel(GL10.GL_SMOOTH);
```

This code enables lighting, enables GL_LIGHT0, and then sets the color and brightness of the light. Finally, the light is positioned in 3D space. In addition, we enable GL_COLOR_MATERIAL so the color set for drawing the objects is used with the lighting. We also enable the smooth shading model, which helps remove the visual transition between triangles on the same face. You can use color material definitions for fancier lighting and more realistic-looking surfaces, but that is beyond the scope of this book.

Here is the drawing code for our cube, assuming we now have a full vertex array of all 24 points and an index array defining the order in which they should be drawn:

```
gl.glEnableClientState(GL10.GL_NORMAL_ARRAY);
gl.glVertexPointer(3, GL10.GL_FLOAT, 0, mVertexBuffer);
gl.glNormalPointer(GL10.GL_FLOAT, 0, mNormalBuffer);
gl.glDrawElements(GL10.GL_TRIANGLES, indices.length,
GL10.GL_UNSIGNED_BYTE, mIndexBuffer);
```

Notice that the normal array and normal mode are now turned on. Without this, the lighting won't look right. As with the other arrays, this has to be assigned through a fixed buffer in Java, as this code demonstrates:

```
float normals[] = {
    // front
    0, 0, 1, 0, 0, 1, 0, 0, 1, 0, 0, 1,
    // back
    0, 0, -1, 0, 0, -1, 0, 0, -1, 0, 0, -1,
    // top
    0, 1, 0, 0, 1, 0, 0, 1, 0, 0, 1, 0,
    // bottom
    0, -1, 0, 0, -1, 0, 0, -1, 0, 0, -1, 0,
    // right
    1, 0, 0, 1, 0, 0, 1, 0, 0, 1, 0, 0,
    // left
    -1, 0, 0, -1, 0, 0, -1, 0, 0, -1, 0, 0 };
mNormalBuffer = getFloatBufferFromFloatArray(normals);
```

The preceding code uses one of the helper methods we talked about previously to create a FloatBuffer. We use a floating point array for the normals. This also shows the normals and how each vertex must have one. (Recall that we now have 24 vertices for the cube.) You can create various lighting effects by making the normals not actually perpendicular to the surface, but for more accurate lighting, it's usually better to just increase the polygon count of your objects or add textures. Figure 20.4 shows the solid cube, now shaded to show depth better.

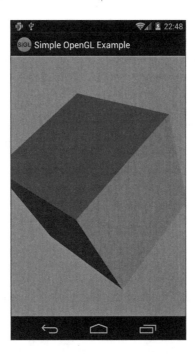

Figure 20.4   A cube with a light shining from the right to shade it.

Texturing Your Objects

Texturing surfaces, or putting images on surfaces, is a rather lengthy and complex topic. It's enough for our purposes to focus on learning how to texture with Android, so we use the previously lit and colored cube and texture it.

First, texturing needs to be enabled, as shown in the following code:

```
mGL.glEnable(GL10.GL_TEXTURE_2D);
int[] textures = new int[1];
mGL.glGenTextures(1, textures, 0);
```

This code enables texturing and creates an internally named slot for one texture. We use this slot to tell OpenGL what texture we operate on in the next block of code:

```
gl.glBindTexture(GL10.GL_TEXTURE_2D, textures[0]);
Bitmap bitmap = BitmapFactory.decodeResource(
    c.getResources(), R.drawable.android);
Bitmap bitmap256 = Bitmap.createScaledBitmap(
    bitmap, 256, 256, false);
GLUtils.texImage2D(GL10.GL_TEXTURE_2D, 0, bitmap256, 0);
bitmap.recycle();
bitmap256.recycle();
```

You've probably begun to wonder what happened to Android-specific code. Well, it's back. OpenGL ES needs bitmaps to use as textures. Lucky for us, Android comes with a `Bitmap` class that can read in nearly any format of image, including PNG, GIF, and JPG files. You can do this straight from a `Drawable` resource identifier, too, as demonstrated in the preceding code. OpenGL requires that textures be square and have sides that are powers of two, such as 64 x 64 or 256 x 256. Because the source image might or might not be in one of these exact sizes, we scale it again with just a single Android method call. If the source image weren't square, though, the original aspect ratio is not kept. Sometimes it is easier to scale down with the original aspect ratio and add colored padding around the edges of the image instead of stretching it, but this is beyond the scope of this example.

Finally, `GLUtils.texImage2D()` assigns an Android `Bitmap` to an OpenGL texture. OpenGL keeps the image internally, so we can clean up the `Bitmap` objects with a call to the `recycle()` method.

Now that OpenGL ES knows about the texture, the next step is to tell it where to draw the texture. You can accomplish this through using a texture coordinate buffer. This is similar to all the other buffer arrays in that it must be assigned to a fixed Java buffer and enabled. Here is the code to do this with our cube example:

```
float texCoords[] = {
    1,0, 1,1, 0,1, 0,0,
    1,0, 1,1, 0,1, 0,0,
    1,0, 1,1, 0,1, 0,0,
    1,0, 1,1, 0,1, 0,0,
    1,0, 1,1, 0,1, 0,0,
    1,0, 1,1, 0,1, 0,0,
    };
mCoordBuffer = getFloatBufferFromFloatArray(texCoords);
gl.glEnableClientState(GL10.GL_TEXTURE_COORD_ARRAY);
gl.glTexCoordPointer(2, GL10.GL_FLOAT, 0, mCoordBuffer);

draw(gl);
```

As promised, this code creates a fixed buffer for the texture coordinates. We set the same ones on each face of the cube, so each vertex has a texture coordinate assigned to it (`0,0` is the lower-left portion of the texture and `1,1` is the upper-right). Next, we enable the `GL_TEXTURE_COORD_ARRAY` state and then tell OpenGL which buffer to use. Finally, we draw the cube. Now, we left the code the same as before, which produces the output you see in Figure 20.5 (left). The coloring does still apply, even with textures. If coloring is not applied, the output looks like what you see in Figure 20.5 (right).

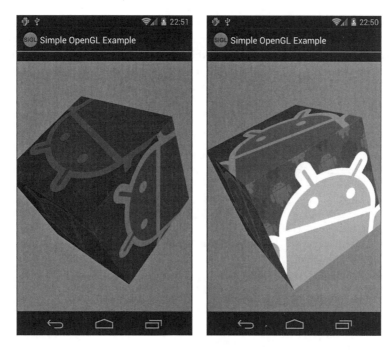

Figure 20.5   A red colored cube with texture (left) and the same cube
without red coloring (right).

Interacting with Android Views and Events

Now that you have gone through this introduction to OpenGL ES on Android, you
have seen how to draw 3D objects on the screen. Actually, these 3D objects are drawn
on a SurfaceView, which has all the typical Android attributes found on View widgets.
We now use these attributes to interact with the rest of the application.

First, we show you how to send information from the OpenGL thread back to the
main thread to monitor performance. Then, we give an example of how to forward key
events from the main thread to the OpenGL thread to control the animation on the
screen.

Enabling the OpenGL Thread to Talk to the Application Thread

The Android SDK provides a helper class for running code on another thread. The
Handler class can allow a piece of code to run on a target thread—the thread that the
Handler was instantiated in. For the purpose of this example, you do this in the
Activity class:

```
public final Handler mHandler = new Handler();
```

This enables the OpenGL thread to execute code on the Activity thread by calling the post() method of the Handler. This enables us to act on other View objects on the screen that we can't act on from outside of the Activity thread on the OpenGL thread. For this example, the frame rate of the scene rendered is calculated in the OpenGL thread and then posted back to the Activity thread. Here is a method that does just that:

```
public void calculateAndDisplayFPS() {
    if (showFPS) {
        long thisTime = System.currentTimeMillis();
        if (thisTime - mLastTime < mSkipTime) {
            mFrames++;
        } else {
            mFrames++;
            final long fps =
                mFrames / ((thisTime-mLastTime)/1000);
            mFrames = 0;
            mLastTime = thisTime;
            mHandler.post(new Runnable() {
                public void run() {
                    mFPSText.setText("FPS = " + fps);
                }
            });
        }
    }
}
```

The calculateAndDisplayFPS() method is called from within the animation loop of the OpenGL thread. The math is fairly straightforward: the number of frames divided by the duration for those frames in seconds. Then, we take that and post it to the Handler for the Activity thread by creating a new Runnable object that applies a String to the TextView that holds the current frame rate.

However, doing this for every iteration causes the performance to drop substantially. Instead, a counter tracks the number of frames drawn, and we do the calculation and display every time the duration of mSkipTime has gone by. A value of 5000ms has worked well to avoid influencing the performance too much by simply measuring the performance. Figure 20.6 shows the display with the frame rate.

Figure 20.6   A textured, lit, shaded cube with the frame rate displayed.

Enabling the Application Thread to Talk to the OpenGL Thread

Now let's look at the reverse situation. We want the main application thread to communicate with the OpenGL thread. We can use a `Handler` to post code to the OpenGL
thread for execution. However, if we are not going to execute any OpenGL code, we
aren't required to run it in the OpenGL thread context. Instead, we can add a key event
handler to the `SurfaceView` to either speed up or stop the animation in the OpenGL
thread.

A `SurfaceView` needs to be the current focus before it receives key events. A couple
of method calls configure this:

```
setFocusable(true);
setFocusableInTouchMode(true);
```

Setting focusable for both touch modes enables key events to come in regardless of
the mode. Now, within the `SurfaceView`, key event handlers need to be implemented.
First, we implement a handler for toggling the frame rate on and off. The following is a
sample implementation of the `onKeyDown()` method override:

```
public boolean onKeyDown(int keyCode, KeyEvent event) {
    switch (keyCode) {
        case KeyEvent.KEYCODE_F:
            mGLThread.toggleFPSDisplay();
        return true;
    }
    return super.onKeyDown(keyCode, event);
}
```

When the user presses the F key, a call to the `toggleFPSDisplay()` method of the OpenGL ES thread is made. This merely changes the state of the `boolean` flag and then updates the text field status. The `onKeyDown()` method is called multiple times if the key is held, toggling the display until the key is released. There are multiple methods to prevent this, such as just handling it within `onKeyUp()` or using different keys to enable and disable the state.

The next control we provide to the user is the ability to pause the animation while the P key is held down. Add the following case statement to `onKeyDown()`:

```
case KeyEvent.KEYCODE_P:
    mGLThread.setAnim(false);
    return true;
```

Here, the state is forced to false regardless of how many times `onKeyDown()` is called. Next, an implementation of `onKeyUp()` is needed to resume the animation when the user lifts his finger:

```
public boolean onKeyUp(int keyCode, KeyEvent event) {
    switch (keyCode) {
        case KeyEvent.KEYCODE_P:
            mGLThread.setAnim(true);
            return true;
    }
    return super.onKeyUp(keyCode, event);
}
```

Again, the value is forced and set to true so that when the user lifts his finger off the key, the animation resumes regardless of the current state. An `if` statement around the inner part of the entire `while()` animation loop can pause the entire rendering in this example.

In these examples, the code does not actually run in the OpenGL thread to change the state of the flags. This is acceptable for the following reasons:

- The values are set in this way exclusively (no concurrency problems).
- The exact state of the flags is unimportant during the loop.
- No calls to OpenGL are made.

The first two reasons mean that we don't have to perform thread synchronization for the functionality to work acceptably and safely. The last reason means that we don't need to create a `Handler` on the OpenGL thread to execute OpenGL calls in the proper thread. There are many circumstances where these aren't met. Discussing thread synchronization is not within the scope of this chapter, however. Standard Java methods are available for doing this.

Cleaning Up OpenGL ES

It is necessary for your application to clean up OpenGL when your application is done using it. This happens when the application quits or the `Activity` has changed in some way. The recommended process for gracefully shutting down OpenGL is to reset the surface and context, destroy the surface and context you configured, and then terminate the EGL instance. You can do this with the following code:

```
private void cleanupGL() {
    mEGL.eglMakeCurrent(mGLDisplay, EGL10.EGL_NO_SURFACE,
        EGL10.EGL_NO_SURFACE, EGL10.EGL_NO_CONTEXT);
    mEGL.eglDestroySurface(mGLDisplay, mGLSurface);
    mEGL.eglDestroyContext(mGLDisplay, mGLContext);
    mEGL.eglTerminate(mGLDisplay);
}
```

First, `eglMakeCurrent()` removes the surface and context that were used. Next, `eglDestroySurface()` and `eglDestroyContext()` release any resources held by OpenGL for the surface and the context. Finally, OpenGL is terminated through a call to `eglTerminate()`. If OpenGL runs in a separate thread, the thread can now be terminated as well.

It is up to the application to clean up OpenGL properly. There are no helper methods available for managing all of it automatically in the Android lifecycle as there are with `Cursor` objects and the like.

Using `GLSurfaceView` (Easy OpenGL ES)

Several new classes were introduced with Android 1.5 (API Level 3) that you can use to simplify application OpenGL ES implementation. The `GLSurfaceView` and `GLSurfaceView.Renderer` classes effectively require less code to write so that you can focus on the actual GL drawing process instead of the implementation details and upkeep necessary to handle OpenGL ES calls. Essentially, the `GLSurfaceView` class handles the EGL initialization, threading, and calls in to a user-defined `Renderer` class. The `Renderer` class handles the drawing and GL initialization.

Tip

The code examples provided in this section are taken from the
`ShowAndroidGLActivity.java` class in the SimpleOpenGL application. The source
code for this application is provided for download on the book's websites.

To use the `GLSurfaceView` class, you must either extend it or instantiate
it directly. Either way, you then need to provide an implementation of a
`GLSurfaceView.Renderer` class. The `Renderer` class must contain appropriate callbacks
for drawing and GL initialization. Additionally, the `Activity` must pass `onPause()` and
`onResume()` events on to the `GLSurfaceView`. The EGL initialization is handled by the
`GLSurfaceView` object, and threading is used to offload the processing away from the
main thread.

The following code demonstrates an entire `Activity` that duplicates the colorful triangle we drew earlier in this chapter, as shown in Figure 20.2:

```java
public class AndroidOpenGL extends Activity {
CustomSurfaceView mAndroidSurface = null;

protected void onPause() {
    super.onPause();
    mAndroidSurface.onPause();
}

protected void onResume() {
    super.onResume();
    mAndroidSurface.onResume();
}

protected void onCreate(Bundle savedInstanceState) {
    super.onCreate(savedInstanceState);

    mAndroidSurface = new CustomSurfaceView(this);
    setContentView(mAndroidSurface);
}

private class CustomSurfaceView extends GLSurfaceView {
    final CustomRenderer mRenderer = new CustomRenderer();

    public CustomSurfaceView(Context context) {
        super(context);
        setFocusable(true);
        setFocusableInTouchMode(true);
        setRenderer(mRenderer);
    }
```

```java
    public boolean onKeyDown(int keyCode, KeyEvent event) {
        switch (keyCode) {
        case KeyEvent.KEYCODE_P:
            queueEvent(new Runnable() {
                public void run() {
                    mRenderer.togglePause();
                }
            });
            return true;
        }
        return super.onKeyDown(keyCode, event);
    }
}

private class CustomRenderer implements
    GLSurfaceView.Renderer {
    TriangleSmallGLUT mTriangle = new TriangleSmallGLUT(3);
    boolean fAnimPaused = false;

    public void onDrawFrame(GL10 gl) {
        if (!fAnimPaused) {
            gl.glClear(GL10.GL_COLOR_BUFFER_BIT |
                GL10.GL_DEPTH_BUFFER_BIT);
            gl.glRotatef(1f, 0, 0, 1f);

            if (mTriangle != null) {
                mTriangle.drawColorful(gl);
            }
        }
    }

    public void togglePause() {
        if (fAnimPaused == true) {
            fAnimPaused = false;
        } else {
            fAnimPaused = true;
        }
    }

    public void onSurfaceChanged(GL10 gl, int width,
        int height) {
        gl.glViewport(0, 0, width, height);

        // configure projection to screen
        gl.glMatrixMode(GL10.GL_PROJECTION);
        gl.glLoadIdentity();
```

```
        gl.glClearColor(0.5f, 0.5f, 0.5f, 1);
        float aspect = (float) width / height;
        GLU.gluPerspective(gl, 45.0f, aspect, 1.0f, 30.0f);
    }

    public void onSurfaceCreated(GL10 gl,
        EGLConfig config) {
        gl.glEnableClientState(GL10.GL_VERTEX_ARRAY);

        // configure model space
        gl.glMatrixMode(GL10.GL_MODELVIEW);
        gl.glLoadIdentity();
        GLU.gluLookAt(gl, 0, 0, 10f, 0, 0, 0, 0, 1, 0f);
        gl.glColor4f(1f, 0f, 0f, 1f);
    }
}}
```

As you can see, this code demonstrates creating a new `GLSurfaceView` and a new
`GLSurfaceView.Renderer`. The end result, with proper implementation of the triangle
drawing class (included with the book code and discussed earlier in this chapter), is a
spinning triangle that the user can pause with the press of the P key. The
`GLSurfaceView` implementation contains its own renderer, which is less generic than
assigning it externally, but with the key handling we implemented. The two classes must
work closely together.

The `GLSurfaceView` implements key handling by overriding the `onKeyDown()`
method of the regular `View` class. The action is passed on to the `Renderer` through a
helper method called `queueEvent()`. The `queueEvent()` method passes the `Runnable`
object on to the `Renderer` thread held by the `GLSurfaceView`.

Next, the `Renderer` implementation provides the drawing in the `onDrawFrame()`
method. This is either called continuously or on demand, depending on the render mode
set via a call to the `GLSurfaceView.setRenderMode()` method. The implementation
of `onSurfaceChanged()` is now where we set up the screen projection—an appropriate
place because this method is called on orientation or size changes of the surface. Then, in
`onSurfaceCreated()`, the basic GL configuration is performed, including setting client
states and static data, such as the model view.

All EGL configuration is now performed internally to `GLSurfaceView`, so the application need not worry about it. If, however, the application needs to perform custom
configuration of the EGL, the `EGLConfig` object is passed to the `onSurfaceCreated()`
method and is used to perform such custom configuration.

If you choose to use this method to bring up a GL surface on Android, the implementation of the rendering code doesn't need to change at all.

Using OpenGL ES 2.0

Android began supporting Open GL ES 2.0 in Android 2.2 (API Level 8), although applications that leveraged the Android NDK can use 2.0 features as early as API Level 5 with NDK Release 3. In this section, we discuss the Android Java API support for OpenGL ES 2.0. Support also remains for OpenGL ES 1.x and for good reason. Open GL ES 2.0 is not backward compatible with OpenGL ES 1.x. The different OpenGL ES versions provide different methods of handling 3D graphics:

- OpenGL ES 1.x provides a fixed function rendering and texturing pipeline. That is to say, the math used to transform, light, and color a scene is all the same—fixed functions.

- OpenGL ES 2.0 replaced the fixed functions with vertex and fragment shader programs written, of course, by you, the developer. Writing the shader programs provides much more flexibility, but does incur a bit more overhead on the development side.

The choice of which version of OpenGL ES to use is yours. In this section, we show you how to initialize and get a basic OpenGL ES 2.0 program up and running. Using the NDK method is discussed in Chapter 21.

Tip

Many of the code examples provided in this section are taken from the SimpleOpenGL2 application. The source code for this application is provided for download on the book's websites.

Configuring Your Application for OpenGL ES 2.0

If you're going to use the Android OpenGL ES 2.0 APIs and aren't planning on supporting alternate code paths, you need to specify two items in your manifest file: Your application requires Android 2.2 or higher using the `<uses-sdk>` tag and that it requires OpenGL ES 2.0 using the `<uses-feature>` tag.

```
<uses-sdk
    android:targetSdkVersion="8"
    android:minSdkVersion="8" />
<uses-feature
    android:glEsVersion="0x00020000" />
```

Requesting an OpenGL ES 2.0 Surface

Start by creating your custom `SurfaceView`, which you usually do within the `Activity` class `onCreate()` method, as follows:

```
mAndroidSurface = new CustomGL2SurfaceView(this);
setContentView(mAndroidSurface);
```

Of course, you need to implement the `CustomGL2SurfaceView` class. In our sample project, we did this as an inner class of the `Activity`, for convenience:

```
private class CustomGL2SurfaceView extends GLSurfaceView {
    final CustomRenderer renderer;

    public CustomGL2SurfaceView(Context context) {
        super(context);
        setEGLContextClientVersion(2);
        renderer = new CustomRenderer();
        setRenderer(renderer);
    }
}
```

The most important line of code here is the call to the `setEGLContextClientVersion()` method. This call is made in order to request an EGL context for OpenGL ES 1.x (when the parameter is 1) or OpenGL ES 2.x (when the parameter is 2). Then the custom renderer is set.

Although it might seem confusing, the `Renderer` methods take `GL10` objects. How, then, are you to make OpenGL ES 2.0 calls? The answer turns out to be simple: The `GLES20` class is entirely static. Just ignore the `GL10` parameters and make calls directly to the `GLES20` class.

The `CustomRenderer` class starts out by initializing the vertices, much as we did earlier. Then, when the `onSurfaceCreate()` method is called, we can initialize the shader programs, as follows:

```
@Override
public void onSurfaceCreated(GL10 unused, EGLConfig unused2) {
    try {
        initShaderProgram(R.raw.simple_vertex, R.raw.simple_fragment);
        initialized = true;
    } catch (Exception e) {
        Log.e(DEBUG_TAG, "Failed to init GL");
    }
}
```

The two resource identifiers, `simple_vertex` and `simple_fragment`, simply reference two text files stored as a raw resources. Now, let's look at the initialization of the shaders:

```
private int shaderProgram = 0;
private void initShaderProgram(int vertexId, int fragmentId)
    throws Exception {
    int vertexShader =
        loadAndCompileShader(GLES20.GL_VERTEX_SHADER, vertexId);
    int fragmentShader =
        loadAndCompileShader(GLES20.GL_FRAGMENT_SHADER, fragmentId);
```

```
    shaderProgram = GLES20.glCreateProgram();
    if (shaderProgram == 0) {
        throw new Exception("Failed to create shader program");
    }
    // attach the shaders to the program
    GLES20.glAttachShader(shaderProgram, vertexShader);
    GLES20.glAttachShader(shaderProgram, fragmentShader);
    // bind attribute in our vertex shader
    GLES20.glBindAttribLocation(shaderProgram, 0, "vPosition");
    // link the shaders
    GLES20.glLinkProgram(shaderProgram);
    // check the linker status
    int[] linkerStatus = new int[1];
    GLES20.glGetProgramiv(shaderProgram, GLES20.GL_LINK_STATUS,
        linkerStatus, 0);
    if (GLES20.GL_TRUE != linkerStatus[0]) {
        Log.e(DEBUG_TAG, "Linker Failure: "
            + GLES20.glGetProgramInfoLog(shaderProgram));
        GLES20.glDeleteProgram(shaderProgram);
        throw new Exception("Program linker failed");
    }
    GLES20.glClearColor(0.5f, 0.5f, 0.5f, 1);
}
```

This process does not change substantially for different shaders. Recall that OpenGL ES 2.0 requires both a vertex shader and a fragment shader. First, we load the text for each shader and compile them. Then, we create a new shader program reference, attach both shaders to it, assign an attribute position to our only input parameter, and link the program. Finally, checks are made to confirm that the program linked successfully.

The loading of each shader is handled by our loadAndCompileShader() method. Here is a sample implementation of this method:

```
private int loadAndCompileShader(int shaderType, int shaderId)
    throws Exception {
    InputStream inputStream =
        AndroidGL2Activity.this.getResources().openRawResource(shaderId);
    String shaderCode = inputStreamToString(inputStream);
    int shader = GLES20.glCreateShader(shaderType);
    if (shader == 0) {
        throw new Exception("Can't create shader");
    }
    // hand the code over to GL
    GLES20.glShaderSource(shader, shaderCode);
    // compile it
    GLES20.glCompileShader(shader);
    // get compile status
    int[] status = new int[1];
```

```
    GLES20.glGetShaderiv(shader, GLES20.GL_COMPILE_STATUS, status, 0);
    if (status[0] == 0) {
        // failed
        Log.e(DEBUG_TAG, "Compiler Failure: "
            + GLES20.glGetShaderInfoLog(shader));
        GLES20.glDeleteShader(shader);
        throw new Exception("Shader compilation failed");
    }
    return shader;
}
```

The `loadAndCompileShader()` method reads in the raw resource as a string. Then the source is handed over to `GLES20` via a call to the `glShaderSource()` method. Finally, the shader is compiled with a call to `glCompileShader()`. The result is checked to make sure the compile was successful. OpenGL ES 2.0 holds the binary results internally so that they can be used later during linking.

The `onSurfaceChanged()` method should look quite familiar—it changes little. The viewport is reconfigured for the new display metrics and then the clear color is set. Note again that you can simply use the static `GLES20` calls rather than the `GL10` parameter.

```
@Override
public void onSurfaceChanged(GL10 unused, int width, int height) {
    Log.v(DEBUG_TAG, "onSurfaceChanged");
    GLES20.glViewport(0, 0, width, height);
    GLES20.glClearColor(0.5f, 0.5f, 0.5f, 1);
}
```

Finally, we're ready to render the triangle. The scene is rendered each time the system calls our `onDrawFrame()` implementation.

```
@Override
public void onDrawFrame(GL10 unused) {
    if (!initialized) {
        return;
    }
    GLES20.glClear(GLES20.GL_COLOR_BUFFER_BIT);
    GLES20.glUseProgram(shaderProgram);
    GLES20.glVertexAttribPointer(0, 3, GLES20.GL_FLOAT, false, 12,
        verticesBuffer);
    GLES20.glEnableVertexAttribArray(0);
    GLES20.glDrawArrays(GLES20.GL_TRIANGLES, 0, 3);
}
```

At this point, the code should also appear familiar. The primary difference here is the call to the `glUseProgram()` method, where we must pass in the numeric identifier of the program we compiled and linked. The final result is simply a static (motionless) triangle on the screen. It's not very exciting, considering the amount of code required. The flexibility of the shaders is powerful, but many applications don't need the extra flexibility that comes with using OpenGL ES 2.0, either.

By now, you might be wondering what the shaders look like. Because the resource system of Android just uses the part of the filename before the extension, we decided to name our shader files very clearly so we could easily tell what they were: `simple_vertex.shader` and `simple_fragment.shader`. These are two of the simplest shaders one can define.

First, let's look at the vertex shader because it's first in the pipeline:

```
attribute vec4 vPosition;
void main()
{
    gl_Position = vPosition;
}
```

This has a single input, `vPosition`, which is simply assigned to the output. No transformations are applied, and we're not doing any texturing. Now let's turn our attention to the fragment shader:

```
precision mediump float;
void main()
{
    gl_FragColor = vec4(0.0, 1.0, 0.0, 1.0);
}
```

This shader is even simpler. It's assigning a fixed color to the output. In this case, it's assigning green to the output.

Shader definitions can be quite complex. Implementing lighting, texturing, fog effects, and other interesting OpenGL ES 2.0 features that can't be fashioned using the fixed pipeline of OpenGL ES 1.x is far beyond the scope of this book. However, we'd recommend picking up a book on OpenGL ES 2.0, such as *OpenGL ES 2.0 Programming Guide* by Aaftab Munshi, Dan Gisnburg, and Dave Shreiner (Addison-Wesley, 2008, ISBN: 0321502795) or *OpenGL SuperBible* by Richard S. Wright, Jr., Nicholas Haemel, Graham Sellers, and Benjamin Lipchak (Addison-Wesley, 2010, ISBN: 0321712617), or finding resources online.

Working with RenderScript

RenderScript is a set of high-performance graphics and computation APIs that was introduced in Android 3.0 (API Level 11). RenderScript uses a C language (C99, specifically) for writing scripts. Through intermediate compilation, RenderScript is designed to run on a variety of processor architectures, providing a means of writing performance-critical code that the system later compiles to native code for the processor it can run on. This can be the device CPU, a multi-core CPU, or even the GPU. As of this writing, only the CPU is a target.

RenderScript is based on the C programming language. If you're not familiar with C, we recommend that you get familiar with it first before trying to use RenderScript. Although RenderScript is not OpenGL, nor does it require that you use it for graphics rendering, the concepts for using it are similar to OpenGL concepts. And, indeed, the underlying graphics rendering is done with OpenGL ES 2; however, RenderScript exposes only a subset of the functionality available in OpenGL ES. Therefore, familiarity with OpenGL and 3D graphics terminology helps here, as it has for the other portions of this chapter.

Although RenderScript is more limiting than using OpenGL ES in the 3D rendering area, the addition of compute-only RenderScript adds some welcome capabilities. Drawing a quick 3D scene using RenderScript might be more efficient in terms of coding than using OpenGL. Using RenderScript for heavy computation or image manipulation might be faster to develop and it might perform better than similar NDK solutions (due to automatic distribution across hardware cores). Unlike developing with the Android NDK, you don't have to worry about the underlying hardware architecture. In fact, when it comes to NDK limitations, such as no support for Google TV, RenderScript has fewer. It does work on Google TV.

Tip

The code examples provided in this section are taken from the SimpleRenderscript application. The source code for this sample application is provided for download on the book's websites.

Defining RenderScript Functionality

So, let's see an example of an Android application that leverages Renderscript. Let's assume you start with an existing Android project in Eclipse. RenderScript files are stored in your source tree as files that have the .rs file suffix. For example, we are going to create a simple snowflake animation, so we add a file called snow.rs.

A Tip for Source Control

RenderScript generates an intermediate binary file in the res/raw directory. For example, snow.rs creates a file called snow.bc (bc for LLVM bitcode, the intermediate binary format). This file should not be checked in to source control. We recommend adding an ignore definition for your source control to keep all .bc files out.

RenderScript files begin with a definition of the RenderScript version; the only valid value is 1, currently. This is followed by the Java package name associated with your application. Next, you add your #include statements for the RenderScript headers your application needs (in this example, we use the rs_graphics.rsh header to access some simple graphics functions).

```
#pragma version(1)
#pragma rs java_package_name(com.androidbook.simplerenderscript)
#include "rs_graphics.rsh"
```

Now let's define some global variables. First, we define the mesh. It maps to the `Mesh` object on the Java side, which is where we initialize the memory for it. A mesh is similar to a vertex buffer in OpenGL. For this example, the mesh is made up of points, but we define that in Java later. While you're at it, create a couple of variables to hold wind and gravity values.

```
rs_mesh snowMesh;
typedef struct __attribute__((packed, aligned(4))) Snow {
    float2 velocity;
    float2 position;
    uchar4 color;
} Snow_t;
Snow_t *snow;
float2 wind;
float2 grav;
```

RenderScript has two special functions: `root()` and `init()`. The `root()` function is the rendering loop. It is called each time the system needs to draw the scene. The return value defines whether the script runs once (return 0) or at N-millisecond intervals (return N). If the hardware can't keep up with the requested frequency, then `root()` runs as often as it can. The `init()` function is automatically called once when the script loads and is a good place to initialize variables and other state parameters. Initialize the wind and gravity in the `init()` function:

```
void init() {
    grav.x = 0;
    grav.y = 18;
    wind.x = rsRand(50)+20;
    wind.y = rsRand(4) - 2;
}
```

Initialize the snow in its own helper function. Because the mesh is allocated in Java, we first determine how big it is with a call to the `rsAllocationGetDimX()` function to get the array dimensions so we know how many points we're initializing. The function takes an `rs_allocation`, which is basically a reference to the memory being managed by RenderScript. Next, iterate over each structure and set some random values for the snowflake data, so the snow will appear natural (or at least evenly distributed).

```
void initSnow() {
    const float w = rsgGetWidth();
    const float h = rsgGetHeight();
    int snowCount = rsAllocationGetDimX(rsGetAllocation(snow));
```

```
    Snow_t *pSnow = snow;
    for (int i=0; i < snowCount; i++) {
        pSnow->position.x = rsRand(w);
        pSnow->position.y = rsRand(h);
        pSnow->velocity.y = rsRand(60);
        pSnow->velocity.x = rsRand(100);
        pSnow->velocity.x -= 50;
        uchar4 c = rsPackColorTo8888(255, 255, 255);
        pSnow->color = c;
        pSnow++;
    }
}
```

At this point, we make a two-line root() function that draws the scene as-is. It draws the same every time, of course.

```
int root() {
    rsgClearColor(0.0f, 0.0f, 0.0f, 0.0f);
    rsgDrawMesh(snowMesh);
    return 0;
}
```

The rsgClearColor() function is basically the same as the glClear() function of OpenGL. Then we call the rsgDrawMesh() function, passing in the mesh we've configured. This is somewhat like a call to glDrawArrays() of OpenGL.

Let's update the root() function to animate the snowflakes. Begin by clearing the drawing area using the rsgClearColor() function. Then, for some simple pseudo-physics–style simulation, iterate over each snowflake and apply its current velocity and wind to its position, then adjust the velocity based on gravity acceleration. Finally, check to see whether any snowflakes have fallen off the bottom of the screen and move them back to the top of the screen as needed. Finally, redraw the updated mesh using the rsgDrawMesh() function.

```
int root() {
    rsgClearColor(0.0f, 0.0f, 0.0f, 0.0f);
    float dt = min(rsGetDt(), 0.1f);

    float w = rsgGetWidth();
    float h = rsgGetHeight();

    int snowCount = rsAllocationGetDimX(rsGetAllocation(snow));

    Snow_t *pSnow = snow;
    for (int i=0; i < snowCount; i++) {

        pSnow->position.x += ((pSnow->velocity.x +wind.x) * dt);
        pSnow->position.y += ((pSnow->velocity.y +wind.y) * dt);
```

```
        if (pSnow->position.y > h) {
            pSnow->position.y = 0;
            pSnow->position.x = rsRand(w);
            pSnow->velocity.y = rsRand(60);
        }

        pSnow->velocity.x += (grav.x)*dt;
        pSnow->velocity.y += (grav.y)*dt;

        pSnow++;
    }
    rsgDrawMesh(snowMesh);
    return 30;
}
```

Tip

When you save the script project file in Eclipse, the builders automatically create a file
called snow.bc in the /res/raw directory. This automatically generated file should not
be checked into source control, nor should it be modified. In addition, some Java files are
created in the /gen folder. These are the interface files used for calling into the script
from Android.

Now that the script is created, we need to initialize it for use from within your
Android classes. To do this, we created a helper Java class called SnowRS.java. In it, we
allocate the memory for the snow flakes, initialize the script, and bind the mesh and
snow flake allocation to it. This class also uses a RenderScriptGL object.

```
public class SnowRS {
    public static final int SNOW_FLAKES = 4000;
    private ScriptC_snow mScript;

    private Resources mResources;
    private RenderScriptGL mRS;

    public SnowRS() {
    }

    public void stop() {
        mRS.bindRootScript(null);
    }

    public void start() {
        mRS.bindRootScript(mScript);
    }
```

```
public void init(RenderScriptGL rs, Resources res) {
    mRS = rs;
    mResources = res;
    mScript = (ScriptC_snow) createScript();
}

public ScriptC createScript() {
    ScriptField_Snow snow = new ScriptField_Snow(mRS, SNOW_FLAKES);
    Mesh.AllocationBuilder smb = new Mesh.AllocationBuilder(mRS);
    smb.addVertexAllocation(snow.getAllocation());
    smb.addIndexSetType(Mesh.Primitive.POINT);
    Mesh sm = smb.create();

    ScriptC_snow script;
    script = new ScriptC_snow(mRS, mResources, R.raw.snow);
    script.set_snowMesh(sm);
    script.bind_snow(snow);
    script.invoke_initSnow();
    return script;
}
}
```

Let's take a closer look at the createScript() method, as that's where the memory and rendering initialization take place. First, it initializes a structure array of 4,000 snowflakes. This is then used to create a Mesh object used for rendering. The rendering construct is set to POINT, so each snowflake shows up as a pixel on the screen. Next, the script itself is created and initialized using the raw resource entry created by the Eclipse builder. Then, we assign the Mesh and the array allocation into the script via the calls set_snowMesh() and bind_snow(), respectively. Finally, we initialize the snow with a call to the initSnow() function we created earlier by calling invoke_initSnow(). The script does not start running at this point, but the init() function has been called. To get the script running, call bindRootScript() on the script object, as seen in the start() method.

Rendering to a Custom View Control

The Android SDK provides just the means we need to display our RenderScript: the RSSurfaceView class. Implement a class called FallingSnowView that extends the RSSurfaceView class, like this:

```
public class FallingSnowView extends RSSurfaceView {
    private RenderScriptGL mRSGL;
    private SnowRS mRender;

    public FallingSnowView(Context context) {
        super(context);
    }
```

```
    @Override
    public void surfaceChanged(SurfaceHolder holder, int format,
        int w, int h) {
        super.surfaceChanged(holder, format, w, h);
        if (mRSGL == null) {
            RenderScriptGL.SurfaceConfig sc =
                new RenderScriptGL.SurfaceConfig();
            mRSGL = createRenderScriptGL(sc);
            mRSGL.setSurface(holder, w, h);
            mRender = new SnowRS(w, h);
            mRender.init(mRSGL, getResources(), false);
            mRender.start();
        }
    }


    @Override
    protected void onDetachedFromWindow() {
        if (mRSGL != null) {
            mRSGL = null;
            destroyRenderScriptGL();
        }
    }
}
```

The magic here is in the surfaceChanged() method. Here we create a
RenderScriptGL object from the SurfaceHolder incoming parameter. Next, the
SnowRS object is instantiated and rendering is started with the start() method. To
clean up, we call the destroyRenderScriptGL() method in the
onDetachedFromWindow() callback method.

You now have everything in place to use the FallingSnowView class in your
Activity class. The onCreate() method of your Activity class can be as simple as
this:

```
public class SimpleRenderscriptActivity extends Activity {
    private FallingSnowView snowView;

    @Override
    public void onCreate(Bundle savedInstanceState) {
        super.onCreate(savedInstanceState);
        snowView = new FallingSnowView(this);
        setContentView(snowView);

    }

    @Override
    protected void onResume() {
        super.onResume();
```

```
            snowView.resume();
    }

    @Override
    protected void onPause() {
        super.onPause();
        snowView.pause();
    }
}
```

A frame of the resulting scene is shown in Figure 20.7.

Figure 20.7   The snow is falling in our RenderScript animation example.

There you go. You have now mastered the basics of initializing RenderScript and rendering to the screen. All of this was done in the context of a simple particle system simulating pixel-sized snowflakes. RenderScript can do a lot more, though. You can use a
RenderScript for graphics rendering or computational purposes. You can use it to apply
graphical effects to bitmaps or add shaders to leverage device graphics hardware to draw
the scene differently. You can move the pseudo-physics for the snow to its own compute
RenderScript. You can set up transformations to draw in a 3D space. You can configure
textures to draw. You can set shaders called programs in RenderScript using the OpenGL
shader language GLSL. See the Android SDK documentation for more details.

Summary

In this chapter, you learned the basics for using OpenGL ES from within an Android application. You also learned about the different versions of OpenGL ES supported by the Android platform and the high-performance graphics and compute features available as part of RenderScript.

You learned about several ways to use OpenGL ES in your Android applications. You learned how to initialize OpenGL ES in its own thread. Then you learned how to draw, color, and light objects using a variety of OpenGL and Android helper methods. You then learned how your application thread and the OpenGL thread can interact with each other. Finally, you learned how to clean up OpenGL.

Creating fully functional 3D applications and games is a vast topic, more than enough to fill entire books. You have learned enough to get started drawing in three dimensions on Android and can use the knowledge to apply general OpenGL concepts to Android. The reference section that follows contains links to more information to help you deepen your OpenGL ES knowledge.

References and More Information

Khronos OpenGL ES overview:
  http://www.khronos.org/opengles/
OpenGL ES 1.1 API documentation:
  http://www.khronos.org/opengles/sdk/1.1/docs/man/
OpenGL ES 2.0 API documentation:
  http://www.khronos.org/opengles/sdk/2.0/docs/man/
OpenGL ES information:
  http://www.opengl.org
Android Dev Guide: "RenderScript":
  http://d.android.com/guide/topics/renderscript/index.html
Android Dev Guide: "RenderScript Graphics":
  http://d.android.com/guide/topics/renderscript/graphics.html
Android Dev Guide: "RenderScript Compute":
  http://d.android.com/guide/topics/renderscript/compute.html
Android Dev Guide: "RenderScript Runtime API Reference":
  http://d.android.com/guide/topics/renderscript/reference.html

21

Using the Android NDK

Although Android applications are primarily written in Java, there are times when developers need or prefer to leverage native C or C++ libraries. The Android Native Development Kit (NDK) provides the tools necessary to include and use native libraries in your Android applications. In this chapter, you learn under what circumstances the Android NDK should be considered and how to configure and use it.

Determining When to Use the Android NDK

Most Android applications are written solely in Java using the Android SDK and run within the Dalvik VM. Most applications run smoothly and efficiently in this fashion. However, there are situations when calling in to native code from Java can be preferable. The Android NDK provides tool-chain support for compiling and using native C and C++ libraries in conjunction with your Android Java applications. This is usually done for one of two reasons:

- To perform processor-intensive operations such as complex physics, which can be implemented more efficiently in C and C++, offering substantial performance improvements.
- To leverage existing code, usually in the form of shared or proprietary C or C++ libraries, when porting is not ideal. This is often the case when trying to support multiple platforms with a single code base.

Warning

The native libraries created by the Android NDK can be used only on devices running Android 1.5 and higher. You cannot develop applications that use the Android NDK for older platform versions. Currently Android NDK cannot be used on Google TV devices.

Calling in to native code from Java involves some tradeoffs. Application developers must consider their application design carefully, weighing the benefits of using the NDK versus the drawbacks, which include

- Increased code complexity
- Increased debugging complexity
- Performance overhead for each native code call
- More complex build process
- Developers required to be versed in Java, C/C++, and JNI concepts

Although developers can write entire applications in C or C++, not all of the Android APIs are available directly in native code. If your application requires complex math, physics, graphics algorithms, or other intensive operations, the Android NDK might be right for your project. Your libraries can take advantage of a number of stable native C and C++ APIs, including

- C library headers (libc)
- Math library headers (libm)
- The zlib compression library headers (libz)
- 3D graphics library headers (OpenGL ES 1.1 and 2.0)
- A CPU features library for detecting device CPU features at runtime
- Other headers for C++, logging, JNI, and more

The full list of stable APIs that your code can take advantage of is found in the documentation downloaded with the NDK in the STABLE-APIS.HTML file.

Installing the Android NDK

You can install the Android NDK on Windows, Mac OSX, or Linux operating systems that have the Android SDK and tools properly installed. You also need to install or have already installed

- GNU Make 3.81 or later (http://www.gnu.org/software/make/)
- GNU Awk (Gawk) or Nawk (http://www.gnu.org/software/gawk/)
- Cygwin 1.7 or later (Windows only, http://www.cygwin.com)

You can download the Android NDK from the Android developer website at http://d.android.com/sdk/ndk/. As of Android NDK r7, the Windows installer contains everything needed to perform all NDK operations, except ndk-gdb, without the need for Cygwin. That is to say, if you don't need to debug (for instance, on a build machine) or don't need the use of gdb, no additional tools need to be installed on Windows machines.

Exploring the Android NDK

The Android NDK contains a number of different tools and files, specifically

- Native system libraries and headers that are forward-compatible with the Android platform (1.5 and beyond)
- Tools for compiling and linking native libraries for ARMv5TE and ARMv7-A devices (x86 coming soon)
- Build files for embedding native libraries into Android applications
- Native debugging using ndk-gdb
- NDK documentation in the /docs subdirectory
- NDK sample applications in the /samples subdirectory

Running an Android NDK Sample Application

The best way to familiarize yourself with the Android NDK is to build one of the sample applications provided, such as hello-jni. To do this, take the following steps:

1. Build the hello-jni native library, located in the NDK /samples/hello-jni subdirectory, by typing the following on the command line: **ndk-build**.
2. In Eclipse, import the existing project from the /samples/hello-jni/project/ subdirectory of the NDK installation directory by choosing New, Android Project, and then choosing the Create from Existing Source option. Do a clean build on the project.
3. Create a Debug Configuration for the project.
4. Create an appropriate AVD if necessary. Run the application as normal.
5. If you get errors, you might need to do a "Clean project" in Eclipse after running an ndk-build clean and ndk-build again. It's not uncommon for Eclipse's state to get out of sync with the build status of the native library.

Creating Your Own NDK Project

Now let's look at an example of how to set up and use the NDK for your own Android applications using Eclipse. To create a new Android application that calls into native code, take the following steps:

1. Begin by creating a new Android project in Eclipse.
2. Navigate to your project directory and create a subdirectory called /jni. Inside this directory, place two C files: native_basics.c and native_opengl2.c.

3. In the /jni subdirectory, create a file called Android.mk. A sample Android.mk file might look like this, the one used in our sample application:

```
LOCAL_PATH := $(call my-dir)
include $(CLEAR_VARS)
LOCAL_LDLIBS := -llog -lGLESv2
APP_ABI := all
LOCAL_MODULE    := simplendk
LOCAL_SRC_FILES := native_basics.c native_opengl2.c
include $(BUILD_SHARED_LIBRARY)
```

4. Edit the Android.mk file and make any build changes necessary. By default, only the ARMv5TE instruction set will be targeted. For our sample, this is not necessary. You might want to target a narrower number of devices, but use ARMv7 code to gain native floating point operations to possibly improve math performance. The use of all for APP_ABI also currently includes x86 architecture targets.

5. Build the native library and embed it in your Android application by navigating back to the project directory and running the ndk-build script. You might need to set up the path to this batch file; the ndk-build script is located in the ndk install directory.

6. In Eclipse, update your application manifest file. Be sure to set the <uses-sdk> tag with its android:minSdkVersion attribute set to a value of 3 or higher. In our sample, we ultimately add OpenGL ES 2.0, so we've set these to 8.

7. Create an Eclipse Debug Configuration and any necessary AVDs as normal.

Tip

Many of the code examples provided in this chapter are taken from the SimpleNDK application. The source code for this application is provided for download on the book websites.

Calling Native Code from Java

There are three main steps necessary to add a call from Java to native code, as follows:

1. Add a declaration for the new function in your Java class file as a native type.

2. Add a static initializer for the library that the native function will be compiled into.

3. Add the function of the appropriate name, following a specific naming scheme to the native source file.

This isn't as complex as it sounds, but we go through each step now. The SimpleNDK project has a class called NativeBasicsActivity.java. Let's start there by adding the declaration for the native function. The following declaration must be added to the class:

```
private native void basicNativeCall();
```

Now, make sure that the native library with this function is loaded. This doesn't need to happen for every call, just for each library. In the `Android.mk` file, we identified the library as `simplendk` (the value of `LOCALE_MODULE`), so we load that library. Add this static initializer to the `NativeBasicsActivity` class:

```
static {
    System.loadLibrary("simplendk");
}
```

Finally, the function needs to be added to the `native_basics.c` file in the native library that's being compiled. Each function must follow a specific naming convention. Instead of dots, each part of the function name is separated using an underscore, as follows:

```
Java_package_name_ClassName_functionName
(JNIEnv *env, jobject this, your vars...);
```

For the example, that means our function looks like this:

```
void Java_com_androidbook_simplendk_NativeBasicsActivity_basicNativeCall
    (JNIEnv *env, jobject this)
{
    // do something interesting here
}
```

That's a lengthy function name, but you get errors if you name it incorrectly. This function is now called whenever the Java method declared as `basicNativeCall()` is invoked. But how will you know? Add the following line to the function and then make sure to include `"android/log.h"` in the `native_basics.c` file:

```
__android_log_print(ANDROID_LOG_VERBOSE, DEBUG_TAG, "Basic call");
```

And there you have it! Your first call from Android Java to C native. If you're familiar with JNI, you might realize that it's mostly the same. The main difference is which libraries are available. If you're familiar with JNI, you should find using the NDK fairly straightforward.

Handling Parameters and Return Values

Now that you can make a basic native call, let's pass some parameters in to C and then return something. We make a simple little C function that takes a format string that works with the `stdio sprintf()` call and two numbers to add. The numbers are added, placed in the format string, and a new string is returned. Although simplistic, this demonstrates the handling of Java objects and reminds us that we need to manage memory properly in native C code.

```
jstring Java_com_androidbook_simplendk_NativeBasicsActivity_formattedAddition
    (JNIEnv *env, jobject this, jint number1,
    jint number2, jstring formatString)
```

```
{
    // get a C string from a Java string object
    jboolean fCopy;
    const char * szFormat =
        (*env)->GetStringUTFChars(env, formatString, &fCopy);
    char * szResult;
    // add the two values
    jlong nSum = number1+number2;
    // make sure there's ample room for nSum
    szResult = malloc(sizeof(szFormat)+30);
    // make the call
    sprintf(szResult, szFormat, nSum);
    // get a Java string object
    jstring result = (*env)->NewStringUTF(env, szResult);

    // free the C strings
    free(szResult);
    (*env)->ReleaseStringUTFChars(env, formatString, szFormat);
    // return the Java string object
    return(result);
}
```

The JNI environment object is used for interacting with Java objects. Regular C functions are used for regular C memory management.

Using Exceptions with Native Code

Native code can throw exceptions that the Java side can catch as well as check for exceptions when making calls to Java code. This makes heavy use of the JNIEnv object and might be familiar to those with JNI experience. The following native function throws an exception if the input number parameter isn't a certain value:

```
void Java_com_androidbook_simplendk_NativeBasicsActivity_throwsException
    (JNIEnv * env, jobject this, jint number)
{
    if (number < NUM_RANGE_MIN || number > NUM_RANGE_MAX) {
        // throw an exception
        jclass illegalArgumentException =
            (*env)->FindClass(env, "java/lang/IllegalArgumentException");
        if (illegalArgumentException == NULL) {
            return;
        }
        (*env)->ThrowNew(env, illegalArgumentException,
            "What an exceptional number.");
    } else {
        __android_log_print(ANDROID_LOG_VERBOSE, DEBUG_TAG,
            "Nothing exceptional here");
    }
}
```

The Java declaration for this, as you might expect, needs a throws clause.

```
private native void throwsException(int num)
    throws IllegalArgumentException;
```

Basically, the exception class is found through reflection. Then, the `ThrowNew()` method of the JNIEnv object is used to do the actual throwing of the exception.

To show how to check for an exception in native C code, we need to also show how to call a Java method from C. The following block of code does just that:

```
void Java_com_androidbook_simplendk_NativeBasicsActivity_checksException
    (JNIEnv * env, jobject this, jint number)
{
    jthrowable exception;
    jclass class = (*env)->GetObjectClass(env, this);
    jmethodID fnJavaThrowsException =
        (*env)->GetMethodID(env, class, "javaThrowsException", "(I)V");
    if (fnJavaThrowsException != NULL) {
        (*env)->CallVoidMethod(env, this, fnJavaThrowsException, number);
        exception = (*env)->ExceptionOccurred(env);
        if (exception) {
            (*env)->ExceptionDescribe(env);
            (*env)->ExceptionClear(env);
            __android_log_print(ANDROID_LOG_ERROR,
                DEBUG_TAG, "Exception occurred. Check LogCat.");
        }
    } else {
        __android_log_print(ANDROID_LOG_ERROR,
            DEBUG_TAG, "No method found");
    }
}
```

The call to the `GetMethodID()` function is best looked up in your favorite JNI reference or online. It's basically a reflective way of getting a reference to the method, but the fourth parameter must be supplied correctly. In this case, it takes a single integer and returns a void.

Because the method returns a void, use the `CallVoidMethod()` function to actually call it and then use the `ExceptionOccurred()` function to check to see whether the method threw an exception. If it did, the `ExceptionDescribe()` function actually writes the exception out to LogCat, but it looks slightly different from a normal exception output. Then the exception is cleared so it doesn't go any further.

The Java method being called, `javaThrowsException()`, is defined as follows:

```
@SuppressWarnings("unused") // is called from native
private void javaThrowsException(int num)
    throws IllegalArgumentException {
    if (num == 42) {
```

```
        throw new IllegalArgumentException("Anything but that number!");
    } else {
        Log.v(DEBUG_TAG, "Good choice in numbers.");
    }
}
```

The use of the @SuppressWarnings option is due to the fact that the method is never called directly from Java, only from native code. You can also use this process of calling Java methods for Android SDK methods. However, remember that the idea of using NDK is generally to increase performance. If you find yourself doing many Android calls, the performance might be improved by simply staying on the Java side of things and leaving algorithmically heavy functionality on the native side.

Using Native Activities

While most uses of Android NDK involve calling native code through JNI, it is possible to build a fully native activity and, indeed, a fully native application. This is useful for applications that don't use the Android APIs much, such as ports of existing games. Many APIs are available, however. Read more about creating a fully native application in the NDK documentation file NATIVE_ACTIVITY.HTML.

Improving Graphics Performance

One of the most common reasons to use the Android NDK is to leverage the OpenGL ES 1.1 and 2.0 native libraries to perform complex math calculations that benefit from native code and speed up the porting process. Although you can use the Java APIs in the Android SDK to provide OpenGL ES support, some developers with core graphics libraries built in C or C++ might prefer to use the NDK. Here are some tips for developing and using graphics libraries provided with the Android NDK:

- OpenGL ES 1.1 native libraries are guaranteed on Android 1.6 (API Level 4) and higher; OpenGL ES 2.0 native libraries are guaranteed on Android 2.0 (API Level 5) and higher. Make sure you include "GLES2/gl2.h" and, optionally, include "GLES2/gl2ext.h" to get access to the functions. They are named in the standard OpenGL way (for example, glClearColor).
- Use the <uses-sdk> manifest tag to enforce the minimum SDK supported by the OpenGL ES version your application leverages.
- Use the <uses-feature> manifest tag to specify which version of OpenGL ES your application leverages so that the Android Market can filter your application and provide it only to compatible devices.

For example, the following block of code is how the drawFrame() method from Chapter 20, "Developing Android 3D Graphics Applications," would look in the NDK. You can find this code in the SimpleNDK project:

```
const GLfloat gVertices[] = {
    0.0f, 0.5f, 0.0f,
    -0.5f, -0.5f, 0.0f,
    0.5f, -0.5f, 0.0f
};

void Java_com_androidbook_simplendk_NativeOpenGL2Activity_drawFrame
    (JNIEnv * env, jobject this, jint shaderProgram)
{
    glClear(GL_COLOR_BUFFER_BIT);
    glUseProgram(shaderProgram);
    glVertexAttribPointer(0, 3, GL_FLOAT, GL_FALSE, 12, gVertices);
    glEnableVertexAttribArray(0);
    glDrawArrays(GL_TRIANGLES, 0, 3);
}
```

This is called from the onDrawFrame() method of our CustomRenderer class. Because this is the code that runs in a tight loop, it makes sense to implement it with native code. Of course, this particular implementation doesn't benefit at all, but if we had done a bunch of complex math, transformations, and other algorithmically heavy code, it could possibly be faster. Only testing on actual devices can determine for each case what is or isn't faster, though.

A Comparison to RenderScript

In Chapter 20, we talked about RenderScript with respect to graphics. Although that's a common use of RenderScript, it can also be used for computational purposes. As one of the reasons for using Android NDK is also for computational purposes, there is some overlap. However, RenderScript has a couple of advantages that are compelling when you're not using existing C code.

First, unlike NDK code, RenderScript code is compiled for the target device once on the device. This means you don't have to worry about new CPU architectures that come out. In addition, when support for GPU is added (OpenCL-style computation), your code will automatically start using it. This also simplifies your build system. Second, RenderScript makes it easy to leverage multiple cores. Many calls do this automatically, but there are explicit calls for dividing work. Combined, if all you're looking for from native code is a performance boost, RenderScript might be an excellent choice.

Summary

The Android NDK provides helpful tools that enable developers to call into native C and C++ libraries on devices running Android 1.5 and higher. Installing the Android NDK toolset is a relatively straightforward process. Using the Android NDK involves creating build scripts in order to include shared native libraries in your Android application package files. Although using the Android NDK is not necessary for every application, certain types of applications might benefit greatly from its use.

References and More Information

Android NDK download site:
   http://d.android.com/sdk/ndk/index.html
Google discussion group: "Android NDK":
   http://groups.google.com/group/android-ndk
JNI reference book:
   http://java.sun.com/docs/books/jni/html/jniTOC.html

22

Extending Android Application Reach

Android applications can be extended far beyond traditional functional boundaries to integrate tightly with the rest of the operating system. Developers can use a number of other platform features to improve the usefulness of an application. In this chapter, you learn about the various ways to enhance your applications and extend their reach, making them even more powerful and compelling to your users.

Enhancing Your Applications

One of Android's most compelling features as a platform is its approach to application interoperability. Unlike the mobile development platforms of the past, which allowed each simple application to run in its own little bubble, Android allows applications to share data and functionality with other applications and the rest of the operating system in a secure and reasonable fashion. After you've developed your core application, it's time to give some thought to how to extend the application's reach beyond the traditional use case, which is

1. User launches the app.
2. User runs the app.
3. User closes the app.

Although it's certainly necessary to support that particular scenario, it's not the only way that users can interact with your app or its features. The Android framework includes a number of ways to move beyond this paradigm. You can extend and enhance Android applications in a variety of ways, including

- Exposing small segments of application functionality in the form of App Widgets, which can reside on the user's Home screen.

- Providing users with an interactive background associated with your application in the form of a live wallpaper.

- Making application content searchable across the device, as discussed in Chapter 23, "Enabling Application Search."

- Enabling your application to act as a content type handler, exposing the capability to process common types of data such as pictures or videos.

- Enabling different application entry points using intent filters above and beyond the default activity to launch.

- Acting as content providers, exposing internal data for use by other applications and taking advantage of other content providers to enhance your applications. See Chapter 4, "Building Android Content Providers," for more details.

- Acting as a broadcast receiver to react to important events that occur and by broadcasting application events of interest to other applications. See Chapter 5, "Broadcasting and Receiving Intents," for more details.

- By acting as a service, providing data services and special functionality to other applications, as discussed in Chapter 2, "Working with Services."

This is where we encourage you to think outside the box and consider how to extend the reach of your applications. By doing so, you keep your application fresh in your users' minds so they continually rely on your application and don't forget about it. Now let's look at some of the options listed in more detail.

Warning

Another way you can make content-rich applications more readily available to users is with the use of live folders. Introduced in Android 1.5 (API Level 3), it was discontinued in Android 3.0 (API Level 11) due to security reasons. The Android team recommends using App Widget Collections instead, but they are available only in devices running Android 3.0 (API Level 11) and later.

Working with App Widgets

Introduced in API Level 3, the App Widget provides a level of application integration with the Android operating system previously not available to mobile developers. Applications that publish App Widgets are called App Widget providers. A component that can contain an App Widget is called an App Widget *host*. An *App Widget* is a lightweight, simply featured application (such as a desktop plug-in) that can be installed on a host such as the Home screen.

An App Widget is normally tied back to some underlying application. For example, a calendar application might have an App Widget that shows the current date and enables the user to view the scheduled events of the day. Clicking on a specific event might launch the full calendar application to that date, enabling the user to access the full range of application features. Similarly, a music application might provide a simple set of controls within an App Widget, enabling the user to easily start and stop music playback from his Home screen. We provide a simple App Widget implementation as part of the code that accompanies this book; this App Widget displays information about the United States Homeland Security Advisory System's threat level (red/severe, orange/high, yellow/elevated, blue/guarded, green/low)—this type of App Widget might be appropriate for a travel application.

An App Widget can be updated at regular intervals with fresh content. This makes App Widgets ideal for secondary application features, whereas notifications that launch into the full application functionality might be more appropriate for events that require a speedy user response.

Creating an App Widget

Consider whether or not your application should include App Widget functionality. Although App Widgets are small in size and light on functionality, they allow the user access to application functionality straight from the Home screen. App Widgets also serve to keep users using the application by reminding them that they installed it. Some applications allow only one instance of an App Widget to run (such as the music player), whereas others might allow multiple instances of the same App Widget to be placed simultaneously, though generally showing different content (such as a picture frame).

You need to make the following changes to your application to support App Widgets:

- Provide an XML App Widget configuration.
- Determine whether the App Widget requires a configuration activity.
- Provide an `AppWidgetProvider` class implementation.
- Provide a `Service` class implementation to handle App Widget content updates, as needed.
- Update the application Android manifest file to register the App Widget provider information and any information about the update service.

Now let's look at some of these requirements in greater detail.

Tip

The code examples provided in this section are taken from the SimpleAppWidget application. The source code for this application is provided for download on the book's websites.

Creating an App Widget Configuration

First, your application must provide an XML App Widget definition. You can store this definition in the project's resources in the `/res/xml` directory. Let's take a closer look at an example of an App Widget definition, as defined in `/res/xml/simple_widget_info.xml`:

```
<?xml version="1.0" encoding="utf-8"?>
<appwidget-provider
```

```
    xmlns:android="http://schemas.android.com/apk/res/android"
    android:minWidth="146dp"
    android:minHeight="72dp"
    android:updatePeriodMillis="28800000"
    android:initialLayout="@layout/widget"
    android:previewImage="@drawable/widgetPreview">
</appwidget-provider>
```

This simple App Widget definition is encapsulated in the `<appwidget-provider>`
XML tag. The `minWidth` and `minHeight` attributes dictate the size of the App Widget
(a dimension, here in `dp`), and the `updatePeriodMillis` attribute is used to define
how often the App Widget content is refreshed (using the App Widget update service)—
in this case, once every eight hours. The App Widget layout definition is referenced using
the `initialLayout` attribute—we talk more about this layout file in a few moments.
Finally, a preview of the App Widget is provided with the `previewImage` field. This is
useful in Android 3.0 and later where selecting images is done from the preview image
rather than a list.

Note

An App Widget cannot be updated more frequently than every 30 minutes (1,800,000 milliseconds). Ensure that the `updatePeriodMillis` attribute of your App Widget provider
reflects this limitation. This limit has testing implications. You might consider a tool to
force an update or some sort of Refresh button that users might benefit from, as well.

If your widget must break this limit, which you should only do for a very good reason, you
must implement the timer yourself. Keep in mind the effect on battery life and performance this decision might have.

To draw nicely on the Home screen, the App Widget dimensions must follow certain
guidelines. The Home screen is divided into cells of a particular size. When the user
attempts to install an App Widget, the system checks to make sure there is enough space
(as dictated by the minimum width and height values of the App Widget).

Tip

The basic formula for determining the size of your App Widget is to multiply the number of
cells you want by 74, and then subtract two. In our case, we want an App Widget two cells
high and two cells wide. Therefore, we use a size of ((74×2)–2) or 146. For a nice write-up
on App Widget design guidelines, see the Android website at http://d.android.com/guide/
practices/ui_guidelines/widget_design.html.

There are a number of other attributes available in the `<appwidget-provider>` tag.
For example, you can specify the `Activity` class used to configure the App Widget
using the `configure` attribute, which is especially useful when you support multiple
simultaneous App Widget instances (see the App Widget write-ups on our book's blog
for more advanced App Widget implementations). For a complete list of available App

Widget provider configuration details, see the class documentation for the android.appwidget.AppWidgetProviderInfo class.

Determining Whether the App Widget Requires a Configuration Activity

Generally speaking, if there is more than one instance of an App Widget, each instance should look or behave differently. This isn't a strict requirement; if each instance of the App Widget looks and acts the same, users quickly catch on and install only one instance at a time.

However, if you want to differentiate between App Widget instances, you need to provide each with settings, and thus, you must create a configuration activity. This configuration activity is a normal activity, but it will read in certain Intent extras upon launch. The configuration activity must be defined in the App Widget XML configuration.

Each time a new App Widget instance is created, the configuration Activity is launched. The Activity is launched with the unique App Widget identifier, passed in via the launch intent's EXTRA_APPWIDGET_ID extra. The Activity, on completion, must set this value back in the result intent along with result status, such as RESULT_OK.

The configuration activity should not only let the user configure options on this particular App Widget instance, but it should also update the RemoteViews object, as the App Widget will not receive an update event when it's first created with a configuration Activity set in the XML configuration. Subsequent updates receive the update event, though.

Creating an App Widget Provider

An App Widget is basically a BroadcastReceiver that handles particular actions. As with a broadcast receiver, the primary interaction with an App Widget happens through the onReceive() method. However, the default AppWidgetProvider class handles onReceive() and, in turn, delegates operations to its other methods, which you then implement.

Implementing the AppWidgetProvider Class

The AppWidgetProvider class simplifies the handling of these actions by providing a framework for developers to implement App Widgets. An AppWidgetProvider implementation requires the following methods:

- The onEnabled() method is called when the App Widget is created. This is a good place to perform any configuration shared for the entire widget provider. This method is called once for the first App Widget instance added to the widget host (usually the home screen).

- The onDisabled() method is called when the App Widget is disabled. This method is called only after all App Widget instances for this provider are removed from the App Widget host. For example, if there were five App Widgets for this provider on the home screen, this method would be called only after the user removed the fifth and final App Widget.

- The `onUpdate()` method is called at regular intervals, depending on the update frequency specified in the App Widget configuration file. This frequency uses an in-exact timer, so do not rely on this frequency being precise. If you need precision updates, consider scheduling updates using the `AlarmManager` class. This method is called with a list of widget identifiers. Each identifier references a unique App Widget instance in the App Widget host. The App Widget provider implementation must differentiate between each instance and, typically, store different configuration values for each as well.

- The `onDeleted()` method is called when a particular instance of this App Widget is deleted.

Using Remote Views

Android App Widgets do not run in the application process, but in the host's process. Therefore, the App Widget uses the `RemoteViews` class to define its user interface. The `RemoteViews` class supports a subset of the overall `View` hierarchy, for display in another process. Generally speaking, you want to configure the `RemoteViews` object and send it to the App Widget Manager during the `onUpdate()` method. However, you also need to update it when an instance is created and a configuration activity exists.

View hierarchies defined using `RemoteViews` can contain only a limited set of controls, including `Button`, `ImageButton`, `ImageView`, `TextView`, `AnalogClock`, `Chronometer`, `ProgressBar`, `ListView`, `GridView`, `StackView`, `ViewFlipper`, and `AdapterViewFlipper` controls and only in `FrameLayout`, `LinearLayout`, or `RelativeLayout` layouts. Objects derived from these controls cannot be used, either. The `RemoteViews` configuration should be kept as simple as possible because access to its view hierarchy is controlled through helper methods, such as `setImageViewResource()`, `setTextViewText()`, `setProgressbar()`, `setShort()`, `setString()`, `setChronometer()`, and `setRemoteAdapter()`. In short, you can generate an XML layout definition for an App Widget, but you must be careful to use only controls that are supported by the `RemoteViews` class.

Let's look at the incredibly simple layout definition used by the threat level App Widget, as defined in the resource file `/res/layout/widget.xml`:

```xml
<?xml version="1.0" encoding="utf-8"?>
<RelativeLayout
    xmlns:android="http://schemas.android.com/apk/res/android"
    android:layout_height="match_parent"
    android:layout_width="match_parent"
    android:id="@+id/widget_view">
    <TextView
        android:layout_width="wrap_content"
        android:layout_height="wrap_content"
        android:id="@+id/widget_text_threat"
        android:layout_centerInParent="true">
    </TextView>
</RelativeLayout>
```

Nothing too complex in this layout, eh? A single `TextView` control, which displays the threat level information, is encapsulated in a `RelativeLayout` control. Now your layout can be loaded programmatically into a `RemoteViews` object for use in the App Widget provider. Don't worry, things get more complex when we cram that layout into a `RemoteViews` object and act upon it across processes.

To load a layout resource (such as `widget.xml` defined earlier) into a `RemoteViews` object, you can use the following code:

```
RemoteViews remoteView =
    new RemoteViews(context.getPackageName(), R.layout.widget);
```

When you want to update the text in that layout's `TextView` control, you need to use the `setTextViewText()` method of the `RemoteViews` class, like this:

```
remoteView.setTextViewText(R.id.widget_text_threat, "Red alert!");
```

If you want the user to be able to click in the `RelativeLayout` control of the App Widget display and to launch the underlying application, use the `setOnClickPendingIntent()` method of the `RemoteViews` class. For example, the following code creates a pending intent that can launch the `SimpleAppWidgetActivity` activity:

```
Intent launchAppIntent =
    new Intent(context, SimpleAppWidgetActivity.class);
PendingIntent launchAppPendingIntent = PendingIntent.getActivity(
    context, 0, launchAppIntent,
    PendingIntent.FLAG_UPDATE_CURRENT);
remoteView.setOnClickPendingIntent
    (R.id.widget_view, launchAppPendingIntent);
```

Finally, when the `RemoteViews` object is all set up, the App Widget provider needs to tell the App Widget Manager about the updated `RemoteViews` object:

```
ComponentName simpleWidget = new ComponentName(context,
    SimpleAppWidgetProvider.class);
AppWidgetManager appWidgetManager =
    AppWidgetManager.getInstance(context);
appWidgetManager.updateAppWidget(simpleWidget, remoteView);
```

To update the appropriate App Widget, the `AppWidgetManager` object requires its component name. The App Widget Manager then updates the content of the specific named App Widget using the contents of the `RemoteViews` object you provide in the `updateAppWidget()` method. Each time the `RemoteViews` object is updated, it is rebuilt. Although this usually happens infrequently, keep them simple for good performance.

Note

Unfortunately, the complete implementation of the `AppWidgetProvider` class provided in `SimpleAppWidget` is too lengthy for print. See the `SimpleAppWidgetProvider` class in that sample project for the full details of how the threat level App Widget works.

Updating an App Widget

When the `onUpdate()` method of the App Widget provider is called, a list of identifiers is passed in. Each identifier references a particular App Widget instance for this provider. That is, a user can add any number of App Widgets of a particular kind to a host. It's up to you, though, how they will differ. During the update event, each identifier must be iterated over and update each of the `RemoteViews` objects individually (that is, if you support different instances simultaneously).

An App Widget must be responsive during the update event because it is being executed from the UI thread of the host process. When the updates are done, there is no guarantee that the App Widget Provider object stays around. Therefore, if an App Widget refresh requires any lengthy blocking operations, it must use a service so that it can create a thread to perform these operations in the background.

In our threat level App Widget example, we already have a service that performs some network operations to download updated threat level data. This service is perfect for the needs of an App Widget and the application, so they can share this service. Convenient, huh?

Creating an App Widget Update Service

Most App Widgets do not contain static content, but are updated from time to time. Normally, an Android service is used to enable App Widget content updates. The service performs any necessary update-related tasks, including spawning threads, connecting to the Internet, and so on. The App Widget provider's `onUpdate()` method, which is called at the App Widget update interval, is a great place to start this update service. After the service has done its job, it should shut itself down until the next time fresh content is needed. Let's revisit the threat level App Widget, which uses two services:

- The `SimpleDataUpdateService` class runs at the App Widget update interval (started in the `onUpdate()` method of the App Widget provider). The service connects to the Internet, checks the current threat level, and stores the result in the application's shared preferences. Finally, the service shuts itself down. It might be helpful to consider the application as the "owner" of this service—it provides information for both the application and the App Widget by saving data to the shared preferences.

- The `PrefListenerService` class listens for changes in the application's shared preferences. In addition to using the `onUpdate()` method, this service is started when the App Widget is enabled, thus allowing it to be updated whenever the data changes (for example, when the underlying application modifies the shared preference by checking the threat level itself). When the threat level preference changes, this service triggers a call to the `updateAppWidget()` method of the App Widget provider, which updates the `RemoteViews` object for the App Widget—bypassing the frequency limitations of the App Widget Manager. It might be helpful to consider the App Widget as the "owner" of this service—it runs in the App Widget lifecycle and exists only to update the content of the App Widget.

Certainly, there are simpler ways to update your App Widget. For example, the App Widget can use its one service to do the work of downloading the threat level data and updating the App Widget content, but then the application is left to do its own thing. The method described here illustrates how you can bypass some of the update frequency limitations of App Widgets and still share content between App Widgets and their underlying applications.

Tip

Updating the `RemoteViews` object need not happen from within the App Widget provider. It can be called directly from the application, too. In this example, the service created for downloading the threat level data is used by the application and App Widget alike. Using a service for downloading online data is a good practice for a number of reasons. However, if there was no download service to leverage, we could have gotten away with just one service. In this service, fully controlled by the App Widget, we would have not only done the download but also then updated the `RemoteViews` object directly. Doing this would have eliminated the need for listening to the shared preferences changes from the App Widget service, too.

Configuring the Android Manifest File for App Widgets

For the Android system to know about your application's App Widget, you must include a `<receiver>` tag in the application's Android manifest file to register it as an App Widget provider. App Widgets often use services, and these services must be registered in the Android manifest file with a `<service>` tag like any other service. Here is an excerpt of the Android manifest file from the `SimpleAppWidget` project:

```
<receiver android:name="SimpleAppWidgetProvider"
    android:label="@string/widget_desc"
    android:icon="@drawable/threat_levels_descriptions">
    <intent-filter>
        <action android:name=
            "android.appwidget.action.APPWIDGET_UPDATE" />
    </intent-filter>
    <meta-data
        android:name="android.appwidget.provider"
        android:resource="@xml/simple_widget_info" />
</receiver>
<service android:name="SimpleDataUpdateService" />
<service android:name="SimpleAppWidgetProvider$PrefListenerService" />
```

Notice that, unlike a typical `<receiver>` definition, a `<meta-data>` section references an XML file resource. The `<receiver>` tag includes several bits of information about the App Widget configuration, including a label and icon for the App Widget, which is displayed on the App Widget picker (where the user chooses from available App Widgets on the system). The `<receiver>` tag also includes an intent filter to handle the `android.appwidget.action.APPWIDGET_UPDATE` action, as well as a `<meta-data>` tag that references the App Widget configuration file stored in the XML resource directory. Finally, the services used to update the App Widget are registered.

Installing an App Widget

After your application has implemented App Widget functionality, a user (who has installed your application) can install it to the Home screen using the following steps:

1. From the Home screen, click to the button to show all applications.
2. Choose the Widgets tab, as shown in Figure 22.1.

Figure 22.1   Using the Widget picker to install an App Widget on the Home screen.

3. From the Widget menu, choose the App Widget you want to include by pressing and holding. Users can see the preview image here. Set the preview to something useful—generally what the widget will look like in a typical situation.

4. Drag the App Widget to the place you want it and release, as shown in Figure 22.2.

Figure 22.2   A simple App Widget being placed on the Home screen that displays NTAS alerts.

Becoming an App Widget Host

Although somewhat less common, applications might also become App Widget hosts. App Widget hosts (`android.appWidget.AppWidgetHost`) are simply containers that can embed and display App Widgets. The most commonly used App Widget host is the Home screen. For more information on developing an App Widget host, see the Android SDK documentation.

Working with Live Wallpapers

In addition to still image wallpapers, Android supports the notion of a live wallpaper. Instead of displaying a static background image on the Home screen, the user can set an interactive, or live, wallpaper that can display anything that can be drawn on a surface, such as graphics and animations. Live wallpapers were introduced in Android 2.1 (API Level 7).

Your applications can provide live wallpapers that use 3D graphics and animations as well as display interesting application content. Some examples of live wallpapers include

- A 3D display showing an animated scene portraying abstract shapes
- A service that animates between images found on an online image-sharing service
- An interactive pond with water that ripples with touch
- Wallpapers that change based on the actual season, weather, and time of day

Tip

Programmatic installation of still image wallpapers is discussed in Chapter 14, "Using Android Multimedia APIs."

Creating a Live Wallpaper

A live wallpaper is similar to an Android Service, but its result is a surface that the host can display. You need to make the following changes to your application in order to support live wallpapers:

- Provide an XML wallpaper configuration.
- Provide a `WallpaperService` implementation.
- Update the application Android manifest file to register the wallpaper service with the appropriate permissions.

Now let's look at some of these requirements in greater detail.

Tip

The code examples provided in this section are taken from the SimpleLiveWallpaper application. The source code for this application is provided for download on the book's websites. If you'd like more examples, including ones that use RenderScript for fancier graphics, check out the open source code here (http://code.google.com/p/android-dc-tutorial-projects/source/browse/#svn%2Ftrunk%2FStarsLiveWallpaper or http://goo.gl/NXODt) and here (http://code.google.com/p/android-mt-tutorials/source/browse/#svn%2Ftrunk%2FFallingSnow or http://goo.gl/DoPgc) that we've provided.

Creating a Live Wallpaper Service

The guts of the live wallpaper functionality are provided as part of a `WallpaperService` implementation, and most of the live wallpaper functionality is driven by its `WallpaperService.Engine` implementation.

Implementing a Wallpaper Service

Your application needs to extend the WallpaperService class. The most important method the class needs to override is the onCreateEngine() method. Here is a sample implementation of a wallpaper service called SimpleDroidWallpaper:

```java
public class SimpleDroidWallpaper extends WallpaperService {
    private final Handler handler = new Handler();

    @Override
    public Engine onCreateEngine() {
        return new SimpleWallpaperEngine();
    }
    class SimpleWallpaperEngine extends WallpaperService.Engine {
        // Your implementation of a wallpaper service engine here...
    }
}
```

There's not much to this wallpaper service. The onCreateEngine() method simply returns your application's custom wallpaper engine, which provides all the functionality for a specific live wallpaper. You can also override the other wallpaper service methods, as necessary. A Handler object is initialized for posting wallpaper draw operations.

Implementing a Wallpaper Service Engine

Now let's take a closer look at the wallpaper service engine implementation. The wallpaper service engine handles all the details regarding the lifecycle of a specific instance of a live wallpaper. Much like the graphics examples used in Chapter 20, "Developing Android 3D Graphics Applications," live wallpaper implementations use a Surface object to draw to the screen.

There are a number of callback methods of interest in the wallpaper service engine:

- You can override the onCreate() and onDestroy() methods to set up and tear down the live wallpaper. The Surface object is not valid during these parts of the lifecycle.

- You can override the onSurfaceCreated() and onSurfaceDestroyed() methods (convenience methods for the Surface setup and teardown) to set up and tear down the Surface used for live wallpaper drawing.

- You should override the onVisibilityChanged() method to handle live wallpaper visibility. When invisible, a live wallpaper must not remain running. This method should be treated much like an Activity pause or resume event.

- The onSurfaceChanged() method is another convenience method for Surface management.

- You can override the onOffsetsChanged() method to enable the live wallpaper to react when the user swipes between Home screens.

- You can override the `onTouchEvent()` method to handle touch events. The incoming parameter is a `MotionEvent` object—we talk about the `MotionEvent` class in detail in the gestures section of Chapter 8, "Handling Advanced User Input." You also need to enable touch events (off by default) for the live wallpaper using the `setTouchEventsEnabled()` method.

The implementation details of the live wallpaper are up to the developer. Often, a live wallpaper implementation uses OpenGL ES calls to draw to the screen. For example, the sample live wallpaper project included with this book includes a live wallpaper service that creates a `Bitmap` graphic of a bug droid, which floats around the screen, bouncing off the edges of the wallpaper boundaries. It also responds to touch events by changing its drift direction. Its wallpaper engine uses a thread to manage drawing operations, posting them back to the system using the `Handler` object defined in the wallpaper service.

Tip

Your live wallpaper can respond to user events, such as touch events. It can also listen for events where the user drops items on the screen. For more information, see the documentation for the `WallpaperService.Engine` class.

Note

Unfortunately, the wallpaper engine implementation of the sample application, SimpleLiveWallpaper, is far too lengthy for print due to all the OpenGL ES drawing code. However, you can see its implementation as part of the sample code provided for download on the book's websites. Specifically, check the `SimpleDroidWallpaper` class.

Warning

You should take into account device responsiveness and battery life when designing live wallpapers. Unlike your application where you can simply perform lengthy operations off the main thread, live wallpapers take away performance from the home screen and use battery life regardless of what thread the operation takes place in.

Creating a Live Wallpaper Configuration

Next, your application must provide an XML wallpaper definition. You can store this definition in the project's resources in the `/res/xml` directory. For example, here is a simple wallpaper definition called `/res/xml/droid_wallpaper.xml`:

```xml
<?xml version="1.0" encoding="utf-8"?>
<wallpaper xmlns:android="http://schemas.android.com/apk/res/android"
    android:thumbnail="@drawable/live_wallpaper_android"
    android:description="@string/wallpaper_desc" />
```

This simple wallpaper definition is encapsulated in the `<wallpaper>` XML tag. The description and thumbnail attributes are displayed on the wallpaper picker, where the user is prompted to select a specific wallpaper to use.

Configuring the Android Manifest File for Live Wallpapers

Finally, you need to update the application's Android manifest file to expose the live wallpaper service. Specifically, the `WallpaperService` needs to be registered using the `<service>` tag. The `<service>` tag must include several important bits of information:

- The `WallpaperService` class
- The `BIND_WALLPAPER` permission
- An intent filter for the `WallpaperService` action
- Wallpaper metadata to reference the live wallpaper configuration

Let's look at an example. Here is the `<service>` tag implementation for a simple live wallpaper:

```
<service
    android:label="@string/wallpaper_name"
    android:name="SimpleDroidWallpaper"
    android:permission="android.permission.BIND_WALLPAPER">
    <intent-filter>
        <action
            android:name="android.service.wallpaper.WallpaperService" />
    </intent-filter>
    <meta-data
        android:name="android.service.wallpaper"
        android:resource="@xml/droid_wallpaper" />
</service>
```

In addition to the service definition, you also need to limit installation of your application to API Level 7 and higher (where support for live wallpapers exists) using the `<uses-sdk>` manifest tag:

```
<uses-sdk android:minSdkVersion="7" android:targetSdkVersion="yy" />
```

Keep in mind that your live wallpaper might use APIs (such as OpenGL ES 2.0 APIs) that require a higher `minSdkVersion` than API Level 7. You might also want to use the `<uses-feature>` tag to specify that your application includes live wallpaper support, for use in Android Market filters:

```
<uses-feature android:name="android.software.live_wallpaper" />
```

Installing a Live Wallpaper

After you've implemented live wallpaper support in your application, you can set a live wallpaper on your Home screen using the following steps:

1. Long-press on the Home Screen.
2. From the menu, choose the Live Wallpapers option, as shown in Figure 22.3 (left).

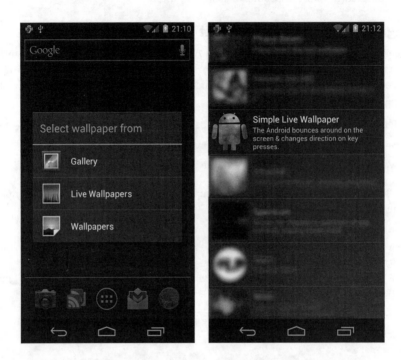

Figure 22.3   Installing a live wallpaper on the Home screen.

3. From the Live Wallpaper menu, choose the live wallpaper you want to include, as shown in Figure 22.3 (right). Here you can see the values you configured in droid_wallpaper.xml. Make these indicative of what the wallpaper is and does.
4. After you've chosen a wallpaper, it is shown in preview mode. Simply choose the Set Wallpaper button to confirm you want to use that live wallpaper. The live wallpaper is now visible on your Home screen, as shown in Figure 22.4.

Figure 22.4   A simple live wallpaper on the Home screen background
that bounces a colorful bug droid around.

Acting as a Content Type Handler

Your application can act as a content type filter—that is, handle common intent actions
such as VIEW, EDIT, or SEND for specific MIME types.

Tip

See the android.content.Intent class for a list of standard activity actions.

A photo application might act as a content type handler for VIEW actions for any
graphic formats, such as JPG, PNG, or RAW image file MIME types. Similarly, a social
networking application might want to handle intent SEND actions when the underlying
data has a MIME type associated with typical social content (for example, text, graphic,
or video). This means that any time the user tries to send data (with the MIME types
that the social networking application was interested in) from an Android application
using an intent with action SEND, the social networking application is listed as a choice
for completing the SEND action request. If the user chooses to send the content using the
social networking application, that application has to launch an Activity to handle the

request (for example, an activity that uploads the content to the social networking website to share).

Finally, content type handlers make it easier to extend the application to act as a content provider, provide search capabilities, or include App Widget features. Define data records using custom MIME types, so that no matter how an intent fires (inside or outside the application), the action is handled by the application in a graceful fashion.

To enable your application to act as a content type handler, you need to make several changes to your application:

- Determine which `Intent` actions and MIME types your application needs to be able to handle.

- You need to implement an `Activity` that can process the `Intent` action or actions that you want to handle.

- You need to register that `Activity` in your application's Android Manifest file using the `<activity>` tag as you normally would. You then need to configure an `<intent-filter>` tag for that `Activity` in your application's Android Manifest file, providing the appropriate `Intent` action and MIME types your application can process.

Determining Intent Actions and MIME Types

Let's look at a simple example. For the remainder of this chapter, we make various modifications to a simple field notes application that uses a content provider to expose African game animal field notes; each note has a title and text body (the content itself comes from field notes on African game animals that we wrote up years ago on our nature blog, which is very popular with grade-schoolers). Throughout these examples, the application acts as a content type handler for `VIEW` requests for data with a custom MIME type:

`vnd.android.cursor.item/vnd.androidbook.live.fieldnotes`

Tip

MIME types come in two forms. Most developers are familiar with MIME types, such as `text/plain` or `image/jpeg` (as defined in RFC2045 & RFC2046), which are standards used globally. The Internet Assigned Numbers Authority (IANA, at http://www.iana.org) manages these global MIME types.

Developers frequently need to create their own MIME types, but without the need for them to become global standards. These types must still be sufficiently unique that MIME type namespace collisions do not occur. When you're dealing with Android content providers, there are two well-defined prefixes that you can use for creating MIME types. The `ContentResolver.CURSOR_DIR_BASE_TYPE` prefix ("vnd.android.cursor.dir") is for use with directories or folders of items. The `ContentResolver.CURSOR_ITEM_BASE_TYPE` prefix ("vnd.android.cursor.item") is for use with a single type. The part after the slash must then be unique. It's not uncommon to pattern MIME types after package names or other such unique qualifiers.

Implementing the Activity to Process the Intents

Next, the application needs an `Activity` class to handle the `Intent` objects it receives. For the sample, we simply need to load a page capable of viewing a field note. Here is a sample implementation of an `Activity` that can parse the `Intent` data and show a screen to display the field note for a specific animal:

```java
public class SimpleViewDetailsActivity extends Activity {
    @Override
    protected void onCreate(Bundle savedInstanceState) {
        super.onCreate(savedInstanceState);
        setContentView(R.layout.details);
        try {
            Intent launchIntent = getIntent();
            Uri launchData = launchIntent.getData();
            String id = launchData.getLastPathSegment();
            Uri dataDetails = Uri.withAppendedPath
                (SimpleFieldnotesContentProvider.CONTENT_URI, id);
            Cursor cursor =
                managedQuery(dataDetails, null, null, null, null);
            cursor.moveToFirst();
            String fieldnoteTitle = cursor.getString(cursor
                .getColumnIndex(SimpleFieldnotesContentProvider
                .FIELDNOTES_TITLE));
            String fieldnoteBody = cursor.getString(cursor
                .getColumnIndex(SimpleFieldnotesContentProvider
                .FIELDNOTES_BODY));
            TextView fieldnoteView = (TextView)
                findViewById(R.id.text_title);
            fieldnoteView.setText(fieldnoteTitle);
            TextView bodyView = (TextView) findViewById(R.id.text_body);
            bodyView.setLinksClickable(true);
            bodyView.setAutoLinkMask(Linkify.ALL);
            bodyView.setText(fieldnoteBody);
        } catch (Exception e) {
            Toast.makeText(this, "Failed.", Toast.LENGTH_LONG).show();
        }
    }
}
```

The `SimpleViewDetailsActivity` class retrieves the `Intent` that was used to launch the `Activity` using the `getIntent()` method. It then inspects the details of that intent, extracting the specific field note identifier using the `getLastPathSegment()` method. The rest of the code simply involves querying the underlying content provider for the appropriate field note record and displaying it using a layout.

Registering the Intent Filter

Finally, the `Activity` class must be registered in the application's Android manifest file and the intent filter must be configured so that the application accepts only intents for specific actions and specific MIME types. For example, the `SimpleViewDetailsActivity` would be registered as follows:

```
<activity
    android:name="SimpleViewDetailsActivity">
    <intent-filter>
      <action
          android:name="android.intent.action.VIEW" />
        <category
            android:name="android.intent.category.DEFAULT" />
        <data android:mimeType =
           "vnd.android.cursor.item/vnd.androidbook.live.fieldnotes" />
    </intent-filter>
</activity>
```

The `<activity>` tag remains the same as any other. The `<intent-filter>` tag is what's interesting here. First, the `<action>` tag defines the matching criteria an `Intent` object will need to specify in order to be handled by this application. The name property of the `<action>` tag specifies the type of action, in this case the `VIEW` action. The `<category>` tag is set to `DEFAULT`, which is most appropriate, and finally, the `<data>` tag is used to filter `VIEW` Intents further to only those of the custom MIME type associated with field notes.

Summary

The Android platform provides a number of ways to integrate your applications tightly into the operating system, enabling you to extend your reach beyond traditional application boundaries. In this chapter, you learned how to extend your application by creating App Widgets, live wallpapers, and more. The Android APIs provide many ways that applications can integrate into the system and take part in the user experience at many levels.

References and More Information

Android Dev Guide: "App Widgets":
    http://d.android.com/guide/topics/appwidgets/index.html
Android technical articles: "Live Wallpapers":
    http://d.android.com/resources/articles/live-wallpapers.html

23

Enabling Application Search

Android devices boast powerful search features, thanks to the search framework that was built into the Android SDK from the beginning. Application developers can enable search features in their applications in a variety of ways, including exposing app data on device-wide searches, providing relevant search suggestions, enabling voice search, and more. In this chapter, you become familiar with some of the most common ways apps can leverage the Android search framework.

Making Application Content Searchable

If your application is content rich, either with content created by users or with content provided by you, the developer, then integrating with the search capabilities of Android can provide many benefits and add value to the user. The application data becomes part of the overall device experience, is more accessible, and your application can be presented to the user in more cases than just when they launch it.

Developers can implement powerful search features in their applications using the Android framework. There are two ways that search capabilities are generally added to Android applications:

- Applications implement a search framework that enables their activities to react to the user pressing the Search button, requesting a search, and performing searches on data within that application.

- Applications can expose their content for use in global, system-wide searches that include application and web content.

Search framework features include the capability to search for and access application data as search results, as well as the ability to provide suggestions as the user types search criteria. Applications can also provide an `Intent` to launch when a user selects specific search suggestions.

> **Tip**
>
> The code examples provided in this section are taken from the SimpleSearchIntegration application. The source code for this application is provided for download on the book's websites.

Let's revisit the African field notes application we discussed in the previous chapter. This application uses a simple content provider to supply information about game animals. Enabling search support in this application seems rational; it enables the user to quickly find information about a specific animal simply by pressing the Search button or using a search widget. When a result is found, the application needs to be able to apply an `Intent` for launching the appropriate screen to view that specific field note—the perfect time to implement a simple content type handler that enables the application to handle "view field note" actions, as shown in Figure 23.1.

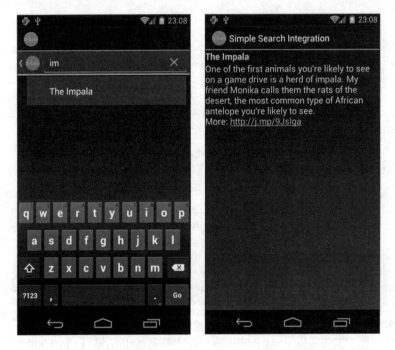

Figure 23.1   Handling in-application searches and search suggestions.

Enabling Searches in Your Application

You need to make a number of changes in your application to enable searches. Although these changes might seem complex, the good news is that if you do it right, enabling global searches later is simple. Searching content generally necessitates that your application exposes a content provider, or at the very least, it has some sort of underlying database that can be searched in a systematic fashion.

Note

The search framework provided by the `SearchManager` class
(`android.app.SearchManager`) does not actually perform the search queries—that is
up to you, the developer. The `SearchManager` class simply manages search services and
the search dialog controls. How and what data is searched and which results are returned
are implementation details.

To enable in-application searches, you need to:

- Develop an application with data, ideally exposed as a content provider.
- Create an XML search configuration file.
- Implement an `Activity` class to handle searches.
- Configure the application's Android manifest file for searches.

Now let's look at each of these requirements in more detail.

Creating a Search Configuration

Creating a search configuration for your application simply means that you need to create an XML file with special search tags. This search configuration file is normally stored
in the xml resource directory (for example, `/res/xml/searchable.xml`) and referenced in the searchable application's Android manifest file.

Enabling Basic Searches

The following is a sample search configuration that the field notes application might use,
stored as an application resource file

```
<?xml version="1.0" encoding="utf-8"?>
<searchable
    xmlns:android="http://schemas.android.com/apk/res/android"
    android:label="@string/app_name"
    android:hint="@string/search_hint"
    android:searchSettingsDescription="@string/search_settings_help">
</searchable>
```

The basic attributes of the search configuration are fairly straightforward. The `label`
attribute is generally set to the name of your application (the application providing the
search result). The `hint` attribute is the text that shows in the `EditText` control of the
search box when no text has been entered—a prompt. You can further customize the
search dialog by customizing the search button text and input method options, if desired.

Enabling Search Suggestions

If your application acts as a content provider and you want to enable search suggestions—those results provided in a list below the search box as the user types in search
criteria—then you must include several additional attributes in your search configuration. You need to specify information about the content provider used to supply the

search suggestions, including its authority, path information, and the query to use to return search suggestions. You also need to provide information for the Intent to trigger when a user clicks on a specific suggestion.

Again, let's go back to the field notes example. Here are the search configuration attributes required to support search suggestions that query field note titles:

```
android:searchSuggestAuthority =
    "com.androidbook.simplesearchintegration.SimpleFieldnotesContentProvider"
android:searchSuggestPath="fieldnotes"
android:searchSuggestSelection="fieldnotes_title LIKE ?"
android:searchSuggestIntentAction="android.intent.action.VIEW"
android:searchSuggestIntentData="content://com.androidbook.simplesearch
➥integration.SimpleFieldnotesContentProvider/fieldnotes"
```

The first attribute, searchSuggestAuthority, sets the content provider to use for the search suggestion query. The second attribute defines the path appended to the Authority and right before SearchManager.SUGGEST_URI_PATH_QUERY is appended to the Authority. The third attribute supplies the SQL WHERE clause of the search query (here, only the field note titles, not their bodies, are queried to keep search suggestion performance reasonably fast). Next, an Intent action is provided for when a user clicks a search suggestion, and then finally the Uri used to launch the Intent is defined.

You can also set a threshold (android:searchSuggestThreshold) on the number of characters the user needs to type before a search suggestion query is performed. Consider setting this value to a reasonable number like 3 or 4 characters to keep queries to a minimum (the default is 0). At a value of zero, even an empty search field shows suggestions—but these are not filtered at all.

Each time the user begins to type in search criteria, the system performs a content provider query to retrieve suggestions. Therefore, the application's content provider interface needs to be updated to handle these queries. To make this all work properly, you need to define a projection in order to map the content provider data columns to those that the search framework expects to use to fill the search suggestion list with content. For example, the following code defines a project to map the field notes unique identifiers and titles to the _ID, SUGGEST_COLUMN_TEXT_1 and SUGGEST_COLUMN_INTENT_DATA_ID fields for the search suggestions:

```
private static final HashMap<String, String>
FIELDNOTES_SEARCH_SUGGEST_PROJECTION_MAP;
static {
    FIELDNOTES_SEARCH_SUGGEST_PROJECTION_MAP =
        new HashMap<String, String>();
    FIELDNOTES_SEARCH_SUGGEST_PROJECTION_MAP.put(_ID, _ID);
    FIELDNOTES_SEARCH_SUGGEST_PROJECTION_MAP.put(
        SearchManager.SUGGEST_COLUMN_TEXT_1, FIELDNOTES_TITLE + " AS "
        + SearchManager.SUGGEST_COLUMN_TEXT_1);
    FIELDNOTES_SEARCH_SUGGEST_PROJECTION_MAP.put(
```

```
        SearchManager.SUGGEST_COLUMN_INTENT_DATA_ID, _ID + " AS "
        + SearchManager.SUGGEST_COLUMN_INTENT_DATA_ID);
}
```

Each time search suggestions need to be displayed, the system executes a query using the `Uri` provided as part of the search configuration. Don't forget to define this `Uri` and register it in the content provider's `UriMatcher` object (using the `addURI()` method). For example, the field notes application used the following `Uri` for search suggestion queries:

```
content://com.androidbook.simplesearchintegration.
➥SimpleFieldnotesContentProvider/fieldnotes/search_suggestion_query
```

By providing a special search suggestion `Uri` for the content provider queries, you can simply update the content provider's `query()` method to handle the specialized query, including building the projection, performing the appropriate query, and returning the results. Let's take a closer look at the field notes content provider `query()` method:

```
@Override
public Cursor query(Uri uri, String[] projection, String selection,
    String[] selectionArgs, String sortOrder) {
    SQLiteQueryBuilder queryBuilder = new SQLiteQueryBuilder();
    queryBuilder.setTables(SimpleFieldnotesDatabase.FIELDNOTES_TABLE);
    int match = sURIMatcher.match(uri);
    switch (match) {
    case FIELDNOTES_SEARCH_SUGGEST:
        selectionArgs = new String[] { "%" + selectionArgs[0] + "%" };
        queryBuilder.setProjectionMap(
            FIELDNOTES_SEARCH_SUGGEST_PROJECTION_MAP);
        break;
    case FIELDNOTES:
        break;
    case FIELDNOTE_ITEM:
        String id = uri.getLastPathSegment();
        queryBuilder.appendWhere(_ID + "=" + id);
        break;
    default:
        throw new IllegalArgumentException("Invalid URI: " + uri);
    }
    SQLiteDatabase sql = database.getReadableDatabase();
    Cursor cursor =
        queryBuilder.query(sql, projection, selection,
            selectionArgs, null, null, sortOrder);
    cursor.setNotificationUri(getContext().getContentResolver(), uri);
    return cursor;
}
```

This `query()` method implementation handles both regular content queries and special search suggestion queries (those that come in with the search suggestion `Uri`). When the search suggestion query occurs, we wrap the search criteria in wildcards and use the handy `setProjectionMap()` method of the `QueryBuilder` object to set and execute the query as normal. Because we want to return results quickly, we search only for titles matching the search criteria for suggestions, not the full text of the field notes.

Tip

Instead of using wildcards and a slow `LIKE` expression in SQLite, we could have used the SQLite FTS3 extension, which enables fast full-text queries. With a limited number of rows of data, this is not strictly necessary in our case and it requires creating tables in a different and much less relational way. Indices are not supported, so query performance might suffer. See the SQLite FTS3 documentation at http://www.sqlite.org/fts3.html.

Enabling Voice Search

You can also add voice search capabilities to your application. This enables the user to speak the search criteria instead of type it. There are several attributes you can add to your search configuration to enable voice searches. The most important attribute is `voiceSearchMode`, which enables voice searches and sets the appropriate mode. The `showVoiceSearchButton` value enables the little voice recording button to display as part of the search dialog, the `launchRecognizer` value tells the Android system to use voice recording activity, and the `launchWebSearch` value initiates the special voice web search activity.

To add voice support to the field notes sample application, add the following line to the search configuration:

```
android:voiceSearchMode="showVoiceSearchButton|launchRecognizer"
```

Other voice search attributes you can set include the voice language model (free form or web search), the voice language, the maximum voice results, and a text prompt for the voice recognition dialog.

Requesting a Search

Up until Android API Level 11, most Android devices had a physical Search button. From within your application, this button can be pressed and the search dialog comes up (Figure 23.1, left). The search dialog can also be triggered by calling the `onSearchRequested()` method of the `Activity` class.

With API Level 11 and later, the Search button is gone. Instead, applications must add a Search button themselves. The best way to do this is with the `SearchView` class. With this class, an expandable search area can easily be added to the action bar. Take, for example, the following implementation of `onCreateOptionsMenu()`, found in the sample app:

```
@Override
public boolean onCreateOptionsMenu(Menu menu) {
    MenuInflater inflater = getMenuInflater();
    inflater.inflate(R.menu.menu, menu);

    SearchManager searchManager =
        (SearchManager) getSystemService(Context.SEARCH_SERVICE);
    SearchView searchView = (SearchView) menu.findItem(R.id.menu_search)
        .getActionView();
    searchView.setSearchableInfo(searchManager
        .getSearchableInfo(new ComponentName(this,
                SimpleSearchableActivity.class)));
    searchView.setIconifiedByDefault(true);
    return true;
}
```

Here's the corresponding menu resource file:

```xml
<?xml version="1.0" encoding="utf-8"?>
<menu xmlns:android="http://schemas.android.com/apk/res/android" >
    <item
        android:id="@+id/menu_search"
        android:actionViewClass="android.widget.SearchView"
        android:icon="@drawable/ic_menu_search"
        android:showAsAction="ifRoom|collapseActionView"
        android:title="@string/menu_search"/>
</menu>
```

The result of this `SearchView` configuration is shown in Figure 23.2. The Action Bar receives the menu item with the search icon (Figure 23.2, left). When the search item is clicked, the search field appears right in the Action Bar, and the suggestions appear right below (Figure 23.2, right).

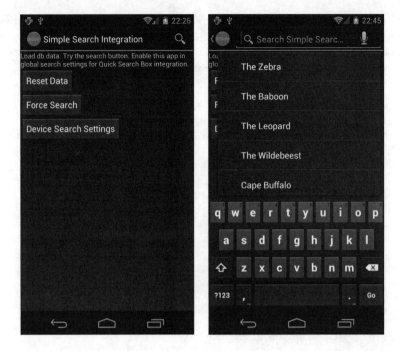

Figure 23.2   Use `SearchView` to search right from the Action Bar.

Creating a Search Activity

Next, you need to implement an `Activity` class that actually performs the requested searches. This `Activity` is launched whenever your application receives an `Intent` with the action value of `ACTION_SEARCH`.

The search request contains the search string in the extra field called `SearchManager.QUERY`. The `Activity` takes this value, performs the search, and then responds with the results.

Let's look at the search `Activity` from our field notes example. You can implement its search activity, `SimpleSearchableActivity`, as follows:

```
public class SimpleSearchableActivity extends ListActivity {
    @Override
    protected void onCreate(Bundle savedInstanceState) {
        super.onCreate(savedInstanceState);
        Intent intent = getIntent();
        checkIntent(intent);
    }

    @Override
    protected void onNewIntent(Intent newIntent) {
```

```
        // update the activity launch intent
        setIntent(newIntent);
        // handle it
        checkIntent(newIntent);
    }

    private void checkIntent(Intent intent) {
        String query = "";
        String intentAction = intent.getAction();
        if (Intent.ACTION_SEARCH.equals(intentAction)) {
            query = intent.getStringExtra(SearchManager.QUERY);
            Toast.makeText(this,
                "Search received: " + query, Toast.LENGTH_LONG)
                .show();
        } else if (Intent.ACTION_VIEW.equals(intentAction)) {
            // pass this off to the details view activity
            Uri details = intent.getData();
            Intent detailsIntent =
                new Intent(Intent.ACTION_VIEW, details);
            startActivity(detailsIntent);
            finish();
            return;
        }
        fillList(query);
    }

    private void fillList(String query) {
        String wildcardQuery = "%" + query + "%";
        Cursor cursor =
            managedQuery(
                SimpleFieldnotesContentProvider.CONTENT_URI,
                null,
                SimpleFieldnotesContentProvider.FIELDNOTES_TITLE
                + " LIKE ? OR "
                + SimpleFieldnotesContentProvider.FIELDNOTES_BODY
                + " LIKE ?",
                new String[] { wildcardQuery, wildcardQuery }, null);
        ListAdapter adapter =
            new SimpleCursorAdapter(
                this,
                android.R.layout.simple_list_item_1,
                cursor,
                new String[] {
                    SimpleFieldnotesContentProvider.FIELDNOTES_TITLE },
                new int[] { android.R.id.text1 });
        setListAdapter(adapter);
    }
```

```
@Override
protected void onListItemClick(
    ListView l, View v, int position, long id) {
    Uri details = Uri.withAppendedPath(
        SimpleFieldnotesContentProvider.CONTENT_URI, "" + id);
    Intent intent =
        new Intent(Intent.ACTION_VIEW, details);
    startActivity(intent);
    }
}
```

Both the onCreate() and onNewIntent() methods are implemented because the
Activity is flagged with a launchMode set to singleTop. This Activity is capable of
bringing up the search dialog when the user presses the Search button, like the rest of
the activities in this example. When the user performs a search, the system launches the
SimpleSearchableActivity—the same Activity the user was already viewing. We
don't want to create a huge stack of search result activities, so we don't let it have more
than one instance on top of the stack—thus the singleTop setting.

Handling the search is fairly straightforward. We use the search term provided for us
to create a query. Using the managedQuery call, the results are obtained as a Cursor
object that is then used with the SimpleCursorAdapter object to fill the ListView
control of the Activity class.

For list item click handling, the implementation here simply creates a new VIEW
intent and, effectively, lets the system handle the item clicking. In this case, the details
activity handles the displaying of the proper field note. Why do this instead of launching
the class activity directly? No reason other than it's simple and it's well tested from other
uses of this launch style.

When a user clicks on a suggestion in the list, instead of an ACTION_SEARCH, this
activity receives the usual ACTION_VIEW. Instead of handling it here, though, it's passed
on to the details view Activity as that activity is already designed to handle the drawing of the details for each item—no reason to implement it twice.

Configuring the Android Manifest File for Search

Now it's time to register your searchable Activity class in the application manifest file,
including configuring the intent filter associated with the ACTION_SEARCH action. You
also need to mark your application as searchable using a <meta-data> manifest file tag.

Here is the Android manifest file excerpt for the searchable activity registration:

```
<activity
    android:name="SimpleSearchableActivity"
    android:launchMode="singleTop">
    <intent-filter>
        <action android:name="android.intent.action.SEARCH" />
    </intent-filter>
    <intent-filter>
```

```
                <action android:name="android.intent.action.VIEW" />
        </intent-filter>
        <meta-data
            android:name="android.app.searchable"
            android:resource="@xml/searchable" />
</activity>
```

The main difference between this `<activity>` tag configuration and a typical activity is the addition of the intent filter for intents with an action type of SEARCH. In addition, some metadata is provided so that the system knows where to find the search configuration details.

Next, let's look at an example of how to enable the Search button for all activities in the application. This `<meta-data>` block needs to be added to the `<application>` tag, outside any `<activity>` tags.

```
<meta-data
    android:name="android.app.default_searchable"
    android:value =
        "com.androidbook.simplesearchintegration.SimpleSearchableActivity" />
```

This `<meta-data>` tag configures the default activity that handles the search results for the entire application. This way, pressing the Search button brings up the search dialog from any activity in the application. If you don't want this functionality in every activity, you need to add this definition to each activity for which you do want the Search button enabled.

Note

Not all Android devices have a Search button. If you want to guarantee search abilities within the application, consider adding other ways to initiate a search, such as adding a Search button to the application screen or providing the search option on the options menu.

Enabling Global Search

After you have enabled your application for searches, you can make it part of the global device search features with a few extra steps. Global searches are often invoked using the Quick Search Box. In order to enable your application for global search, you need to

- Begin with an application that already has in-application search capabilities as described earlier.
- Update the search configuration file to enable global searches.
- Include your application in global searches by updating the Search settings of the device.

Now let's look at these requirements in a bit more detail. Let's assume we're working with the same sample application—the field notes. Figure 23.3 shows the global search box, as initiated from the Home screen.

Figure 23.3   Application content is included in global search results,
such as when the user presses the Search button while on the
Home screen.

Updating a Search Configuration for Global Searches

Updating an existing search configuration is simple. All you need to do is add the
`includeInGlobalSearch` attribute in your configuration and set it to `true` as follows:

```
android:includeInGlobalSearch="true"
```

At this point, you should also ensure that your application is acting as a content type handler for the results you provide as part of global searches (if you haven't already). That way, users can select search suggestions provided by your application. Again, you probably want to leverage the content type handler functionality again, in order to launch the application when a search suggestion is chosen.

Tip

You can initiate a global search using the `SearchManager.INTENT_ACTION_
GLOBAL_SEARCH` intent.

Updating Search Settings for Global Searches

However, the user has ultimate control over what applications are included as part of the global search. Your application is not included in global searches by default. The user must include your application explicitly. For your application's content to show up as part of global searches, the user must adjust the device Search settings. The user makes this configuration from the Home screen, Search, Overflow menu, Settings, Searchable Items menu, as shown in Figure 23.4.

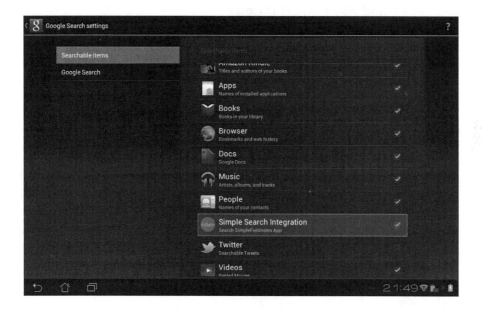

Figure 23.4   Configuring device search settings to include content from
your application.

If your application has content that is appropriate for global searches, you might want to include a shortcut to these settings so that users can easily navigate to them without feeling like they've left your application. The `SearchManager` class has an intent called `INTENT_ACTION_SEARCH_SETTINGS` for this purpose:

```
Intent intent = new Intent(SearchManager.INTENT_ACTION_SEARCH_SETTINGS);
startActivity(intent);
```

This intent launches the Settings application on the Search settings screen, as shown in Figure 23.4. As you can see, searches—whether they are in-application searches or global searches—allow application content to be exposed in new and interesting ways so that the user's data is always just a few keystrokes (or spoken words) away.

Summary

The Android search framework enables applications to expose their data so that the user can find information easily and efficiently through a consistent interface. Applications can enable in-application searches, search suggestions, voice searching, and more. Often, applications with content providers and application databases are the simplest to enable for search, so using these common design practices will work to your advantage.

References and More Information

Android Dev Guide: "Search":
   http://d.android.com/guide/topics/search/index.html
Android SDK Documentation on the SearchManager class:
   http://d.android.com/reference/android/app/SearchManager.html
Android SDK Documentation on the SearchView class:
   http://d.android.com/reference/android/widget/SearchView.html
Android SDK Documentation on the SearchRecentSuggestions class:
   http://d.android.com/reference/android/provider/SearchRecentSuggestions.html
Android SDK Documentation on searchable configuration files:
   http://d.android.com/guide/topics/search/searchable-config.html

24

Working with Cloud to Device Messaging

Does your application need to connect to a server and download data to keep its content fresh? Does the data come in at random times, as opposed to on a schedule (once-a-day news article download)? Are you considering implementing a polling mechanism so that your Android application can routinely check your application server for new content? If this is the case, you might want to look into Google's Cloud to Device Messaging (usually referred to as C2DM) service instead, because it can save you a lot of work and results in more efficient use of the user's device resources. In this chapter, we talk about this third-party service, which is available to Android developers when targeting devices that include the Google experience.

An Overview of C2DM

C2DM is a messaging service offered by Google that supports push-style messaging. It basically allows third-party developers like you to use a single messaging service on the device instead of creating one. The C2DM service is free to use, but it has certain requirements, quotas, and limitations you should be aware of.

Warning

C2DM is a Google Labs-style project, which means it can be changed or discontinued at any time. The Android Cloud to Device Messaging team reserves the right to change the service, quotas, and other features of C2DM at any time. That said, many of their own applications use the service, so it isn't likely to disappear anytime soon.

The C2DM service was introduced in Android 2.2 (API Level 8). It allows users to push data to applications efficiently. Instead of your application constantly checking for new data on its application server, a notification can be initiated from the server side. This has substantial positive ramifications in terms of device power usage and application responsiveness.

Note

Using Google's C2DM service basically means you're using the shared messaging channel that Google developed for its own Android applications, such as Gmail. This cuts down on the number of individual applications constantly staying "awake" in order to poll their application servers and check for new stuff.

Understanding C2DM Message Flow

Here are the basics for how the C2DM messaging process works. To push data to an application, the developer's application server sends a simple notification to Google's C2DM servers via HTTP using a registration token that a specific application installation received when it registered. Google's servers handle the message delivery details, pushing the data to the user's device when it becomes available on the network. The shared messaging channel on the user's Android device receives the message and sends out a broadcast. Your application implements a broadcast receiver, so it can wake up, receive the message, and inspect its contents. Your application can then take whatever action is necessary, such as contacting its application server for more information or to download additional content.

Understanding the Limitations of the C2DM Service

Because this is a free service and all applications on the device use the same service to communicate with the Google messaging servers, there are a number of limitations for using C2DM. Some of these limitations include the following:

- The C2DM service requires Android 2.2 or higher.
- The C2DM service is available only on Android devices that have the Google experience. The device must have the Android Market installed, and users must be signed in to their Google account. This means that devices such as the Amazon Kindle Fire cannot take advantage of such services and so developers must use other alternatives.
- The messages pushed to the device must be simple; they are not intended to deliver the data "payload" so much as to inform an application that it has new data available so that it can wake up and retrieve that data itself, using whatever means necessary. The size limit for messages at the time of this writing is 1024 bytes.
- As with many messaging services, messages are not absolutely guaranteed to be delivered. Your application should not be reliant on any one specific message to perform its core duties. You're better off using the service for generic messages such as, "There's new content for the app to download," than for specifics such as, "Download new content called ABC." Any specifics can be handled when your application wakes up and communicates with your application's server directly.

- As with many messaging services, the C2DM service is not intended for time-critical situations. Messages are delivered in a timely manner, but there is no time limit. Therefore, it's not appropriate for alarm apps and the like.

- Google has imposed certain message quotas for the C2DM service in order to ensure good quality service for all users. Quotas are tied to the developer's sender account and apply to all applications tied to that account. There are *global quotas* (number of messages sent to all devices in total) and *device quotas* (number of messages sent to a specific device) for a given time period. The default global quota for a new account is 200,000 messages a day, which is reasonable for small to midsize applications. Developers whose applications become popular and require higher quotas can request quota increases. You can find out more about quotas on the C2DM website at http://code.google.com/android/c2dm/quotas.html.

- Of course, C2DM service requires the user to have a network-enabled device. The good news is that Google has created a robust push mechanism that stores your messages to be sent to the device and is fault tolerant enough to handle sporadic network connectivity frequently experienced with mobile devices. Still, your users may incur data charges for network activity, as normal.

These limitations are pretty reasonable for most small- and medium-sized applications that are published on the Android Market. Given how straightforward the implementation is, we see no reason not to use the C2DM service. If your application user base outgrows the service, that's a great problem to have.

If your application cannot work within these limitations, you need to use an alternative method of communicating with your application. See the alternatives discussed at the end of this chapter for some options.

Signing Up for C2DM

To use Google's C2DM service, you need to sign up for a sender account. This is the account you use for communication between your application server and the Google C2DM services, which send the message to the client Android device. You can sign up at http://code.google.com/android/c2dm/signup.html.

Note

When you incorporate C2DM services into your Android applications, you are subject to additional terms of service, so make sure you read the fine print carefully to ensure your application complies with the rules.

When you sign up for a C2DM sender account, you need to agree to the terms of service. You are then asked to fill out a form that describes how you, the developer, plan to use the C2DM service, including information about your application and your contact information. This form is submitted for review by the Android Cloud to Device Messaging team.

Tip

This process used to take awhile, but the last time we ran through it, we received a response within 10 minutes.

Incorporating C2DM into Your Applications

After you have registered with Google and your application has been accepted, you will receive an email detailing your sender account privileges. It might take a day or two before you can send messages through the Google C2DM servers, but you can take this time to familiarize yourself with the documentation and sample code available at the C2DM Google Project website at http://code.google.com/android/c2dm/.

Integrating C2DM Services on the Android Client Side

The basic process for integrating C2DM into your Android application is as follows:

1. Your application requires several C2DM-specific permissions.
2. If C2DM messaging is required by your application, you will want to set the minimum SDK supported by your application to API Level 8.
3. Your application must register to receive C2DM messages from a specific sender identifier.
4. The registration on the client side results in an application identifier that must be delivered to the server and stored for future use.
5. Your application must implement a broadcast receiver.
6. Your application is responsible for retrieving any data payload that is spawned by a C2DM message arriving. The message itself needs to be simple.
7. Your application must unregister to stop receiving C2DM messages.

Integrating C2DM Services on the Android Application Server Side

The process sending notifications to Google's C2DM servers is as follows:

1. Your application server must support HTTPS. Your application server should also be able to queue message requests and ideally, perform exponential back offs.
2. Your application server needs to maintain an authentication token and refresh it occasionally.
3. To send a message to the C2DM servers, your application server must create an HTTP POST message. This message must include information about the registration identifier, auth token, message data, and message delivery behavior details.
4. The application server should be able to handle numerous response codes (successful and erroneous) from the C2DM servers.
5. Your application must unregister to stop receiving C2DM messages.

For more information on how to configure your application server for C2DM messaging, see the C2DM documentation at http://code.google.com/android/c2dm/index.html#server.

Exploring the C2DM Sample Applications

Google provides two sample applications that help illustrate how to use C2DM. One is the popular Chrome to Phone application. The other is an application called JumpNote. Both are open source. Chrome to Phone is available for download on Android Market as is its companion extension for Chrome.

Chrome to Phone allows the user to use an extension on Chrome to send a URL down to a device that runs the Android application. It does so by sending a C2DM message. The source code for all aspects of the project can be downloaded and reviewed at http://code.google.com/p/chrometophone/.

JumpNote is a notepad style online app with an Android client. C2DM is used to provide notifications to automatically synchronize the notes between the two applications. It provides a good example of a multi-platform app using Android, Google Web Toolkit, and Google App Engine. The source code and compiled binary can be viewed and downloaded at http://code.google.com/p/jumpnote/. JumpNote is also a good example of syncing.

What Alternatives to C2DM Exist?

In some cases, the C2DM service may not be right for your application. Perhaps you are targeting devices that do not include the Google experience and do not have the Android Market installed, or your application requires more intensive message traffic than the C2DM service currently allows. In this case, you are perfectly welcome to implement your own messaging solutions. Some options include:

- Implement a simple server polling solution in a background service. This works well for infrequent messages or messages that aren't time sensitive.

- Leverage a messaging protocol such as Extensible Messaging and Presence Protocol (XMPP).

- Check the app markets your application is published through. Some third-party app markets are now publishing their own push services for use by their subscribers. For example, Amazon provides notification services as part of their Amazon Web Services SDK for Android. These services can incur fees to the developer and the user.

Summary

There are numerous third-party APIs and services that can be used to create robust and interesting applications on the Android platform. One service that can greatly improve the experience your users have with their Android devices is the Cloud to Device Messaging push service available from Google. This service allows applications to share a messaging channel, making for better battery life and more responsive applications.

References and More Information

Google Code Project: "Android Cloud to Device Messaging Framework":
    http://code.google.com/android/c2dm/
Android developers blog: "Cloud to Device Messaging":
    http://android-developers.blogspot.com/2010/05/android-cloud-to-device-messaging.html
Amazon Web Services SDK for Android:
    http://aws.amazon.com/sdkforandroid/

## 25

Managing User Accounts and Synchronizing User Data

Android is cloud-friendly. Android applications can integrate tightly with remote services, helping users transition seamlessly. Android applications can synchronize data with remote cloud-based (Internet) services using sync adapters. Developers can also take advantage of Android's cloud-based backup service to protect and migrate application data safely and effectively. In this chapter, you learn about the account and synchronization features to sync data to built-in applications and how to protect application data using the backup and restore features available in Android.

Managing Accounts with the Account Manager

From a user perspective, the Android 2.0 platform introduced many exciting new device features. For instance, the user can register and use multiple accounts for email and contact management. This feature was provided through a combination of new synchronization and account services that are also available to developers. Although you can use the account and synchronization packages with any kind of data, the intention seems to be to provide a way for developers and companies to integrate their business services with the system that synchronizes data to the built-in Android applications.

Android user accounts are manipulated using the classes available in the android.accounts package. This functionality is primarily designed for accounts with services that contain contact, email, or other such information in them. A good example of this type of online service is a social networking application that contains friends' contact information, as well as other relevant information such as their statuses. This information is often delivered and used on an Android device using the synchronization service (we talk more about synchronization later in the chapter).

First, we talk about accounts. Accounts registered with the Android account manager should provide access to the same sort of information—contact information, for the most part. Different accounts can be registered for a given user using the Android AccountManager class. Each account contains authentication information for a service, usually credentials for a server account somewhere online. Android services, such as the synchronization services built in to the platform, can access these accounts, mining them for the appropriate types of information (again, primarily contact details, but also other bits of data such as social networking status).

Let's look at how using account information provided via the `AccountManager` and `Account` classes works. An application that needs to access the server can request a list of accounts from the system. If one of the accounts contains credentials for the server, the application can request an authentication token for the account. The application would then use this token as a way to log in to the remote server to access its services. This keeps the user credentials secure and private while also providing a convenience to the user in that they only need to provide their credentials once, regardless of how many applications use the information. All these tasks are achieved using the `AccountManager` class. A call to the `getAccountByType()` method retrieves a list of accounts and then a call to the `getAuthToken()` method retrieves the token associated with a specific account, which the application can use to communicate with a password-protected resource, such as a web service.

On the other side of this process, authenticating credentials against the backend server are the account providers. That is, the services that provide users with accounts and with which user information is authenticated so the applications can get the auth tokens. In order to do all of this (handle system requests to authenticate an `Account` object against the remote server), the account provider must implement an account authenticator. Through the authenticator, the account provider requests appropriate credentials and then confirms them with whatever account authentication operations are necessary— usually an online server. To implement an account authenticator, you need to make several modifications to your application. Begin by implementing the `AbstractAccountAuthenticator` class. You also need to update the application's Android Manifest file, provide an authenticator configuration file (XML), and provide an authenticator preference screen configuration in order to make the authentication experience as seamless as possible for the user.

Tip

Learn more about creating system-wide accounts in the Android SDK documentation for the `AbstractAccountAuthenticator` class. Learn more about using accounts in the Android SDK documentation for the `AccountManager` class. Also see the Android Training documentation on remembering users (http://developer.android.com/training/id-auth/index.html).

Synchronizing Data with Sync Adapters

The synchronization feature available in the Android SDK requires the use of the accounts classes we talked about earlier. This service is principally designed to enable syncing of contact, email, and calendar data to the built-in applications from a backend datastore—you're "adapting" backend server data to the existing content providers. That is, the service is not generally used for syncing data specific to your typical Android application. In theory, applications can use this service to keep generic data in sync, but they might be better served by implementing synchronization internally. You can do this using the `AlarmManager` class to schedule systematic data synchronization via the network, perhaps using an Android service.

If, however, you are working with data that is well suited to syncing to the internal applications, such as contacts or calendar information that you want to put in the built-in applications and content providers, implementing a sync adapter makes sense. This enables the Android system to manage synchronization activities.

The account service must provide the sync adapter by extending the `AbstractThreadedSyncAdapter` class. When the sync occurs, the `onPerformSync()` method of the sync adapter is called. The parameters to this method tell the adapter what account (as defined by the `Account` parameter) is being used, thus providing necessary authentication tokens (auth token, for short) for accessing protected resources without the need for asking the user for credentials. The adapter is also told which content provider to write the data to and for which authority, in the content provider sense, the data belongs to.

In this way, synchronization operations are performed on their own thread at a time requested by the system. During the sync, the adapter gets updated information from the server and synchronizes it to the given content provider. The implementation details for this are flexible and up to the developer.

Tip

Learn more about creating sync adapters by checking out the Sync Adapter sample application on the Android developer website:
http://d.android.com/resources/samples/SampleSyncAdapter/.

Using Backup Services

Android backup services were introduced in Android 2.2 (API Level 8). Applications can use the backup system service to request that application data such as shared preferences and files be backed up or restored. The backup service handles things from there, sending or retrieving the appropriate backup archives to a remote backup service.

Backup services should not be used for syncing application content. Backup and restore operations do not occur on demand. Use a synchronization strategy such as the sync adapter discussed earlier in this chapter in this case. Use Android backup services only to back up important application data.

Tip

Many of the code examples provided in this section are taken from the SimpleBackup application. The source code for this application is provided for download on the book's websites. Also, you need to use the `adb bmgr` command to force backups and restores to occur. For more information on `adb`, see Appendix A, "The Android Debug Bridge Quick-Start Guide."

Choosing a Remote Backup Service

One of the most important decisions when it comes to backing up application data is deciding where to back it up to. The remote backup service you choose should be secure, reliable, and always available. Many developers will likely choose the solution provided by Google: Android Backup Service.

Note

Other third-party remote backup services might be available. If you want complete control over the backup process, you might want to consider creating your own. However, this is beyond the scope of this book.

For your application to use Android Backup Service, you must register your application with Google and acquire a unique backup service key for use within the application's manifest file. You can sign up for Google's backup service at the Android Backup Service website: http://code.google.com/android/backup/signup.html.

Warning

Backup services are available on most, but not all, Android devices running Android 2.2 and higher. The underlying implementation might vary. Also, different remote backup services might impose additional limitations on the devices supported. Test your specific target devices and backup solution thoroughly to determine that backup services function properly with your application.

Registering with Android Backup Service

After you have chosen a remote backup service, you might need to jump through a few more hoops. With Google's Android Backup Service, you need to register for a special key to use. After you've acquired this key, you can use it in your application's manifest file using the `<meta-data>` tag in the `<application>` block, like this:

```
<meta-data android:name="com.google.android.backup.api_key"
    android:value="KEY HERE" />
```

Implementing a Backup Agent

The backup system service relies on an application's backup agent to determine what application data should be archived for backup and restore purposes.

Providing a Backup Agent Implementation

Now it's time to implement the backup agent for your particular application. The backup agent determines what application data to send to the backup service. If you only want to back up shared preference data and application files, you can simply use the `BackupAgentHelper` class.

> **Tip**
>
> If you need to customize how your application backs up its data, you need to extend the `BackupAgent` class, which requires you to implement two callback methods. The `onBackup()` method is called when your application requests a backup and provides the backup service with the appropriate application data to back up. The `onRestore()` method is called when a restore is requested. The backup service supplies the archived data and the `onRestore()` method handles restoring the application data.

Here is a sample implementation of a backup agent class:

```
public class SimpleBackupAgent extends BackupAgentHelper {
    @Override
    public void onCreate() {
        // Register helpers here
    }
}
```

Your application's backup agent needs to include a backup helper for each type of data it wants to back up.

Implementing a Backup Helper for Shared Preferences

To back up shared preferences files, you need to use the `SharedPreferencesBackupHelper` class. Adding support for shared preferences is straightforward. Simply update the backup agent's `onCreate()` method, create a valid `SharedPreferencesBackupHelper` object, and use the `addHelper()` method to add it to the agent:

```
SharedPreferencesBackupHelper prefshelper = new
➡SharedPreferencesBackupHelper(this,
    PREFERENCE_FILENAME);
addHelper(BACKUP_PREFERENCE_KEY, prefshelper);
```

This particular helper backs up all shared preferences by name. In this case, the `addHelper()` method takes two parameters:

- A unique name for this helper (in this case, the backup key is stored as a `String` variable called `BACKUP_PREFERENCE_KEY`).
- A valid `SharedPreferencesBackupHelper` object configured to control backups and restores on a specific set of shared preferences by name (in this case, the preference filename is stored in a `String` variable called `PREFERENCE_FILENAME`).

That's it. In fact, if your application is backing up only shared preferences, you don't even need to implement the `onBackup()` and `onRestore()` methods of your backup agent class.

Tip

Got more than one set of preferences? No problem. The constructor for `SharedPreferencesBackupHelper` can take any number of preference filenames. You still need only one unique name key for the helper.

Implementing a Backup Helper for Files

To back up application files, use the `FileBackupHelper` class. Files are a bit trickier to handle than shared preferences because they are not thread-safe. Begin by updating the backup agent's `onCreate()` method, create a valid `FileBackupHelper` object, and use the `addHelper()` method to add it to the agent:

```
FileBackupHelper filehelper = new FileBackupHelper(this, APP_FILE_NAME);
addHelper(BACKUP_FILE_KEY, filehelper);
```

The file helper backs up specific files by name. In this case, the `addHelper()` method takes two parameters:

- A unique name for this helper (in this case, the backup key is stored as a `String` variable called `BACKUP_FILE_KEY`).
- A valid `FileBackupHelper` object configured to control backups and restores on a specific file by name (in this case, the filename is stored in a `String` variable called `APP_FILE_NAME`).

Tip

Got more than one file to back up? No problem. The constructor for `FileBackupHelper` can take any number of filenames. You still need only one unique name key for the helper. The services were designed to back up configuration data, not necessarily all files or media. There are currently no guidelines for the size of the data that can be backed up. For instance, a book reader application might back up book titles and reading states, but not the book contents. Then, after a restore, the data can be used to download the book contents again. To the user, the state appears the same. It is intended for state and configuration files, not large data files, though.

You also need to make sure that all file operations in your application are thread-safe as it's possible a backup will be requested while a file is being accessed. The Android website suggests the following method for defining a lock from a simple `Object` array within your `Activity`, as follows:

```
static final Object[] fileLock = new Object[0];
```

Use this lock each and every time you perform file operations, either in your application logic or in the backup agent. For example:

```
synchronized(fileLock){
    // Do app logic file operations here
}
```

Finally, you need to override the `onBackup()` and `onRestore()` methods of your backup agent, if only to make sure all file operations are synchronized using your lock for thread-safe access. Here we have the full implementation of a backup agent that backs up one set of shared preferences called `AppPrefs` and a file named `appfile.txt`:

```
public class SimpleBackupAgent extends BackupAgentHelper {
    private static final String PREFERENCE_FILENAME = "AppPrefs";
    private static final String APP_FILE_NAME = "appfile.txt";
    static final String BACKUP_PREFERENCE_KEY = "BackupAppPrefs";
    static final String BACKUP_FILE_KEY = "BackupFile";

    @Override
    public void onCreate() {
        SharedPreferencesBackupHelper prefshelper = new
            SharedPreferencesBackupHelper(this,
            PREFERENCE_FILENAME);
        addHelper(BACKUP_PREFERENCE_KEY, prefshelper);
        FileBackupHelper filehelper =
            new FileBackupHelper(this, APP_FILE_NAME);
        addHelper(BACKUP_FILE_KEY, filehelper);
    }
    @Override
    public void onBackup(ParcelFileDescriptor oldState,
        BackupDataOutput data, ParcelFileDescriptor newState)
        throws IOException {
            synchronized (SimpleBackupActivity.fileLock) {
                super.onBackup(oldState, data, newState);
            }
    }
    @Override
    public void onRestore(BackupDataInput data, int appVersionCode,
        ParcelFileDescriptor newState) throws IOException {
            synchronized (SimpleBackupActivity.fileLock) {
                super.onRestore(data, appVersionCode, newState);
```

```
        }
    }
}
```

To make the `doBackup()` and `doRestore()` methods thread-safe, we simply wrapped the super class call with a synchronized block using your file lock.

Registering the Backup Agent in the Application Manifest File

Finally, you need to register your backup agent class in your application's manifest file using the `android:backupAgent` attribute of the `<application>` tab. For example, if your backup agent class is called `SimpleBackupAgent`, you register it using its fully qualified path name as follows:

```
<application
    android:icon="@drawable/icon"
    android:label="@string/app_name"
    android:backupAgent="com.androidbook.simplebackup.SimpleBackupAgent">
```

Backing Up and Restoring Application Data

The `BackupManager` system service manages backup and restore requests. This service works in the background, on its own schedule. Applications that implement a backup agent can request a backup or restore, but the operations might not happen immediately. To get an instance of the `BackupManager`, simply create one in your `Activity` class, as follows:

```
BackupManager mBackupManager = new BackupManager(this);
```

Requesting a Backup

An application can request a backup using the `dataChanged()` method. Generally, this method should be called any time application data that is to be archived changes. It can be called any number of times, but when it's time to back up, the backup takes place only one time, regardless of how many times `dataChanged()` was called before the backup.

```
mBackupManager.dataChanged();
```

Normally, the user does not initiate a backup. Instead, whenever important application data changes, the `dataChanged()` method should be called as part of the data saving process. At some point in the future, a backup is performed "behind the scenes" by the backup manager.

Warning

Avoid backing up sensitive data to remote servers. Ultimately, you, the developer, are responsible for securing user data, not the backup service you employ. Although some services might encrypt data for you, if it's data sensitive to you or your users, you can always add a layer of encryption yourself.

Requesting a Restore

Restore operations occur automatically when a user resets his device or upgrades after "accidentally" dropping his old one in a hot tub or runs it through the washing machine (happens more often than you'd think). When a restore occurs, the user's data is fetched from the remote backup service and the application's backup agent refreshes the data used by the application, overwriting any data that was there.

An application can directly request a restore using the `requestRestore()` method as well. The `requestRestore()` method takes one parameter: a `RestoreObserver` object. The following code illustrates how to request a restore:

```
RestoreObserver obs = new RestoreObserver(){
    @Override
    public void onUpdate(int nowBeingRestored, String currentPackage) {
        Log.i(DEBUG_TAG, "RESTORING: " + currentPackage);
    }

    @Override
    public void restoreFinished(int error) {
        Log.i(DEBUG_TAG, "RESTORE FINISHED! ("+error+")");
    }

    @Override
    public void restoreStarting(int numPackages) {
        Log.i(DEBUG_TAG, "RESTORE STARTING...");
    }
};

try {
    mBackupManager.requestRestore(obs);
} catch (Exception e) {
    Log.i(DEBUG_TAG,
        "Failed to request restore. Try adb bmgr restore...");
}
```

Tip

Testing of backup services is best done on a device running Android 2.2 or later, in conjunction with the `adb bmgr` command, which can force an immediate backup or restore to occur.

Summary

Android applications do not exist in a vacuum. Users demand that their data be accessible (securely, of course) across any and all technologies they use regularly. Phones fall into hot tubs (more often than you'd think), and users upgrade to newer devices. The Android platform provides services for keeping local application data synchronized with remote cloud services and protecting application data using remote backup and restore services.

References and More Information

Wikipedia on cloud computing:
   http://en.wikipedia.org/wiki/Cloud_computing
Android reference on the `AccountManager` class:
   http://d.android.com/reference/android/accounts/AccountManager.html
Android sample app, Sample Sync Adapter:
   http://d.android.com/resources/samples/SampleSyncAdapter/
Android Dev Guide: "Data Backup":
   http://d.android.com/guide/topics/data/backup.html
Google's Android Backup Service:
   http://code.google.com/android/backup/index.html

26

Internationalizing Your Applications

There are now hundreds of Android devices on the market worldwide. In this chapter, you learn how to design and develop Android applications for foreign users and markets. This involves following design principles that make for easy internationalization, such as using alternative string resources for different languages and leveraging locale-aware classes for format-sensitive data like date and time formats. Finally, we talk a bit about publishing applications in foreign countries.

Internationalizing Applications

Android users hail from many different parts of the world. They speak different languages, use different currencies, and format their dates in different ways—just to name a few examples. Android application internationalization generally falls into three categories:

- Providing alternative resources such as strings or graphics for use when the application runs in different languages
- Implementing locale-independent or locale-specific code and other programmatic concerns
- Configuring your application for sale in foreign markets

We already discussed how to use alternative resources in *Android Wireless Application Development Volume I: Android Essentials*, but perhaps another example is in order. Let's look at an application that loads resources based upon the device language settings. Specifically, let's consider a simple application that loads different string and graphic resources based on the language and region settings of the device.

Internationalization Using Alternative Resources

Let's look at two examples of how to use alternative resources—this time, to localize an application for a variety of different languages and locales. By language, we mean the linguistic variety such as English, French, Spanish, German, Japanese, and so on. By locale, we are getting more specific, such as English (United States) versus English (United Kingdom) or English (Australia). There are times when you can get away with just providing language resources (English is English is English, right?) and times when this just won't work.

Our first example is theoretical. If you want your application to support both English and French strings (in addition to the default strings), you can simply create two additional resource directories called /res/values-en (for the English strings.xml) and /res/values-fr (for the French strings.xml). Within the strings.xml files, the resource names are the same. For example, the /res/values-en/strings.xml file can look like this:

```xml
<?xml version="1.0" encoding="utf-8"?>
<resources>
    <string name="hello">Hello in English!</string>
</resources>
```

Whereas, the /res/values-fr/strings.xml file would look like this:

```xml
<?xml version="1.0" encoding="utf-8"?>
<resources>
    <string name="hello">Bonjour en Français!</string>
</resources>
```

A default layout file in the /res/layout directory that displays the string refers to the string by the variable name @string/hello, without regard to which language or directory the string resource is in. The Android operating system determines which version of the string (French, English, or default) to load at runtime. A layout with a TextView control to display the string might look like this:

```xml
<?xml version="1.0" encoding="utf-8"?>
<LinearLayout
    xmlns:android="http://schemas.android.com/apk/res/android"
    android:orientation="vertical"
    android:layout_width="match_parent"
    android:layout_height="match_parent">
    <TextView
        android:layout_width="match_parent"
        android:layout_height="match_parent"
        android:text="@string/hello" >
</LinearLayout>
```

The string is accessed programmatically in the normal way:

```
String str = getString(R.string.hello);
```

It's as easy as that. So, we move on to a more complex example, which illustrates how you can organize alternative application resources to provide functionality based on the device language and locale.

Tip

The code examples provided in this chapter are taken from the SimpleInternationalization application. The source code for this application is provided for download on the book's websites.

Again, this application has no real code to speak of. Instead, all interesting functionality depends upon the judicious and clever use of resource folder qualifiers to specify resources to load. These resources are

- The default resources for this application include the application icon stored in the /res/drawable directory, the layout file stored in the /res/layout directory, and the strings.xml string resources stored in the /res/values directory. These resources are loaded whenever there isn't a more specific resource available to load. They are the fallbacks.
- There are English string resources stored in the /res/values-en directory. If the device language is English, these strings load for use in the default layout.
- There are French Canadian string resources stored in the /res/values-fr-rCA directory. If the device language and locale are set to French (Canada), these strings load for use within the layout. But wait! There's also an alternative layout stored in the /res/layout-fr-rCA directory, and this alternative layout uses a special drawable graphic (the Quebec flag) stored in the /res/drawable-fr-rCA directory.
- Finally, there are French string resources stored in the /res/values-fr directory. If the device language is French (any locale except Canada), these strings load for use in the default layout.

In this way, the application loads different resources based on the language and locale information, as shown in Figure 26.1. This figure shows the project layout, in terms of resources, and what the screen might look like when the device settings are set to different languages and locales.

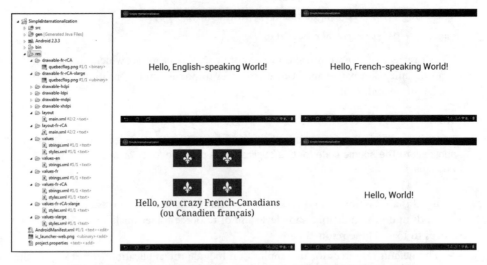

Figure 26.1   Using alternative resources for different language string resources. Locales set to, clockwise from top left: English (any), French (any but Canadian), anything but French or English, and French-Canadian.

Changing the Language Settings

Generally, a device ships in a default language. In the United States, this language is English (United States). Users who purchase devices in France, however, are likely to have a default language setting of French (France), while those in Britain and many British territories would likely have the language set to English (United Kingdom)—that said, Australia and New Zealand have their own English settings and Canada has both an English (Canada) option and a French (Canada) language option.

To change the locale setting on the emulator or the device, you need to perform the following steps:

1. Navigate to the Home screen.
2. Press the Menu button.
3. Choose the Settings option.
4. Scroll down and choose the Language & input settings (see Figure 26.2, top).
5. Choose the Select Language option (see Figure 26.2, top).
6. Select the locale you want to change the system to; for example, French (France), English (United States), or English (United Kingdom), shown as in Figure 26.2, bottom.

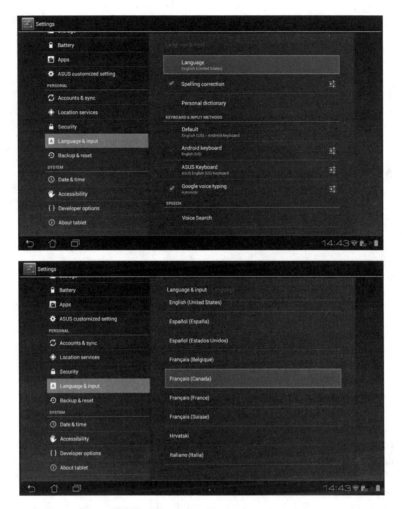

Figure 26.2   Changing device language settings.

Make sure you memorize the steps (and related icons, such as the Settings icon, shown in Figure 26.3) required to change the language settings, as you need to navigate back to this screen in that foreign language, in order to change the settings back.

Figure 26.3   The Settings icon in English and French (left) and the
Settings menu in French (right).

Tip

You can also create custom locales for testing using the Custom Locale application,
available on the Android Emulator. For example, you might want to create a Spanish locale
for Mexico. When you use a custom locale, the emulator displays in its default language
but the current locale is detected as your custom locale, allowing you to localize your
application.

Internationalization forces design choices on the development team. For example, will
you build one big project for all languages or will you break the applications up by
region? For some projects with light internationalization, you might be able to get away
with one project with all internationalized resources. For deep internationalization, you
might need to reorganize projects so that no application becomes too large or cumbersome for the user.

Because much of the work for application localization revolves around alternative
resources, this means that this work might fall not to a developer who knows how to use
Eclipse and the Android tools well, but to a designer who needs some training on how
Android internationalization works, how resources can be layered, and the drawbacks of
over-internationalizing (resulting in large package files with many graphics and such).
On the plus side, this leaves developers free to do what they do best: developing code.

Finally, you've likely noticed that the Android alternative resource structure isn't perfect—especially for countries with multiple official (and unofficial) languages. It is possible to work around these issues, when necessary, by loading graphics programmatically
based on the current locale setting on the device, but this should be attempted only
when absolutely necessary.

Tip

While testing on real hardware is the only way to be sure that your internationalization works the way you expect, the Graphical Layout designer in Eclipse allows you to preview alternate resources.

Implementing Locale Support Programmatically

There are times in which you should ensure that your application code is "locale-aware." Often, this means writing code that is flexible enough to run smoothly regardless of the locale. However, when your application needs to be locale-aware—for example, to download appropriate content from a remote application server—you should rely on locale-friendly methods.

Tip

To determine the device locale, developers can use the `getDefault()` method of the `java.util.Locale` class. Similarly, you can use the `getAvailableLocales()` method to retrieve a list of locales available on the device. Not all locales are supported on all devices; device manufacturers and operators might include only a subset of all locales supported by the Android operating system. For example, you might see devices sold in the United States that support only English and Spanish. You might also want to check out the `android.content.res.Configuration` class for more information on device configuration, including locale settings.

Here are some pointers for developing applications that work in a variety of locales:

- Begin by accepting that different parts of the world have different ways of expressing common information. Respect these differences and support them when feasible.
- Apply standard methods for internationalizing Java applications.
- Most localization issues with application code revolve around the use and formatting of strings, numbers, currencies, dates, and times. Audio and video containing speech is also routinely localized.
- Don't make assumptions about character encodings or what locale your application runs in.
- Always use locale-friendly methods when they are available. Often, a class has two versions of a method: one that uses the current locale and another that includes a locale parameter that you can use when necessary to override behavior.

Tip

There are a number of utility classes and methods provided in the Android SDK for a locale- and region-specific string (start with the `String.format()` method), date manipulation (start with the `java.text.DateFormat` utility class), and phone number formatting (start with the `android.telephony.PhoneNumberUtils` class). Note also that many classes have methods that take a `Locale` parameter, enabling the developer to override behavior for other than the current locale.

Publishing Applications for Foreign Users

After you've designed and developed an application that targets different locales, you need to make sure you can distribute the application to them easily. The Android Market has fairly sophisticated settings available for publishing and selling applications in a variety of countries around the world. This is due to the fact that Google Checkout has worked out the tax and export situations with these countries. Developers can create application listings in a variety of languages and easily target the users they desire. Other markets, such as the Amazon Appstore, are available to a much more limited set of users. See the specific publication channels you wish to use for details about where they distribute applications.

Summary

By internationalizing your Android applications, you enable your applications to reach the maximum number of users. Internationalization requires a multifaceted approach and is best done as part of the application design process. Application assets like strings should be organized by language or region in the appropriate alternative resource directories. You also want to ensure that locale-dependent information like dates, times, and currencies are displayed appropriately, regardless of the region. Finally, be aware that once you internationalize your applications, you must still manage their internationalized application profiles on various publication channels, such as the Android Market.

References and More Information

Android Dev Guide: "Alternative Resources":
    http://d.android.com/guide/topics/resources/providing-resources.html#AlternativeResources
Android Dev Guide: "How Android Finds the Best-Matching Resource":
    http://d.android.com/guide/topics/resources/providing-resources.html#BestMatch
ISO 639-1 Languages:
    http://www.loc.gov/standards/iso639-2/php/code_list.php
ISO 3166-1-alpha-2 Regions:
    http://www.iso.org/iso/country_codes/iso_3166_code_lists/

## 27

An Overview of Third-Party In-App Billing APIs for Android

Developers can monetize their Android applications in a variety of ways. In addition to selling applications outright, developers can integrate billing APIs into their applications in order to sell specific content. In this chapter, we discuss some of the in-app billing APIs available to Android developers, how they might be used, and what some of their limitations are.

What Is In-App Billing?

The freemium business model—where apps are published free of charge but contain content for purchase—is perhaps the most popular way to monetize Android applications these days. Users are more likely to sample a free application, and if the content is sufficiently interesting, they are more likely to pay for it.

Developers can implement freemium applications in a variety of ways. For example,

- A role-playing game might provide a shop where users can purchase items. These items might be available for free in the game if the user is willing to play longer, or the user can purchase items if he doesn't have the time or inclination.

- That same game might want to provide content that is solely available for purchase. For example, perhaps you can customize your character's appearance only if you have the privilege.

- A platform game might entice users with a couple of free levels or a time limit (three-day trial), and then provide more levels or game play time for purchase thereafter.

- A wallpaper, ringtone, music, or video download application might allow the user to browse and preview content and then purchase only the content he wants.

- A cloud-based music storage application might limit the number of songs that can be stored, unless the user upgrades to a purchased storage plan (unlimited or a tiered setup).

- A photo filter app might enable only certain features, such as the ability to share photos with friends, when the user pays up. That same photo filter app might sell new filters right in the app, as they become available.

- A messaging application might want to enable little extras, such as emoticons or video sending, for users who pay for them.

- A developer might want to provide tiered or priority service to those willing to pay for it. This might mean anything, from "faster" service (usage of a higher-performance server, for example). Maybe a user can buy VOIP support calls that are handled right from the app.

- A developer might want to accept donations from users who like their app. They could even "vote" with their dollars to get more features in the next update to the application.

These are just a few of the many ways that in-app purchases can make the monetization of Android applications that much more achievable. Think creatively.

Using In-App Billing

Android developers have numerous options when it comes to designing freemium applications. Most choose to use one of the several well respected services provided that offer libraries for handling secure in-app purchases. Many in-app billing services work only for applications published by specific providers.

Developers are responsible for managing the content they wish to sell to the user through the billing APIs. In-app billing is nontrivial to implement. There are third-party APIs to use, limitations to consider, security and export concerns, and usually substantial code to write—code that needs to be unique and private to your application to help avoid reverse engineering, piracy, and exploitation of your valuable content.

We discuss several specific in-app billing opportunities for developers in this chapter:

- The Android Market's in-app billing APIs
- The Amazon Appstore's in-app billing beta program
- The PayPal billing APIs available from the X.com eCommerce program

All billing APIs have several things in common:

- All in-app billing APIs use a secure connection to complete a financial transaction. This means all billing APIs require the INTERNET permission and a working network connection to function properly.

- All implementations of billing APIs are only as secure as your code is. Protect your digital signatures and any billing API keys provided to you, the developer. Your implementation of billing features should be unique and obfuscated to help avoid piracy and exploitation of your application.
- All in-app billing services that we know of charge commission or fees for use.
- All in-app billing APIs impose addition terms of service and limitations on your applications. We strongly recommend reading the fine print and consulting your financial and law experts if you have questions.
- In-app billing may be tied to a particular device feature, such as having Android Market or Amazon Appstore installed.
- All applications that leverage billing APIs must be careful to comply with international law in terms of taxes, export, and local laws regarding financial transactions.

Note

For these reasons, we do not provide sample applications for the in-app billing mechanisms discussed in this chapter, but we have reviewed the sample applications provided with each technology and are confident they are adequate for most developers. If you were hoping for working samples in this book, we have to tell you to completely change them anyway, otherwise they wouldn't be very secure.

Leveraging Android Market In-App Billing APIs

The Android Market has an in-app billing system that enables you to sell content from within applications. You need an Android Market developer account and Google Checkout/Wallet Merchant account to use these APIs and they have a number of requirements and limitations, such as:

- You can use the APIs only for applications that are published through the Android Market. These can be free or paid applications.
- You can sell digital content using only these APIs. You cannot use them to sell physical goods or services. (This is not an auction payment service, for example.)
- The 30 percent commission fee applies to in-app purchases, just as it does for selling applications on the Android Market.
- You can test your applications before you publish them using test accounts you create with your Android Market publisher account.
- The in-app billing APIs have a number of system requirements you need to comply with. It is available for devices running Android 1.6 (API Level 4) and higher. Other system requirements also exist.

For more information about the Android Market in-app billing APIs, see the Android "Android Market In-app Billing Dev Guide" link in the "References and More Information" section at the end of this chapter.

Note

There is an excellent sample application that illustrates how to use the Android Market in-app billing services that is worth looking over. You can find out more about the sample application at http://d.android.com/guide/market/billing/billing_integrate.html#billing-download. It is available for download from the Android SDK Manager under Extras, Google Market Billing package.

Leveraging Amazon Appstore In-App Billing APIs

With the success of Android-powered eBook readers such as the Amazon Kindle Fire, developers are looking to monetize applications published through venues other than the Android Market. Amazon runs its own Android application marketplace in the form of the Amazon Appstore for Android. Amazon is currently running a closed beta program for in-app purchasing. This technology is appropriate for developers publishing on the Amazon Appstore only. If you are interested in joining this program, we recommend signing up here: http://www.amazon.com/gp/html-forms-controller/AmazonAppstore-IAPrequest.

Note

At the time of this writing, the Amazon Appstore was available only in the United States.

Leveraging PayPal Billing APIs

PayPal is a popular eCommerce service that facilitates financial transactions between somewhat trusted parties. X.commerce (http://www.x.com) is an eCommerce initiative that combines the eBay technologies such as PayPal services into a suite of products that are accessible via libraries. They publish a set of Mobile Payment Libraries that can be used to integrate PayPal functionality into your Android applications. You can download the libraries at their website (see the direct link in the "References and More Information" section at the end of this chapter). We recommend reading over the *Mobile Payment Libraries—Getting Started Guide for Android* documentation. The library documentation is available online, as well as developer forums and a test sandbox for development purposes.

Note

To publish applications that leverage the Mobile Payments Library, you need to create an X.com developer account and submit your applications for review. You can submit and manage your applications from the X.com website. After your application has been approved, you will receive a key for use with the APIs.

Leveraging Other Billing APIs

There are other billing APIs available for use on the Android platform. If you happen to prefer a specific financial service, see whether they have (or are developing) a mobile API! As always, read the fine print. Third-party libraries, especially those that deal with finances, often have additional terms of use. Also, be aware that you, as the developer, are often responsible for handling taxes and tariffs and other financial law compliance, especially when exporting your application to other countries.

Summary

The Android SDK provides many useful user interface components, which developers can use to create compelling and easy-to-use applications. This chapter introduced you to many of the most useful controls and discussed how each behaves, how to style them, and how to handle events from the user.

References and More Information

Wikipedia discussion on the freemium business model:
   http://en.wikipedia.org/wiki/Freemium
Android Market In-app Billing Dev Guide:
   http://d.android.com/guide/market/billing/index.html
Amazon Appstore In-app Billing API Closed Beta Program:
   http://www.amazon.com/gp/html-forms-controller/AmazonAppstore-IAPrequest
X.commerce Mobile Payment Libraries:
   https://www.x.com/developers/paypal/products/mobile-payment-libraries
X.commerce Getting Started Guide for Android:
   https://www.x.com/developers/paypal/documentation-tools/quick-start-guides/mobile-payments-library-android/

## 28

Enabling Application Statistics with Google Analytics

Most Android developers want to know what their users are up to. How long do users spend in the application? How often do they use it? What features of the application are they using and not using? Is the user interface designed so that users can find what they need? What sorts of devices are users using? In this chapter, we discuss how application developers can use the Google Analytics SDK for Android to collect and track information about their application users in a consistent, robust fashion.

Creating a Google Account for Analytics

To send data to the Google Analytics service and later access the statistics your application gathers on the Google Analytics Dashboard, you need to create a developer account at http://www.google.com/analytics. Much like your Android Market account, your Google Analytics account must be tied to an underlying Google Account. The accounts are free to start.

Note

The account setup is primarily targeted at website statistics tracking, but mobile developers use the same workflow so don't get confused and think you're in the wrong place.

As part of the account creation, you'll be asked to log in with your Google account. Then you'll be prompted to enter some information. When you are prompted to enter a website for tracking purposes, choose a fake name (ideally including the name of your app and company domain, such as http://simplestats.androidbook.com). You also need to set the territory and time zone you want to normalize statistics to. Next, you enter contact information for the account. Finally, you need to agree to the terms of service.

Tip

For the same reason as with the Android Market, it's recommended that you create your Google Analytics account with a generic Google Account, such as one for a company entity, as opposed to an individual's account, so you're not trying to track down a specific person's log in information on a weekend, and so on. It's just more professional that way. The analytics account settings can be used to add other people to it, too.

The resulting account creation generates a block of JavaScript for dropping into your "website" for tracking. For mobile developers, you're interested only in the unique Web Property or UA number associated with your account. This number is located in the JavaScript and starts with UA- followed by some numbers. Save off this information—you will need to use this number in your application to send statistics to the proper Google Analytics account. You can create different accounts with different tracking identifiers from your Google Analytics account, or use the same one for all your apps. It depends on what you want out of the reports.

Tip

Many of the code examples provided in this chapter are taken from the SimpleStats application. The source code for this application is provided for download on the book's websites.

For that reason, you may be greeted with an empty dashboard when you first log in to your account, as shown in Figure 28.1.

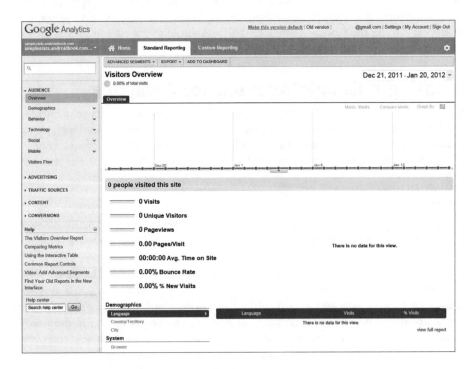

Figure 28.1   The Google Analytics Dashboard (no data).

Adding the Library to Your Eclipse Project

Now you're ready to download the Google Analytics SDK for Android. This library is now available via the Android SDK Manager. When installed, the library is located in the SDK directory under extras, Google, analytics_sdk.

Note

At the time of this writing, we used the Analytics SDK for Android release 2 with Version 1.4.2 listed in the ReadMe.txt file.

Create a /libs directory in your Android project and copy the libGoogleAnalytics.jar file to that directory from its installed directory. To use the Google Analytics SDK for Android, you need to add the library to your Android project. To integrate the SDK into your Eclipse project, follow these steps:

1. Add the libGoogleAnalytics.jar to your project.

2. Add two permissions to your Android manifest file.

Adding the jar file to your project in Eclipse is easy. Simply:

1. Click on the Project properties for your Android project.

2. Under the Java Build Path settings, select the Libraries tab.

3. Click the Add JARs button and choose the jar within the /libs directory.

Because you are sending information over the network, you need to add two permissions to your application. To do this, follow these steps:

1. Click the Permissions tab of the Android manifest file for your application.

2. Add the permission called android.permission.INTERNET.

3. Add the permission called android.permission.ACCESS_NETWORK_STATE.

4. Save your Android manifest file.

You can now start using the classes in the Google Analytics SDK for Android.

Tip

There is also a simple library to help generate basic application tracking events, called Easytracker library. You basically have all your Activity classes inherit from the TrackedActivity class and it does all the tracking for you. This is a simple, all-or-nothing solution, allowing you to avoid collecting data from your applications manually, as we describe later in this chapter. Find out more at http://code.google.com/p/analytics-api-samples/downloads/list.

Collecting Data from Your Applications

Now that you've created an account and added the Google Analytics SDK for Android library to your project, you're ready to start using it to track events and other information in your application. To start tracking in an `Activity` class, retrieve an instance of the `GoogleAnalyticsTracker`. You typically want to start tracking in the `onCreate()` method of your `Activity`, track various events throughout your `Activity` lifecycle, and stop tracking in your `onDestroy()` method. To start tracking, supply your UA account number and an interval (seconds) at which to dispatch events to the server, such as this:

```
GoogleAnalyticsTracker tracker = GoogleAnalyticsTracker.getInstance();
tracker.startNewSession("UA-1234567-89", 30, this);  // Param1 is UA num
```

You can also start a session with a specific dispatch interval in seconds. At each dispatch interval, all queued up tracking activity is dispatched to the Google Analytics servers. You can also manually force a dispatch using the `dispatch()` method, but you want to minimize your dispatches (batch them) to avoid draining the device battery or connecting too often to the Internet.

When you're done tracking, stop the tracker:

```
tracker.stopSession();
```

Stopping a tracking session is commonly performed in the `onDestroy()` callback method of your `Activity` class.

Tip

Logging to the `GoogleAnalyticsTracker` event tracking class is a blocking operation that uses an underlying database. Calls should not occur on the main UI thread. As with some other APIs, such as OpenGL, the `GoogleAnalyticsTracker` class requires all tracking calls to be made on the same thread.

Logging Different Events

Now that you have the SDK set up and working with your application, you want to look into the different types of events you can log with the Google Analytics SDK for Android. You can log page views, events, eCommerce events, and other useful information. The logging methods are flexible enough that you can adapt them to your needs.

Warning

Google Analytics was originally developed to track website statistics, not app stats. Therefore, some of the method names lean in that direction. You simply adapt the call content for your own needs. For example, page views might better be called screen loads, or Activity or Fragment loads, when used with Android. How you map this user activity in your application is up to you.

During a valid tracking session, you can track page views by supplying the name of the page or screen:

```
tracker.trackPageView("/ClickTracker-Main-Screen");
```

You can also track events by specifying a category, action, label, and value (all developer-defined fields):

```
tracker.trackEvent("Clicks", "Button", "Red", 0);
```

Using the Google Analytics Dashboard

After users begin to use your application, the statistics are collected for each of the event hooks you have put in place in your application. This data is then sent to the Google Analytics servers and it's time to head over to the Google Analytics Dashboard and interpret the results.

Tip

Luckily, some of the statistics collected by Google Analytics are now shown in real time. Earlier versions had up to a 24-hour delay between when you log an event and when it shows up in the data on the Dashboard. Real-time statistics are still in beta at the time of this writing.

When your data has been collected and run through the Google Analytics servers, your Dashboard should show the data on the Home screen overview, as shown in Figure 28.2.

You can review the page view details by clicking on the Standard Reporting tab and choosing Content, Overview, as shown in Figure 28.3.

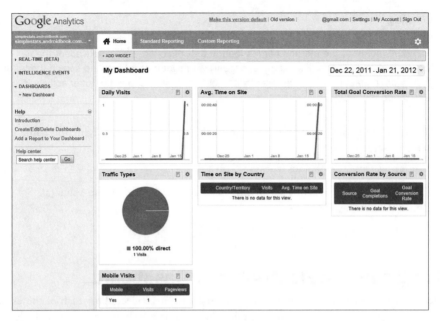

Figure 28.2   The Google Analytics Dashboard (with data).

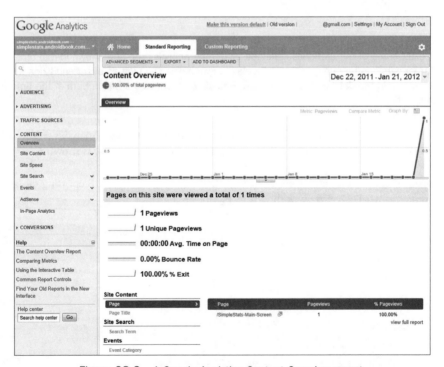

Figure 28.3   A Google Analytics Content Overview report.

You can drill down to the individual button click events by clicking on the Standard Reporting tab and choosing Content, Events, Overview and then drilling down by clicking on the Top Events, Event Label link. This displays the Red and Blue button click events, as shown in Figure 28.4.

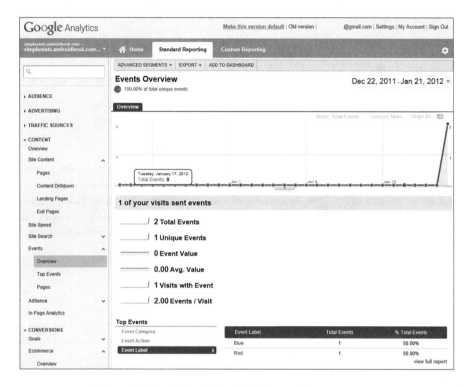

Figure 28.4   A Google Analytics Events Overview report.

The Google Analytics Dashboard has a variety of useful features. We recommend reading through the documentation and messing around with where you put your event hooks in the application prior to publication, as you may want to adjust your analysis strategy to get the reports you desire. For a nice general Google Analytics reference, we recommend *Sams Teach Yourself Google Analytics in 10 Minutes* by Michael Miller (Sams Publishing, 2010, ISBN-13: 9780672333200).

Gathering eCommerce Information

You can also use the Google Analytics SDK for Android to track eCommerce data. This data includes store transactions, purchase data, and other useful information for eCommerce services, which can just as easily include tracking in-app billing data or virtual purchases in a game.

> ### Note
> This type of tracking is not enabled by default. You need to log in to your Google Analytics Dashboard and enable E-Commerce Tracking under the profile settings of your specific account.

Logging eCommerce Events in Your Applications

To start tracking eCommerce information, you must still instantiate the tracker as with other types of events. Then, when you are processing in-app payments or the like, you can use the `Transaction` class to log information about a user purchase. Basically, think of a `Transaction` as a shopping cart instance, and the `Item` class is used to specify the individual items purchased in the cart. Here is the sample code necessary to build up a transaction with two items for purchase.

```
String orderID = "1001" + new Date().toString();

Transaction.Builder transactionBuilder = new Transaction.Builder(
    orderID,
    2.99) ;

transactionBuilder.setStoreName("My Game Store");
transactionBuilder.setShippingCost(0);
transactionBuilder.setTotalTax(0);
mTracker.addTransaction(transactionBuilder.build());
```

Both the `Transaction` and `Item` classes have helper `Builder` classes.

```
// Item #1
Item.Builder itemBuilder = new Item.Builder(
    orderID,
    "SKU_123",
    1.99,
    1);

itemBuilder.setItemCategory("GAME CREDITS");
itemBuilder.setItemName("1 Game Credit");
mTracker.addItem(itemBuilder.build());

// Item #2
Item.Builder itemBuilder2 = new Item.Builder(
```

```
orderID,
"SKU_345",
0.99,
1);

itemBuilder2.setItemCategory("LIFE POINTS");
itemBuilder2.setItemName("1 Life Point");
mTracker.addItem(itemBuilder2.build());
```

When you're ready to commit the transaction and dispatch the results to the Google Analytics servers, simply use the `trackTransactions()` method of the `GoogleAnalyticsTracker` class.

```
mTracker.trackTransactions();
```

Reviewing eCommerce Reports

After you have logged some eCommerce events, you can check out the reports on the Google Analytics Dashboard (assuming you enabled eCommerce tracking in your profile). You can find these reports on the Standard Reporting tab, under the Conversions, Ecommerce. Figure 28.5 shows an Ecommerce Overview report after a single click of the Buy button in the sample application running the Transaction code shown earlier.

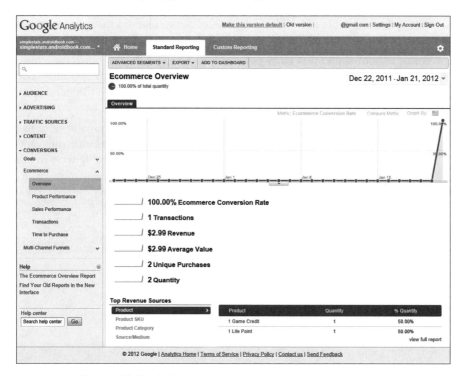

Figure 28.5   A Google Analytics Ecommerce Overview report.

Tracking Ad and Market Referrals

The SDK supports several types of campaign tracking, which allows you to keep track of installation referrals through the Android Market and otherwise. To participate in the Android Market campaign tracking, see the online documentation: http://code.google.com/apis/analytics/docs/mobile/android.html#campaigns.

Gathering Statistics

Now let's talk about some strategies, as well as tips and tricks, for gathering relevant, useful statistics with Google Analytics. Much of the "magic" involves dropping statistics-gathering hooks at clever places in your specific applications. The trick is to place your event hooks at exactly the right places in your application that mean something to you, the developer. Place the hooks in the wrong code locations, and you're going to generate erroneous statistics. It's a bit of an art to do this well, and it's not really something we can give you examples for, but we can talk about some common-sense approaches. For example:

- Develop, document, and test your event tracking strategy and make it consistent. When you track events, you can provide a category, action, label, and value. Use these features consistently throughout your application so that the creation of reports is done in a similar fashion, regardless of who added the event hooks in that part of the application. We see a lot of tracking solutions that generate tons of data but little of real value.

- Know all your application entry points. Most users launch your application from the application tray, but you might have other entry points as well, via notifications or live folders and other intents. If you're trying to log application launches, you need to log for each entry point to get an accurate result.

- Remember your application and `Activity` lifecycle events. You might want to log each time an `Activity` runs. Make sure you do this in a callback that runs only once per `Activity`, such as the `onCreate()` callback. You probably want to avoid logging in `onResume()`, as it may be called repeatedly during the lifetime of an `Activity`. Even so, keep in mind something as simple as rotating the screen will result in a new call to `onCreate()`.

- Gather only the statistics you need, and don't store them if you can avoid it. Gathering excessive information from the user creates and exacerbates a number of issues regarding performance and privacy.

- Consider tracking behavior rather than page views. For example, ranking the difficulty of a game can be done through tracking actions of restarting, dying, quitting frequently, opening help or forum links, and so on. Higher frequencies of these compared to a "completion" action might indicate a higher level of difficulty. In a newsreader application, tracking views that last longer than 30 seconds or involve scrolling down to more content might be more useful than just loading up an article. In fact, behavior is often what analytics tries to glean from page views. You're writing a full application and can more directly indicate behavior through careful creation of tracking events.

- Always verify your assumptions that any unique data you use is unique. Timestamps are not globally unique. Handset device identifiers are available on smartphones, but not tablets and other types of devices.

Protecting Users' Privacy

When you collect user statistics, you need to make sure that the users are aware of your activities, so that privacy concerns are addressed. The Google Analytics Terms of Service require that you indicate to your application users that you reserve the right to anonymously track and report a user's activity inside of your application. By signing up for a Google Analytics account, you agree to these terms. Send only anonymous information to the Google Analytics servers that can be aggregated. Do not send private user information. This isn't the only item you must comply with in the terms of service, of course. Be sure to read and understand it before adding instrumentation to your code with many calls.

Summary

The Google Analytics SDK for Android is an effective way to generate helpful information about how users are using your applications. It's flexible, powerful, and easy to integrate into your applications. As with any logging, you should always inform your users that you are tracking their behavior in the application and have a well understood privacy policy. How you take advantage of the Google Analytics SDK for Android depends on what you're hoping to determine from your users. Heavy analytics may be appropriate for beta projects, whereas lightweight informational logging might be more appropriate for published applications.

References and More Information

Google Analytics documentation:
   http://code.google.com/apis/analytics/
Google Analytics account signup (requires a Google account):
   http://www.google.com/analytics/sign_up.html

Google Analytics documentation for event tracking:
   http://code.google.com/apis/analytics/docs/tracking/eventTrackerGuide.html
Google Analytics documentation for eCommerce tracking:
   http://code.google.com/apis/analytics/docs/tracking/gaTrackingEcommerce.html
Google Analytics documentation on tracking campaigns:
   http://code.google.com/apis/analytics/docs/mobile/android.html#cacampaig
The Easytracker library for Android, Version 1.0:
   http://code.google.com/p/analytics-api-samples/downloads/list

## 29

Protecting Applications from Software Piracy

Android application developers face numerous threats to success in the real world. Apps can be illegally copied and made available for download in alternative locations. A free application might be exploited, causing damage to a brand and leveraging valuable product resources like server bandwidth. All apps are vulnerable to hacking, resulting in rogue downloads with embedded malware, or using knowledge learned to hack a server or other underlying service. Unfortunately, this malicious behavior does happen. Protecting yourself is an ongoing battle; the opposition is constantly improving its methods and you need to stay a step ahead. In this chapter, we talk about some of the ways you can protect yourself from becoming a victim of software piracy.

All Applications Are Vulnerable

Perhaps you've heard some of the startlingly high statistics about the number of mobile applications that are illegally downloaded each year. For the application developer, this loss in revenue, in addition to the other ramifications of software piracy, is staggering; most developers try to take some steps to protect their intellectual property.

All applications deserve protection whether they are paid or free. Just because you're giving away the software doesn't mean that it doesn't contain valuable intellectual property or revenue-making content that you should protect. The last thing you want is for your awesome technology to be copied, misused, or misrepresented simply because you left your work unprotected. This applies to your brand and professional reputation as well. They are all pieces in this puzzle.

The truth is, there is no such thing as a truly invulnerable app (or developer), but you can make your app a hard target. Android developers have various actions they can take to help protect their Android applications from exploitation. Some of these methods include:

- Use secure coding practices
- Obfuscate your binary code using ProGuard
- Leverage the License Verification Library (LVL)

Let's talk about each of these methods in more detail.

Using Secure Coding Practices

As usual, the first step to developing and publishing secure applications is to make it a priority and use common sense. Take a hard look at your application design, look for its vulnerabilities. Where is data stored? How is it accessed? What is plaintext and readable? How would you exploit your application?

Begin by battening down the hatches. Keep developer keys and digital signatures safe so that your development identity cannot be easily exploited. Make sure the passwords that protect these assets are not "password." The same goes for application server accounts and credentials.

Applications that send data over the network can suffer exploitation in a variety of ways. Start by ensuring that your application servers are secure; use strong passwords and all the safeguards you should to protect any network resource. Network sniffing can be a problem so it's important to safeguard any communication between your application and its server. Here are some tips for protecting network communications and resources:

- Don't send any information across the network unless it's absolutely necessary.
- Don't store any private user information remotely unless it's absolutely necessary.
- Don't use predictable or spoofable network communication protocols.
- Use secure network protocols, such as HTTPS and SSL (or TLS), even when data is not sensitive.

Repeat Offenders

In a game, someone might be able to gain points, levels, experience, swords of smiting, or anything else that is useful, simply by performing the same or similar network command multiple times. If the method for performing the action is easily determined through sniffing, the smart user might decide to write a script to do the work for them, regardless of whether the network content is encrypted or not. Although they have a valid account, and have possibly even paid for the game, they will give themselves an unfair advantage against other users. Some cheaters simply do this for their own benefit, while other more entrepreneurially minded cheaters may monetize their findings and provide them to others. Make sure your network communication is sufficiently unpredictable to avoid these repeat offenders.

Obfuscating with ProGuard

Android applications are written in Java. Java is especially susceptible to reverse engineering due to the fact that it supports reflection, or the capability to look up code objects at runtime by name. These labels are kept when the application is compiled. When someone has knowledge of what your application does and the ability to systematically inspect the elements of your code in a human-readable fashion, it takes only a short amount of time to unwind your hard work and exploit it.

Android developers can use the ProGuard tool to make code more difficult to interpret and understand. ProGuard obfuscates, shrinks, and optimizes your code. The end result is a smaller, more secure application package file. Enabling ProGuard is simple in Eclipse with the ADT plug-in. For Android developers, there's little excuse not to provide at least this moderate level of protection to your application source code.

Tip

Using ProGuard changes the code inside the packages and may have implications about how your application works. Be sure to thoroughly test the release version of your application prior to release.

ProGuard processing occurs when you export a signed or unsigned APK file using the Android tools in Eclipse. Besides the added protection of obfuscation, package files are often reduced in size. We routinely see package size reductions of around 25 percent. Surely users will appreciate the faster downloads and more free space on their devices.

Configuring ProGuard for Your Android Applications

ProGuard is an open source tool for compacting and obfuscating compiled Java code. From a protection point of view, the resulting binary files are much harder, but not impossible, to reverse engineer. Android projects created with the ADT plug-in for Eclipse include a default ProGuard configuration file, called `proguard.cfg`. To enable ProGuard, add the following configuration line to the `project.properties` file:

```
proguard.config=proguard.cfg
```

Note

The `project.properties` file says not to make changes, otherwise they'll be erased. Don't worry. This change won't be erased even if you edit the Android settings for the project. At least, it never has been for us and this is the way suggested by the Android team.

ProGuard is now enabled, but only when you use the Android Tools to export a signed or unsigned package with a release version of the application. However, there are several common scenarios when the default ProGuard configuration file doesn't work. During the export process, ProGuard may display some errors. One common error looks like this:

```
[2011-05-31 16:52:07 - HoneycombFragments] Warning:
android.support.v4.app.ActivityCompatHoneycomb: can't find referenced method 'void
invalidateOptionsMenu()' in class android.app.Activity
[2011-05-31 16:52:07 - HoneycombFragments] Warning:
android.support.v4.app.ActivityCompatHoneycomb: can't find referenced method 'void
dump(java.lang.String,java.io.FileDescriptor,java.io.PrintWriter,java.lang.String[
])' in class android.app.Activity
[2011-05-31 ,16:52:07 - HoneycombFragments] Warning:
android.support.v4.view.MenuCompatHoneycomb: can't find referenced method 'void
setShowAsAction(int)' in class android.view.MenuItem
```

The error messages go on to talk about how the classes are inconsistent. This might happen when you try to use ProGuard on a project using the Android compatibility library. The warnings, all of which end in `CompatHoneycomb`, are for compatibility classes that are used to call the Honeycomb versions of methods. This only happens when they are available. For compiles to previous SDK versions, as you probably are with the compatibility library, these warnings can be safely ignored by adding the following warning suppression line to your ProGuard configuration file (`proguard.cfg`):

```
-dontwarn **CompatHoneycomb
```

Then, in a manner similar to the existing `-keep` statements that exist in the file by default, you'll want to include classes that you use. For instance, if you're using fragments, you'd want to add this line:

```
-keep public class * extends android.support.v4.app.Fragment
```

This keeps any unreferenced class that extends the `Fragment` class. If you've referenced only your fragments through XML, this is absolutely required.

After you have edited the `proguard.cfg` file to suit your project, you're ready to test your application thoroughly. Going through the trouble will help protect your application from tampering and reverse engineering, regardless of your distribution method.

Dealing with Error Reports After Obfuscation

Now that your Android application source code is obfuscated, your error reports will also be obfuscated making debugging release builds difficult by design. Luckily, the ProGuard tool outputs a file named `mapping.txt` that can later be used to de-obfuscate the error report. In the SDK tools directory, there is a directory name called `/proguard`. In that directory, you'll find a tool called `retrace`. This tool takes an obfuscated stack trace and makes it readable again. The `mapping.txt` file is stored in a directory named `/proguard`, which is found in the root of your project.

There's one important caveat, though. Every time you make a release, the `mapping.txt` file is recreated. It's not necessarily the same every time. This means that each time you actually release an application to users, you need to keep the `mapping.txt` file and keep which release it goes with. Otherwise, stack traces are basically useless to you. Needless to say, keep your `mapping.txt` files secure so they are not exploited either.

Leveraging the License Verification Library

Let's look at another scenario. Let's imagine that you have developed a killer application and published it a month ago on the Android Market. So far it has been downloaded 25,000 times. But wait! There are 100,000 unique users according to your server logs. Welcome to the world of software piracy. One solution is to live with it and be happy that your application is good enough that people took the time to steal it. Another solution is to fight back; you can start by using the License Verification Library (LVL) to further protect your application from piracy.

Tip

The LVL verifies only Android Market purchases and is not a solution for developers who have published free apps, including those with in-app billing or those using alternative markets.

The LVL is available for download through the Android SDK Manager. The library works only with the Android Market and is meant for paid applications. If you distribute your application through other means, you need to use a separate licensing scheme and you might need to provide separate binaries to support these differing means.

It's up to you to determine whether it's worth the effort using LVL with your specific project. Unlike ProGuard, the LVL is not a turn-key solution; it takes time and effort to get it set up, integrated with your application, and working properly. You have to manage keys, policies, and testing. In addition, even the LVL is prone to exploitation itself. As a public shared library, LVL code compiles the same way against all applications. While obfuscation through ProGuard does help, even that leaves similar patterns for pirates to look for and take advantage of. Identical Java code through ProGuard turns into identical obfuscated code and, ultimately, identical binary. A person looking to crack the licensing can do so much faster if multiple apps use the exact same code patterns, thus you'll want to modify what you can.

The consensus is that modifying the LVL codebase to make it different from all other implementations used by other parties, while keeping the functionality, is your best defense. For that reason, we aren't going to provide code examples here—you'd just have to change them. Instead, we recommend that if you think the LVL is right for you, consult the Google examples provided with the library, available at http://d.android.com/guide/publishing/licensing.html.

Other Anti-Piracy Tips

If piracy is a huge concern for you or your company, there are other methods to help protect your applications. Although piracy can never be stopped completely, here are a few things you might be able to do to combat it:

- Use in-app billing on a free app. Careful control over features that can be enabled through in-app billing allows more users to try your app for free, while the features that must be paid for are protected by requiring accurate billing information. The leak of your compiled binary will no longer be devastating.

- Update your application with great features frequently. Creating an awesome application means supporting your application and adding new features. If this is done frequently, you create more work for those trying to pirate your app while giving an incentive to people to pay and get updates more frequently.

- Block old versions of your application from accessing server resources. If you know a particular version has been pirated and you provide free updates (as most mobile apps do), simply push out an update and provide a message to users of the old version that they must update to continue.

- Price your services and apps appropriately. If your application is overpriced for what it is, it's more likely to be pirated by people who won't pay that amount. Priced correctly and people will be happy to pay for it.

- Provide free trial versions of your app or, if your app is highly valuable and priced correctly, provide cheap trial editions. Without any way to evaluate a paid app, users who actually do want to evaluate the app first may search for a pirated version. If that version actually works, there's little incentive for them to go out and buy the full version.

Although none of these methods are full-proof, the point is to provide a great experience to the user that will bring in more paying users in total. Make people want to pay for what you're offering rather than want to find a workaround to not pay.

Summary

In this chapter, you have learned a variety of straightforward methods to protect your Android applications from theft and tampering. Although no method is perfect, there's no reason to make yourself an easy target. Use common-sense techniques for securing your applications, protect your network communication from cheaters, obfuscate with ProGuard, and consider validating application licensing with the LVL. The longer it takes for your application to be cracked and stolen, the more likely those software pirates will simply turn to easier prey.

References and More Information

Android Dev Guide: "Designing for Security":
   http://d.android.com/guide/practices/security.html
Android Tools, ProGuard:
   http://d.android.com/guide/developing/tools/proguard.html
ProGuard Manual:
   http://proguard.sourceforge.net/index.html#manual/ (http://goo.gl/a6mpW)
Android Dev Guide: "Application Licensing":
   http://d.android.com/guide/publishing/licensing.html
Android development blog article on securing Android LVL applications:
   http://android-developers.blogspot.com/2010/09/securing-android-lvl-
applications.html (http://goo.gl/l0mn)
"Evading Pirates and Stopping Vampires Using LVL, In-App Billing, and App Engine":
   http://www.youtube.com/watch?v=TnSNCXR9fbY

The Android Debug Bridge Quick-Start Guide

The Android Debug Bridge (ADB) is a client-server tool that interacts directly with Android devices and emulators using a command-line interface. You can use this tool, which is provided as part of the Android SDK, to manage and interact with emulator and device instances connected to a development machine and view logging and debugging information. ADB also provides the underpinnings for other tools, such as the Android Plug-In for Eclipse (ADT) and Dalvik Debug Monitor Service (DDMS). This Quick-Start Guide is not complete documentation of the ADB functionality. Instead, it is designed to get you up and running with common tasks. See the ADB documentation provided with the Android SDK for a complete list of features.

Much of the functionality provided by the ADB (such as the LogCat Android logging utility or pushing and pulling files using the File Explorer) is closely integrated into the development environment through DDMS and ADT. Developers might prefer to use these friendly methods to interact with devices and emulators; however, you can use ADB for automation and scripting purposes. You can also use ADB to customize functionality, instead of relying on the defaults exposed through secondary tools.

Listing Connected Devices and Emulators

You can use ADB to list all Android devices and emulator instances connected to a development machine. To do this, simply use the `devices` command of the `adb` command line. For example:

```
adb devices
```

This command lists the emulators and devices attached to this machine by their serial number and state (offline or device). For emulator instances, the serial number is based on their unique port numbers. For example, in this case, we have one emulator instance (Port 5554) and one Android device:

```
C:\>adb devices
List of devices attached
emulator-5554   device
HT841LC1977     device
```

Directing ADB Commands to Specific Devices

When you know the serial number of the device you want to connect to, you can issue commands as follows:

```
adb -s <serial number> <command>
```

For example, to get the state of a specific device, type

```
adb -s emulator-5554 get-state
```

Instead of using the -s flag with a unique serial number, you can also use the -d flag to direct a command to the *only* device instance connected or the -e flag to direct a command to the *only* emulator instance, provided you have only one of each type connected. For example, if we have only one Android phone connected, we can query its serial number as follows:

```
adb -d get-serialno
```

Starting and Stopping the ADB Server

Sometimes you might need to manually restart the ADB server process. We have, for example, needed to do this when we've had an emulator instance running for a long time and have repeatedly connected and disconnected the debugger, eventually resulting in a loss of LogCat logging. In this case, you might want to kill and restart the ADB server (and perhaps Eclipse).

Stopping the ADB Server Process

To terminate the ADB server process, use the kill-server command. For example, type

```
adb kill-server
```

Starting and Checking the ADB Server Process

You can start the ADB server using the start-server command.

```
adb start-server
```

You can also use the start-server command to check whether the server is running. If the server isn't running when other commands are issued, it is started automatically.

Listing ADB Commands

To get a list of all ADB commands, type

```
adb help
```

You can also simply type adb without any arguments to get a list of all other commands available through the adb shell.

Issuing Shell Commands

ADB includes a shell interface (ash) where you can interact directly with the device and issue commands and run binaries. The ash shell has your typical file access commands, such as pwd and ls.

Tip

For more information on the ash shell, check out the Linux Blog Man at http://www.thelinuxblog.com/linux-man-pages/1/ash

Issuing a Single Shell Command

You can issue a single shell command without starting a shell session using the following command:

```
adb shell <command>
```

For example, to list all the files in the /sdcard/download directory on the emulator, type

```
adb -e shell ls /sdcard/download
```

Using a Shell Session

Often you might want to issue more than one command. In this case, you might want to start a shell session. To do so, simply type

```
adb shell
```

For example, to connect to a specific device instance by serial number and start a shell session, type

```
adb -s emulator-5554 shell
# <type commands here>
# exit
```

You can then issue commands. Ending your session is as easy as typing exit.

Tip

If you connect to a device instead of the emulator, you might see a $ as a prompt instead of a # prompt. This indicates user-level access, but the commands, such as logcat and monkey, work as described.

Using the Shell to Start and Stop the Emulator

Stopping the emulator makes it stop responding, although it still displays on your development machine. To stop the emulator, you can issue the `stop` command in the ADB shell.

```
adb -s emulator-5554 shell stop
```

You can then restart the emulator using the `start` command:

```
adb -s emulator-5554 shell start
```

You could also perform these commands from within a shell session, like this:

```
adb -s emulator-5554 shell
# stop
# start
```

> **Tip**
>
> You can also use the shell interface to run built-in command-line programs such as
> `sqlite3` to examine SQLite application databases and `monkey` to stress test an applica-
> tion. You can also install custom binaries on the emulator or device. We talk more about
> this later in the appendix. That said, you can only run `sqlite3` on the device shell if the
> device is rooted, which we do not recommend, although many people do it.

Copying Files

You can use the ADB command line to copy files to and from your hard drive to an
Android device. You need to know the full path information to the file you want to
copy. File operations are subject to your user permissions (locally and remotely).

Sending Files to a Device or Emulator

You can copy files to the device using the `push` command, as follows:

```
adb push <local file path> <remote file path on device>
```

For example, to copy the file `Pic.jpg` from the local hard drive to a device's SD
Card download directory, use the following command:

```
adb -s HT841LC1977 push c:\Pic.jpg /sdcard/download/Pic.jpg
```

Retrieving Files from a Device or Emulator

You can copy files from the device using the `pull` command, as follows:

```
adb pull <remote file path on device> <local file path>
```

For example, to copy the file `Lion.jpg` to your local hard drive from a device's SD Card download directory, use the following command:

```
adb -s HT841LC1977 pull /sdcard/download/Lion.jpg C:\Lion.jpg
```

Tip

If you put picture files onto your SD Card—virtual or otherwise—using this method, you might need to force the Android operating system to refresh using the Media Scanner (available in the Dev Tools application on the Emulator).

Installing and Uninstalling Applications

You can use ADB to install and uninstall packages (applications) on a given Android device or emulator. Although the Eclipse plug-in does this for developers automatically, this functionality is useful for developers not using the Eclipse and for those developers and testers who want to create automated build procedures and testing environments. ADB can also be used to install third-party application packages, including those that are self-distributed and not found on application stores such as the Android Market.

Note

All Android applications are installed as packages created with the Android Asset Packaging Tool (aapt). This is the tool used by the Eclipse plug-in as well.

Installing Applications

To install applications, first create an Android package (.apk) file, and then use the install command:

```
adb install <apk file path>
```

For example, to install the sample application Snake on the emulator, you can use the following command:

```
adb -e install C:\android-sdk\samples\Snake\bin\Snake.apk
821 KB/s (17656 bytes in 0.021s)
      pkg: /data/local/tmp/Snake.apk
Success
```

Reinstalling Applications

You can use the `-r` to reinstall the application package without overwriting its data. For example, you can now reinstall the Snake application without losing your data by using the following command:

```
adb -e install -r C:\Snake.apk
```

Uninstalling Applications

To uninstall an Android application, you need to know the name of its package:

```
adb uninstall <package>
```

For example, to uninstall the MyFirstAndroidApp application from the emulator, you can use the following command:

```
adb -e uninstall com.androidbook.myfirstandroidapp
```

Tip

You might use this command often if you switch between computers and, thus, switch signatures frequently.

Working with LogCat Logging

Android logging information is accessible through the LogCat utility. This utility is integrated into DDMS and Eclipse (using the ADT plug-in), but you can also access it directly from the ADB command line using the following command:

```
adb logcat <option> <filter>
```

This type of command is best done from within the adb shell.

Displaying All Log Information

For example, you can display all LogCat logging information from the emulator instance by opening the shell and typing the logcat command:

```
adb -e shell
# logcat
```

By default, the logging mode is set to brief. For example, the following is an Informational (I) log message (brief mode) from the debug tag called *AppLog* from process ID 20054:

```
I/AppLog(20054): An Informational Log message.
```

Including Date and Time with Log Data

Another useful mode is the time mode, which includes the date and time the log message was invoked. To change the logging mode, use the -v flag and specify the format. For example, to change to time mode, use the following adb shell command:

```
# logcat -v time
```

The resulting log messages are formatted with the date and time, followed by the event severity, tag, process ID, and log message:

```
01-05 21:52:22.465 I/AppLog(20054): Another Log Message.
```

Filtering Log Information

All the log information available through the LogCat tool can be overwhelmingly verbose. Most of the time, a filter or two is required to sift out only the messages you want to view. Filters are formatted tags and event priority pairs. The format for each filter is

```
<Tag Name>:<Lowest Event Priority to Print>
```

For example, a filter to display Informational log messages (and higher-priority messages including Warnings, Errors, and Fatal messages) from log messages tagged with the string `AppLog` would look like this:

```
AppLog:I
```

Tip

You can also use the asterisk (*), which means "all." So if you use an asterisk on the Tag side of the filter, it means "All tags." If you put it on the Event Priority side, it's much like using the V priority—the lowest priority, so all messages display.

Filtering by Event Severity

You can create filters to display only log events of a certain severity. The severity types (from lowest priority or most verbose to highest priority or least verbose) follow:

- Verbose (V)
- Debug (D)
- Info (I)
- Warning (W)
- Error (E)
- Fatal (F)
- Silent (S)

For example, the following shell command displays all Errors and Fatal errors but suppresses warnings, informational messages, debug messages, and verbose messages:

```
# logcat *:E
```

Tip

In API Level 8, a new type of error was created called a `wtf` error. These errors are generated using the `Log.wtf()` method. In this case, *wtf* supposedly stands for "What a terrible failure." This log method should be used to report events that should never happen. See the `Log` class documentation for more details.

Filtering by Tag

You can use multiple filters, ending with a catch-all. Perhaps you want to see all messages from a specific application (a specific tag) and no others. In this case, you want to create a filter to show all messages for a given tag and another filter to suppress all other tags. We also change into time mode, so we get the date and time of the logged events messages. The following `shell` command displays all `AppLog`-tagged logging information and suppresses all other tags:

```
# logcat -v time AppLog:V *:S
```

This filter is roughly equivalent to this other command line:

```
# logcat -v time AppLog:* *:S
```

The resulting log messages are formatted with the date and time, followed by the event severity, tag, process ID, and message:

```
01-05 21:52:22.465 I/AppLog(20054): Another Log Message.
```

Clearing the Log

You can clear the emulator log using the `-c` flag:

```
adb -e logcat -c
```

Or, you can clear it from the ADB shell like this:

```
# logcat -c
```

Redirecting Log Output to a File

You can redirect log output to a file on the deviceusing the `-f` flag. For example, to direct all informational logging messages (and those of higher priority) from the emulator to the file `mylog.txt` in the `sdcard` directory, you can use the following ADB shell command:

```
# logcat -f /sdcard/mylog.txt *:I
```

Note

This file is stored on the emulator or device. You need to pull it onto your desktop either using ADB or the DDMS File Explorer.

Accessing the Secondary Logs

Android has several different logs. By default, you look at the main log. However, an events log and a radio log also exist. You can connect to the other log buffers using the -b flag. For example, to connect to the event log to review events, type

```
# logcat -b events
```

The radio log is similarly accessed as follows:

```
# logcat -b radio
```

Controlling the Backup Service

Android 2.2 introduced a backup service that applications can use to archive important data in case of a factory reset or lost device. This service normally runs in the background, backing up data and restoring it on its own schedule. However, you can use the bmgr shell tool to prompt the backup service to do its thing, which is helpful for testing backup functionality. You can check to see whether the Backup Manager is enabled using the following ADB shell command:

```
# bmgr enabled
Backup Manager currently disabled
```

You can enable the Backup Manager from the ADB shell as follows:

```
# bmgr enable true
Backup Manager now enabled
```

Tip

The user can enable and disable the Backup Manager on a specific device by navigating to the backup settings, accessed via Settings, Privacy, Backup, and Restore.

Forcing Backup Operations

From the ADB shell, you can schedule a backup using the following command:

```
# bmgr backup <package>
```

For example, you can schedule a backup of the SimpleBackup application data as follows:

```
# bmgr backup com.androidbook.simplebackup
```

The previous commands only schedule the backup to occur at some point in the future. You can trigger all scheduled backup tasks with the following command:

```
# bmgr run
```

Forcing Restore Operations

From the ADB shell, you can force a restore using the following command:

```
# bmgr restore <package>
```

For example, you can force a restore of the SimpleBackup application data as follows:

```
# bmgr restore com.androidbook.simplebackup
```

Unlike the `backup` command, the restore command immediately causes a restore operation.

Wiping Archived Data

From the ADB shell, you can wipe archived data for a specific application using the following command:

```
# bmgr wipe <package>
```

For example, you wipe out all archived backup data from the SimpleBackup application as follows:

```
# bmgr wipe com.androidbook.simplebackup
```

Generating Bug Reports

You can create a rather verbose bug report to attach to application defects using the `bugreport` command. For example, to print the debug information for the sole emulator instance running on your development machine, use

```
adb -e bugreport
```

To print the debug information for the sole phone connected via USB, you issue this command instead:

```
adb -d bugreport
```

Using the Shell to Inspect SQLite Databases

You can use the standard `sqlite3` database tool from within the ADB shell. This tool enables you to inspect and interact directly with a SQLite database on the emulator. For a thorough explanation of the `sqlite3` tool, see Appendix B, "The SQLite Quick-Start Guide."

Using the Shell to Stress Test Applications

You can use the Exerciser/Monkey tool from within the ADB shell to send random user events to a specific application. Think of it as handing your phone (or emulator) to a monkey (or a baby, or a baby monkey) and letting it push random keys, causing random events on the phone—events that can crash your application if it doesn't handle them correctly. If your application crashes, the monkey application stops and reports the error, making this a useful tool for quality assurance.

Letting the Monkey Loose on Your Application

To launch the monkey tool, use the following ADB shell command:

```
# monkey -p <package> <options> <event count>
```

For example, to have the monkey tool generate five random events in the GroceryList application in the emulator, do the following:

```
adb -s emulator-5554 shell
# monkey -p com.androidbook.grocerylist 5
```

Listening to Your Monkey

You can watch each event generated by using the verbose flag -v. For example, to see which events you send to the preceding GroceryList application, use this command:

```
adb -s emulator-5554 shell
# monkey -p com.androidbook.grocerylist -v 5
```

Here is the important output from this command:

```
:SendKey: 21   // KEYCODE_DPAD_LEFT
:Sending Trackball ACTION_MOVE x=-4.0 y=2.0
:Sending Trackball ACTION_UP x=0.0 y=0.0
:SendKey: 82   // KEYCODE_MENU
:SendKey: 22   // KEYCODE_DPAD_RIGHT
:SendKey: 23   // KEYCODE_DPAD_CENTER
:Dropped: keys=0 pointers=0 trackballs=0
// Monkey finished
```

You can tell from the verbose logging that the monkey application sent five events to the GroceryList application: a navigation event (left), two trackball events, the Menu button, and then two more navigation events (right, center).

Directing Your Monkey's Actions

You can specify the types of events generated by the monkey application. You basically give weights (percentages) to the different types of events. The event types available are shown in Table A.1.

Table A.1   Monkey Event Types

Event Type	Description	Default Percentage	Command Line Flag	Event ID (As shown in Verbose mode)
Touch	Up/Down event on a single screen location	15%	`--pct-touch`	0
Motion	Down event on a single location, followed by some movement; then an `Up` event in a different screen location	10%	`--pct-motion`	1
Trackball	Trackball events, which are sometimes followed by a `Click` event	15%	`--pct-trackball`	2
Basic Navigation	Up, Down, Left, Right	25%	`--pct-nav`	3
Major Navigation	Menu, Back, Center of DPAD, and such	15%	`--pct-majornav`	4
System Key	Home, Volume, Send, End, and such	2%	`--pct-syskeys`	5
Activity Switch	Randomly switch to other activities	2%	`--pct-appswitch`	6
Other Events	Key presses other buttons	16%	`--pct-anyevent`	7

To use a different mix of events, you need to include the event type's command–line flag as listed in Table A.1, followed by the desired percentage:

```
# monkey [<command line flag> <percentage>...] <event count>
```

For example, to tell the `monkey` tool to use only touch events, use the following command:

```
# monkey -p com.androidbook.grocerylist -pct-touch 100 -v 5
```

Or, let's say you want just Basic and Major navigation events (50%/50%):

```
# monkey -p com.androidbook.grocerylist -pct-nav 50 -pct-majornav 50
-v 5
```

You get the picture.

Training Your Monkey to Repeat His Tricks

For random yet reproducible results, you can use the seed option. The seed feature enables you to modify the events that are produced as part of the event sequence, yet you can rerun sequence in the future (and verify bug fixes, for example). To set a seed, use the -s flag:

```
# monkey -p <package> -s <seed> -v <event count>
```

For example, in the command we used previously, we can change the five events by setting a different starting seed. In this case, we set a seed of 555:

```
# monkey -p com.androidbook.grocerylist -s 555 -v 5
```

Changing the seed changes the event sequence sent by the monkey, so as part of a stress test, you might want to consider generating random seeds, sending them to the monkey, and logging the results. When the application fails on a given seed, keep that seed (and any other command-line options, such as event type percentages) when you log the bug and rerun the test later to verify the bug fix.

Keeping the Monkey on a Leash

By default, the monkey generates events as rapidly as possible. However, you can slow down this behavior using the throttle option, as follows:

```
# monkey -throttle <milliseconds> <event count>
```

For example, to pause for 1 second (1000 milliseconds) between each of the five events issued to the GroceryList application, use the following command:

```
# monkey -p com.androidbook.grocerylist -v -throttle 1000 5
```

Learning More About Your Monkey

For more information about the monkey commands, see the Android SDK Reference website at http://d.android.com/guide/developing/tools/monkey.html. You can also get a list of commands by typing monkey without any command options, like this:

```
adb -e shell monkey
```

Installing Custom Binaries via the Shell

You can install custom binaries on the emulator or device. For example, if you spend a lot of time working in the shell, you might want to install BusyBox, which is a free and useful set of command-line tools available under the GNU General Public License and has been called "The Swiss Army Knife of Embedded Linux" (thanks, Wikipedia, for that little fact). BusyBox provides a number of helpful and familiar UNIX utilities, all packaged in a single binary—for example, utilities such as find and more. BusyBox provides many useful functions (although some might not apply or be permissible) on Android, such as the following:

```
[, [[, addgroup, adduser, adjtimex, ar, arp, arping, ash, awk,
basename, bunzip2, bzcat, bzip2, cal, cat, catv, chattr, chgrp,
chmod, chown, chpasswd, chpst, chroot, chrt, chvt, cksum, clear,
cmp, comm, cp, cpio, crond, crontab, cryptpw, cut, date, dc, dd,
deallocvt, delgroup, deluser, df, dhcprelay, diff, dirname, dmesg,
dnsd, dos2unix, du, dumpkmap, dumpleases, echo, ed, egrep, eject,
env, envdir, envuidgid, ether-wake, expand, expr, fakeidentd, false,
fbset, fdflush, fdformat, fdisk, fgrep, find, fold, free, freer-
amdisk, fsck, fsck.minix, ftpget, ftpput, fuser, getopt, getty,
grep, gunzip, gzip, halt, hdparm, head, hexdump, hostid, hostname,
httpd, hwclock, id, ifconfig, ifdown, ifup, inetd, init, insmod,
install, ip, ipaddr, ipcalc, ipcrm, ipcs, iplink, iproute, iprule,
iptunnel, kbd_mode, kill, killall, killall5, klogd, last, length,
less, linux32, linux64, linuxrc, ln, loadfont, loadkmap, logger,
login, logname, logread, losetup, ls, lsattr, lsmod, lzmacat,
makedevs, md5sum, mdev, mesg, microcom, mkdir, mkfifo, mkfs.minix,
mknod, mkswap, mktemp, modprobe, more, mount, mountpoint, mt, mv,
nameif, nc, netstat, nice, nmeter, nohup, nslookup, od, openvt,
passwd, patch, pgrep, pidof, ping, ping6, pipe_progress, pivot_root,
pkill, poweroff, printenv, printf, ps, pscan, pwd, raidautorun,
rdate, readlink, readprofile, realpath, reboot, renice, reset,
resize, rm, rmdir, rmmod, route, rpm, rpm2cpio, run-parts, runlevel,
runsv, runsvdir, rx, sed, seq, setarch, setconsole, setkeycodes,
setlogcons, setsid, setuidgid, sh, sha1sum, slattach, sleep, soft-
limit, sort, split, start-stop-daemon, stat, strings, stty, su,
sulogin, sum, sv, svlogd, swapoff, swapon, switch_root, sync,
sysctl, syslogd, tail, tar, taskset, tcpsvd, tee, telnet, telnetd,
test, tftp, time, top, touch, tr, traceroute, true, tty, ttysize,
udhcpc, udhcpd, udpsvd, umount, uname, uncompress, unexpand, uniq,
unix2dos, unlzma, unzip, uptime, usleep, uudecode, uuencode, vcon-
fig, vi, vlock, watch, watchdog, wc, wget, which, who, whoami,
xargs, yes, zcat, zcip
```

All you need to do is install the binary (which is available online) using the following steps:

1. Download the BusyBox binary (at your own risk, or compile it for yourself). You can find the binary online at http://benno.id.au/blog/2007/11/14/android-busy-box, where Benno has kindly hosted it for you. (Thanks, Benno!)

2. Make a directory called /data/local/busybox/ on your emulator using the ADB shell; for example, adb -e shell mkdir /data/local/busybox/.

3. Copy the BusyBox binary to the directory you created; for example, adb -e push C:\busybox /data/local/busybox/busybox.

4. Launch the ADB shell; for example, adb -e shell.

5. Navigate to the BusyBox directory; for example, #cd /data/local/busybox.

6. Change the permissions on the BusyBox file; for example, #chmod 777 busybox.

7. Install BusyBox; for example, #./busybox -install.

8. Export the path for ease of use. Note: You need to reset the PATH for each session; for example, #export PATH=/data/busybox:$PATH.

You can find out more about BusyBox at http://www.busybox.net.

B

The SQLite Quick-Start Guide

The Android System allows individual applications to have private SQLite databases in which to store their application data. This Quick-Start Guide is not a complete documentation of the SQLite commands. Instead, it is designed to get you up and running with common tasks. The first part of this appendix introduces the features of the `sqlite3` command-line tool. We then provide an in-depth database example using many common SQLite commands. See the online SQLite documentation (http://www.sqlite.org) for a complete list of features, functionality, and limitations of SQLite.

Exploring Common Tasks with SQLite

SQLite is a lightweight and compact, yet powerful, embedded relational database engine available as public domain. It is fast and has a small footprint, making it perfect for phone system use. Instead of the heavyweight server-based databases such as Oracle and Microsoft SQL Server, each SQLite database is within a self-contained single file on disk.

Android applications store their private databases (SQLite or otherwise) under a special application directory:

```
/data/data/<application package name>/databases/<databasename>
```

For example, the database for the PetTracker application provided in this book is found at:

```
/data/data/com.androidbook.PetTracker/databases/pet_tracker.db
```

The database file format is standard and can be moved across platforms. You can use the Dalvik Debug Monitor Service (DDMS) File Explorer to pull the database file and inspect it with third-party tools such as SQLite Database Browser 2.0, if you like.

Tip

Application-specific SQLite databases are private files accessible only from within that application. To expose application data to other applications, the application must become a content provider.

Using the `sqlite3` Command-Line Interface

In addition to programmatic access to create and use SQLite databases from within your applications, you can also interact with the database using the familiar command-line `sqlite3` tool, which is accessible via the Android Debug Bridge (ADB) remote shell.

The command-line interface for SQLite, called `sqlite3`, is exposed using the ADB tool, which we cover in Appendix A, "The Android Debug Bridge Quick-Start Guide."

Launching the ADB Shell

You must launch the ADB shell interface on the emulator or device (if it is rooted) to use the `sqlite3` commands. If only one Android device (or emulator) is running, you can connect by simply typing

```
c:\>adb shell
```

If you want to connect to a specific instance of the emulator, you can connect by typing

```
adb -s <serialNumber> shell
```

For example, to connect to the emulator at port 5554, you would use the following command:

```
adb -s emulator-5554 shell
```

Connecting to a SQLite Database

Now you can connect to the Android application database of your choice by name. For example, to connect to the database we created with the PetTracker application, we would connect like this:

```
c:\>adb -e shell
# sqlite3 /data/data/com.androidbook.PetTracker/databases/pet_tracker.db
SQLite version 3.6.22
Enter ".help" for instructions
sqlite>
```

Now we have the `sqlite3` command prompt, where we can issue commands. You can exit the interface at any time by typing

```
sqlite>.quit
```

Or, type

```
sqlite>.exit
```

Commands for interacting with the `sqlite3` program start with a dot (.) to differentiate them from SQL commands you can execute directly from the command line. This syntax might be different from other programs you are familiar with (for example, MySQL commands).

Warning

Most Android devices don't allow running the `sqlite3` command as emulators do. Rooted devices do allow this command.

Exploring Your Database

You can use the `sqlite3` commands to explore what your database looks like and inter-act with it. You can

- List available databases.
- List available tables.
- View all the indices on a given table.
- Show the database schema.

Listing Available Databases

You can list the names and file locations attached to this database instance. Generally, you have your main database and a temp database, which contains temp tables. You can list this information by typing

```
sqlite> .databases
seq name file
--- ---- --------------------------------------------------
0   main /data/data/com.androidbook.PetTracker/databases/...
1   temp
sqlite>
```

Listing Available Tables

You can list the tables in the database you connect to by typing

```
sqlite> .tables
android_metadata table_pets      table_pettypes
sqlite>
```

Listing Indices of a Table

You can list the indices of a given table by typing

```
sqlite>.indices table_pets
```

Listing the Database Schema of a Table

You can list the schema of a given table by typing

```
sqlite>.schema table_pets
CREATE TABLE table_pets (_id INTEGER PRIMARY KEY
AUTOINCREMENT,pet_name TEXT,pet_type_id INTEGER);
sqlite>
```

Listing the Database Schema of a Database

You can list the schemas for the entire database by typing

```
sqlite>.schema
CREATE TABLE android_metadata (locale TEXT);
CREATE TABLE table_pets (_id INTEGER PRIMARY KEY
AUTOINCREMENT,pet_name TEXT,pet_type_id INTEGER);
CREATE TABLE table_pettypes (_id INTEGER PRIMARY KEY
AUTOINCREMENT,pet_type TEXT);
sqlite>
```

Importing and Exporting the Database and Its Data

You can use the sqlite3 commands to import and export database data and the
schema; you can also interact with it. You can

- Send command output to a file instead of STDOUT (the screen).
- Dump the database contents as a SQL script (so you can recreate it later).
- Execute SQL scripts from files.
- Import data into the database from a file.

Note

The file paths are on the Android device, not your computer. You need to find a directory on
the Android device in which you have permission to read and write files. For example,
/data/local/tmp/ is a shared directory.

Sending Output to a File

Often, you want the sqlite3 command results to pipe to a file instead of to the screen.
To do this, you can type the output command followed by the file path to which the
results should be written on the Android system. For example

```
sqlite>.output /data/local/tmp/dump.sql
```

Dumping Database Contents

You can create a SQL script to create tables and their values by using the dump command. The dump command creates a transaction that includes calls to CREATE TABLE
and INSERT to populate the database with data. This command can take an optional
table name or dump the whole database.

Tip

The dump command is a great way to do a full archival backup of your database.

For example, the following commands pipe the dump output for the `table_pets` table to a file, and then set the output mode back to the console:

```
sqlite>.output /data/local/tmp/dump.sql
sqlite>.dump table_pets
sqlite>.output stdout
```

You can then use DDMS and the File Explorer to pull the SQL file off the Android file system. The resulting `dump.sql` file looks like this:

```
BEGIN TRANSACTION;
CREATE TABLE table_pets (
_id INTEGER PRIMARY KEY AUTOINCREMENT,
pet_name TEXT,
pet_type_id INTEGER);

INSERT INTO "table_pets" VALUES(1,'Rover',9);
INSERT INTO "table_pets" VALUES(2,'Garfield',8);
COMMIT;
```

Executing SQL Scripts from Files

You can create SQL script files and run them through the console. These scripts must be on the Android file system. For example, let's put a SQL script called `myselect.sql` in the `/data/local/tmp/` directory of the Android file system. The file has two lines:

```
SELECT * FROM table_pettypes;
SELECT * FROM table_pets;
```

We can then run this SQL script by typing

```
sqlite>.read /data/local/tmp/myselect.sql
```

You see the query results on the command line.

Importing Data

You can import formatted data using the `import` and `separator` commands. Files such as CSV use commas for delimiters, but other data formats might use spaces or tabs. You specify the delimiter using the `separator` command. You specify the file to import using the `import` command.

For example, put a CSV script called `some_data.csv` in the `/data/local/tmp/` directory of the Android file system. The file has four lines. It is a comma-delimited file of pet type IDs and pet type names:

```
18,frog
19,turkey
20,piglet
21,great white shark
```

You can then import this data into the `table_pettypes` table, which has two columns: an `_id` column and a `pet_type` descriptor. To import this data, type the following command:

```
sqlite>.separator ,
sqlite>.import /data/local/tmp/some_data.csv table_pettypes
```

Now, if you query the table, you see it has four new rows.

Executing SQL Commands on the Command Line

You can also execute raw SQL commands on the command line. Simply type the SQL command, making sure it ends with a semicolon (;). If you use queries, you might want to change the output mode to column so that query results are easier to read (in columns) and the headers (column names) are printed. For example

```
sqlite> .mode column
sqlite> .header on
sqlite> select * from table_pettypes WHERE _id < 11;
_id        pet_type
---------- ----------
8          bunny
9          fish
10         dog
sqlite>
```

You're not limited to queries, either. You can execute any SQL command you see in a SQL script on the command line if you like.

> **Tip**
>
> We've found it helpful to use the `sqlite3` command line to test SQL queries if our Android SQL queries with `QueryBuilder` are not behaving. This is especially true of more complicated queries.

You can also control the width of each column (so text fields don't truncate) using the `width` command. For example, the following command prints query results with the first column five characters wide (often an ID column such as `_id`), followed by a second column 50 characters wide (text column).

```
sqlite> .width 5 50
```

> **Warning**
>
> SQLite keeps the database schema in a special table called `sqlite_master`. You should consider this table read-only. SQLite stores temporary tables in a special table called `sqlite_temp_master`, which is also a temporary table.

Using Other `sqlite3` Commands

A complete list of `sqlite3` commands is available by typing

```
sqlite> .help
```

Understanding SQLite Limitations

SQLite is powerful, but it has several important limitations compared to traditional SQL Server implementations, such as the following:

- SQLite is not a substitute for a high-powered, server-driven database.
- Being file-based, the database is meant to be accessed in a serial, not a concurrent, manner. Think "single user"—the Android application. It has some concurrency features, but they are limited.
- Access control is maintained by file permissions, not database user permissions.
- Referential integrity is not maintained. For example, foreign key constraints are parsed (for example, in `CREATE TABLE`) but not enforced automatically. However, using trigger functions can enforce them.
- `ALTER TABLE` support is limited. You can use only `RENAME TABLE` and `ADD COLUMN`. You may not drop or alter columns or perform any other such operations. This can make database upgrades a bit tricky.
- Trigger support is limited. You cannot use `FOR EACH STATEMENT` or `INSTEAD OF`. You cannot create recursive triggers.
- You cannot nest transaction operations.
- Views are read-only.
- You cannot use `RIGHT OUTER JOIN` or `FULL OUTER JOIN`.
- SQLite does not support stored procedures or auditing.
- The built-in functions of the SQL language are limited.
- See the SQLite documentation for limitations on the maximum database size, table size, and row size. The Omitted SQL page is helpful (http://www.sqlite.org/omitted.html) as is the Unsupported SQL Wiki (http://www.sqlite.org/cvstrac/wiki?p=UnsupportedSql).

Learning by Example: A Student Grade Database

Let's work through a student "Grades" database to show standard SQL commands to create and work with a database. Although you can create this database using the `sqlite3` command line, we suggest using the Android application to create the empty Grades database, so that it is created in a standard "Android" way.

The setup: The purpose of the database is to keep track of each student's test results for a specific class. In this example, each student's grade is calculated from their individual performance on

- Four quizzes (each weighted as 10 percent of overall grade)
- One midterm (weighted as 25 percent of overall grade)
- One final (weighted as 35 percent of overall grade)

All tests are graded on a scale of 0–100.

Designing the Student Grade Database Schema

The Grades database has three tables: Students, Tests, and TestResults.

The Students table contains student information. The Tests table contains information about each test and how much it counts toward the student's overall grade. Finally, all students' test results are stored in the TestResults table.

Setting Column Datatypes

`sqlite3` has support for the following common datatypes for columns:

- INTEGER (signed integers)
- REAL (floating point values)
- TEXT (UTF-8 or UTF-16 string; encoded using database encoding)
- BLOB (data chunk)

Tip

Do not store files such as images in the database. Instead, store images as files in the application file directory and store the filename or URI path in the database.

Creating Simple Tables with AUTOINCREMENT

First, let's create the Students table. We want a student id to reference each student. We can make this the primary key and set its AUTOINCREMENT attribute. We also want the first and last name of each student, and we require these fields (no nulls). Here's our SQL statement:

```
CREATE TABLE Students (
id INTEGER PRIMARY KEY AUTOINCREMENT,
fname TEXT NOT NULL,
lname TEXT NOT NULL );
```

For the Tests table, we want a test id to reference each test or quiz, much like the Students table. We also want a friendly name for each test and a weight value for how much each test counts for the student's final grade (as a percentage). Here's our SQL statement:

```
CREATE TABLE Tests (
id INTEGER PRIMARY KEY AUTOINCREMENT,
testname TEXT,
weight REAL DEFAULT .10 CHECK (weight<=1));
```

Inserting Data into Tables

Before we move on, let's look at several examples of how to add data to these tables. To add a record to the Students table, you need to specify the column names and the values in order. For example

```
INSERT into Students
(fname, lname)
VALUES
('Harry', 'Potter');
```

Now, we're going to add a few more records to this table for Ron and Hermione. At the same time, we need to add a bunch of records to the Tests table. First, we add the Midterm, which counts for 25 percent of the grade:

```
INSERT into Tests
(testname, weight)
VALUES
('Midterm', .25);
```

Then we add a couple quizzes, which use the default weight of 10 percent:

```
INSERT into Tests (testname) VALUES ('Quiz 1');
```

Finally, we add a Final test worth 35 percent of the total grade.

Querying Tables for Results with SELECT

How do we know the data we've added is in the table? Well, that's easy. We simply query for all rows in a table using a SELECT:

```
SELECT * FROM Tests;
```

This returns all records in the Tests table:

```
id    testname         weight
----- ---------------- ------
1     Midterm          0.25
2     Quiz 1           0.1
3     Quiz 2           0.1
4     Quiz 3           0.1
5     Quiz 4           0.1
6     Final            0.35
```

Now, ideally, we want the weights to add up to 1.0. Let's check using the SUM aggregate function to sum all the weight values in the table:

```
SELECT SUM(weight) FROM Tests;
```

This returns the sum of all weight values in the Tests table:

```
SUM(weight)
-----------
1.0
```

We can also create our own columns and alias them. For example, we can create a column alias called fullname that is a calculated column: It's the student's first and last names concatenated using the || concatenation.

```
SELECT fname||' '|| lname AS fullname, id FROM Students;
```

This gives us the following results:

```
fullname          id
------------      --
Harry Potter       1
Ron Weasley        2
Hermione Granger   3
```

Using Foreign Keys and Composite Primary Keys

Now that we have our students and tests all set up, let's create the TestResults table. This is a more complicated table. It's a list of student-test pairings, along with the score.

The TestResults table pairs up student IDs from the Students table with test IDs from the Tests table. Columns, which link to other tables in this way, are often called *foreign keys*. We want unique student-test pairings, so we create a composite primary key from the student and test foreign keys. Finally, we enforce that the scores are numbers between 0 and 100. No extra credit or retaking tests in this class!

```
CREATE TABLE TestResults (
studentid INTEGER REFERENCES Students(id),
testid INTEGER REFERENCES Tests(id),
score INTEGER CHECK (score<=100 AND score>=0),
PRIMARY KEY (studentid, testid));
```

Tip

SQLite does not enforce foreign key constraints, but you can set them up anyway and enforce the constraints by creating triggers. For an example of using triggers to enforce foreign key constraints in SQL, check out the FullDatabase project provided on the book's websites for Chapter 3.

Now it's time to insert some data into this table. Let's say Harry Potter received an 82 percent on the midterm exam:

```
INSERT into TestResults
(studentid, testid, score)
VALUES
(1,1,82);
```

Now let's input the rest of the students' scores. Harry is a good student. Ron is not a good student, and Hermione aces every test (of course). When they're all added, we can list them. We can do a SELECT * to get all columns or we can specify the columns we want explicitly like this:

```
SELECT studentid, testid, score FROM TestResults;
```

Here are the results from this query:

studentid	testid	score
1	1	82
1	2	88
1	3	78
1	4	90
1	5	85
1	6	94
2	1	10
2	2	90
2	3	50
2	4	55
2	5	45
2	6	65
3	6	100
3	5	100
3	4	100
3	3	100
3	2	100
3	1	100

Altering and Updating Data in Tables

Ron's not a good student, and yet he received a 90 percent on Quiz #1. This is suspicious, so as the teacher, we check the actual paper test to see if we made a recording mistake. He actually earned 60 percent. Now we need to update the table to reflect the correct score:

```
UPDATE TestResults
SET score=60
WHERE studentid=2 AND testid=2;
```

You can delete rows from a table using the DELETE function. For example, to delete the record we just updated, use the following:

```
DELETE FROM TestResults WHERE studentid=2 AND testid=2;
```

You can delete all rows in a table by not specifying the WHERE clause:

```
DELETE FROM TestResults;
```

Querying Multiple Tables Using JOIN

Now that we have all our data in our database, it is time to use it. The preceding listing was not easy for a human to read. It would be much nicer to see a listing with the names of the students and names of the tests instead of their IDs.

Combining data is often handled by performing a JOIN with multiple table sources; there are different kinds of JOIN operations. When you work with multiple tables, you need to specify which table a column belongs to (especially with all these different id columns). You can refer to columns by their column name or by their table name, then a dot (.), and then the column name.

Let's relist the grades again, only this time, include the name of the test and the name of the student. Also, we limit our results only to the score for the Final (test id 6):

```
SELECT
Students.fname||' '|| Students.lname AS StudentName,
Tests.testname,
TestResults.score
FROM TestResults
JOIN Students
      ON (TestResults.studentid=Students.id)
JOIN Tests
      ON (TestResults.testid=Tests.id)
WHERE testid=6;
```

This gives us the following results (you could leave off the WHERE to get all tests):

```
StudentName          testname        score
------------------   -------------   -----
Harry Potter         Final           94
Ron Weasley          Final           65
Hermione Granger     Final           100
```

Using Calculated Columns

Hermione always likes to know where she stands. When she comes to ask what her final grade is likely to be, we can perform a single query to show all her results and calculate the weighted scores of all her results:

```
SELECT
Students.fname||' '|| Students.lname AS StudentName,
Tests.testname,
Tests.weight,
TestResults.score,
(Tests.weight*TestResults.score) AS WeightedScore
FROM TestResults
JOIN Students
       ON (TestResults.studentid=Students.id)
JOIN Tests
       ON (TestResults.testid=Tests.id)
WHERE studentid=3;
```

This gives us predictable results:

StudentName	testname	weight	score	WeightedScore
Hermione Granger	Midterm	0.25	100	25.0
Hermione Granger	Quiz 1	0.1	100	10.0
Hermione Granger	Quiz 2	0.1	100	10.0
Hermione Granger	Quiz 3	0.1	100	10.0
Hermione Granger	Quiz 4	0.1	100	10.0
Hermione Granger	Final	0.35	100	35.0

We can just add up the Weighted Scores and be done, but we can also do it via the query:

```
SELECT
Students.fname||' '|| Students.lname AS StudentName,
SUM((Tests.weight*TestResults.score)) AS TotalWeightedScore
FROM TestResults
JOIN Students
       ON (TestResults.studentid=Students.id)
JOIN Tests
       ON (TestResults.testid=Tests.id)
WHERE studentid=3;
```

Here we get a nice consolidated listing:

StudentName	TotalWeightedScore
Hermione Granger	100.0

If we wanted to get all our students' grades, we need to use the GROUP BY clause. Also, let's order them so the best students are at the top of the list:

```
SELECT
Students.fname||' '|| Students.lname AS StudentName,
SUM((Tests.weight*TestResults.score)) AS TotalWeightedScore
FROM TestResults
```

```
JOIN Students
     ON (TestResults.studentid=Students.id)
JOIN Tests
     ON (TestResults.testid=Tests.id)
GROUP BY TestResults.studentid
ORDER BY TotalWeightedScore DESC;
```

This makes our job as teacher almost too easy, but at least we're saving trees by using a digital grade book.

```
StudentName              TotalWeightedScore
------------------------ -----------------

Hermione Granger         100.0
Harry Potter             87.5
Ron Weasley              46.25
```

Using Subqueries for Calculated Columns

You can also include queries within other queries. For example, you can list each student and a count of how many tests they passed, where a passing score means higher than 60, as in the following:

```
SELECT
Students.fname||' '|| Students.lname AS StudentName,
Students.id AS StudentID,
(SELECT COUNT(*)
FROM TestResults
WHERE TestResults.studentid=Students.id
AND TestResults.score>60)
AS TestsPassed
FROM Students;
```

Again, we see that Ron needs a tutor:

```
StudentName      StudentID  TestsPassed
-----------      ---------  ----------

Harry Potter     1          6
Ron Weasley      2          1
Hermione Granger 3          6
```

Deleting Tables

You can always delete tables using the DROP TABLE command. For example, to delete the TestResults table, use the following SQL command:

```
DROP TABLE TestResults;
```

Java for Android Developers

This appendix contains examples of a number of Java techniques frequently used in Android applications and by seasoned Java developers but not always found in beginner Java books and tutorials. If you are new to Java, this information, used in conjunction with a good Java reference, can help you develop Android applications quickly and effectively.

Learning the Java Programming Language

Android applications are written in Java, so learn Java first—it's essential. This appendix does not teach you standard Java syntax or object-oriented programming and how the object hierarchy works. For that, you should get good reference materials such as books or websites that work for you, and if necessary, take some classes. (It should go without saying that learning basic programming fundamentals comes first, but experience has shown us many people try to write Android apps without learning any programming fundamentals first. Learning programming language syntax, such as Java is not the same as learning how to program.) Without basic Java skills, you're going to have trouble developing good Android applications. It's like asking someone to write a poem in a foreign language without first learning how to speak the language... or learning what a poem is.

We, the authors, do believe that the Android platform is a good way to learn Java development, but this works only if you are either under the instruction of a teacher who is guiding you through programming and application development topics simultaneously, or you are a real self-starter who looks up things as you go and pulls together resources from a variety of sources outside this book.

Tip

Want a high-level crash course in Java to see what we're talking about? See our online articles, such as "Learn Java for Android Development: Introduction to Java" and "Java Syntax," available at http://mobile.tutsplus.com/tutorials/android/java-tutorial/.

Learning the Java Development Tools

Once you've begun learning the basics of Java programming, you must learn to use the tools associated with development. Many Android developers use the free Eclipse IDE for Android development. This book uses Eclipse in its examples. Get familiar with the tool so that you can easily debug your applications, or at least read the errors generated by them. We frequently receive emails from frustrated beginners who have no idea why their applications are not compiling, but would have been able to figure it out themselves if only they had looked at the errors generated by Eclipse, for simple mistakes like missing semicolons, mismatched brackets, or undefined variables. The Eclipse IDE spits out errors on the Problems tab at the bottom of the screen.

Familiarizing Yourself with Java Documentation

Javadocs are automatically generated Java class documentation files created from the source code. All the Java references associated with the Android SDK is available for download through the Android SDK Manager and online at http://d.android.com/reference/ (the Reference tab on the website). This book refers to various Android SDK classes and interfaces, but if we were to reproduce the class documentation for the entire Android SDK, this book would need to be many, many volumes.

Understand that this book, and any book on Android development for that matter, must be used along with the full class documentation. Android developers must constantly refer to the class documentation to choose the right methods and supply the correct parameters. Do not make the mistake of thinking you can develop applications without this core documentation. You'll get familiar with the most commonly used class documentation as you get up to speed, but with new classes and methods being added all the time, it's not practical to even attempt to memorize all of it.

Understanding Java Shorthand

Now let's talk about some of the less common Java syntax you frequently see used in Android applications for one reason or another. These are techniques and shorthand that are often seen in the field, but rarely covered in your typical Java class or beginner's reference, yet you find them in the simplest of examples on the Android Development website, in our books, and in other references.

Java shorthand is rarely shown in books, which tend to want to spell out each individual coding step, often on its own line, for readability. Some Java professionals prefer that style, whereas others strive to make the perfect, terse line of code that does everything, often at the expense of readability. Here are some examples of Java shorthand you're likely to see in Android applications.

Chaining Methods and Unnecessary Temp Variables

Java developers often want to avoid creating unnecessary variables, especially temp variables that are used once to store the result of a calculation, either in the middle of a larger calculation, or for a return value. Therefore, you are likely to see statements evaluated as return values, like this:

```
int sum(int a, int b)
{
    return (a+b);
}
```

This is equivalent to a longer method with a temp variable, as in the following:

```
int sumVerbose(int a, int b)
{
    int temp = a + b;
    return temp;
}
```

Android developers often take these Java features to the extreme in what is called *method chaining*. This means that the interim values of the methods are not stored in their own named variables, but simply used "on the fly." Here is a typical method chaining example:

```
InputStream isIconData = getResources().openRawResource(R.drawable.icon);
```

This is equivalent to the following:

```
Resources myAppResources = this.getResources();
InputStream isIconData = myAppResources.openRawResource(R.drawable.icon);
```

Note that the `this` keyword has also been dropped. You often see method chaining in *builder* style classes. For example, with the Android `AlertDialog` classes, you can either construct a new `AlertDialog` class and call a bunch of setter methods, or use the `AlertDialog.Builder` class to chain all of the setter methods together, ending with a call to the builder's `create()` method that ultimately returns an `AlertDialog` (not an `AlertDialog.Builder` class, which is used only for chaining). Although you don't have to use method chaining, you should recognize what it is and how to read it, because the Android SDK sample applications (and our books) use this technique frequently.

Looping Infinitely

In Java, you can have empty statements simply by terminating a blank line of code with its semicolon. This trick is often used to specify `for` loop conditionals to create an infinite loop, like this:

```
for (;;) {
    // Loop
}
```

Each of the `for` loop components is an empty statement. This evaluates to be true and therefore the loop continues indefinitely. As with any code design, make sure any infinite loops you create have reasonable exit cases.

There's also a `for-each` syntax you might see with arrays and classes that implement the `Iterable` interface. To use the `for-each` loop syntax, you need to define your loop variable, then put a colon, and then specify the name of your array or class. For example:

```
int aNums[] = { 2, 4, 6 };
for (int num : aNums) {
    String strToPrint = num;
}
```

This is equivalent to the following:

```
int aNums[] = { 2, 4, 6 };
for (int i = 0; i < aNums.length; i++) {
    String strToPrint = aNums[i];
}
```

Note that we've also been lazy about the automatic `toString()` conversion done on the `int` values when assigned to the `String` variables.

Working with Unary and Ternary Operators

Java supports unary operations, which allow the developers to easily increment or decrement variable values by 1 using `++` and `--`. For example:

```
int counter = 1;
counter++;
counter--;
```

This code is equivalent to the following:

```
int counter = 1;
counter = counter + 1;
counter = counter - 1;
```

Unary operators can appear before (prefix) or after (postfix) the variable. The location of the operator dictates whether the operation happens before or after the rest of the expression is evaluated. For example, the following code shows how unary operators work by manipulating a variable called `counter` using Android logging:

```
int counter = 0;
Log.i(DEBUG_TAG, "The counter value is ="+counter++);     // prints 0
Log.i(DEBUG_TAG, "The counter value is ="+counter);       // prints 1
Log.i(DEBUG_TAG, "The counter value is ="+counter--);     // prints 1
```

```
Log.i(DEBUG_TAG, "The counter value is ="+counter);        // prints 0
Log.i(DEBUG_TAG, "The counter value is ="+(++counter));    // prints 1
Log.i(DEBUG_TAG, "The counter value is ="+--counter);      // prints 0
```

There are also a number of other unary operators, such as +=, -=, *=, /=, %=, ^=, >>=, <<=, &=, |=. Java also supports ternary operators for if-else shorthand. You might see conditional statements followed by a question mark (?), then a statement to evaluate whether the conditional is true, then a colon (:) and another statement to evaluate whether the conditional is false. The result of a ternary operator is the value of the evaluated statement. Here's an example of a ternary operator in use in a simple conditional evaluation:

```
int lowNum = 1;
int highNum = 99;
int largerNum = lowNum < highNum ? highNum : lowNum;
```

This code is equivalent to the following:

```
int lowNum = 1;
int highNum = 99;
int largerNum;
if(lowNum < highNum)
{
    largerNum = highNum;
} else {
    largerNum = lowNum;
}
```

Working with Inner Classes

You (hopefully) learned about the object-oriented programming and class hierarchy in your basic Java instruction, but not all instructors or books talk about inner classes, or perhaps more importantly, anonymous inner classes.

An *inner class* is a class whose scope and definition is encompassed in another class. Most classes in Java are top-level classes. These classes, and the objects they define, are standalone. You can also create nested classes to encapsulate and define subordinate objects that make sense only in the context of the outer class. Nested classes are called inner classes. Inner classes can have all the features of a regular class, but their scope is limited. Inner classes have another benefit: They have full access to the class in which they are nested. This feature makes inner classes perfect for implementing adapter or builder functionality, as you frequently see them used in Android.

Inner classes exist only to help the developer organize code; the compiler treats inner classes just like any other class, except that the inner classes have a limited scope, and are therefore tethered to the class they are defined with.

Here is an example of a top-level class with two inner classes:

```
public class Car {
    // Car fields, including variables of type Engine and Wheels
    // Misc car methods

    class Engine
    {
        // Car engine fields
        // Get/Set engine methods
        // Functional engine method (goForward, goReverse, etc.)
        // Can access Car fields/methods
    }

    class Wheels
    {
        // Car wheel fields
        // Get/Set wheel methods (getTirePressure, etc.)
        // Functional wheel method (turnRight, turnLeft, etc.)
        // Can access Car fields/methods
    }
}
```

The Car class has two inner classes: Engine and Wheels. Although all user-related data and functionality can be defined in the Car class, using the inner classes to compartmentalize functionality can make code easier to read and maintain. The inner classes Engine and Wheels also have access to the protected/private fields and methods available within the Car class, which they might not otherwise have due to security, if they were defined as standalone classes. Remember that you cannot use or instantiate the Engine or Wheels classes except with an instance of the Car class, but the inner classes can access any fields or methods available in the outer class Car, as needed.

Tip

One specific use for inner classes is as static inner classes. A *static inner* class defines behavior that is not tied to a specific object instance, but applies across all instances.

Let's look at another way inner classes are used. Android developers often use anonymous inner classes to define specialized listeners, which register callbacks for specific behavior when an event occurs, on-the-fly. For example, to listen for clicks on a Button control, the developer uses the setOnClickListener() method, which takes a single parameter: a View.OnClickListener object. You can define an entirely new MyOnClickListener class, or you can simply define the class inline in code, without naming it at all (thus, the anonymous part). The following code uses the anonymous inner class technique to create, define, and assign a custom View.OnClickListener to a Button control:

```
Button aButton = (Button) findViewById(R.id.MyButton);
aButton.setOnClickListener(new View.OnClickListener() {
    public void onClick(View v) {
        // User clicked my button, do something here!
    }
});
```

Similarly, you often see threading done in a similar fashion:

```
new Thread() {
    public void run()
    {
        doWorkHere();
    }
}.start();
```

This code defines a new `Thread` class, implements the `run()` method, and starts the thread, all in one "line" of code.

Handling Other Android Java-isms

Java is an evolving language. Some older reference books do not cover the latest the language has to offer, and different developers have different coding styles. We have tried to make our examples easy to read, even if that means they are a bit verbose. If you find other Android Java-isms, let us know by contacting us at the email provided in the Introduction to this book.

Architecting Android Apps: An Example

Sometimes the easiest way to learn something new is to take it apart and then put it back together again. In this appendix, we do just that; we provide a sample implementation of an Android application called Nearly Handsfree Slideshow (NH Slideshow, for short) and deconstruct it, explaining each component in terms of features, user interface, and what's going on "under the hood." This appendix might make more sense after you've mastered some of the concepts of this book, but feel free to peruse it even if you're just getting started.

Application Overview

A common past time of mobile users is showing off images on their devices—the proud parent, the traveler, the teenage narcissist. Why not allow users to create groups of images and display them, all while using their voice? Starting from this basic idea, a simple application is born. Using voice commands, such as "start slideshow" or "add image," the user controls an application and displays a slideshow of existing images or adds new images from the device. But why nearly handsfree? Why not truly handsfree? Simply put, unless we rewrote various components that can be leveraged via a simple `Intent`, the application can't be fully handsfree. The system's built-in image picker isn't voice assisted, for instance. Just don't confuse this with the type of hands-free interface that is needed in a car. ;)

The Nearly Handsfree Slideshow Application Design

Nearly Handsfree Slideshow is simple in concept and leverages many Android components discussed in this book. The application supports API Level 14 to take advantage of some of the more recent updates to the Android platform. A database stores the organization of the images into slideshows. A content provider gives easy access to the database.

An `IntentService` is used for processing images. `SharedPreferences` are used for a variety of settings and configuration options. An `AsyncTask` is used for image decoding.

> **Tip**
>
> The source code for the complete Android app (Nearly Handsfree Slideshow) is available on the companion CD as well as the exclusive book website (http://www.informit.com/BNandroidVol12).

The NH Slideshow Components Explained

The NH Slideshow application has a number of different components. These components are all used from a single, primary `Activity` class called `NearlyHandsfreeSlideshowActivity`, which drives the main screen.

Each component handles important behavior in an attempt to follow platform best practices, remaining responsive, seamless, and accessible (as much as a slideshow app can be). Following are the components:

- **The Database:** A simple SQLite database handles the storage of the image locations and slideshow names.
- **The Content Provider:** The database functionality is accessed through a content provider, enabling access to the data from other application components without needing to know database specifics.
- **The Shared Preferences:** A set of application preferences are used to store user and internal settings in a persistent way.
- **The Task Queue Intent Service:** This simple service handles lengthy image operations, such as storing a small version of each image to speed up loading, reduce storage usage, and keep a version around in case the original source is deleted.
- **External Components:** Various external system features and components, such as voice recognition and Gallery image picking, are used.
- **The CursorLoader:** A loader is used to manage the data cursor to the slideshow content, efficiently handling the slideshow image queries.
- **The Slideshow Task:** This `AsyncTask` is used to decode images without blocking the main UI thread.
- **The Main screen:** This screen ties everything together, displaying the current active slideshow and handling voice commands.

Now let's look at each component of the NH Slideshow application in more detail.

The Database

The database stores all of the data needed to organize the slideshows and find the images on the local storage.

Overview

The `SQLiteOpenHelper` class helps manage application database details, creating a new database if one does not exist, defining the database schema, and handling queries and database operations such as inserting, updating, and deleting records.

Under the Hood

The application database, `SlideshowDatabase`, extends from the `SQLiteOpenHelper` class. This application requires a simple database with two tables: `table_slideshows` and `table_images`. The slideshows table, `table_slideshows`, contains an identifier column and a name column. The name is the label, or tag, of the slideshow. The images table, `table_images`, contains a unique identifier (id) column, an image path column, and a slideshow identifier column. The image path is an absolute path to the image. The slideshow identifier is basically a foreign key into the `table_slideshows` table.

The Content Provider

The content provider provides access to the underlying application database through a set of well-established methods for creating and querying the data.

Overview

This application could have accessed its database directly, but best practices in Android recommend that application databases by managed by a content provider. The content provider exposes only the aspects of the database your application requires in a standard way that can later be used in other ways and by other applications, if you like.

Under the Hood

The `SlideshowContentProvider` class extends the base `ContentProvider` class and provides the following access to the underlying database. You can:

- Insert new image records into an existing album, which updates the `table_images` table.
- Query for all slideshows using the `SlideshowContentProvider.CONTENT_URI`.
- Query for all images in a slideshow using the `SlideshowContentProvider.CONTENT_URI` with an appended path of the `id` of the slideshow.

The `SlideshowContentProvider` functionality is accessed during the slideshow to query for images to display. It's updated after the result from an image picker returns.

The Shared Preferences

Shared preferences are a great place to store small amounts of persistent data. In other words, it stores data, settings, and configuration that you want to be saved even if the user closes down the application and restarts it at a later date.

Overview

In NH Slideshow, shared preferences are used to store state information about the currently active slideshow.

Under the Hood

A helper class, called `Settings`, handles all of the details of using shared preferences with the application. Although already simple, this abstracts the use to allow for named getters and setters (such as `getSlideshowName()` and `setSlideshowName()`).

The Task Queue Intent Service

An `IntentService` is ideal for managing operations in the form of an asynchronous task queue. Using a full-fledged `Service` (such as an `IntentService`) instead of an `AsyncTask` allows each task to be completed outside the boundaries of any particular `Activity`. It allows the operations performed in an `IntentService` to run their completion almost without interruption of user behavior.

Overview

The `TaskQueueIntentService` class, which extends the `IntentService` class, provides background handling of lengthy image operations and any other lengthy tasks that future features might require. After the user picks an image from device storage, the image is scaled down to screen sized and cached locally by the `TaskQueueIntentService`.

Under the Hood

The `TaskQueueIntentService` class defines various commands, or tasks, that can be performed. For example, the image processing for a gallery image is handled with `COMMAND_PROCESS_PICKED_IMAGE` command. Any additional information about the task request is pulled out of the incoming `Intent` via its `extra` data, such as the name of the slideshow that an image is added to.

The image processing is relatively straightforward. The image is read from device storage into a `Bitmap` object. A scaled `Bitmap` of the appropriate size for the slideshow is created from original via a call to the `Bitmap.createScaledBitmap()` method. Then the new, smaller `Bitmap` is written out to private application storage using the `compress()` method of the `Bitmap` class. We've used the WEBP format to use as little storage space as possible. We're also confident that the decoding of WEBP is as fast as possible on the device because Google created the format and provided native support on Android.

External Components

Android has a great system for leveraging components external to an application. Through the use of intents, an application can easily use activities and services created by other developers or provided by the system.

Overview

In the NH Slideshow application, components for speech recognition and image picking are used. Using these specific features of the Android platform implies certain application requirements. For example, speech recognition works only when the user has a network connection because the speech recognition engine uses remote resources to decode speech.

Under the Hood

When the user wants the NH Slideshow application to listen to and respond to a command, the application launches an `Intent` with a `RecognizerIntent.ACTION_RECOGNIZE_SPEECH` action. The resulting recognized text comes back in an array of `String` objects. The application searches through this array for any recognized commands. For example, the command "add image to trees" would be detected as a `String` that begins with the "add image to" command and the "trees" word would be treated as the slideshow tag target. This then launches into another external component, the image picker.

The NH Slideshow application uses an `Intent` to access the system image picker to let the user choose which images they want in a particular slideshow. This is done by launching an `Intent` with action `Intent.ACTION_PICK` and a URI pointing to the image content such as the device's external image storage, found at `android.provider.MediaStore.Images.Media.EXTERNAL_CONTENT_URI`.

The CursorLoader

The `NearlyHandsfreeSlideshowActivity` class, which uses the `CursorLoader` class and implements the `LoaderManager.LoaderCallbacks<Cursor>` callback class, is used to perform image slideshow queries on a background thread.

Overview

Loaders are a relatively new feature of the Android platform that enable easy asynchronous loading of data in an `Activity` class. The `CursorLoader` is a special type of loader that works great with content provider queries.

Under the Hood

The `NearlyHandsfreeSlideshowActivity` class begins initializing the loader during its `onCreate()` method. Even accessing a simple content provider is considered a blocking operation, so the loader handles all of the details of performing the query off the main thread. When the `Cursor` is ready, it's handed off to the Slideshow Task, an `AsyncTask` object talked about in the later section named, "The Slideshow Task."

When a new image is added to a named slideshow, the content provider notifies any listeners of the changed data. The `Cursor` automatically updates and the new image shows up if it's in the currently active slideshow.

The `Cursor` object is also kept across configuration changes, meaning, for instance, that when the screen orientation changes, the `Cursor` does not need to be queried again.

The Slideshow Task

The `AsyncTask` class is a great way to perform operations off the main UI thread asynchronously with simple communications back to the main thread, as necessary.

Overview

The `SlideshowTask` class (which extends `AsyncTask`) loads an image from a file into a `Bitmap` object, which is not an instant operation so it must be performed off the main thread. An `AsyncTask` object is great for this.

Under the Hood

The `SlideshowTask` class is defined as an inner class of the main activity (and is thus limited in scope). It takes a `Cursor` to the current slideshow results and uses the `onProgressUpdate()` callback method to send a `Bitmap` back to the UI thread for display within the `ImageSwitcher`.

The Main Screen

The main screen, driving by the `NearlyHandsfreeActivity`, serves as the initial entry point for the application and provides access to the bulk of its functionality. Each of the underlying components is used by this class to bring the application together.

Overview

The main screen of the application has the following features:

- Displays the currently active slideshow
- Provides a button for launching voice recognition to enter command mode
- Provides an action bar menu (options menu) for a subset of actions for users who don't want to use their voice
- Layout contains an `ImageSwitcher` control that displays each image within a slideshow

Under the Hood

As the primary activity of the application, the `NearlyHandsfreeActivity` class is the driver of most of the behavior of the application. When the activity first starts, it checks to see whether there is an active slideshow in the application preferences and, if so, uses a `CursorLoader` to begin loading up the images to display in the slideshow. Meanwhile on the main UI thread, an `ImageSwitcher` begins to display each image in the slideshow.

The user can choose to enter command mode by pressing the `Button` control at the bottom of the screen, which launches the speech recognition intent and captures the command. The `NearlyHandsfreeActivity` parses the command and the appropriate action is taken. Two simple commands are supported:

- Changing the active slideshow by saying "show <slideshow name>." When this command is processed by the `NearlyHandsfreeActivity` in its `onActivityResult()` method, the application database is queried for images and then the new slideshow begins to display. The active slideshow name is saved in the application's shared preferences.

- Adding a new image to a slideshow by saying "add image" or "add image to <slideshow name>". When this command is processed by the `onActivityResult()` method, the image picker intent is launched and the user can select an image from device storage.

Index

B

H

M

O

512   sending